das

WILD TIGERS & TAME FLEAS

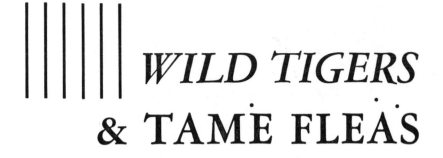

WILD TIGERS & TAME FLEAS

BILL BALLANTINE

Rinehart & Company, Inc.   New York   Toronto

Published simultaneously in Canada by
Clarke, Irwin & Company, Ltd., Toronto

w

To my favorite mammal, Miss W.

CONTENTS

WILD TIGERS & TAME FLEAS

"What kind of a movie was it, Mama-Whiskers?" called our five-year-old son, Toby, from his bed, as we tiptoed in, trying not to wake the exhausted young lady acrobat who was our baby sitter.

"It was all about a circus in Russia, a country far away," said Roberta. "There were big bears taller than Mama" (she is a six-footer) "all dressed up like tea-cozys, and they danced and rode piggy-back on bicycles; and a red fox jumped through a hoop with a rooster perched on it and didn't even eat the rooster; and a rabbit played a drum with his hind leg; and bears went way up in the air on a merry-go-round; and a lady lion tamer lay down on a rug made of real live lions; and there was a little train with penguin passengers; and weasels and a funny dancing ostrich, and . . ."

"Aw, go on," said our tousle-head. "You're just making it all up to fool me." Then he crawled back under the covers to make his return trip to dreamland.

This Little Pig Went to Circus

🐷 "Vater, it be kommen," said the fuzz-cheeked lad, the oldest of six standing at the edge of the sidewalk by the fluted metal pole on top of which was a huge stern clock flanked by cast-iron cherubs. The soft warming sun, hitting the panes of the ground-floor windows of the building behind, threw a reflection of golden backwards letters over the bumpy rose bricks: Walter & Brothers, McGregor's Finest Haberdashery.

It was stuffily hot as only a summer morning can be in the flats of Iowa along the Mississippi. And it was a good time ago—1868.

Down the street came the muffled sound of a band. The boys leaned farther over the curbstone, to catch the first dusty brass notes, the smallest kid (going on four) holding tight to his father's thick, horny fingers. The big man felt in his leather apron pocket for a large, thin paper folded against his German-silver watch. The pass to the circus, the Special Family Pass, which he had earned doing a harness repair job for the Besitzer, a handsome gentleman with bushy goatee.

A resplendent, gleaming black buggy drawn by two powdery white horses hove into view, at the reins in high stovepipe hat the man with the goatee, owner and principal star of Dan Rice's Italian-

American Circus whose showboat had tied up at dawn, alongside the *Lady Franklin*, the ferryboat to Prairie du Chien. Beside Dan Rice sat a lean, golden-colored pig with a silken clown ruff around its neck. *"Vater!"* shouted the littlest boy, *"Ein kleines komisches Schwein!"* Mr. Rice, touching tips of fingers to brim of hat, saluted the father and his tingling half-dozen, who didn't notice that their hero was just a bit tipsy.

Following the buggy came two chaps mounted on horses and carrying American flags. Next, the creaking bandwagon, pulled by a clatter of twelve dappled greys with harness jangling, chest brasses bouncing. The seven or eight unshaven musicians atop this gilded rolling palace created a cacaphony of sound fit to burst the starched blouses of the excited children standing at curbside. Now came four open animal dens: lions, tigers, hyenas and three sleek, spotted leopards, each group of beasts under control of an intrepid trainer. Following were nine beplumed medieval knights in shining armor bravely prancing on caparisoned steeds of black and white; six velveted Ladies of the Court followed sedately after on chestnut mares. Close on their heels was Dan Rice's famous trained talking horse, the blind, beautiful Excelsior, and a lumbering elephant wearing a jewel-studded hood, draped in a splendiferous tassled blanket of flowing silk, a great swaying howdah of gold high on its back. At the tail end of the procession rattled a donkey cart barely managed by a white-faced, red-nosed, blue-stockinged clown. The kids waited until the last bit of delight had vanished into thin air.

"Sehr schön," said Johann, the smallest one. "Golly Jehossafras!"

That afternoon August the harness maker locked his shop and took his six sons to the circus at "Half-Past Two O'Clk P.M." in a tent in the field back of Otto Klussmann's Feed Store. It was a splendorous never-to-be-forgotten experience. Dan Rice's circus program that matinee in McGregor didn't include the maestro's famous stunt of catching a cannon ball on the back of his neck, a feat he had picked up as a boy from a French strong man making his pitch next to the Rice's livery stable. But Dan performed some of the jig-time steps taught him long ago by his mother, daughter of a Methodist minister. He answered questions by quoting Shakespeare, did a bit of comedy bareback riding, and offered to whup any three members of the audience barehanded rough-and-tumble all-to-once. "The Psychological Idiosyncrasies of the Danish Prince Hamlet" were recited; there was a "Repretoire of Comic Duetts by the High

Priest of Momus"; and the blind horse, Excelsior, performed ecstatically as the Winged Pegasus. And, of course, there were comedy didoes by the trained pig, for Dan Rice was known from one end of the land to the other as the first man in America to train and exhibit the farmer's lowly friend, the hog. In McGregor, Iowa, this was by far the most-talked-of act of the entire bill. Little Johnny clapped his hands in glee, saying over and over, "*Vater! Vater! Ein kleines Schwein clown! Ein kleines komisches Schwein!*"

To the harness maker's oldest boy, Albrecht, the Dan Rice Circus was a visitation sent by Gott in Himmel himself. He steamed over. After the show had pulled stakes and floated on down the river, young Al taught himself to ride bareback on a neighbor's plow horse, to ground-tumble, walk a clothesline, to hang by one big toe from a broomstick trapeze and to become a ventriloquist. The seventeen-year-old's rabid enthusiasm infected the five younger boys and they formed a troupe that met all boats with a penny-gathering set-to of somersaults and hand-walking. Thirteen years after the visit of the Dan Rice Circus to McGregor, Iowa, these acrobatic Rüngeling brothers, who had become seven, took to the road with a haphazard show of their own, leaving behind their only sister, Ida. The Ringling Bros Classic and Comic Concert Co. went on tour the following season (the young men no longer talked in terms of years) as Ringling Brothers Grand Carnival of Fun, featuring that "Rising Young Dutch Comedian" young John in a program of "songs, positions, jokes, sayings, hibdy-dibdy fazes, and his roaring dance in Big Wooden Shoes."

It may seem unusual that the Ringling brogans were set on the tanbark trail by America's premier pig trainer, an alcoholic clown with a forty-eight-people show on a leaky river boat, but Dan Rice, at the time of his visit to McGregor, Iowa, was more than just another itinerant buffoon. He was America's first great clown, approaching the peak of a brilliant career, a born wag with a rich singing voice and vitriolic sense of humor. In his circus costume of red-striped tights, blue star-flecked leotard, high hat and goatee, he is reputed to have been the inspiration of our patriotic folk figure, Uncle Sam. With earthy, witty barbs aimed at social mores and the political climate he epitomized the wisecracking Yankee-Doodle clodhopper. He was the Will Rogers of his day, the popular idol of a wound-licking nation that needed one. Besides being an entertainer, Dan Rice was a serious political personality, having run unsuccessfully for

Congress (likely the only clown in history who failed to make it) and campaigned for the election to the Presidency of Zachary Taylor. Rice had strong aspirations himself for that highest office of the land. He was a strong abolitionist and a crusader against Southern secession. His antisecession speech, made in Philadelphia just before the outbreak of hostilities between the states, to an audience that included 350 flinty Southern medical students, is famous. (It included such inflammatory statements as "White folks are just as good as colored, as long as they behave themselves.") Such high-ups as A. Lincoln, Robert E. Lee, James Gordon Bennett, William Cullen Bryant, Jefferson Davis and Horace Greeley were pleased to call Mr. Rice, Dan.

It is not strange that Dan Rice had a finger in the first stirrings of the Greatest Show on Earth. He was a man accustomed to being associated with circus pioneering. His first sponsor, Gilbert R. "Doc" Spalding, an Albany druggist turned showman who organized the first Dan Rice Circus in 1848, was the supreme innovator of outdoor show business. Spalding's brilliant ideas were largely responsible for the transformation of the one-horse tent-opera into a three-ring-circus spectacle. Many of that astute gentleman's mid-nineteenth-century methods are still a working part of the modern, canvas-covered world. "Doc" devised the standard method of enlarging the circus round top by the insertion of middle pieces, exactly as Grandma used to enlarge the dining table on family Sundays by the addition of extra leaves. Spalding also originated the quarter poles which, by taking up slack between center and side poles, made possible the enormous circus Big Tops. He substituted oil lamps for the more dangerous candelabras and concocted the jacks-and-stringers system of portable seats, still employed by most outdoor shows. And in 1858 "Doc" Spalding moved the American circus for the first time by railroad. Dan Rice, the protégé of such a circus-wise genius, must have seemed to the Rüngeling offspring a good fellow to emulate.

Rice himself, at the age of seventeen, had taken his first fatal step into show business by training the only animal he was able to get hold of—a pig. He became half owner of one named Lord Byron and got himself a job with porcine partner on a little traveling puppet show—$16 a month, grits-&-gravy. That was in 1840, twenty-nine years before his stopover in McGregor, at which time Rice was earning more than Honest Abe himself—upwards of a thousand a week.

The trained pig Dan Rice brought to McGregor was a lean, muscular one, much like the acorn-grubbing "woods" pigs of the emigrant pioneers. The porker clown that so enthralled young Johnny Rüngeling did a number of entertaining stunts. He balanced on both front and back legs; rolled a vinegar barrel by trotting hind-legged against it; treadled on the convex hooped sides as it rolled. The "learned" pig answered questions by gutteral grunts, did simple sums with number cards, and spelled D-A-N R-I-C-E, P-I-G, C-O-R-N and McGreggor (with two g's), nudging letter cards with his stubby snout. From a box of assorted flags, he chose Old Glory and waved it aloft in his mouth. With his clown boss the educated pig worked a teeter-totter and did a figure-eight weave between the walking man's legs as Professor Rice stridently sang his favorite ballad, "Root, Hog, or Die."

The pig is not the most acceptable of domestic animals to place before the public as a performer, since man has long cherished the idea that pigs is pigs. While actors and ham have always been synony-mous in the theater, the feeling persists that pig hams should con-fine their performing to the smokehouse. Man seldom feels the same chumminess for pigs that he shows his other domestic creatures. The horse, mule and ox work for him; the cow and goat furnish milk, butter and cheese and are picturesque in pasture; the sheep clothes him; the dog, a real friend, protects his possessions and blindly adores him. But the pig somehow is regarded simply as a food-factory, devoid of charm or personality. The very qualities which man culti-vates for profit in a hog, grossness and sensuality, make the animal repellent to him.

However, Dan Rice had some precedent in introducing the unlikely hog to America as a circus entertainer. Pig actors had ap-peared in the Royal Courts of Europe as early as the fifteenth cen-tury. There is record of the ailing Louis XI, King of France, being cheered by a group of piglets dancing to bagpipes. For the amuse-ment of his crew, Christopher Columbus in 1502 during his fourth voyage to America on his flagship, *Capitana*, staged a blood-bout between a Costa Rican peccary and a crippled jungle monkey. In ancient England at wakes and fairs a great sport was "pig running," the forerunner of our own greased-pig chases. During the eighteenth century pigs took part in British pantomimes, and various "learned pigs" helped their clever owners gather in the shillings of the gullible. These clairvoyant porkers seemingly had intellect enough to make predictions, tell fortunes and answer questions, usually by nudging cards or by picking them out by mouth. The secret lay in training the hogs to respond to the almost inaudible click of the questioner's fingernail.

"Learned pigs" were being exhibited in London as late as the middle of the nineteenth century. Some of them were fakes. One such distinguished example, shown at the Hyde Park Exhibition in 1851, was named Madame Maudie Stevens, the "pig-faced lady." The Madame was neither lady nor pig but a medium-sized brown bear whose face and upper forelegs had been cleanly shaven. White elbow-length gloves covered the lower forelegs and a white-fox muff concealed the forepaws. The shaven bear, dressed in a concealing fashionable frock, a stole over her shoulders, poke bonnet covering the head, sat at a table on a chair whose seat had been removed. Underneath sat a boy, who jabbed the bear's exposed buttocks with a sharp wand each time the showman asked during his lecture, "Is that not correct, Madame?" The "Professor" explained the unearthly grunts by telling his audience that the young lady was unable to utter human speech due to the peculiar formation of her jaws. The climax of the exhibition came when, in answer to a question concerning matrimony, the hidden persuader jabbed extra vigorously so that the bear became really outraged. Whereupon the showman would pass the hat, saying, "Now, now, Madame Stevens, there's no need to be upset just because I asked a simple question."

The trained pig was actually the first truly native-trained animal performer of the American circus, which at first was predominantly an exhibition of equitation skills, the horses—already educated—imported from England and France. The trained porker appeared in the American circus ring in the early 1830's, about the same time as the first arena of trained imported wild animals. Until that time beasts had been confined to menagerie exhibitions whose development was independent of the equestrian circus. The first record of a wild animal imported to this country is that of a lion brought into staid Boston in 1716. This leonine visitor was followed to the same city in 1721 by a camel, and in 1733 a polar bear bugged the eyes of Bean-towners. The first elephant landed in New York City in 1796. The exhibitors of wild animals in those days were strolling animal men with one or two specimens: a grizzled trapper leading a subdued bear out of the woods; a sailor in from the Gold Coast or the Indies with a ring-tailed monkey on his tattooed shoulder; an occasional wombat, eagle, or owl. Busking of the beasts (entertaining for handouts) took place in tavern yards and taprooms for a sprinkle of groats, a meal, and glass of port or a tankard of ale, a home-smoked ham, a demijohn of rum. This crude form of itinerant animal show soon developed into organized menageries, primitive caravans of creaking wagons. By the early 1820's at least a score of them were riding the ruts of the eastern seaboard from Alabama to Maine and inland to the Appalachians.

The menagerie didn't join up with the circus until 1851, and even then the animals were exhibited separately and for an additional admission price, naturally. Aside from this valuable economic advantage, animals gave an indisputable moral tone to the circus, which in those times, even more than now, was regarded as one of the more successful road companies of that brimstone impresario, Lucifer. It was not considered sinful to collect animals, for the godly had always done so, Noah having established a precedent of sorts; nor was it wicked to look at animals on Sunday, the Holy Day. The small contribution—extracted for maintenance only, of course—was considered negligible.

There is possibly some deep-seated connection between religion and the performing pig, for the Egyptians had pig images as long ago as 3400 B.C. In the religions of the ancient Syrians, Phrygians, Greeks and, later, the Hebrews, the pig has had its ups and downs, being alternately vilified and honored.

The Jewish rejection of pig meat as a food, while stemming from the Biblical code of forbidden food sources set forth in Leviticus 11, undoubtedly has been influenced as well by factors of economy and hygiene. Hogs were not considered economically feasible by the wandering tribes of Israel since the animal could not survive travel in the hot, arid land of Egypt. Sheep and cattle were taken instead. Hygienically, pigs were known to transmit undulant fever and the Egyptians believed that drinking pig milk gave men leprosy. They knew, without knowing why, that pork sometimes brought on an inflammatory muscular disease that we now know as trichinosis. The health factor was probably the strongest reason for the taboo on hog flesh, since few of the forbidden animals mentioned in the Levitical list are even passably edible. But, Leviticus notwithstanding, I still consider escargots pretty fair eating.

Through history the pig has never had more than a meager sort of unstable respectability, but perhaps the pig was chosen for the role of patsy because of its reputation for durability; its back was broad enough to take slanderous treatment, for the hog is one of the toughest residents of this tough old world. Swine have been rooting around the globe ever since it started to cool off, and the pig is the most primitive form of domestic animal in existence today, its evolutionary structural change having been less than that of any other farm or barnyard animal. The farmer's daughter has actually undergone more changes.

The domestic pig family, *Suidae,* from which the porcine circus performers are selected, had its origin in the Oligocene epoch, a chunk of time which began sixty million years ago and is still going great guns. That earliest pig antecedent was a tusked hog called *Propalaeochoerus.* Propo begat another mouthful called *Palaeochoerus* (according to the German paleontologist, H. G. Stehlin). In its official family tree, *Sus* is the name of the domestic pig, and its rootin' cousins are African river hogs and bush pigs, wild boar of India and Europe, the ugly African wart and forest hogs, the Babirussa (tripletusked hog of the Celebes), and the pigmy hogs of the Himalayas. The only thing known about the word "pig" is that it comes from the Dutch word *"bigge"* whose roots are hopelessly lost in the low-German linguistic jungles.

The first record of the breeding and raising of swine is an order of the Chinese Emperor Fo-Hi in 3468 b.c., although the Orientals are believed to have domesticated the pig at least five hundred years prior to that date. Pigs were first used by man as scavengers; history, being a little lax on piggery, does not record when man learned that the hog was good to eat. There is, of course, that childhood classic of the Chinese boy burning his finger by sticking it into the family pig charred by an unfortunate stable fire, licking it quickly to cool it off and thereby discovering that roast pork is delicious.

Pigs were among the very first animals imported to America. They were brought in to be eaten, not to amuse the Indians by rolling rum barrels, teeter-tottering or spelling V-I-R-G-I-N-I-A D-A-R-E. On his second voyage to America in 1493, Christopher Columbus brought eight porkers, the progenitors of all the hogs that later overran the Spanish Indies. The pig didn't reach the mainland of North America until the Spanish conqueror, Hernando Cortés, arrived with swine, not on his first 1519 expedition to Mexico, but later, when the points of the cacti had been dulled a little. In the spring of 1539, Hernando de Soto landed thirteen pigs on the Florida gold coast near what is now Boca Grande. They multiplied rapidly, according to a report of a summertime battle the following year between De Soto's Spanish Christians and the heathen Indians in Alabama, which lists as casualties: 2,500 Indians and 18 Christians killed; 150 Christians with 700 arrow wounds; 12 horses dead, 70 wounded; 400 swine lost.

In 1607, after a number of abortive attempts, the British Virginia Company was able to set up at Jamestown, Virginia (the state that was to become the ham center of the United States), a colony of 60 hogs which in two years increased to 600 head. Some pigs landed on Plymouth Rock along with the Pilgrims in 1620, and a few years later the Puritans of the Massachusetts Bay Colony devised the nose ring to prevent hogs from rooting. Along about that time pigs were arriving in droves in the Middle Atlantic area, the careful Dutch shipping boatloads to New Amsterdam in pens floored with sand. Toward the end of the seventeenth century the Spanish missions of California were well stocked with pigs derived from a Chinese breed. They were mainly fat producers, the fat not mixing with lean, as those early Californians abhorred butter and preferred every dish swimming in lard. The lard of the mission pigs went almost to the bone and was peeled off as blubber is peeled from a whale. Just before the dawn of the eighteenth century (1699) the French were introducing *le cochon* to their Mississippi river and Gulf settlements.

The pigs that went along on the great western migrations of the early nineteenth century, by keelboat on the rivers and overland along the same trails that carried P. T. Barnum, Davy Crockett, Jenny Lind and Lafayette, were the prototypes of the trained circus pigs. The emigrant pigs, which were called "woods" hogs, had all the qualities that make a perfect circus trouper. They were good travelers, good foragers, resourceful, self-reliant and fiercely independent—they were emphatically individualists. They minded their own business, insisted on their rights, and were fearless rough-and-tumble battlers, not cringing before man or beast. They seldom perished in the rough elements, had tremendous endurance, generally triumphing over hardship and adversity, and they tolerated all sorts of scurrilous nicknames such as "acorn gatherer," "prairie racer," "stump rooter," "alligator" and "razorback." The "woods" hog could hold its own against all comers—wildcats, coyotes, venomous snakes, foxes and the lone wolf. They made perfect performing porkers, having all the muscle tone and agility necessary to be a star of the circus ring. From the sturdy "woods" hogs came the famous trained pig, Lord Byron, and all the other graduates of Dan Rice's porcine academy.

From his lowly beginning as a pig tricker America's most famous clown did well. That season of his inspirational appearance before the Rüngeling brothers in McGregor, Iowa, he made a net profit of $125,000. Two years later he embarked on what was likely the most spectacular venture of his tempestuous career. He outfitted a magnificent circus river boat called the *Great Paris Pavillion* for a grand tour of the Mississippi and made a trunkful of money. Before very long, however, the great joey's drinking habits began to breathe down his neck. His health tottered, business reverses set in (he dropped $80,000 in the panic of '73) and soon there was bankruptcy for the second helter-skelter time in his life, a period regarded blithely by Rice as an "experience." In 1879, fire destroyed all the assets of Dan Rice except his trained horse, Excelsior, and one pig. The impoverished clown journeyed to San Francisco, began anew, prospered enough to build another floating circus opera and went back to the river. But his weakness for booze-heisting continued to corrode Dan Rice. Sobriety clauses began to appear in his contracts and finally he was drawn completely inside the bottle he loved not wisely but too well, and died in 1900—broke and derelict—at the age of seventy-seven. Few remembered the fabulous clown or any of his superbly trained pig actors. *The New York Times* rated Dan (Mr. Daniel McClaren) a perfunctory, two-paragraph obit, skimming lightly over his career: jockey, cardsharp, one-third owner of a livery stable, half owner of an educated pig, jig dancer, balladeer, strong man, star performer of a score of circuses, owner of several, anti-secessionist and abolitionist, friend of A. Lincoln and Jeff Davis; builder of a thirty-five-thousand-dollar Southern war monument, founder of churches for ex-slaves, twice bankrupt, temperance lecturer.

The year Dan Rice joined out in heaven, the Ringling Bros—those McGregor, Iowa, kids into whose shoes he had shaken the accursed sawdust—were, on eighty-odd railroad cars, taking golden bites from the rich eastern territory of the old master showman, James A. Bailey, whose fabulous Barnum & Bailey Circus was busy gathering in the sheaves in Europe. The boys had no time for looking backwards to their boyhood hero, the pig trainer. The Ringling show had just completed its first tour of California with an ark of animals the like of which Dan Rice had never dreamed: elephants, camels, lions 'n tigers; a hippopotamus, an ibex, an antelope; leopards, pumas, hyenas; water buffalo, elk, deer and zebu; grizzly bears, kangaroos and llamas; aviaries, reptile dens and cages of anthropoid apes. Almost everything in the zoologist's book from *Artiodactyla* to *Equus grevyi,* the zebra, but not one member of the family *Suidae* —no trained pigs. Little Johnny Rüngeling, now grown into the formidable Mr. John, apparently had forgotten the *"ein kleiner* ring-tailed *Komischer"* that so amused him on that summer afternoon long ago.

Dan Rice slid into his decline, but the spoor of the trained pig became stronger across America as the nation stepped over the star-spangled threshold of the twentieth century. Every little mud-show had its troupe of porkers and there were scads of racing razorbacks; the grunters of Farmer Burns became famous at country fairs; Rhinelander's Pigs became a fixture in vaudeville. Perhaps the greatest pig trainer of the period was Lil Kerslake (Li'l for little; he was a short man), who joined out with his barnyard beauties along about 1904 on the Great Wallace Shows. This was a small but substantial enterprise owned by Ben Wallace, which had been spawned in that famous nest of the American circus, Peru, Indiana, in 1884, one of its founders being the great minstrel man, Al G. Fields. Among the center-ring stars of the Wallace contingent was a troupe of gymnasts, the Nelson family, whose feats were unparalleled in the circus world. (Mr. Wallace had a standing offer of $10,000 to anyone who duplicated the tricks of his famous family of kinkers [circus performers].) P. T. Barnum had imported the troupe from England in 1881, rather unwillingly, as part of a deal to acquire a more desirable act, the Lovely Madame Fogardus' Clever Canines and Feathered Sweethearts. Madame—who specialized in wand-balancing and poses plastiques—backstage was plain Emma, wife of muscular, mustachioed Robert, chief of the Nelson acrobatic clan. She was also the mother of its handsome, stalwart stellars, Robert and Arthur, whose wives and children made up the rest of the troupe of fifteen. Destined to bear the escutcheon of the American trained pig into our time was a yet-to-be-born great-grandson of Madame Fogardus, matriarch of all the Nelsons. While trouping through India, Robert the younger had married Adele Wilson, daughter of the proprietor of a small British circus. She had added to the act two top-mounters, Adele and Artie.

The other brother's wife, an ex-Ringling tightrope walker named Sarah Warren, had contributed seven members: six females—Rosina, Hilda, Oneida, Theol, Estrella and Carmencita and a lone male, Paul.

Young Adele the second broke the code of the acrobat and married an outsider, a "towner" who was, however, in a related profession, being an orthopedic surgeon. Adele had two sons, naming them Theodore (after her husband) and Robert (after father and grandfather) and dubbing them both circus-Nelsons instead of surgical-Crosbys.

Adele, soon tiring of life among the plaster casts, divorced her doctor and returned to her first love, the circus, rejoining her tumbling family, and rearing her boys on sawdust and spangles.

In 1906, Ben Wallace bought the German Karl Hagenbeck wild Animal Show and renamed his aggregation the Hagenbeck-Wallace Circus. The Nelson Family continued as a star attraction, whirling madly around the hippodrome track, holding down the center ring with Risley-doubles and flip-flaps (55—count 'em—55) three pedestals high. Lil Kerslake's pigs continued to trot, grunt and mess up one of the between-rings stages.

Adele Nelson's younger son, Bobby, became the pig trainer. He remembers seeing Kerslake's stunting porkers for the first time as a kid going on four, just about the same age as Johnny Rüngeling when the Iowa boy first laid eyes on that greatest pig professor of all time, Dan Rice. Robert Nelson, now a man of fifty, is the owner and operator of America's leading trained pig act, which carries the forthright title, Robert Nelson and his Trained Pigs (there are only two others: one presented by cousin Paul; the other by a German dog-and-pony import named Peterson).

Nelson, brought up under his family's acrobatic thumb, wasn't able to break away to pigs until he was almost a man (by his standards this was not quite sixteen). Once he got the rosin off his hands, he lost no time in rounding up a herd of swine and applying to them what he had soaked up in years of watching the veteran Lil Kerslake and son Fred. Soon Nelson's Nimble Barrows were enthralling the summer jams in Luna Park at New York's inimitable amusement compound, Coney Island, and working winter dates on indoor circuses.

The young act eventually was booked into Venezuela, stranded there, and the educated porkers were sold for lion feed. Nelson was financially rescued by his mother and her new husband, elephant trainer Louis Reed.

After seven wearing years as a free-lance acrobat Bob Nelson was attracted back to Luna Park, and there he met up with pigs again. They weren't educated, but they brought him good luck. For while working at a novelty concession that employed pigs, Nelson happened onto the secret that has become his most valuable asset in pig training: a method of keeping hogs small, arriving at maturity one third the size they would ordinarily reach. This revelation was handed to him on a gin-soaked breath while he was handling something called in the trade, a "pig chute." It's a booth in which shoats are lined up in small box-pens on a high platform leading to the top of a chute. The customer pitches baseballs at a target to trip a piglet door, whereupon the escaping animal skitters to the chute, slides down and runs into a little house. It's a simple pastime, but it makes money.

Nelson was manipulating this affair one afternoon, when a former operator, a woman who had been sacked for overtippling while on duty, appeared in a sodden state and asked the young man, "What're you feedin' 'em to keep 'em small?"

"A little whiskey," joshed Nelson, never dreaming there was a more respectable growth retarder.

"C'm'ere you," snuffled the ex-chuter, leaning heavily on the counter. "You look like a good guy, a gemnelman—I'm gonna tell you my secret. But you must pormise cross your heart, your murver's grave, never never reveal it."

Nelson was amused and decided to humor the inebriated soul.

She whispered in his ear. Now he was amazed. The stunting ingredient was so simple, he was surprised he hadn't ever thought of it. It was something available over many a counter—which kind of counter he will not say. Nor will he say whether the potion is powder, liquid or solid. In fact he won't say anything at all about the magical method except that the diminishing influence is on bone structure and that cruelty is in no way involved. At six months the Nelson pigs weigh from 125 to 150 pounds; ordinarily a pig that age tips the beam at about 300 pounds.

"I dose them right up to maturity," Nelson explained to me. "That's thirty to thirty-six months—I had to call Cornell University to find out, so I'd know when to stop feeding the stuff. . . . No, I didn't tell them what it is."

He doesn't remember the name of his benefactor or know where the old doll got her knowledge. I asked him about this once and got a circus-sensible answer, "She never volunteered," he said, "and I never asked."

At some time or other almost everyone in circus business has tried to pry Nelson's well-guarded secret from him. The most persistent seeker has been Felix Adler, the Ringling Bros clown, who models his clown face after that of a pig and whose trademark is a piglet which slides a chute for a reward of milk slurped from a nippled bottle. I have seen Felix, who is normally not an easy spender, set up the boiler-makers for Bobby until they were running out his ears, in hopes that the stiff drink would lubricate his tongue, but no matter how pie-eyed the keeper of the pig secret became, he remained true to his gin-fuzzed godmother. It has been more than thirty years since she whispered in Bobby Nelson's ear, but he has never betrayed her confidence, not even to his own mother.

After his brief ham-and-egger stint at Coney Island, Bobby tried to get up another pig act, but he never seemed able to garner enough cash or credit to frame it properly and soon fell back on the old family trade, acrobatics.

"In nineteen thirty-five," he told me, "I was back with the Nelson famliy and in 'thirty-six—where was I? . . . Oh, yes, I think I held out too long for a raise that year and didn't get it. I went to visit the Tom Mix show in Albany, and he saw me in the backyard (he knew me from the Floto show) and he asked me, 'Can you still do a flip-flap?' I told him sure, and he said, 'Let's see.' I did and he said, 'You're hired.' I got fifteen dollars a week in an acrobatic act with five girls."

Throughout World War II Nelson was a physical training instructor for the Air Force at Miami Beach, Florida. Following the war, in 1947, he was back doing flip-flaps and doubling as a fill-in clown on the Ringling Bros Barnum & Bailey Circus. He took as much of this menial grubbing as he could and, in 1950, pulled his stakes and his savings account for another go at the trained pigs.

This time he clicked. He bought a big red truck, built props, had costumes made, hired a helper and began to do just fine on one of the large indoor circuses, the Polack Bros. Western Unit, which performs mainly under the sponsorship of the Ancient Arabic Order of the Nobles of the Mystic Shrine.

On a brisk October night, along about 3 A.M., Nelson, his helper and his exhausted pig actors were making a long overland jump between Denver, Colorado and Enid, Oklahoma. The act had wound up a good but tiring week due to the mountain city's high altitude. The heavily loaded truck lurched toward the dawn with the helper driving. Dozing beside him on the front seat, Nelson was slumped against the door. A sudden sharp curve shifted his dead weight onto the door handle. It sprang. The door whipped open. Bob flopped through the dark rushing space and thudded to the roadside. The driver, making a frantic grab for his falling boss, lurched against the steering wheel, turning it just enough to roll the truck's right rear wheels over Nelson's left leg, the seven-ton load crushing it into the gravelly ground rock.

Bobby wakened with a scream of pain. The driver managed to get him back into the truck cab, leaving a lot of his bone ground into the gravel. Nelson, more concerned by his discovery of a broken arm than by the pulverized leg, of which he was only vaguely aware, gritted his teeth and called up the trouper courage of all the sainted Nelsons back to his great-grandfather namesake and Madame Fogardus. He hung on like a "woods" hog. The foot was almost completely severed.

After nearly three agonizing years in hospitals in various parts of the country, Nelson emerged with one leg several inches shorter than the other. He knew he could never again be a circus acrobat—perhaps a blessing worth all the misery. As soon as he could hobble about, he began to poke around the countryside of rural Columbia county for some pigs to train.

The family home, an enormous pre-Revolutionary rambler of stone and frame, is near the village of Ghent, between Hudson and Chatham, New York, in the Hudson valley about 130 miles upriver from Manhattan. The proprietor of the local tavern, The Navarra House, a fellow named George Snyder, also drove a Standard Oil Company truck. In mid-May, he bought five six-week-old shoats from a rustic on his oil route for Adele Nelson's son, who paid the going market rate, eleven dollars each. On June first, two years seven and one-half months after his accident, Nelson, still in his cast, began again to be a pig professor.

At the snowy tag end of February I drove upstate to visit the man who was reviving America's first indigenous circus act and to see how he was managing his marvelous gritty comeback.

I found him getting ready to practice his new pigs in a barn on the Ghent-Harlanville road about two miles from the Nelson homestead. The barn is a massive old structure owned by a friendly neighbor, Bill Hublin, who nobly donates its use to Nelson.

"I used the Ghent Town Hall a couple of times," Nelson said, "but there I had to pay for the lights and heat, and anyway they wouldn't go for having me and the pigs in there all winter."

Hublin, not a working farmer, uses the building mainly as a garage, tractor shelter and basketball court for his teen-ager boy and girl. Nelson was practicing his pigs in the low-ceilinged area under the hayloft of the heavy timbered storehouse. Birds chirped in the eaves and a group of noisy boys were ripping through a rough game of basketball on the sub-standard court alongside. Their ball frequently bounced across the pigs' ring carpet, a round canvas piece about thirty feet across—faded green, blue and orange.

"It's one of the old Ringling ring carpets cut down," said Bobby. "It cost sixty-five dollars just to have them orange pieces sewed on, and look how the pigs have rooted them up already. Under the lights it looks like a million. It's flashy and my next one—when I get some dough—I'm gonna have made just exactly like it."

Scattered around the little clearing was a clutter of sleds, bicycles, coils of barbed wire, defunct brooders, beer cases, rusting milk cans, floppy black inner tubes, worn tires, axes, an ominous butcher block and a large straw target. Along one wall hung an array of tools.

Bob turned up a portable radio. "The noise and music gets them used to being with a circus," he explained.

He was wearing a pair of blue coveralls, trimmed in bright red, over a red woolen sport shirt. One sleeve of the jumper bore the telltale remnants of a picked-out embroidered insignia RBB&B. On his balding head was an old grey felt hat, and enormous black rubbers completely covered his shoes. He stripped one off to show me the thick-soled built-up shoe he wears on the foot of his injured leg. When he walked to the truck backed up to the door, he didn't limp at all.

"The only thing is," he said, "I can't jig around so much in the act any more. I used to do little dance steps and all, but now I can't. And another thing—I never in my life wore long-johns, but boy I do now. Got to, to keep warm."

I helped Bob drop the heavy, high endgate of the big red truck, and when he let his pals out of their boxes, which were very clean and dry with shavings, they scampered down the runway which had been shoved through a crack in the barn's sliding doors just big enough for it. Outside in the driveway, between the three-foot-high snowbanks, sat the Hublin family's shiny cars and a small tractor.

"It kind of embarrasses me," said Bob, "his stuff out in the snow and me inside with the pigs. I feel like a nuisance, but he tells me not to worry about it—he doesn't care. He's been like a brother to me."

Nelson, who has the short, stocky stature of the acrobat, single-handedly hauled the heavy runway into the barn to double in brass as teeter-totter board and the incline for a slide.

A wooden frame with upside-down dishpans bolted to it was laid on the floor. It was the pigs' home base—their "seat."

"The pans are the boundary, that's all," said Nelson. "I tried covering them with carpet, but they just rip it off every time."

There were four pans but five pigs. "The fifth one," said Bobby, "is my clown, Abner. I've trained him to wander so that he goes off the stage and roots though the audience. They love it."

Then he distributed the props—low wooden hurdles, a stool, a rolling barrel made from an oil drum, a pair of pedestals which were small editions of elephant spindles, and a steel seesaw fulcrum.

"Seats," yelled the pig master, and the hogs, who were rooting and scuffling among the scattered farm objects, immediately scuttled on their short legs to the pans, placing their front hoofs upon the skiddy enameled surfaces. Professor Nelson picked up his long, supple stock whip, and the pig pupils' recital began.

The first trick was a double pyramid to the stool, with Abner, true to clown tradition, first knocking it over—for which he received a pinch of bread from the trainer's pocket. After another stool knock-over came a four-pig long-mount to the furniture. This, while similar to the elephant trick of the same name, does not have its grace. The pig long-mount with faces squashed into backs and front legs dangling gives somewhat the impression of a multiple mating. After another knock-over two pigs did a hind-leg circular trot around the spindles.

Then came the hurdles, the hogs being able to clear twenty inches. "The highest jump my other pigs ever made," said Nelson, "was forty inches to a table. Only it wasn't an easy free leap like this but more a squat or crouch. They measured it off first then kind of sprung."

Abner came on to knock over the hurdle and got his bread reward.

Then the entire company took turns rolling the barrel with their front feet while Abner, the clown, walked through the moving tube. This was followed by a walking long-mount, which was even more startling than the stabile variety. Annie, the sow, then had a turn trotting on top of the rolling cylinder with a strong assist from Nelson. Abner did his specialty, the figure-eight leg-weave back and forth across the carpet, after which the teeter-totter was set up. This was a really remarkable trick, with a pig on either end of the lever and a third one at the fulcrum, controlling the movement of the board by what seemed to be a voluntary backing up and moving forward.

"I broke this trick alone," said Bob, "when I was still in the cast."

The finish trick of the act was the slide, with all members participating. "They don't like it now," said their prodder, "because in the cold the wax is not slippery enough."

The four pig performers went calmly back to their "scats," but Abner continued on his own to climb the ladder and make the slide, coming for his bread reward after each descent. In training this pig Nelson has defied the sacred maxim of the animal trainer: "The main thing is to teach an animal *not* to do a trick, once he has learned it, unless he gets the cue." Most trainers believe that otherwise the animal simply repeats and repeats until he loses interest and sulks. Each trick, they feel, should be a special event.

"Pigs are different," explained Bobby when I asked about this. "He'll keep that up until I run out of bread, and be ready to go again soon as I get some more."

Pigs are trained together as a group after a brief get-acquainted period. They are broken in on leads, first being taught to take "seat," a basic principle of all animal training—the establishment of a base. Pig teaching is progressive, each trick being added to the routine as it is accomplished. The specialties are broken separately and sand-wiched into the group program.

The hind-leg stand is the hardest position for the pig to achieve, because of its odd build. Somersaults are an impossibility. Walking on top of a rolling cylinder is difficult also because of the pig's long-bodied construction. This trick must be started when the pig is small so that it can become gradually adjusted to the moving curved sur-face. Rolling a ball is another practically impossible stunt for a pig because of its hard hoofs. Pigs, however, can be broken to walking a tightrope (a narrow board, really) and can be taught to hold things in their mouths. The easiest trick to establish is the figure-eight foot-weave, and the most critical time in the entire curriculum of piggery is the day the leads are removed for the first time. If the animals bolt and run, a lot of patient work is undone. Nelson's pigs have bolted only once. That was during a performance in Richmond, Virginia, on an outdoor stage which had become too sun-hot for the pigs' comfort.

"Everything bolted that day," he recounts, "ponies, dogs, sea lions. Everything. At least I brought my pigs back for their sliding finish trick."

I was surprised by the variety of the tricks and the extreme agility of Nelson's hogs and by their size. I had expected either huge fat monsters or cute tiny shoats, but these were workmanlike in-betweens, much like the pioneers' "woods" hogs, lean and muscular. The largest of the Nelson quintet weighed roughly 135 pounds. They were about nine months old. They all had straight erect ears.

"The straight ears is the most important thing in a performing pig," said the modern authority of the art of pig guidance. "For the looks, but especially so they can see well."

Nelson's varsity five gets the best of medical care. Besides diplo-mas, it has certificates of inoculation against the three main hog killers: anthrax, hog cholera and erysipelas. "That's more prevalent now even than cholera," the pig dean said, "and I can't even spell it."

Pigs can get all sorts of other things wrong with them such as the painful black tooth, enteritis, brucellosis (the same as undulant fever in man), tuberculosis (which the pig can get from man), influenza, swinepox and nutritional anemia. The chief parasites of pigs are roundworms, the source of trichinosis. Nelson's ham actors are wormed twice a year, and they take baths in the summertime only. "I don't want them to catch cold," he explains, "since I've conditioned them to go without heat. It makes them hardier."

Pigs eat everything that man eats, except escargots. They will not eat worms, mice, maggots, grasshoppers or weeds. A pig stores about 35 per cent of the energy of its meals in its body; the usual gain is 1 pound of weight for each 3 to 5 pounds of fodder. "Another thing," said Nelson in defense of his favorite animal, "that people say about pigs; that 'eat like a hog' business. It's man that forces a pig to eat so much. He is supposed to turn into a ton of pork in six months. In half a year he's expected to increase his weight by six thousand per cent! Pigs have a very small stomach."

The Grand Sachem of American pigs feeds his tribe a commercial pig and sow mash. When it's very cold, he adds ear-corn to the diet. The group does away with a bucket of apples twice a day, winter and summer. It gets no milk. When performing, feeding time is at dawn and after the night show, which suits the pigs just fine for they are naturally nocturnal feeders. During a layoff they are fed more like people, at 8 A.M. and again at 5 P.M.

By nature the pig is gentle, sweet-tempered and seldom an aggressor. Pigs are not intentional biters, but, to prevent accidents to trainer or public, the tusks of show pigs are cut down to the gum— under anesthetic by a veterinarian. Professor Nelson has high regard for the intelligence of his collegiates. "They are not stupid," he told me, "but they are stubborn. You can't use the whip on them except to remind them you're there. They're like sea lions in that respect— timid and must be treated kindly with very little discipline."

I asked what he looked for in a performing pig prospect. "Conformation mostly," he answered. "If the legs are straight, if they stand on their toes (they're like little toe dancers, you know), wide chest, and, of course, ears that don't flop over their eyes."

Pigs have good eyesight, but they can't see through ears. Their hearing is very good also, and they are able to distinguish pitch. They respond to musical cues. In ancient Italy the swineherds called their droves in from acorn gathering in the oak forests by a single pure note blown on a horn, each herd recognizing its own distinctive call.

One of the most amusing tricks in Nelson's original pig act—a pig rolling out a strip of ring carpet—was based on the pig's keen sense of smell. The trainer simply hid three or four tidbits of bread in the roll. Rooting to get at them, the pig pushed along the carpet.

Nelson said his pig actors were no particular breed but a mixture of Chester White, Duroc, Poland-China, Yorkshire, Berkshire and Hampshire—the last two being, he thought, the source of the straight ears. The clown Abner, who is all white, likely derived from Chester White and Yorkshire. Hank, white with red face, was probably a cross of one of those breeds and a red Duroc. The company probably got its trim, handsome figures from that last breed (numerically one of the leading in the United States), for it is noted for its good back, body, feet and legs, also docility and hardiness. Red, who is a beautiful golden color, presumably had a strong Duroc father or mother. Lum, white with a few black marks, could have been Hampshire-Yorkshire. Annie, the prima-donna sow, is beautifully marked like an Apaloosa horse, white with black inky splotches. She probably had a little Spotted Poland-China in her.

Annie is named for the wife of the innkeeper who procured the troupe for Nelson. "At first," he said, "when she came to see the act practicing, she didn't know whether to be offended or honored. But finally she got to like having a trained pig named for her, and now she's real proud of Annie and loves her dearly." He suddenly flicked his stock whip at the line-up standing at their "seats" and yelled, "Lum, you leave Annie alone!" Then he continued to me, "I don't like having a female in the act. They come in heat every three weeks, and the three days it lasts I have one hell of a time with the boys."

I was impressed with the cleanliness of Nelson's disciples and their silky smooth coats which showed no bristles, although the hairs had a good wiry thickness. "They get currycombed with rubber twice a day," said their manager. "In the layoff season I oil them with any old kind of oil—mineral, baby, even old crankcase oil. It keeps the skin from drying out and scaling." There was no trace of the usual piggy smell about these fellows.

"That's the worst thing people say. 'Dirty as a pig,' " insisted Nelson. "That's a lot of hogwash. Pigs are by nature one of the cleanest animals. You won't see a pig wallow in dirty water if he can have clean. And they like to have a clean, dry bed same as anybody else."

When the pigs had rested some, they were put through the routine again. Then the professor said, "Guess we'll have to stop. I'm running out of bread for Abner, and I don't like to disappoint him for his slides."

He put the chute up to the truck, still refusing my offer to help, and ran the superb swine back into their home on wheels. After they were all snug in their boxes, the pig man observed, "I guess they're just about the luckiest pigs on earth. I looked it up once in the *Farmer's Almanac,* and they estimate there is close to three hundred million pigs in the world. These five can work for me until they get too stiff to be acrobats any more. Most hogs last about six months— and bingo! to the market. I expect I'll have these guys performing about five or six years more."

Back at the old homestead, after we parked the truck, a police dog named Princess romped up to nose Bob's hand. "That's Reed's dog," he said, "she's a pig herder and a bull-hand. She helped Reed break in them baby elephants of Ringling's. You know Reed was past seventy then! He stopped an elephant stampede out in Texas when he was sixty-nine! And look at him! Still going strong, and he's only got a few years to go until he's eighty! My mother worked elephants, you know, after she married Reed. In vaudeville. Keith's. The Orpheum circuit. Loew's. Pantages. Fanchon and Marco time. Publix. Them all. She and Reed had three bulls—Tillie, Myrtle and Jennie. Tillie was the world's only talking elephant. They kept them right in this barn; the floor rings is still here. The farmers call this place the Elephant Farm and that road out there, the Elephant Road."

Princess ran along the snowy driveway toward the old frame house. There was a smell of wood smoke in the air, and the winter sky was a sharp blue above the black streaks of woods. "I'd like someday," mused the pig trainer, "to break in a pig for hunting. They make good pointers but not so good retrievers. You'd have to watch them. Like when they use pigs in France to hunt truffles and mushrooms. They have to get there before the pig gobbles up what he finds. I read of an English hunting pig that would point at anything except rabbits. Pigs can swim, and they could probably even bring in ducks. I bet you I could do it, if I ever get the time." Then he added, "Their tails stay curly when they point."

"In Them Days"

🐚 At first glance you might think Sarasota just another Florida resort town—a bit more old-fashioned than its slick sister cities over on the east coast, perhaps even a bit dowdy compared to those sleek flat-roofed communities with two deep-freeze pheasants in every electric pot, a double garage and swimming pool on every lawn. Flashy super-resort trappings are largely absent from Sarasota. It has an endearing quality of small-town friendliness, the lazy feel of ante-bellum plantation South. The beach motels on the Gulf are as modern as all get out; but downtown the hotels are massive, somnolent grand duchesses; and one, a converted bank building, has the quaint name of Orange Blossom. Neon has not gotten out of hand; bars are dark, quiet and retiring; some of the business streets are shaded by old-fangled galleries, others by trees. There are elegant, pleasantly relaxed shopping centers on the keys in the bay fronting the town. Aged clapboard houses, painted white, with shady screened and latticed verandas, dot sleepy neighborhoods of modest newer homes. There are board fences and tassled hammocks; front doors wrought with aluminum palm trees and flamingos; sunrooms with frosted-glass jalousies. The whole town has an unpretentious, leisurely pace. How nice, you say, the first time you encounter Sarasota—just like New England and the Cape. How very nice!

And then whammo! a five-eighths-nude man bounds into the sky behind one of the modest one-stories, does a somersault against the clouds, drops out of sight and bounds again. There is a trampoline in the backyard, and he is a circus performer practicing. For this quiet little spot on the west coast of Florida has been circus town ever since John Ringling first brought his monster show here to winter in 1926. You awaken to lion roars and the distant trumpetings of elephants. If you look sharp through the palm trees, you might see the stretched nets of a flying-trapeze act—young men and girls in muscles and leotards, cutting naked capers against the blue, blue sky. Around a corner, poking from clusters of sea grape, towering over the banyan trees, you encounter the long, fat, silver barrel of a cannon, its maw broad enough to swallow a man. And this is exactly what it does, for it is the circus cannon of the world famous Zacchini family, who have shot two high-caliber generations the length of the nation's Big Tops and arenas. You will see muscular girls, hanging by their jaws among the pines, gracefully posturing to the precise count, in French, of a celebrated aerialist of another day, vigilant on the earth below, in a well-worn Italian fedora.

You drive past a motel run by the man who stands on his forefinger; another, operated by a couple of ex-sideshow giants. The jolly, moon-faced fellow, writing orders for send-home gift boxes at one of the many fruit dealers, has no arms, only hands growing from his shoulders; during the circus season he is a seal-boy in a sideshow annex. Your waiter in the town's most popular restaurant used to be the chauffeur of Henry Ringling North, younger brother of the fabulous Mr. John's nephew, Mr. Johnny. Underfoot there are midgets, dwarfs and clowns, dour without their putty noses and false smiles. The one-time legal-beagle of the Greatest Show on Earth runs a milk route.

The cigar-counter lady in the leading bank building on the main corner is a willing encyclopedia of circus lore. Even the United States Government is not safe from the inroads of Sarasota's circus folk, for the bland fellow in sun helmet, delivering mail by bicycle cart along

Main Street, is a leading Big Top flying-trapeze leaper who has made good his escape from the increasingly insecure world of the nomads.

I wasn't surprised then, when I was looking for someone in town to tell me about performing pigs, to be taken by a young public-relations executive (formerly a clown) to a rather sedate trailer camp on the edge of town.

"If anybody can tell you about trained pigs," he said, "old John White can. He's trained about every kind of small animal that's trainable."

As soon as I saw Mr. White I remembered that he had been ticket-taker on the gate at the Ringling Bros Winter Quarters, which had just closed for the summer. I never dreamed that he had been an animal trainer. John is a hearty, lean stalwart with a raw-boned craggy face, very sun-browned at the time of our visit. He has a lot of tarnished silver hair, and it was neatly slicked, parted and combed.

"Pigs," he said, almost before we had a chance to slide the screen door closed and squeeze into the small trailer, "didn't mean anything. In them days we had a lot of pig acts."

"Boy, I'm glad you boys came along," said John's wife, a cheerily plump lady some years his junior. "He gets bored to death sitting out here with only towners around, and nobody to cut up jackpots with. Some days I just don't think he can stand it for another minute."

I asked John White if pigs had been his circus specialty.

"No, heck," he said, "my dad always had dogs and mules." And then old John launched into a discourse only slightly interrupted by our questions and scrapbooks hauled out by his wife. Over a couple of fascinating hours I was given an eyewitness picture of the old dog-and-pony show days; learned how to train dogs and mules; had revealed to me the mysteries of the January mule, a tanbark classic whose details I'd not been able to uncover before. I absorbed a firsthand account of the historic Pete Jenkins act, the riding turn that was one of pioneer America's first indigenous contributions to the circus. And John White told me the story of the first Negro to appear on the stage in the Deep South with a white man and woman —himself and his wife—in an act called, "White, Black and Useless," the last-named being a mule.

John White's father, following the pattern of those early circus days, had functioned in nine different acts, and son John followed in his busy footsteps. In his circus days he operated this array: chariot races with greyhounds in the traces and monkey drivers; performing spitz dogs; a jockey act with dogs riding ponies, monkeys riding goats, little dogs riding bigger ones; a high-school trick horse; liberty horse drill; a clown act with two donkeys; a January mule; the traditional Pete Jenkins act; and high-leaping greyhounds. "In the greyhound racing," John said, "the monkeys was belted in and the reins tied onto their hands. We put hundred-pound weights inside the chariots so's they could make the curves on the hippodrome track down by the blues—the bleacher seats."

Leaping greyhounds were all the rage in early sawdust-and-spangles days. One of the most spectacular greyhound displays was that of Madame Lilly Strepetow (a Russian lady now in her declining years and employed by her friends, the Cristiani Circus family, where she is generally useful, usually in tearing tickets for the sideshow and wild animal annex). Mme. Strepetow called her tableau: "The Wild Hunting" A Sport Act Unique All the World Over. Her handbills advertised: "Two own horses, a Hunt of Russian Greyhounds, Splendid Decoration and 36 First-class Dresses." Leaping greyhounds appeared also with the stage show of the Great Herrman, the magician. These were presented by a Mr. John Wingfield and featured The Great Leap—over a pile-up of two tables and one chair. Doberman pinschers are also great leapers, and a chap named Aldo Cristiani (no relation to the circus-owning Cristianis) today has a first-rate act of Dobermans—ten dogs all from the same litter. They do six-foot jumps from ground level without benefit of the usual springboard.

"The springboard ramp is what gives the dog its lift," explained John White. "The ramp, attached to the top of a table, was a carpet-padded, inclined board with an oak piece underneath supporting its middle. The high end was free just like the end of a swimmin' pool diving board. When the dog hit that ramp-end, it gave him a big push into the air. The audience never saw that oak piece; it was our gimmick, and we always hid it with a drape. A' course the dog had to be fearless and strong, and you had to build up his muscles over months. You'd start low and increase the height gradually. And the dog has got to gauge his jump; the one that jumps too fast never gets anywhere. I had one dog, Jiggsy, that went over eleven feet high that way. We never did reach his limit; never took him to capacity—we was afraid to."

White does not believe that every dog can be broken to do the high leap; the ability has to be within the animal. "Breeding don't mean a thing," he explains. "It's just like a race horse; no man can really pick out a race horse. One whose mother was just an old cart horse might be a real whiz-bang. Same in leaping dogs; it's just gotta be there."

When I asked old John if it was easy to break dogs to training, he said, "There's no answer to that. Each dog has a different disposition. It's just like two people; show me how many people can sleep together comfortable—especially two men. The hardest is to break a dog act to give it over to someone else. To work a dog act—in fact any animal act—you have to know the manner of the animal, the little traits—everything."

John said that the somersaulting dog was the hardest to train. In the old days no dog act was complete without at least one somersaulting dog. "It's hard on the dog," said John White, "and it's hard on the man."

"How on the dog?" I asked.

"If I put a rope on you and start throwing you clean over," he answered, "you'd see how on the dog. The soft pad he lands on helps some, and you can support him a little with your hand underneath—but not too much hand. You got to learn him to get away from them hind legs."

Why on the man?

"It's all that stoopin' " explained White. "It's gets you like holy murder in the back."

White had at one time six dogs that somersaulted together on cue; also waltzed and jumped rope in unison. I asked about chastising a dog during training: "Do you spare the rod and spoil the dog?"

"If a dog fights you," said this training authority, "you gotta stop him. If you don't, he'll bite you sooner or later. You got to condition him not to bite if you want to keep him and you out of trouble."

The main thing with dogs, said Mr. White, was to keep them in good physical condition, feeding them once a day, preferably after the night show—in between the matinee and evening performance is considered very bad. The trick dog should have a regular routine and plenty of exercise. His performance does not give the animal enough; there should be runs and walks as well. This conforms to the belief of some ballet dancers that weight must be kept down by regular calesthenics, not by dancing alone.

The easiest trick to teach a dog is sitting up. After his back is strong enough through exercise, the mutt is balanced in a sitting position by holding a light stick under his chin for slight support. To get a dog to hold an object in its mouth, don't touch your stick to the lower jaw; just rest it lightly atop the nose, and the animal will clamp up his bottom jaw onto the object.

John also told me how to make cats box. "You get two male cats," he said, "put collars on them and leather mitts, loose at the front so's they make noise when they slap together. Then two people hold the cats by the leads, and you squeeze the very end of the tails to make the cats punch out. It's a scream. After a while you don't need to squeeze the tails no more. They just spar by themselves.

"Boxing kangaroos I never had much to do with. They're easy to break, they tell me—both them and the wallabies—but I never liked them. They can rip you with their back claws and they pack a good-sized wallop in their tails—all muscle, thick as a trapeze-catcher's biceps and strong as a baseball bat."

John White's notion that breeding is of little importance in leaping dogs seems to hold true for the majority of other circus dogs. Most of the talented canines in trained-dog acts and the trick dogs of clowns are common mutts, for dogs, like small boys, also run away with the circus. Puppy waifs choosing this life of vagabondage usually sniff out jobs in clown alley and enter a world of canine aristocracy. Those adopted by other performers or by work-hands lead carefree enough lives but, by clown-dog standards, insufferably dull ones.

Being a clown-alley dog is great sport. Clown dogs get to dress up like rabbits, elephants and little horses, and sometimes they can even have lights on their tails. They affect spectacles, dangly earrings, and pearl necklaces; learn to hold pipes in their mouths, wear derbies, high silk hats and monocles, and act every bit as important as people. They have custom-made coats, some with spangles, and occasionally wear spats and snowshoes. Their Big Top labor is far from strenuous. They tag along behind their comic bosses, with an occasional flipping somersault, sit-up, dead-doggie, hind-leg trot or front-leg balance. All that some dogs do is rush a clown and bite into his padded rear, these luckiest of all show-bums being called pad-dogs.

Clowns find that the commonest ill-bred mutts usually make the best comedy dogs. Charlie Bell, one of the old-time clown-dog handlers (in recent years he worked the tiny dog-elephants on the Ringling show), once told me that the finest performing dog he ever owned, a terrier named Trixie, was a waif that he stumbled over one dark night on his way to the circus train. Of the full-blooded dogs,

clowns prefer French poodles and dachshunds. They are to the slap-stick born—true harlequins—but most joeys' funds are too hard earned to squander on pedigrees.

The famous clown, Polidor, had a troupe of full-bred Chihuahuas, and his best-remembered stunt was a funeral for a dead flea with the dogs as black-draped mourners. Polidor also had in his repertoire a gag that sticks persistently in every circus buff's memory—"the dog in the stomach." Perhaps it has some association with pre-natal influence. The stunt operated thus: a small dog would leap through a trap door in the rear of an especially built hollow fat-suit worn by the clown, half-circle an inside platform and pop out of the stomach by another trapdoor.

Clown-dogs live in a small world bounded by the edges of the circus community. While they often venture beyond the Big Top stake line, they seldom leave the circus backyard, and they never cross the boundaries of the circus lot alone. They are considered kinkers by the management and bed down wherever their clown-boss sleeps, usually snuggled into the foot of his berth. Clown-dogs eat well, having the pick of cookhouse leavings, and the variety of bones is infinite. Very often a clown will smuggle his dog, hidden in a small valise, into a restaurant and surreptitiously slip him under-the-table handouts. Some of the finest eating places in the country with the strictest "No Pets Absolutely" rule have unwittingly entertained clown-dogs. (Tip to restaurant managers: vague-looking man carrying small beat-up airlines bag is undoubtedly clown in mufti, with dog in bag.)

Clown-dogs are remarkably well disciplined, and in the per-formers' dressing rooms they behave to each other very much in the manner of well-bred neighbors in a New York apartment house—yip-ping a lot but seldom indulging in serious wrangles or mayhem. And the unpardonable sin is *never* committed on trunk corners.

Dogs who are habitual night-crawlers don't have to change their owlish habits too much when they become clowns. They can stay up all night as usual and furthermore, with their master, have honorable entree to all barrooms for a midnight snack, finding it no longer necessary to scavenge the swill pails out back. They can sleep late, until almost noon, and when they are not contributing their in-finitesimal bit to the fine art of buffoonery, they have a choice of in-numerable fragrant places in which to laze around.

While the life of a clown-dog is comfortable, it is confining and somewhat introverted, with little real social exchange—dog to dog. Joeys seldom give their bread-and-butters the opportunity to mix either with the wag-tailed ruffians of the working departments or with the hard-working professionals of the featured performing troupes. The pros are too busy to notice this affront, and the dogs of the roughnecks simply shrug off the enforced segregation. These tatter-demalion wards of the workhands are invariably real toughies, regarding themselves as vastly superior to the actor dogs, especially their clown-brother creampuffs.

The most famous rag-tail roustabout dogs of the modern circus world were Negus, guardian of the menagerie, and Murphy, the ring-stock (horse department) mascot. Negus was all black with white chest and was named by some erudite cage-hand after the Ethiopian sovereign. He and Murphy were such personalities around the circus that they were portrayed in a novel, *Cat Man*, by Edward Hoagland (although Negus's color was changed to fox-red). The dogs were the only ones of all the easily recognizable characters whose names were unaltered in that roistering tale, which gives such an accurate insight to the backstage life of the animal department of a large circus. (Highly recommended in this corner.)

Negus had two main jobs: one to chase kids who tried to free-roll the circus (get in without paying) by crawling under the menagerie sidewall; the other to prevent menagerie workhands from pilfering grapes, oranges, bananas and other delicacies meant for the menagerie's wilder creatures.

Murphy, a curly-haired somewhat-Airedale, was a circus sybarite with no well-defined functions. He usually rode to and from the train atop a carriage in a place of high honor, but he was a great train-misser until his operation. Mr. Murphy, in making romantic night calls around town, was getting left behind too often, causing great inconvenience, so Henderson, the circus veterinarian, was asked to alter Murphy's way of life. Murphy never cared much for Doc after that, though they finally got around to nodding again.

The most repeated circus-dog story, so well known that in the tented world it has become a classic, is based on the fact that usually a circus under canvas looks the same on a hard-clay lot in Okmulgee, Oklahoma, as it does in a grassy field in Columbus, Ohio, each wagon usually being spotted every day in the same position in relation to the other units of the big show—other wagons, midway joints, main entrance, Big Top, sideshow and other tents. This day-to-day sameness is said to have fooled a dog named Red Wagon Nellie, a small Boston bull who belonged half-and-half to the circus treasurer and its auditor.

Nellie made her home in the main office wagon called the Red Wagon, and she was a thoroughly spoiled young bitch. Nearly everybody around the front-end of the show brought Nellie the choicest bones from the cookhouse. When she had too many to chew on, she would bury the extras under the wagon. The next morning at the next stand in another town Nellie would trustfully go to her burying grounds to dig up a bone. She never got over being mystified by the seeming disappearance of her treasures. I never believed this story, crediting it to the lively imagination of a circus press agent, until one night in the dark I lost a key by the Red Wagon. In looking for it by the morning's early light, I suddenly, sheepishly, realized that we were in the next town a hundred and fifty miles away!

While I am very familiar with the domain of the dog on the

circus, I have never known much about circus trick mules, for they were all gone from the Big Top by the time I became a circus addict. So I was glad that day in Sarasota to come across a man who not only knew about trained pigs and dogs but who was also an authority on mules. Few circus-goers know about mules any more. That lovable, snorting war horse of the circus, Roland Butler, when he was Ringling publicity chief, received a letter from a lady in Marblehead, Massachusetts, asking whether mules were able to sit down. Roland knew less about mules than his inquirer, but his answer, a classic bit of *non sequitur*, was taken seriously and forwarded by the trustful lady to the Museum of Comparative Zoology at Harvard University, which carefully filed it. It said in part: ". . . some mules are trained to sit down, some sit down on their own initiatives. The length of time they sit varies the same as it does with other sitting creatures. . . ."

About all I knew about a mule when I called on old John White was that the true mule has a horse-mare mother, an ass father; and that the hinny (hinnus) results from the breeding, never deliberate, of a stallion with an ass. And I knew that mules and hinnys, both male and female, are sterile—with them it's the end of the line.

"There's lots to a mule," said John White. "They're not so strong as a horse, but they have some of his agility and way of movin', and mules ain't as patient as dunkeys but are just as sure-footed."

The only circus mule I remember is one that was worked by a tall, thin, long-legged Ringling Bros clown named Willy Mosier. He would run down the hippodrome track with the mule following him. The instant the clown paused, the mule would scoot between his stilt-like legs from behind, heisting the fellow to its back.

"Sure," said John, "that pick-up was a standard mule trick in them days—only Willy he did it the best. You don't see no pick-*out* mules any more either. My dad had one of the best pick-out mules in the business."

A pick-out mule, pony or horse is one that selects letters or colors from a line-up of them to solve elementary mathematical problems, answer questions or indicate powers of discrimination and intelligence. These trained equines also pick out a handkerchief, scarf, or some other cloth (often a silk flag) from a box which is usually closed by a lid, or from a man's pocket or from other hiding places. Many times such animals have been foisted on the public as truly educated beasts.

For over thirty years a horse named Lady Wonder was presented by her owner—Mrs. C. D. Fonda, a simple farm woman of Richmond, Virginia—as a genuine clairvoyant animal. Lady Wonder exercised her supposed perception for an average of five thousand persons a year until she died of a heart attack in 1957, having granted person-to-horse consultations to one hundred and fifty thousand persons. Questions were three for a dollar, and people flocked to the horse for information, solace and help. Lady Wonder was taken very seriously by everyone but hard-bitten circus people. She was examined by the foremost investigator in America of extra-sensory perception, Dr. J. B. Rhine, of Duke University, who became convinced of her telepathic powers. An honorable Massachusetts district attorney and a chief of police of equal integrity jointly credited Lady Wonder with giving them the clue that led to the finding of the bodies of a pair of missing children. Lady Wonder picked Jack Dempsey to win over Jack Sharkey in the heavyweight title bout of 1927; she was widely patronized by trustful horse-players; her help was sought by oil wild-catters.

An especially skeptical doubting Thomas from the circus was Czeslan (Charles) Mroczkowski, the Polish horse trainer who has been with Ringling Bros and Barnum & Bailey since 1948: Charlie smiled wryly when I asked him one day about Lady Wonder. "You expect people to believe such things?" he said. "That a horse can read minds? Is *clairvoyant?* Maybe the woman trainer is a little, but she is just smart, I think. It's all done with cues, has to be. A horse is not intelligent to spell words. In Europe they have many acts similar. Any horse I could train to do the same thing. Either a slight movement of the body, your arm, hand, finger—anything. Maybe even just the snapping the fingernail. The smallest thing—just depends on what the horse has been broken to—tells him when to stop at an object."

My new circus friend, John White, didn't take much stock in Lady Wonder either. "It's just a trick," he said. "Any of the old mule trainers could do it. My dad's pick-out mule did all them things. He did problems and sums (simple ones a'course), and he picked out names and colors and the handkerchief and flags from the box with the lid on it. And besides he'd take your coat off the rack with his teeth, hold it for you 'til you got into it; then he'd take it off again, brush it and hang it back up. He waited table, did a little Swiss bell ringing, and churned butter. It took an awful lot of breaking for a good mule act. He rode on a swing and a teeter-totter, jumped over two Indian ponies and a dunkey, and finished by leaping over a five-foot gate. And then we'd go into the January act."

The January mule is one of the oldest interludes in the circus. In America it comes down from torchlight days, the favorite of our grandfathers and great-grandfathers and a specialty of every talking clown, from the British Grimaldi through Yankee Dan Rice, until circuses grew too big for clowns to communicate with an audience except by incomprehensible yoicks and furious sallies of madness.

"After the pick-out mule did that five-foot leap over the gate," said John White, beginning to unfold the mystery of the January act to me, "the clown comes in and him and the ringmaster holds a conversation. 'Where did you get that mule?' 'I raised him,' the ringmaster says. 'Yeah, you raised him from my father's barn,' says the clown. 'Bet you a hundred dollars against a bottle of wine he can't jump the bars three times in a row.' The clown pulls out a roll, peels off some stage money and they bet. Then the clown whispers in the mule's ear—pantomiming mostly, saying like if you don't jump when I say I'll give you a big bag of oats. Then he says out loud, 'You ain't gonna jump *are* you?' and the mule shakes his head no. The ringmaster runs the mule around the ring and when the mule gets to the bars the clown yells, 'Whoa! January' (that's why it's called a January mule; it was always the mule's name—don't ask me why). After the mule balks two more times at the bars the ringmaster pretends to be mad and calls out to the clown, 'I'll double the bet if *you* can make him jump.' So then the clown takes the whip, gives the cue and away the mule goes, right over the bars—clean as a whistle. Then the clown says, 'How'd you like to trade him for a larger horse?' and he goes out and comes in with a pony and little buckboard wagon. Right away the pony lays down in the shafts and the ringmaster don't see him. 'Where is he?' and so on—they do *that* bit of cross fire. Then the ringmaster asks is the mule a good driver? So they hitch it to the cart and the clown gives the cue and the mule kicks at the dashboard until the wagon falls apart (it's a breakaway). Then the clown goes out and comes back in with the bucking mule. They do all the old gags—get a gilly [a non-circus person] from the audience to ride him, and a few plants and so forth. Finally the clown says, 'I can ride him' and him and the ringmaster bets again. The clown gets on the mule's back looking toward the tail with his legs straddling the neck, his hands on the mule's shoulders. The mule bucks but naturally cain't throw him off, then it lays down and the clown turns him clean over without ever leaving the neck and the mule scrambles back up on all fours again and the clown rides him around the ring, picks up the money and out. It's a little bit bigger'n the January act that Dan Rice used, but it was a jim-dandy."

Remnants of this act are seen occasionally, fleeting glimpses during a bareback riding act when the comic, dressed in some outlandish outfit, after many hair-raising and ludicrous attempts to ride a fast-paced horse (invariably dropping his trousers at some point) finally masters the rhythm and finishes nonchalantly on the swift-circling steed with hands in pockets or assuming some other such insouciant attitude. Sometimes there is the traditional strip; more often not.

The incomparable Poodles Hanneford, draped in floor-length coonskin coat, battered derby cocked jauntily over pasty-white face, made a specialty of this stunt in his prime. Poodles' nephew, Tommy Hanneford, performing now in indoor circuses, has devised an "Elvis Presley" version of the same bit; and Giustino Loyal, of the spectacular Loyal-Repenski troupe of pyramiding bareback acrobats, working in an out-sized zoot suit, performs a slightly Latinized translation of the turn.

This segment of the January act derives from a still older bit of circus ring-horse history, the old "Pete Jenkins" routine, which some antiquarians trace back to the original Astley's Circus in England in the 1770's and a skit on horseback called "Billy Button, or The Tailor's Ride to Brantford." This satirized the military tailor, army costumers being notoriously clumsy horsemen. The Pete Jenkins hokum is again an artless joust with the ringmaster, an attempt to make the elegant gentleman appear ridiculous—the oldest dodge of the circus clown. Huckleberry Finn gives the best description I've ever seen of the Pete Jenkins foolishness:

> "Well, all through the circus they done the most astonishing things, and all the time that clown carried on so it most killed the people. The ringmaster couldn't ever say a word to him but he was back at him quick as a wink with the funniest things a body ever said, and how he ever *could* think of so many of them, and so sudden and so pat, was what I couldn't no way understand. Why, I couldn't 'a' thought of them in a year. And by and by a drunk man tried to get into the ring—said he wanted to ride, said he could ride as well as anybody that ever was. They argued and tried to keep him out but he wouldn't listen, and the whole show come to a standstill. Then the

people begun to holler at him and make fun of him, and that made him mad and he begun to rip and tear; so that stirred up the people, and a lot of men begun to pile down off the benches and swarm towards the ring, saying, "Knock him down! throw him out!" and one or two women begun to scream. So, then, the ringmaster made a little speech, and said he hoped there wouldn't be no disturbance, and if the man would promise he wouldn't make no more trouble he would let him ride if he thought he could stay on the horse. So everybody laughed and said all right, and the man got on. The minute he was on, the horse begun to rip and tear and jump and cavort around, with two circus men hanging on to his bridle trying to hold him, and the drunk man hanging to his neck and his heels flying in the air every jump, and the whole crowd of people standing up shouting and laughing till the tears rolled down. And at last, sure enough, all the circus men could do, the horse broke loose and away he went like the very nation, round and round the ring, with that sot laying down on him and hanging to his neck, with first one leg hanging most to the ground on one side and then t'other one on t'other side, and the people just crazy. It warn't funny to me, though; I was all of a tremble to see his danger. But pretty soon he struggled up astraddle and grabbed the bridle and stood! and the horse a-going like a house afire, too. He just stood up there, a-sailing around as easy and comfortable as if he warn't ever drunk in his life—and then he begun to pull off his clothes and sling them. He shed them so thick they kind of clogged the air, and altogether he shed seventeen suits. And then, there he was, slim and handsome and dressed the gaudiest and prettiest you ever saw, and he lit into that horse with his whip and made him fairly hum—and finally skipped off, and made his bow and danced off to the dressing-room, and everybody just a-howling with pleasure and astonishment.

Then the ringmaster he see how he had been fooled, and he *was* the sickest ringmaster you ever see, I reckon. Why, it was one of his own men! He had got up that joke all out of his own head and never let on to nobody. Well, I felt sheepish enough to be took in so, but I wouldn't 'a' been in that ringmaster's place, not for a thousand dollars."

John White's version of the Pete Jenkins classic starts with the simulated drunk (". . . a little silly stupid, but not too much . . .") bringing his chair down from the grandstand to sit by the ring curb.

His actions finally annoy the audience to a point where a policeman, not in on the gag, is called to intercede. The cop hustles the "drunk" out of the tent (". . . we always led him in under the tightwire so's his high round-top hat would get knocked off. Boy! would he burn . . .") and once outside, the "law" is tipped off to the gag. When the rosinback horse is led into the ring, a clown enters and tells the ringmaster that the trick rider has been hurt and cannot appear. The ringmaster to solve the dilemma suggests that the clown substitute. The joey agrees and mounts the horse. Band strikes furious tempo; horse tears around ring; rider quickly jounces off tail end. He calls for slower music. This time around the horse goes so slowly that the clown gradually bounces his way to the front and goes tumbling head over heels off over the neck. " 'Betwixt and between music, then,' he says," explained Mr. White, "and now the drunk stumbles back in and says, 'I can ride.' So they put him up on the horse and he flops right away off the other side with a roll and a crash from the drummer. He crawls back under the belly and gets on again; slides off the back and does the tail-drag for about two times around the ring. Then he lets go, and while he is in the path on hands and knees the horse, coming around again, bears down on him. Well, a' course the audience screams! the horse leaps over him and he runs after it, grabs on, mounts and stands up. Then he strips down and we have a little jockey finish. In them days, suffering cats! it used to knock 'em dead."

Along about the middle of John White's long and full life among the mules and lesser performing denizens of the sawdust ring, he succumbed (in 1919) to the golden lure of vaudeville and left the open road for a spell. He took with him a mule named Useless, a wife named Anne, and an assistant named Harry Jones, a big Jack-Johnson-like Negro who had wandered onto the lot of the Sig Sautelle Circus one summer afternoon fifteen years previously and been hired by White.

Mrs. White was a trouper also—"out of" Middleport, Ohio, her father "out of" Harrisburg, Pa. (Old-timer circus people always refer to their place of origin in that way, never saying "born in.") Anne's family, the McCormicks, were gun-jugglers and sharpshooters. Baby Anne never knew a real pink-ribboned bassinet; her nests were in the trunk trays and canvas sling chairs of red-wheeled wagon circuses. Her beginning year was spent traveling with the circus of W. C. Coup, who had been the very first circus business partner of P. T.

Barnum; her second year of trouping was on the T. K. Burke Circus operated by the clown father of Billie Burke, who later became a celebrated legit actress.

"I had this farm up to Elkton, Maryland," John White told me, "had to get my stuff out of Baltimore; couldn't cut the feed bill there. I said to the wife, I'm gonna get me up a good small novelty act and get out of this consarned mud-show business; live decent for a change."

So White dreamed up a presentation woven from a thousand-and-one nights of sawdust and spangles—a little borrowed from Pete Jenkins, some from the pick-out mule and a bit from the January. The act opened on the afterbeat of the "Anvil Chorus" as the curtain rose on a blacksmith shop. A Negro (Harry Jones) enters dressed in Prince Albert coat and plug hat and pulling a thick hawser. When its entire length is finally hauled from the wings a tiny dog is discovered tied to its end (one of the oldest gags in clown business, and always a good laugh). Let John White explain the rest: "The Negro says to me (I'm the blacksmith) he's looking for Mr. Smith. I play dumb (the audience is away ahead of him). Yeah, Mr. Smith, he says. Oh, I say—catching on—you mean the *black*smith; you want a *job*. Then the wife, dressed up like Sis Hopkins, brings on the mule, dressed in a straw bonnet with his ears sticking out and over-hall pants—she made them herself." ("The first fitting was awful," Mrs. White interjected.)

"They're lined with rubber, so's if he made a mess," continued John. "She asks Harry if he shoes mules and he says, no ma'am, I shoos flies—we had a lot of fast crossfire like that. And that's when we start with the mule. Harry did a lot of funny business with Useless, trying to shoe it. Finally the wife says she can see he can't shoe mules and she's gonna take her mule home. 'Why I bet you can't even *ride* a mule,' she says. Harry and her makes a bet and the money is laid down by the footlights. The mule sneaks over while they're gabbing and eats it (we used toilet paper dyed green with vegetable dye; it dissolves before it even hits the stomach). Well then Harry gets on the mule and it does the bucking and throws him all over the stage. Then he gets on backwards like in the January act, and we do the mule rollover. The finish is a high leap through the back window with the boy on the mule's back. During the blackout the scenery flies and the lights come up on the mule running like all get out on a treadmill in front of a cyclorama."

"Was that the finish of the act?" I asked. John cast me a look of vast disbelief. "Finish? Heck yes, I couldn't put in no more." Then he added, "You had to have a Negro in an act like that. A white man wouldn't have the stability; any kicking—why, he got it. A white guy couldn't have took it."

At first the act wasn't a smash hit. It opened in the Girard Theater, Philadelphia, and the troupe was summarily canned at the end of the first week. The agent told White he'd have to get the act in a little better shape, so he booked the troupe with Dumont's Minstrels, then playing at 9th and Arch streets, same town. (John and his wife were the only whites in the cast.) "Harry," said John, "couldn't sing worth a darn, but he had a marvelous delivery and he looked swell on stage. Finally after three weeks the agent said, 'John I got some time for you'—and we opened at Proctor's in Yonkers for four hundred dollars; I gave the boy fifty. I figured we was doing good; only four pieces of baggage, a mat, the mule and a dog—and we carried him in a grip. Why I was only getting three hundred and fifty a week for my old ten-dog leaping act."

White, Black & Useless became a huge success. "Keith time, Loew's, Pantage's, Moss and that Texas time," said John. "*Texas* time," doubted his wife. "Oh, you mean the Interstate."

White, because of Harry, always had it in his contract that the act wouldn't play below the Mason-Dixon line. Then one day, an enterprising agent (perhaps even forward-looking, but this is doubtful) proposed to book the act into the Deep South, on the Del Mar time. At this point (1919) in the artistic culture of the South, according to John White, no white performer had ever appeared on a Southern stage with a Negro. John said okay, go ahead, he guessed the agent knew what he was doing.

White, Black & Useless opened its Deep South tour at the Lyric Theater in Richmond, Virginia. In going back to those days when he made theatrical history, John White told me, "The white manager come back to our dressing room as we was unpacking; he didn't say nothing, just stood there. 'I know what you're thinking,' I said to him, 'but just wait until it's over and then decide.' And we knocked them cold; they screamed! We played there eleven weeks."

The theater in Columbia, South Carolina, which had a Negro skull mounted on its backstage light-board, at first refused to give Harry Jones a dressing room. After the opening show the management changed its mind.

"We had the same trouble in Mobile, Alabama," said John, "but after the act the stagehands even invited Harry into their soft-ball game out back."

In New Orleans there was more difficulty. "The manager said to me," related John, " 'Mr. White, I don't know if I want to put you on or not.' I said, 'The business is between you and the office. I got mine; it don't mean a thing.' He said, 'What is the newspapers going to say?' That's what he said, 'What is the newspapers going to say?' He was worried. He had all that pit, and from the second balcony on down was white; only the third balcony was Negro. (Fifteen cents, the seats was in them days, way up there; nigger heaven, they called it down South, peanut heaven up North.) I told him to wait, and he said he didn't know.

" 'You want me to hang the scenery?' I asked him. 'Yes.' Well, we knocked them cold; *they* screamed. And crowds of the colored people came around the stage door alley after to see if we really had a Negro on the stage with white folks. They just couldn't believe it was true. The manager was a'scared and made Harry stay inside until the mob went away. Believe me, I was a'scared to read the newspapers. But they was fine."

As a true vaudevillian, John White remembers almost every word of the New Orleans reviews. Dipping into his trunkful of total recall, he said, "In its Palace Theater review the *Picayune* said, 'As fast as we can print words is as fast as White, Black and Useless produced laughs; the funniest act of its kind ever to play New Orleans.' "

The revolutionary Southern tour ended in Cincinnati, and the act went on to play eight years, including fourteen fantastic weeks in England at the Victoria Theater across the street from the Palladium, where the young Marx Brothers were putting the British to the test of American slapstick. "They laid a big egg," said John. "If it hadn't been for that dancer of theirs, they'd have been a flop."

White, Black & Useless closed back in Philadelphia at the Earle Theater in 1927, and the Whites dropped back into circus business with their mule, Useless, who had been very useful, indeed. Harry Jones married and set up housekeeping as far as he could get from the Deep South—in Newport, Rhode Island.

"Them was the days," said John White. "Vaudeville. That's where they had all the cuckoo animal acts. The high-class performers on the bill with an animal act always called that engagement their

'nervous week.' Leaping dogs was a big thing then. They was all
kind of dog acts in them days. Collies, trained Alaskans, wolfhounds,
posing dogs, talking and singing dogs (there was even singing wolves).
Dogs that rode bicycles; ones that made up as ladies and smoked; and
I remember a dachsie dressed up to be an alligator. They even had a
dog troupe that did a one-act drama, 'The Faithless Woman' it was
called. Merian's Dogs. They worked without a trainer onstage and
they did everything: a drunk staggering out of a barroom; a brass
band; a wedding and a funeral; dogs sitting at a restaurant, shooting
pool, playing pinochle. Everything! One act in them days had a dog
that posed on a pedestal all through the act never moving a muscle—
just as still as Grant's Tomb; at the finish when the curtain dropped
and come up again, the trainer'd say to the dog, 'C'mon, let's go,
the act is over,' and it'd leap down, shake hisself and run off. Big
hand because the audience figured the dog had held that pose for
fifteen minutes. But it was a gimmick; the original dog was a dummy
switched to a live dog when the curtain rung down. Good gag.

"Barnold's Drunken Dog got the highest pay in them days, a
thousand a week once from Klaw & Erlanger—ordinarily he rated
three hundred dollars a week. One funny act was Gil Mason and his
dogs; they always did just the *opposite* of what he told them to. And
he had a little monkey that would shiver and shake every time he
said the words, 'Frank Buck.' There was a dog that drew pictures with
a pen tied to his paw. Gautier's Bricklayers was a big hit; they did
a flying trapeze finish and worked without the trainer onstage, same
as Merian's Dogs.

"There was lots of bird acts, mostly cockatoos—they was easy
to train. They raised flags on little flagpoles, hung out the washing
and put out a fire in a little toy house. There was Torcat's Educated
Roosters—a standard act; and Swain's Rats & Cats—a marvelous
act! There weren't too many big animals in vaudeville in them
days—cost too much to ship them around. We had probably the
only act featuring a mule—White, Black & Useless—and there was
a few riding acts like May Wirth, the Hannefords and the Riding
Duttons who wore powdered wigs and dressed up like George Wash-
ingtons. Ella Bradna and her Act Beautiful played wintertime in
vaudeville. I broke the macaws and cockatoo-on-the-horse for that
act for Ella."

This was the illustrious act, brought originally to the Ringling
Bros Circus by Olympia Desval, which starred the equestrienne wife

of the late Fred Bradna (distinguished RBB&B equestrian director) in the center ring for twenty-nine seasons, purported to be the longest such run in circus history. The Act Beautiful was a tableau riding act with horses, dogs, pigeons and other birds, all as white as the driven snow. It featured an outsized MacKenzie husky named Zero and a singing Hungarian midget named Paul Horompo, who had sat many times on the lap of James A. Bailey.

I remember the act very well. Its high point came with the midget as white-faced Harlequin in a white satin outfit, singing a piercing tenor ballad, while Madame Bradna, beautifully gowned in white, aimed a pure white popgun rifle from her comely powder-white shoulder at an almost-white suspended box which contained white pigeons. When the rifle pinged they were released to fly about and eventually settle on various landing points of the Madame herself and on the white carriage drawn by a white horse, with white dogs treadmilling the broad wheels, both inside and out.

One winter evening in Pittsburgh, where the Act Beautiful was filling in some circus off-season time with a theatrical engagement, when the trap sprang, there materialized, along with the birds, a pair of muddy black boots which flopped with a rubbery thud at the feet of a startled Madame Bradna and midget. They belonged to Mullen, the groom, who had a habit of carrying his "wet-weathers" overnight in the pigeon cage and had forgotten that day to remove them.

John White chuckled at this story, which had been passed on to me by the midget. "Around animals in them days you always was good for a lot of laughs."

After his happy vaudeville days, John White answered the call of the calliope again in 1928 and trouped four years on the Downie Bros Circus, a small motorized outfit, and three years with the Al G. Barnes show after it was acquired by John Ringling. He broke in his last group of performing animals, goats, on a small railroad show, the Sparks Circus, in 1947 when he was sixty-four years of age.

"Then we quit," said John.

"But," rejoined his wife, "If I'd 'a' let you, you'd 'a' broke a pig act two years ago."

John, his old eyes sparking back to them days, smiled at Anne McCormick White, by gun-juggler out of sharpshooter.

"Well," he said quietly, "I'd 'a' had use for *you*."

Trouble
Bruin

My friend Steve Colhoun, a top-level photographer, lives a graceful bachelor life on Manhattan's upper East Side, a few blocks from a quietly swank First Avenue bistro named Billy's.

One afternoon on his way to a set of Park Avenue squash racquets Steve stood up to Billy's polished mahogany for a quick beer. Peeping from the breast pocket of his raw silk jacket was a tiny, furry, stuffed bear which a fashion model had playfully given him that morning.

Now, since the passing of Mrs. Billy—a rather stern, buxom lady, who, from her corner table, vigilantly guarded the high social level of the establishment by strident bellow and cane thwack—members of the lower drinking depths sometimes slip into this class-A joint by choice or by mistake. One such stood at Steve's elbow—a coarse fellow with a stubble of beard, bent nose and belligerent jaw—a refugee from the Third Avenue gin mills. He glowered at the tiny pocketed bear. Steve pretended not to notice. Not that he was afraid of the guy (Steve is a plus six-footer), but for heaven's sake why make a scene? The toughie glowered more fiercely. Finally he turned, gave Steve a long go-to-hell look and in a beery blur said, "Say, bud."

"Yes?" Steve answered politely.

"About that bear," said the rough customer.

"Yes?" said Steve again, edging away just a bit and getting on the ready.

"I got one jush like it," said the tough guy. "See?" He dipped grubby thumb and forefinger into his breast pocket, hauled forth an identical little yellow furry bear, and fondled it happily.

In America, bowery bum or gentleman, everybody loves a bear; we are a nation reared on bears. A bear lurks at every mother's knee; the dark forests of childhood rage with them. That inimitable porridge trio—the Big, the Mama-sized and the Little Bear. Mr. Milne's incredible Pooh. And the bear magically transformed into a charming Prince through the unselfish love of Rose Red—or was it Snow White? (Since Disney I have become confused.)

The first animal cuddled in bed by most American boys (and some girls) is a Teddy bear, a ruler of our juvenile culture that even Mickey Mouse has been unable to depose. (An American President, Theodore Roosevelt, wished this favorite childhood creature on us by being photographed on one of his innumerable hunting expeditions holding a bear cub.)

The bear is the trained wild animal that has trudged the tanbark trail longer than any other—the bear and the clown being the only survivors from the earliest Grecian beginnings of the sawdust spectacle. The clown has descended to us from that ancient time in an almost pure line, some of his standard gags today being identical with those endured by Socrates and confreres. The bear's repertoire has been expanded over the ages, but every bruin still specializes in dancing, the antic that launched his tribe in show business. The dancing bears trained by wandering Greek priests from Agyrion in the early part of the fourth century B.C. were likely the world's first wild-animal entertainers, although bruins were present in the menageries of the ancient Egyptians and featured in the mammoth religious festivals and processions.

Romans were not too interested in ursine terpsichore, preferring to use their shaggy creatures in more sinister spectacles called "*venationes*," public exhibitions of brutal killings and beast baitings. For these sadistic occasions the arena was often sprinkled with gold powder and cinnabar, as well as sand and sawdust, and the ill-fated animals were made beautiful by lovely colors and adorned with tinkly bells, gold shrubbery, silver brocaded silks and satins. The bears were sometimes dabbed with a sticky substance so that their rollings would cover them with feathers and straw and bits of fallen martyrs.

The medieval mountebanks and gypsies of middle Europe revived the tradition of the dancing bear, and the first animal performers in the new world were partially tamed native-forest bears shuffling to a turkey trot on the hard clay of tavern courtyards.

Trained monkeys, usually regarded as America's premier animal performers, didn't get here until 1751, long after our first foreign bear had arrived in 1733 at Boston, favorite entry port for most wild animal early arrivals from abroad.

Of all the wild carnivores performing today bears are the favorite. The public dotes on bears, makes over them more than any other wild creature. People seldom talk intimately to lions, tigers, giraffes, rhinos, elephants or camels, but they invariably believe that bears understand every word said to them. This is largely because bears, when spoken to, fix their attention on the speaker. Human vanity is flattered by this seeming animal deference, since other wild beasts tend to ignore mankind. Everybody regards the bear as a delightful cuddlesome creature. This is a large, naïve mistake, for a bear loves nobody and is far from cuddlesome.

Bears are the most vicious, most dangerous of the wild exhibition animals, much more ferocious than the big cats, more treacherous than elephants, and are not to be trusted for one unholy second. Beware of bears! A bear is the world's wisest, most resourceful beast, extremely well-educated in the art of self-preservation, matching the coyote, wolf and white-tailed deer. On this continent bears have survived thirty thousand years longer than the saber-tooth tiger and the American lion. Remains of all three mammals are found in the famous La Brea tar pits of Los Angeles. Bears are the toughest of all carnivores; few animals have been so unmercifully put upon as the bear.

Savage peoples have always feared and respected its power and have done their utmost to eliminate the shaggy monster. Among the wilder Asiatics the extinction program was sometimes carried on under the mantle of holiness. Bear worship is widespread among Siberian tribes with the practice extending as far south as the northernmost parts of Japan, where the Ainu, a primitive people whose culture remains close to the neolithic, still venerate the bear.

Gypsies have been rough on bears. They used to remove most of the danger from their dancing bears by blinding them and conditioned the beasts to stand erect by placing trays of hot coals beneath the front paws to keep the animals from going down on all fours.

But not only the savage races have treated the bear brutally—civilized peoples have done their share as well. The British have been rather beastly. Bearbaiting was legal in England for seven hundred years, from the reign of Henry II. In this popular sport of Britannia's gentlemen, a bear chained to a stake by one hind leg was harassed and attacked by vicious dogs especially trained for this purpose. A popular variation was the whipping of a blinded bear. Sunday was the favorite bearbaiting day and the main arena in London was the "Paris Garden" in Southwark on the south side of the Thames.

The bloody spectacles had royal sanction (Queen Elizabeth, in 1575, attended a soirée involving thirteen bruins) and the chief master of the bear, whose annual salary was sixteen denarii (one d. originally the equivalent of ten asses) was empowered to requisition animals wherever he found them. A bulletin of the day stated:

> Her Majesty is very well. This day she appoints a Frenchman to do feats upon a rope in the Conduit Court. Tomorrow she has commanded the bears, the bull and the ape to be bayted in the tiltyard. Upon Wednesday she will have solemn dauncing.

Although a baited bull's nose was usually blown full of pepper to add fury to the show, this extra fillip was never necessary for the fierce bear. The bull was also allowed a hole in the ground in which to shield his most sensitive parts, nose and lips, but bears were never pandered to in the slightest.

A report from that savage epoch of the bear says:

> It was a sport very pleasant to see; the bear with his pink eyes tearing after his enemies approach; the nimbleness and await of the dog to take his advantage and the force and experience of the bear again to avoid his assaults; if he were bitten in one place how he would pinch in another to get free; that if he were taken once, then by what shift with biting, with clawing, with roaring, with tossing and tumbling, he would work and wind himself from them; and when he was loose to shake

his ears twice or thrice with the blood and the slaver hanging about his physiognomy.

The Puritans tried to put an end to bearbaiting, not particularly because of the cruelty to the animals, but because the exhibition gave pleasure to spectators on the Sabbath. Bearbaiting was finally prohibited by an Act of Parliament—but not until 1835, the same year that Texas proclaimed independence of Mexico and the Cherokees ceded their lands to the United States government for five million dollars and agreed to move their tepees across the Mississippi.

The bear's colossal endurance and hardiness make it a great circus trouper. Other factors which have enabled it to be the most interesting performing beast of the tanbark are its original thought and vigorous enterprise. Only the order of primates taken collectively surpass the bear in both respects. A bear is able to find the weakest area in any thing that relates to its confinement (either man or material) and set itself to destroy it.

Bears have a driving curiosity and take well to tricks. Next to simians they are the most demonstrative of all wild animals and adept in the art of facial and bodily expression. In variety of voice the bear surpasses all other wild creatures (except possibly the elephant), being able to whine, whimper, snort, rumble, blow and sniff, cry, bawl, howl and roar—and to make a horrendous sound by clanking toothy jaws together.

The European brown bear is the species usually seen in the circus ring, as this type responds best to training. However, the Himalayan black bear, a glossy blue-black beauty with a white crescent on its chest, is almost as able a performer as his Occidental cousin, and the Syrian bear is frequently used by circus bear trainers.

Rarely seen in a circus act, for it is a rather nervous cowardly beast, is the Yezo, an unusually large (six-hundred-pound) Old World bear, native to Japan. Seldom found in captivity outside a circus menagerie or zoo are the sloth bear of India and Ceylon; the Kodiak, the Alaskan giant that sometimes reaches a weight of 1600 pounds; and the only South American bear, smallest of the New World beasts (adult 200 pounds), the spectacled bear, which has whitish rings around its eyes. A very rare bear is an inland white one found in northern British Columbia. Called the *Evarctos Kermooei*, it is a species of black bear and not a polar, as might be assumed from its color. The Malayan sun bear is a poor performing risk, for it is by nature hysterical, evil-tempered, aggressive and very savage.

Attempts to train the American black bear and its cinnamon-brown brother have been largely unsuccessful, and it is extremely doubtful that you will ever see a performing grizzly bear. It has been found absolutely impossible to make any kind of actor—good, bad or indifferent—of that fierce fellow. Even the great Karl Hagenbeck, the famous German wild-animal expert, failed after investing a reputed $100,000 in an effort to break an act of grizzlies. Authorities claim that only one grizzly in a thousand has any of the qualities necessary to become a performer. In the wagon-show days of the circus, a chap calling himself Grizzly Bear Charlie purported to exhibit a troupe of these furies, but his bears actually were Russian browns. The scientific name of the grizzly, *Ursus horribilis*, just about describes it. In the wilds the grizzly is feared by all other bears. Its long dense fur, tough as chain mail, makes it fairly invulnerable to attack.

The polar bear, as fierce as the grizzly and just as bloodthirsty, but stupider, more stoic and very awkward to train, is often seen in circus performance. The largest polar bear act in history was one of seventy-five, turned out in 1908 by the Hagenbeck outfit in Germany. For fifteen years they were exhibited by Wilhelm Hagenbeck, who has stated that in all that time only two of the bears ever became fond of their work and that not a single bear ever telegraphed its intentions or revealed its mood by facial expression. The polar bear, an exception to all other bruins, is a notorious poker face, completely expressionless whether angry or pleased. Some trainers find it so difficult to tell one polar bear from another that they identify them by color spots painted on the sides of their snowy heads.

Bears are of the family *Ursidae*, one of the four such groups in the superfamily of *Canoidea*, which, with its sister superfamily, *Feloidea* (housing cat, hyena and civet families), falls under one of the suborders of *Carnivora*, the split-footed or typical carnivores (*Fissipedia*) with pawlike feet and varying cheek teeth. The other suborder is the fin-footed (*Pinnipedia*) or seal group, with paddlelike feet and cheek teeth all the same (sea lions, seals and walruses). The bear family, *Ursidae*, is closely related to the clan of dog, wolf and fox—*Canidae*; and to the tribe which contains raccoons, kinkajous, coatimundis, and pandas—the *Procyonidae*. The fourth family in the group to which the bear belongs is the *Mustelidae*, in which reside most of the unwilling suppliers of *haute monde* fur wraps: the mink, ermine, sable, marten, badger; as well as the ferret, skunk, weasel and wolverine. The two animals which most resemble toy bears, the koala, which is the living image of a Teddy bear, and the wombat, dead ringer for Mr. Pooh, are not bears at all but marsupials.

The word "bear" was brought into the Anglo-Saxon language by the European brown bear, common dancing bear of the gypsies and other itinerant entertainers. It ranges the temperate regions eastward from Spain to the Bering Straits, although eradicated from Great Britain by the end of the eleventh century. *Béras* is the Lithuanian word for brown; *braun* is the German word for that color, and in French and Swedish it is *brun*; Italians say *bruno*. The word meaning bear varies greatly in the various tongues: German, *bär*; French, *ours*; Swedish, *björn*; Italian, *orso*.

The cubs of black and brown bear are born painlessly during the mother's hibernation. (Polars also hibernate; their cubs are born below frost level.) At birth, bear cubs are hairless and tiny, between kitten and squirrel size—sometimes as long as eight or ten inches, weighing from eight ounces to two pounds. The mother remains in a comatose state offering her babies milk and warmth, taking no nutriment herself but that of her younkers' feces, her rectum blocked until spring by a plug of pine needles known as the "tappen." Papa bear, somewhat of a tramp, hibernates apart from his spouse, is not present at the birth of his heirs and never bothers to look in on them once they arrive.

After a spring of snuggling and suckling, furring and growing, the cubs spend summer and their first winter being taught by their solicitous mama. At the beginning of their second winter they are big enough to set out on their own. Soon they are members in good standing of the clan bear.

A bear with every advantage can annihilate a lion or tiger. Roman Proske, famous trainer of big cats, lost two tigers and a lion to bears; a Clyde Beatty tigress was murdered by a bear. But the bear wins against the big cats only in a sneak attack. Given a fair-shake encounter at equal weights, the big cat would emerge victorious, in the opinion of most animal experts, due to its great maneuverability and lightning speed. Bears are not invulnerable. Al G. Barnes, the owner of what was America's most-diversified wild-animal circus, in his memoirs tells of a small zebra dispatching a large grizzly bear to insensibility by one well-planted kick to the forehead; a news story from Europe in the spring of 1957 told of a bear fight on the Willy Hagenbeck Circus, in which an elephant with one blow from its powerful trunk knocked the ambition out of a battling giant polar bear.

The bear is the most dangerous animal to train for circus exhibition. It does not have the quickly rising, quickly ebbing, passionate furies of the big cats; a wronged bear becomes chronically sullen and smoulders until the opportunity arrives to kill his provoker. The average circus bear on hind legs stands close to six feet tall and weighs from 300 to 500 pounds. It has tremendous power, being able, with one swift swipe, to smash a man's rib cage or neatly strip a bloody toupee from his skull. Add to this strength a tireless energy, great destructive enterprise, plus spasmodic treachery and you have a formidable opponent. Bears also have an excellent nose and can scent the slightest fear in a man facing them.

It is widely believed that bear trainers keep their beasts up on hind legs because a bear is unable to attack from that position. This is not true. A bear can attack from any old position—even when flat on its back. An onslaught is seldom launched while standing upright, the beast preferring the more natural, more sure all-fours rush. In its native state a bear rears on its hind legs mostly to explore terrain, but it also gets into this position to reach treed food, to scratch its mark high on the bears' "warning tree" (believed to be a habit of the rutting season) and to do battle with another bear.

A polar bear's attack tactic is to jump a victim and roll over with him; other bears come in head down, suddenly and silently, with no warning, for a relentless grab to draw the man-victim to them, usually going for the legs to drop him to the floor. The Himalayan bear is fond of holding its victim with its front paws while blissfully shredding him with the claws of its back ones. A bear attacking another carnivore first swipes a blow to his foe's head, then seizes him by cheek with teeth, shifting as quickly as possible to the throat. A bear seldom bites lower than the shoulders. In an even match the fracas is carried on head to head, jaws to jaws, the paws doing little damage. When a bear is outclassed, or is taking too much of a larruping, he throws himself to the ground on his back so that he can lash out with all four sets of claws, making an extremely wicked target.

All the bear-men I've talked to have told me that, given a choice of antagonist, they would rather take on a lion than a bear. There are only a few ways to fend off a bear attack. In training, an ordinary kitchen broom, straw-end to the bear, is a simple but effective defense. Fast footwork is a most important factor in working with the lumbering beasts. "Make it mighty plain that you're the boss," Albert Rix, a disciple of Hagenbeck, once explained to me, "and then be always ready to get fast from out the way in case you haven't conwinced the bear." Nothing discourages a really angry bear; he is absolutely relentless when aroused. A blank gun fired in his open jaws only infuriates him further; water simply drives him closer to insanity. Poke a chair at a bear and he will likely take it away from you and splinter its legs over your noggin. Fire, which will swerve an outraged elephant, or a snake, which will dissuade a nasty gorilla, registers zero to a maddened bear. Only a live bullet will successfully stop a bear on a serious rampage.

An attacking bear covers himself well by dropping his head stomachward and hunching his beefy shoulders so that the only thing available for receiving a thwack is his broad heavily muscled back. "That," smiles Rix, a Swede who understands bears very well, "you could hit with a sledge hammer and it make no effect. They try to push you into a corner and then there is no chance. They crush you."

A recommended way to break a bear's hold is to grab and twist his ears; another is to stomp mightily on his toes. If arms are free, a good hard punch on the nose will usually spring the muscle trap, but this takes real nerve—it's so easy to lose a fist. (The powerful jaws of a strong bear are capable of snapping a half-inch iron bar in two.) It was such a blow to a bruin proboscis that gave the Hagenbeck-Wallace Circus its Famous Somersaulting Bear. The attacking bear, on being smacked in defense, went into a complete somersault, so the stunt was promptly added to the repertoire—always cued by a crosscut wind-up. The brave bear trainer who let fly the thunderbolt, a kid just breaking into the big cage, is now a man long known for his mastery of lions and tigers, the celebrated Clyde Beatty.

A bear's long non-retractable claws are as sharp as a big cat's, but the bruin's best weapon is its vicious bite. Bears are what animal handlers call "series biters," making holes rather than removing chunks of flesh. Bite, bite, bite, bite again; relax jaws and chomp in over and over again. A bear latching onto an ankle will bite its way up the leg to the crotch in a matter of seconds. And if a bear chooses to hold tight, nothing powered by a human can open the jaws, for the teeth mortise together tighter than the temple stones of Machu Picchu. The only favorable thing to be said for a bear bite is that it will almost never produce blood poisoning, which usually results from the bite of a lion, tiger or other big cat, causing, in some cases, raging fevers and violent death. Bears, being omnivorous and mainly vegetable feeders, have cleaner mouths than the monster cats, whose teeth always carry putrid remnants of bloody flesh feasts.

With no trouble at all a bear's gigantic jaws can tear an arm from its socket. Ringling Bros Circus Sideshow once featured an Armless Wonder, Jack Hubert, an ex-animal trainer, forced into the world of tented oddities after he had lost the decision first to a lion, then to a polar bear. One of the great wild-beast trainers of all time, Jack Bonavita, a boyhood idol of Clyde Beatty, had his life shortened by a rampaging polar bear. Chubby Gilfoyle, whose bear act gave Beatty his first taste of handling wild animals, was a one-armed trainer, his best whip-wielder sacrificed to an enraged bear.

A bear once forced Clyde Beatty to become involved in a youthful folly of female impersonation. It was his first season on the Hagenbeck-Wallace show. The "Spec," grand pageant of the hippodrome track, was Arabian in theme that year and featured a Valentino-type "Sheik" vocalist mounted on a caparisoned white horse. After sobbing a maudlin ballad about the luscious *petit chou* who had rejected his love, compromised his honor and put egg on his face before Allah, the "Sheik" galloped off through the burning sawdust sands into a spotlight sun and returned with faithless betrayer slung limply across his saddle, at the head of a dazzling exotic procession in splendid bad taste. The lover's lament was then reprised, after which the hapless victim was ceremoniously pushed into the wild animal den. The young lady, an animal trainer in thin disguise, would then carry on with her act, subduing the beasts that had been expected to tear her limb from feckless limb.

As entertainment the production wasn't earth-shaking—but not bad for those tacky velveteen-and-dyed-ostrich-plume days. The hitch was that, while the girl had courage, she was new to the act, and the bear, who hadn't yet accepted her domination, made a practice of rushing to embrace her rudely as soon as she entered the arena. This not only brought unwelcome guffaws at a very serious dramatic moment, which considerably annoyed the Big Top baritone, but also worried the young lady some. She finally became so perturbed by the bussing bear that she refused to continue her role in the masquerade.

The management, looking around the backyard, found no distaff eligibles to step into her turned-up sandals but fell on Beatty, the only capable beast handler who hadn't yet begun to shave. He was cajoled into service, and after sleeves were hastily stitched onto the costume to conceal bulging biceps, Beatty, flimsily veiled, became the naughty nautch girl of the Casbah. He had no intention of becoming marooned in such a spot but endured the agony for the sake of the show. However, Clyde soon sensed that the management was pleased with his portrayal and was making no effort to find a permanent replacement. When he began to find mash notes pinned to his trunk and bouquets of goldenrod and stinkweed on his wagon steps after the act, Beatty made a hasty decision. From then on during the impassioned renunciation the "Sheik" vocalist was tickled unmercifully by his hefty saddle-draped lover-girl. It wasn't long until the beautiful betrayal was written out of the "Spec," and a grateful Beatty went back to full-time beast subjugating.

Beatty once worked the largest bear act ever seen in America, but he has never cared too much for the shaggy fur-balls, although he admits that the bear is the smartest animal he has ever encountered. "It can learn tricks," he told me once, "like no other animal—and more of them. I even taught bears to carry lighted torches in their mouths!"

Besides the great courage needed for bear training a considerable amount of patience is required. Elephants, horses, chimpanzees and most other mammals, excepting porpoises, can be broken to perform standard tricks predetermined by the trainer. Of the carnivores, only dogs are trained by this arbitrary method; training of all the other species is preceded by a long period of careful, steady observation to determine what sort of stunts each particular beast is able to do. In other words the performance is adapted to the animals' capabilities, the beasts first telling the man what they can do best.

Now when the potential of a lion, tiger or smaller cat is learned, the animal can then be *forced* to learn tricks that suit its particular temperament. But a bear cannot be pushed into performing. He can only be *encouraged* to perform an act that he has first indicated is suitable for him; and the stunt must be learned in the bear's own way in his own sweet time. Beating, whipping, coaxing, wheedling, or bribing with food makes absolutely no impression on Herr Bruin.

Bears, like horses, have poor memories for their routines and need to be practiced often. Only occasionally does one come along who absolutely refuses to practice but never misses a cue in performance.

One of the greatest bear trainers the world has ever known is a genial Teuton named Emil Pallenberg, now aged seventy, retired and living in America's circus home town, Sarasota, Florida. The late Fred Bradna, for forty-two years Ringling Bros' Equestrian Director extraordinary, and symbol of the circus's halcyon days, in his memoirs says of Herr Pallenberg:

"Schooled in the early German tradition, he was a martinet, and a violent disciplinarian, but he obtained results—the skating bear, the bicycle-riding bear—which no one has duplicated with equal finesse." Now Bradna classifying Pallenberg as a martinet is simply the *Topf* calling the *Kessel* black, for the great ringmaster was no slouch himself in the fine art of polite tyranny (in his day he used to zing pebbles at lazy clowns to keep them on the *qui vive*), but such tribute from a man notoriously cautious (almost stingy) with praise, gives some indication of the very special and great ability of Pallenberg, *bruin-Meister*.

Emil Pallenberg was the first man to teach a bear to ride a bicycle. It was a lady bear, a beautiful Russian brown creature, and her name was Ella. In my boyhood I greatly admired Ella's pedal pushing. The Pallenbergs were a natty couple in those days (Emil's wife, Cato, always appeared with him): he handsome and slim in pearl-grey derby, riding habit with tattersall vest, three-quarter laced boots, and brisk, waxed mustache; she quietly beautiful with long strands of pearls cascading down peach-blossom bare shoulders, high heels, spangled bodice and flouncy fur-trimmed skirt that ended saucily just below silk-stockinged knees.

While in Sarasota recently I called around to see the Pallenbergs. Gone is derby and tattersall; waistline and mustache have both relaxed. Emil has grown to resemble one of his big bruins (this physiognomical change seems to take place in all animal trainers). He is happily rotund, solid not fat; his full-moon face is serious, quizzically wise and very sun-browned. The great bear-man, after all those years pacing bears on the circus stages, even walks like one of the shaggy creatures. As Emil lumbered ahead of me onto his sunporch, I felt like Goldilocks and half expected to find waiting three bowls of steaming porridge.

"About bears you want to know," he said, as he settled into a creaking wicker chair. "Bears, more than any other animal, are like people; every one is unlike from the other one. They are tougher than they look and they don't like much to be pushed around; but I rather train ten bears than one dog. After two, three times a bear knows what you want him to do. A dog does, too; only do you think a dog will do it? No sir, he is too stubborn; he just don't *want* to understand. Dogs stink, too; bears don't—I could get in the biggest hotel with a bear."

Pallenberg's bears were always females ("Male bears?" he exclaimed in horror. "One heck of a good way to commit suicide"); and they were the most versatile bears the world has ever seen. Besides the bicycle riding for which they were famous, they danced alone, waltzed together, roller skated, rowed boats (land-bound on small wheels), balanced on rolling globes, rocked on hobby horses, bobbed on teeter-totters, balanced on unicycles, walked tightropes, stomped about on stilts, and rode motorcycles. They also played the bass drum, concertina and harmonica (yes, the *harmonica!*); and performed a risley act (foot juggling), in which they lay on their backs and juggled small barrels with their feet (a spectacular idea which Emil had observed at a Russian circus in St. Petersburg in 1913).

Only once was Emil clawed by one of his ferocious performers—during the making of a motion picture as he was saving a Hollywood stunt man from being ripped apart when, in an ill-advised chase, the bear forgot she was acting.

In his lifetime of training, Pallenberg lost only one bear due to poor health. It died of heart failure during an excessive heat spell in the Middle West when the thermometer hit 114 degrees. The Pallenberg troupe had only one really violent fight: a Japanese bear ripped up a black bear named Edith. After she was nursed back to one piece again, Emil retired Edith from the act and made a pet of her.

It is a rare bear that accepts domestication. Besides Pallenberg's Edith, the only other I've ever heard of was a legendary bear of ancient time that killed one of a team of bullocks clearing ground for a new Abbey at Compiègne, France. The brave monks captured the creature and are supposed to have converted it to work in harness with the surviving ox, causing the building to be called for thirteen hundred years thereafter the Abbey of Bear Field.

"You can never tame a wild animal," says Pallenberg, "only train it by control. And never play with trained animals. You lose the discipline—same as with kids. You play with children, and they have no respect for you as a father."

Emil told me that he always preferred to begin his bears' training when they were one year old and, unlike most bear trainers, with an immediate start, eliminating the usual get-acquainted period between man and animal. The quality Pallenberg looks for most in a bear is pep; a too-tame bear presages a sloppy performer and usually has little aptitude for learning. The quickest way of determining whether a bear is suitable for training is by attempting to put a muzzle on the beast. "If I can get on the muzzle," Emil said, "I find out the character of the bear—vicious or not so vicious."

Muzzling is done with the bear's head clamped through an opening in a stockade-like board barrier. The wild beast is carefully tied down for this operation, with a stick placed near the fulcrum of its jaws to prevent biting. This first muzzle is a fairly tight one and when the animal becomes accustomed to it, a looser one is placed over it, so that the more restrictive one can soon be eliminated.

"When first we come to America, we didn't use muzzles," Emil explained. "Most other bear acts then were working with rings in the bears' noses; our bears' mouths were absolutely free. The muzzle is not cruel; it just makes everything safe all around. They wear it only during show time, which is how long?—fifteen minutes, a half hour twice a day. Even muzzled a bear can eat, and they can bite pretty good, too—take your finger off in no time."

The first thing a bear—or any animal—in training must be made to understand is the meaning of "yes" and "no." "Without that you can do nothing," said Pallenberg. "Then you must be always careful to make the same movements. If you do things a new way, even ever so little, most bears get nervous and won't work right. And always you must be very, very careful, for a bear outsmart you every time in every respect. And you be calm; I holler at a bear only if he feels like being stubborn. They won't take forcing; you must talk sweet. And you never use a whip; that is another excellent way to commit suicide. Besides, beating ruins an animal. You must build respect and confidence instead of to break down by force."

Bears are easily startled, being in this respect like sea lions. They are nearsighted, and unusual unexpected things, such as the sudden appearance of a white horse, the shifting of a revolving stage, are apt to knock them off their routine for days.

"I have plenty flops," said Pallenberg. "Many times we—how you say it?—lay the egg. With the music, the ap-plows of the audience, the tent blowing, people walk in front of your act—everything like that—believe me, you got your hands full working with bears."

Emil said the most difficult tricks to teach bears are "the small stuff"—dancing with a doll, picking up things, playing musical instruments, the two most unusual in which Herr Professor Pallenberg tutored his bears being the harmonica and concertina. The latter is fairly simple once the bear accepts the restriction of the wrist loops with which the musical squeeze-box is held—but this takes *some* doing. The mouth-organ trick requires extraordinary patience.

"How you make a bear blow?" asks Emil. "Well, I tell you—you don't make him. You just sit and watch for days and days, sometimes weeks and weeks, sometimes a month for him to blow by himself. All animals will do it sometime; you just have to *be* there when the bear does it. The first time he goes *prr-r-upppt* with his mouth (like a belch) I ignore it. Then I wait and wait until he does it again. This time I praise him; and every time he blows again, I praise him again. Soon he blows just to get a rise out of me. Eventually I hold something up to his mouth; not the mouth-organ yet—just a wooden prop, because the bear's tendency is to grab whatever it is and crush it. After a long, long time he gets used to this prop, and soon he will blow every time I praise him. I substitute the real instrument, and we make beautiful musik together."

The training of roller-skating bears is begun with the skate wheels immobilized, locked tight. "But first," says Emil, "you must have a bear who lets you put the skates on him."

The trainer observes how his protégé walks in the strapped-on skate shoes to see which foot is favored, how the weight is balanced, and so on. Then the skate wheels are adjusted to suit the bear's peculiar kinetics. The system is somewhat like that used in balancing the feet of a race horse.

The balance of a bear on a bicycle is greatly different from that of a man. Bears have a more tense balance, tend to fall more readily, but can describe much smaller circles than a human rider. Pallenberg has had great fun pitting his motorcycling bears against motorcycle policemen in circle-making competition; the bears always win.

Bear bicycle training is an extremely slow process. The training bicycle is heavily built and stationary, firmly guyed to the ground. The trainer depends on bear curiosity to bring the animal to the

ING 's AND BARNU &BAILE
COMBINED SHOWS

ERG'S Wonder BEARS
WALK TIGHT ROPES and RIDE BICYCLES LIKE HU

IING

vehicle. After the bear becomes accustomed to the strange machine, he will approach it and soon is touching it by paw. As in the blowing, the first time is ignored, the second and subsequent times praised. Every two or three days the bear will put a paw on the cycle. Only one paw at a time is worked on. Not until the bear has learned to perfection how to place one paw on the handlebars, is work begun to induce the placing of the other.

Bringing the hind legs to the pedals is the hardest part of the training. After two to three months of laborious work the bear is able to mount the cycle, still stationary. Then it is another month until pedaling is perfected—still in a static position.

Now comes the hardest part of all, to get the bear to move the cycle. This stage requires mostly a mighty strong back, for the job is done exactly as it is for a child learning to wheel. The tutor walks along holding the animal and wheel erect—helping the bear to feel its balance, bears not being natural equilibrists. The course is straight at first but the steering bar is not locked in place; the bear is free to guide the front wheel as he chooses.

Years and years of hard-won experience have gone into the Pallenberg bicycle-riding bears. Emil trained his first cycling bear, the first the world ever saw, on the promenade garden paths of the Cologne Zoo in Germany. He knew none of the finer points of training; the beast was simply directed by guttural commands of "*Nein*" and "*Ja*," the chief training factors being the willing young muscles of Emil and a younger brother, Christian. Emil was a fuzz-cheeked sixteen then, passing his days of yearning as a merchant apprentice in a neighborhood dry-goods emporium.

Emil's older brother, Joseph, an animal sculptor and zoo architect (he devised the world's first pit cages and was a designer for Karl Hagenbeck and Kaiser Wilhelm), had his studio in the Zoological Garden grounds. A zoo keeper had trained some monkeys to ride a bicycle. Joseph the artist was not impressed. He ventured at dinner one evening that he believed, from his knowledge of bear anatomy, that a bruin could be trained to do the same stunt. Emil and Christian, aged twelve, were intrigued by the challenge.

"Every little penny we squeezed together," Emil says, remembering those early days, "to buy our first bear, from the animal dealer Louis Ruhe—not from Hagenbeck, because we know they figure we are just kids and they sell us only outlaws and keep the good bears for themselves training. We come to the zoo by bicycle early every morning at three, four A.M.—long before the gates open to the public. And we practice at night after work; Christian work all day in a machine shop. For one year we do this. All our money went for feed and for bears. We never find a good one; a very big disappointment. We didn't know how to train. Everybody discourage us, even old man Hagenbeck; he say you boys are *sehr verrückt*—much nuts. Every two, three months a new bear; we have so many bears finally we have to shoot them. We just couldn't find the right type."

Then *wunderbar!* Emil happened on Ella, the wonder bear. And after two more years of trial-and-error training, catch-as-catch-can, and after a good many stretches of iron fence had been leveled, several petunia and geranium beds torn up, and after one rather spectacular inundation in the Zoological Gardens' fountain, Ella the bear finally learned to wobble along fairly well on the badly battered bicycle. The boys, greatly heartened, surrounded their cycling star with a small caged menagerie of two leopards, two large lions and one puma and hit the mud-show circuit.

"We find quickly out," Emil told me, "it cost too much; we couldn't afford this type act. So many little shows we go on; they wouldn't feed the animals, didn't pay off. We had a *heck* of a time; I even forget what we call the act that first time. Mother and Father were very much against it. We both had good jobs. 'Why animals?' they asked us."

After six months of barnstorming, Emil was conscripted into the army, but he contrived to be stationed in Cologne and so could continue to develop Ella, the bicycling bear. When his two years of military servitude were up, Emil framed Pallenberg's Gemichte Tiergruppe (mixed animal group), an odd collection of creatures including ". . . two South American greyhounds, a bucking you-naco with riding it two phoenix baboons, those big brown-maned ones with the big snoots—really a riot—and two Russian brown bears." (One of them, of course, the lady cyclist, Ella.) This rag-taggle outfit joined a small circus touring Westphalia and the Rhineland. "A *kliene* lousy outfit," reminisced Emil, "but—face it—we had a lousy little act."

When the talented guanaco was adjudged no better than any other split-hoofed beast, and barred from France due to quarantine restrictions, the act broke up and a crestfallen Emil returned home to take temporary refuge in haberdashery. However, sawdust runs deeper than the ribbon counter, and in 1912 Pallenberg abandoned the niceties of clerking for another go at snorting bears, launching another act.

The following spring, in Rotterdam, Emil met Cato, a foundry owner's daughter. They fell in love. About this same time Christian, the younger brother, renounced the animal kingdom to study engineering, thus forcing Emil to break his contract calling for a two-man act. As a result the bears were temporarily impounded, then freed by the ready reichsmarks of a German theatrical agent, who subsequently booked the outfit into Budapest, Copenhagen, Hamburg and Stockholm. Cato quietly slipped away from home, joined her bear-man in that Swedish city, and they were married. In St. Petersburg, Russia, the animal act's next stand, Cato insisted that Emil fire his nagging malcontent assistant and give her the job.

At first practice with the bears, Cato was bitten on the backside. "I get even!" she threatened the errant bear, and in two weeks she was working the act as well as her young husband. Back in Vienna the Pallenbergs weighed two offers—Russia or the U.S.A.? Cato tossed a krone; it rolled under the bed, but she has always claimed that it proclaimed "America."

In May, 1914, Emil, Cato, Miss Ella and two other bears, Tony and Sasha, sailed on the SS *Krone Prinz Wilhelm* from Bremerhaven, Germany, for Hoboken, U.S.A.

The day the act hit San Francisco war was declared on Germany, and Pallenberg bookings fell off to zero. "But we be lucky," mused Emil. "Just think if we had gone to Russia we would then have been performing bears in Siberia concentration camp!"

After a brief period of ordeal by chauvinism, Emil received an offer on a picture postcard of a job on the Hagenbeck-Wallace circus—$75 a week with upper berth, cookhouse and bear feed included. He accepted by wire.

The following season the Pallenbergs went to work for John Ringling at the old Madison Square Garden in New York City at double the money, same provender and a lower berth. The next season they received $225 per and were moved into a small stateroom. Thereafter a stateroom became a symbol of achievement and the Pallenbergs always managed to latch onto one, increasing its size year by year until finally they were enthroned in a parlor twelve feet long, a phenomenal amount of circus-train space for just two people. One bear act branched into two, then into four, and eventually there were eight bruins in a display that occupied all four stages in the Ringling Big Top.

And later there was a farm in Connecticut with two spare bear rooms, and in 1916, a son Emil Jr. and a housekeeper-nurse to care for him. Eventually (twelve years later), came a daughter, whose unique name, Dibirma, was concocted at a Hollywood luncheon given by cinema comedian Harold Lloyd's mother for Cato and a trio of her girl friends: DIxie Willson, the circus chronicler and sister of Meredith ("Music Man") Willson; BIRd Millman, the wire-walker; and MAy Wirth, queen of bareback riders.

The Pallenbergs left the Ringling aegis in 1929, the year Mr. John, by arrogantly ignoring a conference with Madison Square Garden directors, lost his contract for that desirable showplace to the American Circus Corporation, which controlled five major circuses: Al G. Barnes, Sparks, John Robinson, Hagenbeck-Wallace, and Sells-Floto. To regain his lease, John Ringling was forced to buy out the rival combine for $1,700,000, raising the money from a New York loan company on his personal note. Then Fate lowered the boom on the great circus mogul. John Ringling's wife, Mable, died; the depression blighted the nation; Mr. John went into receivership, suffered a coronary thrombosis, the collapse of the Florida real-estate boom, and was dethroned and stripped of all managerial power by his receivers, whose first economy move was to slough the expensive wild animal acts.

The Pallenbergs and their large assemblage of hungry bruins suddenly found themselves outside—without stateroom, cookhouse, or job. Emil sold all but one of his four bear acts and sank the proceeds and his savings into an ill-fated venture called the Western Vaudeville Fair Association. He soon went broke, and with his remaining bruins hit the road again, managing by Teutonic stubbornness to overcome the strong competition of the acts he had unloaded —all, of course, billing themselves as Pallenberg's Wonder Bears.

For years the "Original" Pallenberg Bears shagged around the country, playing parks and fairs. They had one highly successful Broadway run of sixty-two weeks in a hit musical, "Music in the Air," and eventually scratched a little gold from the pits of Hollywood. Such was the fame of the great Pallenberg that only a few years ago, with but one bear, he was able to command as much as $750 a week. Emil was still trouping at age sixty-four, his last professional appearance being at a South Paris, Maine, county fair. Both he and his wife have borrowed from the bruin its most notable quality—endurance.

Bears are notoriously hardy performers, tenacious and long-lived. Some of the Pallenberg veterans were: Lily, active twenty-four years; Martha (". . . thirty-two years a perfect performer . . ."); and Fritzi, nineteen years. (Fritzi could have trod the boards longer, but, becoming insanely jealous of Madame Pallenberg, had to be shot.) Ella, the famous cyclist, rode her various wheels for twenty-eight years before being retired to the Dusseldorf, Germany, zoo.

"We are just up from having pneumonia," said Mrs. Pallenberg that afternoon of my visit in Sarasota. (At that moment she looked robust enough to enter a six-day bike race.) "We attend two weeks ago the Ringling auction to buy back some of Emil's brother Joseph's bronzes that we long ago gave to Mrs. Charlie, and we catch cold sitting in the drafty tent for three days. It was so sad; all of Edith's *beautiful* things now scattered and gone." She was referring to the recent public auction of the estate of Mrs. Edith Conway Ringling, deceased widow of Charles, the next to last of the original Ringling Bros (died 1926, ten years before the great Mr. John passed on). She was the mother of the late Robert Ringling from whom John Ringling North wrested control of The Greatest Show on Earth in 1947.

"Two hundred seventy-five dollars," said Emil, "I have to pay to get back Joseph's bronzes—a peacock, a sea lion and a buffalo. That is *some* money for us now, but the sculptures mean so much to us."

"I wish," said Cato, "Joseph could have made one of Ella on her bicycle."

"Or one by Snookums on roller skates," added the patriarch of trained bears. "*There* was a performer. She was my last bear, my favorite and best (with my son in Australia now). Snookums could do *all* the tricks of all the others I ever had—combined. I think she must be the best all-round bear *anybody* ever had; and the *only* one in my whole career that was affectionate. All the others were strictly business; you couldn't touch otherwise, except they were performing in the act. Snookums could work fourteen minutes alone—hardly needed me on the stage. Remarkable! And my voice cues always different were, never in the same order—but she always understand."

He sighed and settled further into his wicker chair. The Florida sun was setting into the bay only a few flat lawns away. "I wish

Snookums be here right now with us; then tomorrow I take her fishing with me."

Now, that's a sight I'd give a lot to see. Papa Pallenberg and Snookums Braun drifting along a lazy bayou in a flat-bottomed scow with a case of beer, a watermelon and sack of apples, straw bonnets and portable radio. I wonder which one would wield the rod and line and which would scoop the fish out with his paw?

The Sarasota Masai

One winter morning when I was in Sarasota, Florida, to design the Ringling Bros Circus menagerie and midway, I read in the Sarasota daily *Herald-Tribune* an item stating that a young lion trainer was to be hauled into court to defend his wild animals against the complaints of neighbors who said that the cats roared at night, stank and were a beastly nuisance to the neighborhood.

Now I feel that the smell of lions has a definite something— like the smell of a wet dog. Tiger smell? Well, maybe—though it, too, has its point. To me a circus wouldn't be what it is without its smells. Leather harness. Sweating horses. Sun-heated canvas. The aroma of dry hay along the bull-line. The big cats. Musty dressing-room trunks, reeking of grease paint, five-and-dime store talc, starched clown suits, and rotting oilcloth. Even circus tickets have a special smell, as though they'd been printed with a wilder kind of ink.

I drove out that evening to talk to the beleaguered fellow, whose name was Pat Anthony. He lived pretty far from the built-up part of town—"out on thc skirts," as a dwarf clown I know used to say. The troublesome lions' den was like an outpost on the African plains, situated even beyond the winter quarters of the Cristiani family's circus, which is practically in the next county. All you could see was acres of flat open space dotted with a few lonesome houses. A red trailer truck dwarfed a trim one-story house. Huge letters on the sides of the boxcar trailer said, Pat Anthony's Jungle-bred Wild Lions.

In the back yard stood a circular arena of steel bars, and the tawny lions themselves were lounging in a long row of narrow traveling cages alongside it. A pleasantly plump lady sat reading in a canvas sling-chair under a tree, and I asked her where I'd find Mr. Anthony.

"They've gone to the movies," she said. "I'm the lion-sitter."

"How does one work up to being a lion-sitter?" I inquired, and she said it had been easy—she broke in as a chimpanzee-sitter. Her husband has the best chimp act in the business; Craig's Chimpanzees. I told the sitter I would wait for the lion trainer.

It was pleasant sitting there in the balmy Florida evening with the lions *oo-aahing* every once in a while. A frisky cub was tethered on the grass under a tree and a sign said, "Danger! Lion on leash." The neighbors' houses were all but lost in the open-air vastness. I couldn't even smell their suppers cooking. The Anthonys, Pat and his wife and three kids (two girls six and five and a younger boy), came home about seven thirty, and the lion-sitter went home to her chimps.

After I had established that I was one of his distant circus cousins and not just another repulsive towner, Anthony took me on a short tour of his lion family, and then we sat down under the stars to talk. He peeled off his sports shirt over his black curly head.

"It was hot in that movie," he said. "I wouldn't 've gone except it was the Clyde Beatty picture."

Pat Anthony (born Anthony Patrick Vitanza) is one of those handsome Irish-looking Italians. He told me he was one of nine kids raised by a widowed mother who came from Palermo, Sicily, to Cleveland, Ohio. He was youngest of the boys (has a younger sister) and never knew his father.

"My uncle's tailor shop is what held us all together," he said.

All the kids got through high school, and Pat went on for six months at Ohio State University, thinking he'd like to be a criminal lawyer. "Mom figured that since most of my friends were crooks," he said jokingly, "I oughta have a good career."

I asked Pat about the Sarasota court business. "Them people," he said, "they could go anyplace in the world. I can't. This is circus country. After all, I'm already out in the middle of nowheres. This court order they got out is the first real kick in the pants circus people ever got in Sarasota." He stretched his heavily muscled arms and sniffed.

"My lions don't stink. Can you smell them? I play thee-aters; *ballerinas* follow me. No stink. They're nuts."

He was facing his trouble with typical circus philosophy.

"It's not the first time I've been misunderstood. I studied lion training under the GI bill (I was the first one ever to do that), and they all thought I was psycho—in a very nice way—a battle-fatigue case. You should have heard those damn-fool white-collars at the Los Angeles VA snicker at me. I resented it."

I had heard that the United States Government had officially, though reluctantly, sponsored Anthony's lion-training education. The Los Angeles Veterans Bureau recovered nicely, but some fairly heady correspondence was exchanged before the ambitious ex-GI (a Pacific paratrooper) was permitted to enroll as a student of lion subjugating at Louis Goebel's World Jungle Compound at Thousand Oaks, California, which is up the Malibu Canyon, northwest of Los Angeles.

"I was accepted October twelfth, nineteen forty-eight," said Pat. "I remember the date exactly. I got ninety bucks a month for eighteen months."

When I asked if he had learned everything in such a short time he said, "No, I'm still learning." Then he added, "Look—you got the wrong guy if you want to know about lions. Terrell Jacobs is the lion king. He handled fifty males all at once. He had the only performing black leopard act of its kind ever—that was at the San Francisco World's Fair. He's been in the business over forty years; I'm just a First-of-May novice (circus rookie) compared to him. I bet I haven't handled in my whole career more'n forty lions.

"And Clyde Beatty is like sterling on silver. Clyde surpassed all other trainers with groups; he had forty mixed lions and tigers once,

and even today he works about twenty. He has the largest animal act going. Alongside Clyde I'm just a kid."

The nearly full moon was being sliced into silvery chunks by the steel bars of the arena and the controversial lions had settled down to sleep and dream.

"Clyde was my boyhood hero," said this youthful lion trainer. "Every time the Beatty show came to the Auditorium with the Shrine circus, I'd be there the whole time, watching him and studying the act. As I got older, I kept applying for a job, but he wouldn't hire me. One of the agents with the show suggested Thousand Oaks was a good place to break in, so after the war I stopped off out there and got a job as a cage-hand for Melvin Koontz, the guy that wrastles all the cats for the movies. And then I applied to the VA so I could study to be a real trainer. It took me seven months before I could convince them I wasn't outa my head."

Pat doesn't think his idea of higher education is a bit odd. "A million kids, they want to be lion trainers," he said, "even today with rockets, the TV, cowboys, and shooting at the moon and all."

After his graduation as a full-fledged lion trainer, Pat stayed on at Goebel's compound as an assistant handler.

"Everybody—my teachers and the animals—all strung along with me," he said, "and one day I got the break I was lookin' for. The chief lion trainer broke his leg. The boss went frantic, so he asked me could I at least work one group—they had mountain lions, a mixed male and female and some African males. I told him sure, I could work all three."

And the nervy neophyte did—for six months, until the regular trainer was chipped out of his cast.

"Then in nineteen fifty-three," Pat said, continuing the saga of the government-issue lion trainer, "I got up a little act of my own and played a few small winter dates and pumpkin fairs, but I didn't have too much money, and finally I figured I was on my way out—the cats goin' bad, low on funds. I needed an angel bad."

One was provided, a chap named Walker Dick, who owned the National Bank of Wheeling in Wheeling, West Virginia, and also that town's country club. Walker rounded up fifteen thousand dollars so that his friend Pat could frame a decent act. In 1953 it appeared for the first time on the Hamid-Morton indoor circus.

"In this business you need an angel," said Anthony. "Even Beatty had one, Frank Walters. You must have seen him around; a great big Texas guy in a big hat with buckskin boots and diamonds all over. They say he put up as much as two hundred thousand dollars to Beatty."

I asked Pat how much he figured his own act was worth now. "About fifty grand," he answered without batting an eye. "But I'd never sell it."

Then we got back to his boyhood idol, Beatty. "He's a Buckeye boy, too. Been around cats since nineteen twenty when he run away from home to join out on a little mud-show when it came to Chillicothe. He was born right outside there, at Bainbridge. He told me once he got five bucks a month, cookhouse and shared an upper— with bedbugs. Clyde had his first wild animal act when he was eighteen. That gives him close onto thirty-five years in the big cage, and I bet he goes another fifteen easy. He's still a young man; you should see him—only a little bit grey and just as lean and tough as ever."

Did Pat expect his son to follow his lion-training footsteps? "Bob?" he answered. "He can be a lion tamer or whatever he chooses —cut girls' dresses out if he wants to; I'd let him. No, it wouldn't be no shock, but I'll admit it'd be embarrassing."

Pat stretched his twenty-nine-year-old muscles and took one of the glasses of iced tea his wife brought out on a tray. "But Terrell Jacobs now," he continued, "*there* is the lion man." (Mr. Jacobs was still alive then in 1955; he died aged fifty-four, suddenly, of a heart attack, in his home the day before Christmas 1957.) " 'Terrell Jacobs, the Undisputed King of All Wild Animal Trainers,' they used to bill him," Anthony said, marveling at the memory. " 'Battling Flashing Fangs and Sweeping Claws, Enforces His Will and Desires Upon a Snarling, Roaring Ring of Hate and Fury.' I used to say that instead of prayers when I went to bed at night when I was a kid. Terrell Jacobs has only been on about fifteen circuses, every one from Gentry Bros. on up—the Sells-Floto, Cole Bros., Al G., Kelly-Miller, and even one I bet you never heard of, Holland Classical Circus. He's made most of the big carnies, too: Royal American, World of Mirth, Strates, and a Canuck outfit, the Sullivan World's Greatest Shows. You know about the only thing I know about baseball is that Terrell Jacobs was the first act of the first circus ever to play on a baseball diamond in New York City. Sheba, one of his females, was the first lion ever admitted to Yankee Stadium. She was thirteen years old, and she got nasty if he didn't introduce her first. And man, did he have the scars!—the most of anybody."

I asked how many that would be.

"Well," answered Pat Anthony, "Terrell he has fifty-two just from one leopard alone. He carries about two hundred tooth and claw marks on his body. He's supposed to have to take an intravenous shot against lockjaw every six months all his life. Of course, I don't know for sure if that's true or not, but that's what they say. And you know what he likes best to train with?" Pat laughed. "A kitchen broom!"

Anthony's solid, square chest was marked only with curly black hair, but not all good trainers are free of scars. Every trainer—good, bad or indifferent—gets them sooner or later. It all depends on the breaks and has little to do with skill in the craft. Oscar Konyot, the lion trainer I had known on the Ringling show, is the only man I've ever actually seen being clawed. The accident happened during a between-shows rehearsal as the trainer, a rangy fellow with a Punch-like face, was trying to get a lion to sit up. Konyot was poking at the animal with a whip stock when the beast struck out and back so swiftly that had I winked I would have missed the thrust. (All big cats, except the cheetah, have retractable claws.) The lion's claws caught the trainer on his upper right arm. He paled, grabbed the spot with his free hand, and carefully backed against the bars where he stood quietly until the cage boys could run the cats from the arena— not moving anything except his eyes. I can still see them flicking after each departing cat, ticking them off one by one. When the chute door had closed behind the last tail, Konyot walked unaided out of the cage to the doctor's wagon near the center side entrance to the Big Top. There were only two little rips in his sleeve, but when the shirt was cut away the arm was a bloody mess. The man turned grey when he saw the wound and for the first time wobbled a bit. It took twenty-eight stitches to sew him up. He was quite put out that he couldn't work the night show—being unable to get back to the lot in time due to heavy traffic, after having taken his girl-friend into town for dinner. This was just one of fifty-five scars earned in eleven years.

"Yeah," said Anthony, "fifty-five is a lot of scars, but Konyot, he had a comedy act, didn't he? Mine is a fighting act; it's not near so dangerous."

The late Fred Bradna, who for years was Ringling Bros' equestrian director extraordinary, had told me that Alfred Court, whom *he* considered the greatest modern cat trainer, had never once been seriously hurt and was the gentlest of subjugators, never using a gun or whip.

"If you'll read Court's own book," said Anthony when I spoke of this, "you'll find out he was bad hurt more'n a couple of times. And while it's true he didn't use a blank gun, he did use a whip and a stick sometimes. In training he used a blunt-pointed fork with tin cans tied to it to make noise." (I looked this up later and found that Anthony was quite right. The book, *My Life With the Big Cats*, recounts several crippling accidents: one in which four fangs went completely through Court's thigh, another that caused months of layoff due to blood poisoning. There are also a few rousing descriptions of tigers being whacked by hickory sticks—and lashed.)

"Court," continued Anthony, "he was French. He had a picture act (posing animals in a tableau), and he was plenty good. But you have to use *some* force with a strong animal like a lion or tiger, so they'll learn to respect you. You can make pets outa big cats just so long, then look out. One day they'll get you. There was some guy out in Iowa, name of Hall, had a lion given him by Melvin Koontz, the Hollywood lion wrestler. The animal had the run of the house for two years. Then the cat turned sour, became a man-hater and chased the guy—tried to kill him one day. But he still kept the lion fourteen years more in a cage and outdoor run. . . . Did you ever see that lion that girl out in Texas brings around the show in a station wagon that she's rigged out with bars? I couldn't ever use a cat like that," said Pat Anthony, "even for a seat-warmer. [A cat that simply sits on a pedestal to dress and populate the act but one that does not perform tricks.] I like young lions, lively lions. Most of mine are under four years. They reach five, to move the sons-a-guns you need to shoot off a cannon or a firecracker under them. I don't go for those act-beautifuls where you need the Beacon Storage to move the props. I kick a barrel outa the way or pick up a chair, I do a lot. My act goes snap! snap! snap!"

I asked him what he looked for in a cat; how he picked his scrappers. "If a cat shies away from a stick poked in his face, he's got enough for me," Pat answered. "It indicates he's got good sense, is not what we call a lumberhead. When a cat doesn't shy, he'll be troublesome and have to be trained while restrained by rope and collar. The noise a cat makes means nothing; the noisiest ones often make the best performers. Next I look for good features, especially the eyes. Don't give me no cross-eyed cats! And then the age. I like to get lions at two and one-half or three years old; tigers fifteen months. The sooner you plant the methods the better off you are. You mould the disposition and establish control. That's the most important thing; you lose control, you lose your act."

Talking to Pat Anthony that soft evening under the lush Florida moon, I learned that foremost on any cat-man's curriculum is teaching the animal to stay put, to "seat." And that, in all tricks, it is most important that the primary movement of the cue is always the same, given from the same position with the same stance and tone of voice.

"And I do nothing to make the cat fear me," added the professor. "The minute they fear me, they're gonna nail me. The gun shooting means nothing. The pistol is just a prop; it shoots blanks—as many as I can afford. The noise scares them maybe a little, and you have to watch to shoot up or to one side so's not to burn the cat with the flash."

This young lion trainer told me the easiest big cat trick is the laydown. "You get them pooped, and they lay down by themselves," he said, "and the most difficult is the hind-leg walk. I got one that I'm breaking in for that now."

The one stunt everyone associates with lion training is that of the man putting his head in the beast's mouth. For generations it has been *the* classic lion stunt.

"First of all," said Pat, "it's not much of a feat. Only a lion that is freakishly tame can be used, and no man ever actually puts his head in the mouth. He only places his *face* between the open jaws. Furthermore, he holds the upper jaw securely in one hand, the lower in the other, and if he feels the slightest pressure from either he pulls his kisser back right quick. Then, too, most lions, even healthy ones, have super-halitosis, the worst you ever come across. Nothing is more sickening than the nauseating foul breath of the average lion. But the main reason I don't stick my head in a lion's mouth is because it's a display of stupidity. It belittles the wild animal and knocks down the standard of the act. You tell the public that you're working chickens, you take away the anxiety from the act."

When I asked Pat the difference between lion and tiger attack, he told me that a lion keeps coming, bouncing across the ground, while a tiger is a one-time attacker, leaping only once through the air. If the tiger doesn't connect the first time, it doesn't try again—at least not right away. Lionesses are also leapers. "The best offense against a lion attack," said the lion boy, "is a dodge. If one ever landed on me, I'd try to jam my chair on his head, knock the seat out and cram the legs around his neck. While he's trying to shake loose, I'm making tracks."

I told Anthony that the Roman naturalist, Pliny the Elder, was the first man to note that a lion lashed himself into a fury with his tail, like a bull. The beast was thought to have a sharp prickle in the end of the tail and sure enough, centuries later a German professor named Blumenbach discovered it. The lion prickle is referred to in Homer's *Iliad*. Pat said sure, he'd look it up someday when he didn't have anything else to do.

I was curious as to why Anthony had chosen lions instead of emulating Beatty with a mixed group.

"Well," he explained, "I admit tigers *are* more beautiful, but they cost a hell of a lot more. You can get a lion anywhere from three hundred to six hundred dollars, a tiger, a good one, costs from two thousand to three thousand five hundred. Tigers are smarter, but they don't breed too good in captivity, so they're scarcer. The one I have, Sultan, a male Bengal-Siberian mixture, I got cheap from Trefflich's because the cat was in such bad shape. I only paid fifteen hundred for him. Per pound, big cats are more like gold than beef."

Anthony told me he had chosen the lion as his animal for another, less practical, reason. "Someday soon," he said, "a lion act is going to be a rare novelty, for I think lions are becoming extinct. They used to be in Asia and Greece, but you won't find any there now. And look now how they're being knocked off in Africa, with the Masai pushing them away from the water holes right into the hunters' laps."

While circus people seldom concern themselves with the complexities of world problems, it was natural for Anthony to know of Africa's cattle vs. wild animal dilemma, for this was part of his, the animal, realm. The native Masai, in the constant search for grass and water for their cattle, are driving out Africa's game. The Government's program to eradicate or control animal diseases has caused the cattle of the nomadic tribes to multiply enormously. The Masai have become very rich in cattle; the pasturage, pitifully poor. In some of the National Parks, while hunters and sportsmen with guns are excluded, the Masai inhabitants are not, and this has added to the toll of wild animals, including the lion. When the beasts are driven away from the protected sections into non-protected areas they are soon shot, trapped or poisoned.

The Masai, who are an intelligent, fiercely independent people, are not completely to blame for the dwindling of the Dark Continent's savage beasts. Some of the blame must fall on the heads of the ecologists and a great deal of it on the staggeringly rapid increase in populations, plus the introduction of modern farming methods and industry. These factors, more than any others, have put the seal of death on the once-teeming wildlife of bush and plain over the greater part of the Dark Continent. Farmers and pastoralists have not learned to coexist with wild animals. Statesmen take a typical ward politician's view of the matter of animal preservation. One such bureaucrat has been quoted by Elspeth Huxley, the eminent English writer who has studied the problem, as saying, "Lions and elephants belong to the past. It is sentimental to worry about them. You have no wolves in England. What we want are factories and hydroelectric schemes."

After our discussion of the lion's African death knell, Anthony said, "It's too bad. Soon you'll only be able to see the king of beasts in a circus. That is, if they don't succeed in eliminating circuses—and us too." He got up, stretched into the stars and yawned.

I was happy to see that one of the world's youngest circus wild-animal trainers still held to the deeply rooted idea that the lion is the king of beasts. The Biblical references to the lion as a symbol of power are many. David slew a lion (and a bear) in the preliminaries to his incredible sling-shot kayo of the Philistine giant; Daniel was thrown into the lions' den to prove the superiority of God over King Darius. However, many animal men do not pledge allegiance to the lion as ruler of the jungle kingdom. Some choose the tiger as monarch; others, the African buffalo, a formidable creature of cruel temperament, wicked horns, sharp hoofs and a concrete forehead. The rhinoceros is well armored and powerful, but poor eyesight disqualifies him from the exalted position; and the gorilla, as a champ, is highly overrated. The hippo, although a good fighter, is exceedingly clumsy out of water. There are many sportsmen who feel that the American mountain lion, if larger, would make a formidable challenger for the king of beasts title, as this cat (also called the puma, cougar, catamount and American panther) is a sovereign loner who will not tolerate the slightest interference in his affairs.

The lion holds his despotic jungle sway mainly because of his

great sinuous maneuverability. Though the large head with extra strong jaws is not to be underestimated, the lion is also a good bluffer, making his roars more tremendously resonant by sending them into the ground. The widespread reverence for stalwart lion courage is, according to animal men, largely unwarranted. Morally the lion is only an immense cat, with all the guileful, vindictive qualities of that slinking creature.

In a fair-shake showdown between a full-grown male lion and the same-size, same-sex tiger, animal handlers mostly bet on the lion. Although the tiger is regarded as being more bloodthirsty, treacherous and untamable, the physical differences between the two big cat species are slight, being mainly those of hide, skull and mane. The tiger has no mane, but old male tigers do have long, spreading cheek hair. Much of the lion-tiger difference is in family relations: a lioness never destroys its young; the tigress often does. The lion helps rear his offspring; the tiger forsakes his lady love for gamier affairs. Physically, the lion has better forequarters and the great advantage of his mane because it protects the carotid artery and acts as a tangle for attacking claws or jaws. (Not all male lions have this life preserver however, the Nubian being bare-shouldered and the lion of Central Africa having just a slight ruff on each side of its chin.)

The lion on the average is bigger and heavier than a tiger and in fighting can take more punishment and has infinitely greater endurance. He shifts better in battle, also. The tiger is a razzle-dazzle fighter, biting and lashing, but doing little damage, comparatively speaking. The lion is better on the target, hitting for the back of the neck or spine where he can ruin a tiger with one crunching chomp. However, a tiger is terribly tenacious and has tremendous speed. The lion in fighting uses only one front paw at a time, the tiger uses both.

Clyde Beatty has had to contend with many mortal lion-tiger brawls in his big cage—and the corpses were never lions. Of all those dead tigers, only two were Siberians, the biggest of the breed.

A few days after my evening talk with Anthony on the grassy plains of Sarasota, I attended the Anthony vs. the People battle in the courtroom of Circuit Judge W. T. Harrison. It was a very entertaining session and quite a few innocents learned a lot about *Felis leo*—and the clan circus.

Combatants against the lion master included five males and two females. The males were better on the target, the females more tenacious. All the witnesses complained that their nerves were being eroded by prolonged lack of sleep due to roaring lions; that they were being sickened by nauseating zephyrs wafting from the Anthony estate. The most annoying thing about lions, said the ladies, was that lions roar loudest at approximately 3 A.M. and wake their husbands.

Anthony countered that lions only roar when they are contented and then only for a short period. He contended also that his beasts roar less than five minutes out of every twenty-four hours. And, furthermore, he was sleeping fine except for the occasional barking of a neighbor's dog. And also, only three of his lions are able to roar since a lion under four years old cannot roar. And there is no odor to a lion.

"Everyone knows," he said from the witness stand, "that cats are the cleanest animals there are—cleanest of the human race. Any lion expert will tell you that."

Whereupon the judge called for a lion expert, and a large, sharp-faced gentleman, who had been sittting back against the wall immensely enjoying the whole brabble, sauntered forth. He was Cecil D. Montgomery, Menagerie Superintendent of the Ringling Bros Circus, and he was ready to testify in favor of the lion. However, since he had been observing the proceedings, he was disqualified as a court witness and so was dismissed. Anthony's attorney said he had another animal expert on the premises and sent to the corridor for a fellow who turned out to be the Italian bandmaster of the Cristiani Circus.

The lions' lawyer asked him slowly and carefully, "Now let's get this straight. Are you an animal man?"

"No," the bandman replied honestly and proudly, "I am a musician."

He was dismissed.

After this came a wonderful, feisty old coot, Texas Jim Mitchell, an ex-carnie who runs a very successful tourist attraction, a Snake Farm and Animal Display. Texas Jim was able to get on record a few thousand well-chosen well-salted words in the defense of lions, ending by pointing across the courtroom and declaring to the judge: "If you can smell a lion from here to that door, I'll eat him alive."

Judge Harrison cautioned Mr. Mitchell against making such rash promises while under oath. But Texas Jim countered that, as an old lion keeper, he could assure the court it was no rash statement.

In the next-to-closing spot, the defense offered the county health officer, Dr. W. L. Wright, who testified that while he didn't know much about roaring, he was rightdown certain that neither the lions

nor their premises bore any offensive odors. He stated that the Anthony home was spick and span, and that the entire place fell within
the standards of excellent public health. Keeping a lion, said the
doctor, was no more a health hazard than keeping a horse, as long as
the lion was behind bars.

After a minimum bit of pondering by the judge, a verdict was
handed down, ordering Anthony to remove all "roaring lions" by
February ninth and to keep them removed. This seemed to satisfy
the young lion trainer. I talked with him on the courthouse steps
directly afterward.

"Anyhow," he said, "we open for Hamid-Morton in Memphis on
the thirteenth, so if we have to leave town on the ninth, it's still
okay." Then he added philosophically, "People are just like animals—
you can get used to living around them."

The Anthony lions now live in Tampa, where the water holes
are better and pasturage is not so fenced in.

Mobel Stock, Tiger Teacher

🐾 There has been only a small handful of female wild-animal trainers, and the only one in the history of the world able to break, train and work tigers is the fabulous Mabel Stark, the greatest woman subjugator of jungle beasts of all time.

Miss Stark claims to have broken the only two tiger displays ever trained in this country—one of twelve for the Al G. Barnes Circus in 1919, and one of nine for Ringling Bros in 1922. Every tiger act in America since then has been composed of animals that have received their primary schooling in some other country.

Mabel is one of the grand old-timers of the circus—one of the few hardy perennials left over from the days when the Big Tops bloomed with such magnificent performers as Leitzel, May Wirth, the Flying Concellos, the Loyal-Repenski bareback riders, the cannon-balling Zacchini brothers, and Codona, the angel of the flying triple somersault. According to Mabel's own count, she has been before the public with wild animals of one kind or another, but principally tigers, without an enforced layoff for forty-seven years—since 1911.

Just recently Miss Stark returned from a three-and-one-half-year tour of Japan with her tigers, and in many respects that engagement was her proudest, for the Japanese honored the tiger lady by informally bestowing the title of Teacher upon her. In Nippon land Mabel Stark, tiger trainer, is affectionately known as "Mobel Stock, Teacher."

Miss Stark began her life among the wilder mammalians with a hitch of eleven years on the Al G. Barnes Circus. When that tent-opera was gobbled up by John Ringling, Mabel went along as part of the chattel, remaining under the Ringling banners until 1942, six years longer than the big boss himself, who was trumpeted into the showman's grassy Paradise in 1936.

Miss Stark has made tours to South America and the Hawaiian Islands and spent several years performing for motion pictures, working out of the World Jungle Compound at Thousand Oaks, California. Now and again, Mabel lent ferocious flicker assistance to most of the epics whose scripts called for bloodthirsty tigers. Among her beneficiaries were Sabu ("Song of India"), Cecil B. DeMille ("The Greatest Show On Earth") and Victor Mature ("Demetrius and the Gladiators").

With the rise of the new trend in circuses, the indoor sponsored show, Mabel Stark joined one of the strongest of these new units, the Polack Bros. Western. After three sessions of playing arenas, Shrine auditoriums and basketball courts, she took five of her huge striped tomcats to the Orient for the Japanese tour.

Miss Stark first flung at life as a trained nurse. She doffed the white cap after a vacation visit to a Hollywood movie studio, during which she saw a stunt man wrestle a tiger to a prearranged draw. On being told that it was easy to become a tiger subduer, she bought herself one of the orange and black devils from the Selig Zoo for $350, took him to her backyard in nearby seaside Venice and, in six months of trial and error, had herself a passably trained tiger and a job on the Al G. Barnes Circus exercising horses—to her, a loathsome task. Very soon she butted her way into a goat act, a position which left the ex-Nightingale wide open for kidding remarks about having a strong act, but Mabel's grit and determination soon brought her a small tiger display. Then came a presentation that included two lions as well as the tigers, likely the first mixed group worked by a woman. Mettlesome Mabel soon discovered that, while she found it fairly simple to train that one tiger, it was not easy to become a bonafide wild animal trainer. At the peak of her career, Miss Stark was asked in her dressing room by a gushing lady vistor what it takes to be a tiger trainer. Mabel, who had experienced a rough matinee with her cats, said, "This," and thrust from under her dressing gown horribly scarred legs, clawed and bitten, ankles to thighs.

To this enthralled student of the American circus Mabel Stark has always been a fabulous legend, and I was pleased last summer while in California to have the chance to meet the great battle-scarred veteran face to face after years of merely seeing her seat to arena. The meeting was arranged by an old circus friend, Parley Baer, now a movie actor and television cowboy, husband of an ex-trapeze artist.

Jungle Land (formerly The World Jungle Compound), where Mabel Stark was performing, is beyond Malibu Canyon, and by the time my wife and I arrived, delayed by heavy Sunday traffic and my own underestimation of the tremendous California distances, the place was just about deserted, preparing to close for the day. It was like an old-time Sunday-school-picnic grove. Only here there was the saving grace of animals—elephants, buffalo, lions and even camels. There were lots of them, likely every single one that ever chewed its cud across the burning movie sands of Venice, California.

When I asked a stubbly groundsman where I could find Miss Stark, he growled amiably, "What's 'a matter son, doncha know Mabel? That's her a'sittin' over there on that there bench."

The tiger lady had just finished working her Sunday-afternoon performance and at first was a little miffed that we had missed it. My wife was put out also, tigers being her favorite circus animal, but for an Eastern boy I had done the best I could.

Miss Stark is small and lithe and her high-cheekboned face is very handsome. I am told (and I have seen photographs that prove this) that in her youth she was a real blonde stunner. A daughter of a Kentucky grub-hills tobacco farmer, she admits to sixty-five years, while appearing considerably younger. (She is a trifle sensitive about her age; a journalist friend is in Miss Stark's permanent doghouse for ungallantly reporting as a "grandmother's shawl" the fashionable stole the lady wore to a recent Circus Fans' Association banquet.)

"She looks exactly like a beautiful tiger," my wife whispered in awe as we approached the great lady waiting to hold court on a dilapidated park bench by the gravel roadway opposite her tiny dressing cottage. She needn't have whispered, for I'm sure that Miss Stark would have been highly flattered by such a comparison. Indeed, the feline character of Miss Stark's face was most amazing. Can this be the mark of the born cat trainer? Is there some unplumbed affinity between the lady and the animals she chose for her lifetime associates? It's the sort of fascinating idea the anthroposophists might look into.

The queen of the tigers took quite a casual view of her singularly uncrowded profession.

"Any woman can do what I can do," she said as an opening gambit. "I can't see why not. You just get behind a tiger, he goes forward; move your hand, they go down. I do it with my voice."

It may be a cinch to Miss Stark, but I'm quite sure she has the right wave length and the big cats are tuned in to her.

"I never had a tiger yet I couldn't train into something," she added. "Never threw one out. 'Course some of them you can use just for seat-warmers. Even that handsome one with the little bitty eyes like a rabbit—beautiful but not much brain—I even trained him some."

Mabel told us that she does not like to work with an animal that is not at least her own size.

"Those little bitty things like leopards and pumas get underfoot. And I won't take on anything like the black jaguar that's not thoroughbred. They simply don't have enough learning power. You can't just train tricks into any old tiger that comes up the pike, either. You have to pick your animals."

Cat trainers don't depend much on long-nosed cats, usually nastier than short-nosers. They beware of narrow heads combined with long noses, often the mark of a cat whose parents were a lusting brother and sister. Cross-eyed cats are avoided, for this indicates misbreeding, bringing with it a warped intellect, lack of mental poise and balance and often a predilection to mayhem and murder. There are few things more provoking to a wild-animal trainer than having a killer in the act. Noisy rebels are preferred to silent resenters, the first being a frank and honest delinquent, the other a cat loaded with poisonous mutiny, waiting the chance to sink fangs into his trainer or rake him with claws.

Miss Stark considers one and one half to two years of age the best time to start cats to kindergarten.

"Earlier it is too much like children," she says, "you break their hearts with training." A tiger more than five years old she regards as being too treacherous to attempt training. Females are usually easier to train than males. Though not especially smarter, they are more responsive. Males are die-hards and submit to the will of the trainer only if there is no other way out.

"And after you get your cats picked," continued the tiger lady, "you watch them carefully to see what each one can do best."

A tiger trainer first observes a new cat from outside its traveling cage for one week. Then entrances are practiced from the chute into the big arena, the animal being closely observed from inside the safety-cage entrance. The trainer wants to see if he has a right-hander or a southpaw. The cat's rushes are tested by opening the door slightly at regular intervals. After a few days the trainer has a pretty good idea of the kind of cat he has and whether training can be started with the animal on a freewheeling basis or restrained by collar and lunge rope. When the handler joins a new cat in the big cage for the first time, the beast will stop sharp in his tracks and stare. What it does next is significant. Either the beast leaves the human strictly alone or figures him for a sucker and springs.

"Lion rushes I never minded much," said Miss Stark. "They're just big woof-woof bluffers. If I stand my ground or side-step, they don't try again. But tigers, now, are different. That first rush worries me. You better be damned well prepared to stop a tiger. He don't fool none; he means business. You don't have to kill them; just stand pat and speak sharp enough. You never back up from a tiger. Just like a dog—you back up and he'll keep comin' at you. And if you turn and run, he'll be on you in nothing flat, tearing at your throat, rippin' into your back."

After a cat is accustomed to its new surroundings, the performing arena, the trainer starts its seat breaking by first persuading the animal to mount a solid wooden block. After the animal's natural suspicions are allayed, a sturdy iron-legged pedestal is substituted. Mabel Stark cues her big tyro tigers with a stockyard whip, a rather thick supple affair—never uses the cracking lash-whip.

Early tiger training is exceedingly laborious, for the big cats have one-track minds, able to concentrate on only one thing at a time. And they cannot be worked too long at one stretch; fifteen minutes is plenty at the very first.

The notion that they learn by watching other cats perform is sheer nonsense.

"Sometimes," Mabel said, "it takes me a week just to get a tiger's forepaws onto the block seat." When the ears flatten back and the tail gets nervous, it's time to stop. The cat is not only becoming irritable; it is lethal. It takes about a month to get a new big cat to learn to take his seat.

"You must bring an animal to you by your voice and manner," said Mabel, "not drive it with clubs or whips or lead it with meat. Sure, you can beat a cat into obedience just like you can a kid, or spoil him with meat—but one day you'll get it all back in spades."

Miss Stark's mystic mammal-to-mammal approach is contrary to the methods used by most present-day big-cat trainers, who usually operate on the basis of food reward for good behavior and swift, energetic and physical punishment for misbehavior. Al G. Barnes, the man who gave Miss Stark her first job, had the same kind of rapprochement with wild creatures that Mabel has. He was attuned to even the commonest of animals and possessed a decidedly uncanny ability to make all four-footed beasts understand him. For Mr. Barnes, pouting parrots became eager to recite their entire vocabularies, to sing their most squawking arias, to whisper their most shocking profanities. Even the shy desert coyote carried on moonlight conversations with Barnes. He once taught a jackass to bray on cue; and balky horses, even those not circus-trained, obeyed his every soft-spoken word. An indefatigable car-chasing dog once was cradled in Mr. Barnes' arms for a solemn discussion and explanation of the mechanics of the vehicle, much to the amusement of onlookers. While this lecture didn't entirely stop the mutt's bad habit, nevertheless he never again chased a car when Barnes was in sight.

Some of this brotherliness between man and the animal kingdom surely has been absorbed by Mabel Stark, for that gentle rapport with beasts is very rare. She has somehow passed along her knowledge as well to at least one of her long line of cage boys, a twenty-six-year-old Kansas City kid named Dick McGraw, currently the lion trainer at the St. Louis Zoo, who believes in and loves wild animals in that same way.

Miss Stark's specialty is "center pyramids." Most cat trainers arrange their group tableaus so that, in comparative safety, they face the beasts, posed with their backs to the bars of the arena. But not Miss Mabel. She displays her felines across ring-center and blithely enters into the spectacle with tigers to the right, tigers to the left, tigers behind and above her—a brave show of skill for which she is highly regarded in the profession.

Miss Stark's specialty at the height of her career—never duplicated by anyone else—was a spectacular wrestling match with a tiger. A big fellow named Rajah, who was raised on goat milk (the milk-maid, Mabel herself), was her first grunt-and-groaner. As a cub, his mistress carried him about in a basket with a ribbon around his neck. As an adolescent tiger, he was led about on a leash until the day he quietly reached out and snapped off the head of a passing ostrich. For her tiger-wrestling bout, Mabel wore a suit of white leather, as a frolicsome tiger is terribly dangerous without meaning to be.

Tigers, seldom able to control their strength, can inflict almost as much damage with a playful rake as with a viciously intended one. Mabel once worked for a year in what she describes as a "fog of pain" from an unsuspected brain abscess caused by an unintentional paw swipe by Rajah during one of their wrestling match thrillers.

Besides being the world's only lady wrestler of tigers, Miss Stark is the only trainer, male or female, who has taught a tiger to walk a treadmill, possibly the most difficult of tiger stunts.

A favorite Stark trick, also no bed of roses for trainer or beast, is the "wire-walk" across a heavy cable, the chief difficulty being that tigers do not normally cross their feet when walking. The trick is begun with two parallel planks. To get the tiger across them requires infinite patience.

"Maybe," said Mabel, "the first day he only touches his paw to one plank." After the tiger has progressed to being able to cross the two-plank bridge, one is taken away and the whole process begins again to coax the animal across the single rail. When this has been accomplished, a heavy cable is laid on the board. The tiger continues to walk the plank getting the feel of the steel strand under his feet.

"It's very hard on the foot webs," explained Mabel, "but if you keep the cages clean, there's no danger of infection. The bruises don't need medication; the tigers take care of it themselves."

The cable is raised above the board a little each day until the cat is walking it alone. Then the board is removed.

Miss Stark has made much of adventitious training, some of her best tiger tricks having been stumbled onto. The rollover was an accidental revelation. Miss Stark, boxed in by a tiger, kicked out at him. He rolled over. She kicked again; result, another roll.

"Hey, we got a trick," exclaimed the trainer jubilantly. Though this first roller has long since retired, Mabel still cues her roll-over tigers with a leg-swinging movement.

Miss Stark's first tiger sit-up occurred because, while styling—the

word circus people use to describe the flourish at the end of a trick—
she happened to strike the sensitive nose of one of her big cats with
the stock of a whip. The tiger, surprised by the blow, straightened
onto his haunches into a perfect sit-up.

"Okay," said Mabel, "you can do it accidentally, we'll do it
regular." She still cues her sit-up cats with an up-flung motion of her
arm though she no longer uses the whipstock.

"Kitty," remembers Mabel, "was my best roll-over sit-up cat. To
break the sit-up you must first 'muscle' the backs. Give them a pole at
first to rest on, then switch to a whipstock held in your hands."

Miss Stark is not an advocate of the pistol-packing wild-animal
act.

"I can get just as good a 'bounce' from a cat," she has always
said, referring to the noisy rehearsed charge of a lion or tiger, "just
by raising my hand. Just my voice and the positions I take is enough
to start them 'bouncing.'"

The widely believed notion that the longer a big cat is worked
the more docile it becomes is pure malarkey. It simply develops into
a more dangerous animal by catching onto the trainer's methods, and
is more difficult to scare and bluff. Miss Stark's best wire-walking
tiger, Bill, still working at age fifteen, is as dangerous as ever. Tigers
are usually able to work until they are eighteen.

Miss Stark's life has been a succession of spectacular clawings
and chawings. It is her proud boast that every inch of her body has
been scratched or bitten into battle scars. "I've had broken bones,
been torn to pieces and everything else," she has said. "Lucky my
uniform hides the scars—all except my hand and it's my right one. I
can style with it, but I can't hold a whip any more."

A melee with lionesses, a breed with which Mabel was relatively
unfamiliar, resulted in a weak left hand. An arm broken by feline jaws
was badly joined and had to be rebroken and reset three weeks after
the mishap, which happened during a winter off-season at a commercial fair in California during Mabel's early circus days.

Mabel Stark received her first real tiger mauling along the
Barnes parade route one day when her striped cats finally succeeded
in snarling through a cage-dividing panel that ordinarily kept them
from their trainer. Mabel received deep gashes in her back and side
that morning, and at the hospital the doctor was able to slide his
hand through the hole in her calf between flesh and bone.

The worst mauling of Miss Stark's career took place in 1928 in

Bangor, Maine, while Mabel was on the John Robinson Circus. There had been torrential rains; the ring was slippery, the animals extremely tense. Mabel slipped in the muddy arena, and the moment she went down a tiger named Sheik leaped upon her ripping into her left thigh, almost severing the leg above the knee. Another tiger named Zoo closed in for the kill, and as the tigers tore and fought over the helpless woman, Terrell Jacobs, the lion trainer, rushed to her aid. He finally managed to drive the beasts back into their chute, but not before Miss Stark had suffered: a badly mangled leg, a torn and mashed face, an ankle that remained stiff for many months, a deep hole in her shoulder, a torn deltoid muscle and a hole in her neck uncomfortably close to the jugular vein.

The doctors' sewing bee lasted four hours. The accident put Miss Stark out of business for two months. The face scars were later largely eliminated by plastic surgery.

Mabel almost lost the use of her right hand in a 1951 tiger attack and has been forced ever since to work without benefit of gun or traditional chair-shield, though she can still wield a whip by means of a peculiarly combined body-arm motion of great power.

When attacking, a tiger invariably leaps for the throat. Once a beachhead is established there, the beast rolls onto its back. Then with prey lying on the tiger's stomach, the animal doubles up hind legs to hook its claws into the victim's throat and rip the body wide open with one powerful, kicking thrust.

"When you're working with tigers, you watch for those little tail switches that warn of an attack," explained Mabel. "And you can usually tell in the eyes, but a tiger attack comes quick and sudden —not much warning."

Mabel doesn't worry too much about sex rearing its tawny head in the arena. "I can put a male and female in the act right after breeding them," she says, "and they'll work and not touch each other, just make little purr noises like all cats do when they're happy. *Prrrruppppt. Prrrrupppt.*"

Remembering what Pat Anthony had told me about jamming a chair over an attacking lion's head, I asked Mabel's opinion on this use of the traditional prop.

"Well," she said, "I *throw* a chair an awful lot, but I ain't gonna jam no chair over a tiger's head. If he gets that close, I'm gonna be movin' some other way."

Miss Stark learned the rudiments of animal training with very little outside help, but the phenomenal Hungarian trainer, Louis Roth, pointed her way to a polished performance.

Mr. Roth, like Miss Stark, had the instinctive ability to "read" an arena full of big cats. He had tremendous control over all animals, but his specialty was lions. Roth, who joined the Al G. Barnes Circus in 1910, was the man largely responsible for building that show into the world's greatest animal circus from its gypsy-wagon beginnings, when the main attraction was an animal display consisting of thirteen dogs, two goats and eight upside-down bucket pedestals.

It was likely Roth who taught Mabel Stark how to wrestle a tiger, since he had once exhibited a wrestling lion patterned after such an act observed as a boy in Hungary. Roth himself was able to ride astride a lion; and he trained three lions to ride a horse at the same time, and a leopard to be a zebra jockey.

One of Mabel Stark's most flamboyant stunts was one done in partnership with this doughty Hungarian, who had worked his way up to the big-time big cage from a lowly beginning as a three-dollar-a-week cage boy. In their virtuoso performance Miss Stark, Mr. Roth and a lion-at-liberty named George were hoisted on a platform from barred arena to upper reaches of the Big Top where fireworks were unleashed. It was a real showpiece, unique in its day. The stunt once served to disprove the myth that wild animals are crazed by the sight of blood. On the descent one day Mabel was felled by a piece of falling rigging, which hit her head and drew blood. As the elevator dropped, the lion instead of going mad from the blood smell calmly leaned down and stanched the wound by gently licking it.

One of the most exciting wild-animal acts ever performed by a woman was that of Martha Florine, a contemporary of Miss Stark's. Martha's tour de force was a mad dash into and out of the cage of a ferocious lion named "Wallace, the Untameable." Martha had to accomplish this mighty frenetic folly without the fierce beast nailing her, and this required split-second calculations. It was an exciting and sensational presentation. The lion, attracted to the end of the long eleven-foot cage opposite the small safety-cage entrance, would make a lunging half-somersault to the ceiling as Martha made her sudden appearance. The doughty miss would then scamper under the big cat and pause until he made a return raid and leap. Then she shot under him again and out through the little door to safety. Wallace always tried to beat her to the door, but he never did, although several times Martha was clawed just a bit.

Mabel's choice for the best all-round all-time animal trainer is John Helliot. "And to think," she often says, "he was killed by being run over by a street car."

The queen of all tiger trainers believes that Pete Taylor had the best "fighting act."

The most tigers Miss Stark has ever handled at one time was sixteen on the Al G. Barnes show in 1930; her grandest mixed display was one of fourteen tigers and seven male lions. When Mabel went to Japan in 1954 she took along five tigers; there are now eleven there in the group that she trained and worked. They belong to the Japanese Government, since according to Miss Stark, it is a law that all tigers entering that country must be sold to the state. They are big bruisers, two of them weighing over 750 pounds. (Tigers in America today average 500 pounds for the male; 350 female.)

In Japan, Mabel worked her act one month in each town big enough to hold a circus.

"And some that wasn't," she comments wryly.

"We worked outdoors with no seats; the people sat squatted down on an inclined platform around the cage. They came to see me in any weather; the worse the weather, the more the crowd. The tiger in Japan has religious significance, you know. They'd come in the teeming rain and all squat there under umbrellas (we worked in raincoats); some days we'd have four inches of snow in the arena."

The snowy days were treacherous ones, for big cats hate to get their feet wet or muddy, loathing anything that sticks to their toes. Amazonian Indians frequently capture jaguars by taking advantage of this abhorrence of cats to sticky stuff on their feet. They trap the beasts in a viscid birdlime made of breadfruit or holly bark. The stuff is stickier than flypaper, and the cat becomes so distracted in trying to get it off—so immersed in the inbred cat instinct to be clean—that he is easily netted. It is simply a jungle application of the old-country method remembered by our early-American grandmothers of accustoming a new house tabby to its new home by spreading butter on its paws. In licking off the grease all the cat's other worries cease to exist.

Mabel found the Japanese beast men good workers but feels they will never make top-notch wild-animal trainers.

"I had three good boys, Tiagwa (my number one), Nakiyama and Ouchaba. They were conscientious and thorough, but they had no command in their voices."

It was getting dusk as we talked to Miss Stark. Her tigers, back up the little draw, remembering the jungle, were making their sundown roars.

"I'm going back down there someday soon. 'Mobel Stock, Teacher,' they call me there," she said proudly. "I left a lot of good friends in Japan—and Eddie. You remember him. Eddie Trees. He was menagerie boss for Ringlings for years. We were married ten years. I left him in Japan; he died over there."

It was simply a statement; she expected no sympathy and we were silent. In a little while Mrs. Eddie Trees drifted back from Japan and said, "Well, youngsters, I've got to go eat supper now. There's something on TV tonight I want to see; Clyde Beatty on Ed Sullivan's show. It was nice of you folks to drive up, but next time come in time to see the tigers, too."

On our way back to the city we stopped off to thank our friend Parley, and he said he wished we could know the great Mabel as well as he did. He considered her one of the seven wonders of the world.

"She lives tigers," he said. "She never asks the cage boys to do what she won't do herself. She's out there bright and early mornings to see that there are no mixups or fights, to see that the cats are treated well. Sometimes she even pitches in and helps put up the arena. She does all her own doctoring for the tigers; gives them whatever they need—vitamins, cod-liver oil and lime water and worm medicine. She sees to it that they feed good, too. If she could get them, she'd serve up zebra cutlets and hippo steaks, which they love. As it is, it costs plenty to feed a tiger. One eats about fifteen pounds of horse meat a day six days a week; on the seventh they get milk and eggs. One thing tigers won't do is overeat, but their stomachs need a rest once a week."

Parley took us to the kitchen for drinks.

"Mabel's a great girl. Did she tell you about that time she parted a lion's mane whacking him with a two-inch hickory stick? She laid him out cold, then she cried like a baby because she thought she had killed him."

For a fine moment Parley relished this memory of his trouping days with the great one. "She's the only woman I know," he added, "who can curse like a trooper and still sound like a perfect lady. One day she came by here and said she wished there had been a band out there that day because she'd had a balky cat. 'And you know,' she said, 'there is nothing like some good strong language to get a cat working, but I'm supposed to be a lady in that arena and everyone is too close for me to cuss without a band to cover me up.' "

We filled our glasses again and saluted the world's all-time greatest lady tiger trainer, in the center ring, Fearless Female Subjugator Demonstrating Woman's Triumphal Power Over Ferocious Beasts of the Jungle, PRE-senting! Miss Mabel Stark—a lady and a thoroughbred, with or without cussing.

The Tiger Trainer's Embroidery

It was a hot, tropical, late-February morning at the winter quarters of the Greatest Show on Earth, but far from a lazy one. Frenzied activity of putting together the gigantic circus had begun to spread across the sun-baked acreage, once a fairground. Rehearsals had started on Washington's birthday, and in the outdoor "Madison Square Garden," practice area out behind the horse stables, the "Spec" pageant was being walked through to the wheezing of a small portable organ valiantly trying to be a circus band. Feed wagons, manure haulers and tractors substituted for fancy floats; sports shirts, Levi's and sweat-stained leotards for spangled silks and satins.

The canvas loft hummed with sewing machines; six old ladies were stitching the new season's Big Top. In a meadow between cookhouse and Seat Repair Dept., the mammoth patched and tattered tent of the season past was being lazily unfurled to be used as a practice hall for the well-muscled butterflies of the aerial ballet. From along the siding tracks came clanks and clangs of the car-repair men, the white-blue flicker and metal-melting roar of the welders. This was the circus with its scarlet hair down. This was a time of hard labor.

In the cavernous train shed a crew of painters were daubing at heroic flattering portraits of sideshow freaks and transforming the menagerie cages into delights of crimson and gold, turquoise, magenta and purple. I had gone there that morning, as designer of this part of the circus, to check on the blush pink being slapped onto the walls of the hippopotamuses' rolling den. When I got back to the ticket wagon I was using as my atelier, the costume designers' young assistant was waiting to ask how in hell he could disguise bull-hooks as fairy wands and to slip me the tip-off that after lunch, in closed session, Mr. North's new tiger trainer was to face for the first time the new tigers which had arrived at Quarters only a few days before after a rough month at sea.

I made plans to be on hand, for the new tiger man, a Dane named Trevor Bale, was my next-door neighbor. My wife, Whiskers, and I were living that winter with our kids (boy four, girls three and two, and a just-born boy) a lion's roar from Quarters in a place called Circus City, a trailer park operated by the general manager of the circus, his wife and half sister. (The odd nickname was tagged onto my wife, Roberta, when she was one of the showgirls of the late John Murray Anderson, producer of theatrical extravaganzas and circus spectacles, who was addicted to renaming his friends affectionately to suit his fancy. The sobriquet refers illogically to an uncle who once wrestled professionally under the name of "Whiskers Blake.") The compound was rimmed with apartments which had been made from old circus railroad sleeping cars by the addition of foundations, plumbing and new roofs. Several of these ex-Pullmans were split into two narrow kitchen, bedroom and bath units, and we occupied one of these, separated from the Bales by a mutual beaver-board bedroom wall. We hadn't gotten to know them yet beyond this auditory bedchamber acquaintance, as they had just moved in, but we were aware of a blonde British wife named Renée and three kids; Gloria, eleven, and twins of eight, Elvin and Dawnita. I had some idea of how the tiger man handled *them*, and I wanted to see if he did as well with larger animals, so I managed to be among the handful of privileged assembled that afternoon in the ring barn, a hideous octagonal ancient of concrete block just beyond the dusty ringstock corral.

Both circus veterinarians and the first-aid man were there. Also the menagerie boss, with a few rough-looking cage-hands, one ready with a fire hose (to fend off any tiger attacks); Mr. Pat Valdo, the personnel director, and a few other importants, including his eminence, JRN, and younger brother, Henry, both elegantly tricked out in expertly fitted jodhpurs and expensive Italian sports jackets. The high-ceilinged, dirt-floored, drab room, whose high-up windows had been crudely painted over, was in semidarkness as the wide barn door had been securely closed. There was a crisp feeling of tension. My new neighbor, whom North had been eying during his European junkets for the past seven years, was inside the steel-barred arena, calmly awaiting the release of the demons from their cage chute. His pert waxed mustache gave him a tremendous air of bravado that made him look every inch a beast subjugator, though he wore none of the usual trappings—not even boots. Dressed in a wrinkled pair of ordinary blue pants, he was stripped to the waist and had the chest of a Sandow.

I asked Valdo what the tigers were like. "Big," he said, "but not in too good shape."

The handler accompanying the big cats had been held back by immigration regulations and somehow no instructions had been delivered with the shipment. It turned out that no one knew the names of the animals, which was which, what tricks, if any, they had been broken to—absolutely nothing. Bale signaled to let in the first tiger. The chute's wooden door rattled; the cage boys poked iron rods at the big tawny beast whose evil muzzle appeared at the opening.

"Huhyh! huhyh!" grunted the boys, their irons rattling against the bars. The long striped body slithered into the enclosure. The hearts of men stopped for an instant. Bale took command, daring and intimidating the slinking tiger. Its ears were flattened, the eyes smouldering, the tail twitched softly. There wasn't a sound now. The tiger trainer's tight stomach moved in and out almost imperceptibly. His eyes were riveted to the enormous beast, the knuckles of the fingers holding whipstock and hickory club stretched white. The tiger silently rushed the man and promptly received a stout, piston-quick clout on the nose. Her lip curled in a terrible snarl. She backed off, circled and lunged again. Bale ducked adroitly, then inch by painful inch he forced the big cat back against the bars of the arena. Holding her there with his eyes and whip end he signaled to let in a second tiger. This one was lively, too, but had less fight. After she was huddled near the first, the others were admitted one by one at intervals, the daring Dane studying each long and carefully. They were a wild-looking, snarling bunch, and it took exceptional courage to face them.

Mrs. Bale, standing near me, pale but calm, muttered to herself, "Oh, ducks, don't they look just terrible."

They were giants: three shaggy-haired Siberians, two huge, handsomely striped Bengals and two smaller, less vivid Sumatrans—2800 pounds of stalking, skulking, murderous death. The big cats ignored every command roared from the deep chest.

"These bloody barstards haven't been trained," the tiger man shouted to his new boss, without taking his eye off the beasts. "They don't understand English, French, German, Swedish or even Zulu!"

It took a good two hours to stem the baleful skirmishes, rushes and charges, but finally the tiger trainer had the quivering beasts ranged in some semblance of order around the bars. Then he signaled to a cage boy who rattled the wooden chute door and the big cats slithered out, sultry eyes shooting promises of future mayhem to their subduer. Bale was shining with sweat, his mustache as cocky as ever, and Mr. North seemed pleased with his latest find.

"Do you think we can have an act ready for the opening in the Garden in April?" he asked this newest employe.

"All I can do is all I can do," replied Bale. "That's only a month, and they're in bloody bad shape."

In just one more session the enigmatical tigers were brought to "seat" by the redoubtable Dane. On the sixth day, still so vicious they wouldn't mix with each other, they succeeded in swiping him down twice, inflicting no damage, however.

At the end of two weeks Bale had the cats pretty well in hand, but though every night through our bedroom wall we were regaled with the vivid details of the day's class in tigerology, we still hadn't broken through the Bale family's European reserve. Mrs. Bale was extremely pregnant and this, along with her natural British reticence, kept us from getting very close to the family.

One night my wife poked me awake. "Listen," she said. I did.

"Do you hear it?" she asked. "A baby crying." And soon I did; the gasping *wah-awah-awah* that is the unmistakable cry of a just-born baby.

We heard the water running in our mutual pipes. And little stirrings next door, but no voices. I slid a long side glance out the window but could see no lights on.

"Do you suppose Mrs. Bale has had her baby?" asked my mama-of-four with some alarm. "In the middle of the night with no help?" Then, though we kept our ears peeled for a long while, we heard no more. And I, at least, fell off to sleep.

It was not quite light when my wife poked me again. "Listen," she whispered, "I hear that cry again. Hear it?"

I did. A new baby if I ever heard one—and I have. Then it was very quiet for a long time.

"Get your pants on and go out and look," said Whiskers. "They may need help."

I did. Still no lights, nothing stirring at the tiger trainer's apartment. It was weird. When I came back to bed, Whiskers sat up with great alarm.

"Don't you suppose they need help?"

"Nonsense," I replied. "Go to sleep. If she had the baby, he's an animal man and probably knows just what to do and everything is all right. If they want us they'll call."

"Don't you think you should go and knock on the door?"

"What will I say?" I asked. " 'Mr. Bale did you just have a baby?' He's liable to take a poke at me, and he's a big man. You know how private circus people like to be. Forget it."

But neither of us could and lay awake until light trying to work out the puzzle.

Mrs. Bale appeared at the garbage can the next morning, but she was just as heavily pregnant as ever.

"Well," observed Whiskers, "I guess she didn't. But that *was* a baby. I *know* it was."

Every night after, for a week, we heard the little cries at regular intervals, on the same schedule as that maintained for a new-born suckling. The water ran, the cries quieted, but there was never any light or any talking. Just when we were about to lose our sanity, I had a breakfast flash of inspiration. "Do you suppose," I asked Miss Whiskers, "that those cries could be . . ."

"A tiger!" she cried. "Of course, a baby tiger!"

Our oldest boy, Toby, jumped up from the table. "Daddy! Daddy!" he clapped happily, "you guessed our secret. I knew it all the time. Dawnita told me the first day. They have a little baby tiger that they feed off a bottle."

Whiskers couldn't help telling all this to Mrs. Bale when they accidentally (so she said) met at the garbage can that evening. And from then on we became friendly neighbors and went often to the Bale kitchen for a spot of tea, rum, or a trifle, which is an ungodly heroic sweet that the British concoct.

We began to distinguish Trevor Bale, subjugator of tigers, from Edwin Trevor "Tommy" Bale, man and father. He was born in Copenhagen, of a Danish mother, while the family was trouping with the Circus Schumann. At three he was mixed up in a tiger escape; at five in a tent collapsed by snow. At six he had crossed the English Channel on a sinking boat loaded with circus horses; and had once been saved from death-by-crocodile-bite by a providential kick his father administered to the saurian's jaw (the upper, should this emergency ever arise in your family).

When Trevor was seven, while leading a circus parade dressed in a velvet suit, he was bucked off a mule; and his father swatted him instead of the beast.

"If you do that again, God help you, that's all!" said Père Bale, an uncompromising gentleman who, being angered by a partner's attempt to maneuver him out of top billing, dissolved the arrangement by cutting in two all the paraphernalia (props, riggings, carpets, rings, curtains) of their enterprise, the Royal Empire Stage Circus.

As a boy, Trevor was exposed to all kinds of animals from elephants to geese; and as pets he had a jackdaw, pony, monkey and a very provident dog named Monday, who (according to Bale) died after digging its own grave, a little each day, finally toppling into it on a Tuesday.

The earliest circus Trevor remembers is one he saw as a tyke in Norway, the Buffalo Jack Joyce show, a Scandinavian version of an American horse opera. The program included, "Jack Joyce's Cowboy-trup 'Scener af Livet i Wild West,' Lassokastining, sadling ridning af vilde Beste. Slim Smith, Buffalo Bill's head-cowboy rider bucking Hesten 'Two-Step.' "

The list of circuses in which Bale has been a performer is a long one, but it was in Pagel's South African circus that Trevor Bale reached the zenith of his versatility. He led off with Pagel's Pride of Performing Lions, followed by the inevitable Cowboy Roundup. Then he appeared in Thrills on the Trapeze, accompanied Pagel's Performing Pachyderms and drilled Bella and her Zebra. Next came Pagel's Arabian Dromedaries and Bosco the Wonder Horse, both squired by Professor Bale, followed by The Corona Troupe of Novelty

Riders (all Bale and a yard wide) and the Grand Carousel of thirty horses (E. Bale, Equestrian Director). Trevor also appeared as the Head Roman centurion in the show's finale.

"Something New: Startling-Daring-Enthralling-Spectacular-and-Horrifying! Christian Martyrs & Slaves Condemned to Flames! Lions in Roman Arena! (The Christian Martyrs, Slaves and Lions in Arena not presented at matinees)."

I had heard of this famous Pagel's Circus, having read of it in a British circus book by Lewis Hasting called, *Dragons are Extra*. The author said:

> . . . Madame Pagel, the dominant partner in the concern, was an unforgettable character. She had at one time been one of those fairylike creatures who hop lightly through hoops on the back of a prancing skewbald. But when I knew her this little Lancashire woman had the curves of an outsize Juno, a coruscating temperament and a flow of basic English that would have broken the heart of an old-time sergeant-major. She was the most kind-hearted and generous soul alive and had a wonderful way with animals. She sat at the ticket office when the performance began, and if by any chance you asked for change the ensuing invective would blast you straight into your seat. . . . Herr Pagel, a vast gloomy German, the junior partner in the show, was a lion tamer when he wasn't doing innumerable other chores about the place. He had started his career as a strong man, and his immense thighs and biceps remained to mark this early profession of his. Evil-minded persons claimed that he had taken to the lions' den as the only way to escape Madame his wife. But this was undoubtedly slander. The two were as devoted a couple, after their peculiar fashion, as any in Illyria. . . .
>
> I once had the honor of driving around Bulawayo with Madame Pagel in a large rickety saloon car, while she distributed her various orders and lowered the town's level of Guinness' stout at various houses of call. While we traveled, the admired of all beholders, I sat in the back seat, Madame Pagel drove, and on the other front seat sat a small, melancholy black-maned lion, which Madame Pagel fed from time to time with chocolate creams.

I asked Bale once as we chatted at dusk in Circus City which animal he found the most difficult to train.

"Children," he answered without a moment's hesitation. "Compared to kids, tigers are easy; you know what they're thinking and they don't change their minds."

Bale told me he was training his own youngsters by the same principles that he applies to four-footed animals. He teaches them to accept orders, to have respect for man, to develop tractability, an even disposition and agility.

"And you see that they have good health and teach them to 'seat,' to have a home base." He looked around for his three and, not finding them in sight, filled his massive chest and let loose with a thunderous blast, "EL-VIN! DAWN-NITA! GLO-O-O-RIA!" which must surely have been heard in downtown Sarasota. To really give the call justice a much bolder type face is needed. Try to imagine an ocean liner whistle at six feet, a diesel locomotive at a crossing, and you approximate father Bale's call of the wild.

"Tigers are the most cunning," he went on in a normal tone of voice. "The black panther is a killer, has terrific speed and wizard reactions. A jaguar is stubborn; leopards are, I guess, the swiftest cat. Zebras are wicked and spiteful, and you dasn't work them too hard because they have weak hearts. Same as a kangaroo. If you box a kangaroo, never hit it near the heart or you'll kill it." I told him I'd remember that. "Lions," added Bale, "give the most warning of attack. They have slow way of turning before they strike. Polar bears, they move suddenly in one straight motion with no change of expression. Very dangerous animal—the most, I should say."

One day, getting on to April, Trevor looked in at my wagon at Quarters and said amiably, "Stop by this evening to see our tree. It's only just arrived from England." Tree? I puzzled. A Christmas tree all the way from England? Wasn't that carrying nationalism a bit far—and anyhow wasn't it a little late? So that night after the kids were bedded down, Whiskers and I slipped next door to the tiger trainer's kitchen. The decorations for the twins' February birthday party hadn't been taken down yet. Festoons made of refrigerator silver foil swung from the low ceiling. There was a sprig of tired mistletoe over the sink and some Florida pine around the donnicker (circus word for "toilet") door, but no Christmas tree.

"Have a bit of trifle?" Renée offered, smiling as we scanned the trimmings. "The kids just couldn't bear to have me take them down," she said. "They remind us so much of back home."

Trevor handed me a cardboard folder, saying, "Here's our tree."

He smiled when I looked blank. "Fooled you, didn't I, old chum?" he said. "It's our family Genealogical Tree. Prepared by an old friend back home, Stan Bult, and just come by registered post. Here's the letter with it."

I glanced at the note: "I hope you find it worth framing and hanging in your home. It took a little time to duplicate as the one I keep for my record stretches almost four feet wide . . ."

I unfolded the long sheet of foolscap. There was a conglomeration of names reaching by red ink lines back to great-grandfather William Bale, Naval Tailor, Gosport, Hants born 16—, died 18— m . . . . died 18— aged 105, 6 children. (I could see a few leaves would be missing from this tree.) Among the assemblage of fifty-four relatives, sixteen were annotated as jugglers, six as trick cyclists, and there was a scattering of other specialties—bender, marionettist, wire-walker, musician, equestrienne, roller balancer, Tiller dancer, clown, proprietor. Trevor and his half brother, Harder, were the only wild-animal trainers listed, although there were several trainers of monkeys and dogs.

Trevor's grandfather, Edwin, was tagged a pigeon trainer. He had been, as well, a dog, monkey and pony subjugator; founder of the Yokohama Troupe of simulated Japanese jugglers and the juggling Zanettos; proprietor of the Bale Cycling Troupe; and operator of the Bale Family Circus.

Trevor's father, Edwin George, who had been a trick cyclist and animal trainer (also juggler, musician, clown, ringmaster and circus proprietor) died at the age of seventy-two after training a troupe of performing dogs while on his deathbed.

"Cup of tea?" asked Renée. "Lipton's. A British firm. Back 'ome all the shops is Lipton's. I buy it loose—none of them 'orrible bags."

Tucked in the breakfast nook, Whiskers noticed a cushion beautifully embroidered with a snarling tiger head.

"Did it meself," said the tiger trainer. "I've taught Renée to embroider. Never went to school, but I can cook and take a lorry motor apart and get it back together again. I speak six languages fluently, including Afrikaans and Zulu. An' I can build anything. We just bought a little lot out Fruitville Road, and I'm going to put me up my own house one of these bloody days." Then he brought out the rum bottle. "You'll have a spot in your tea won't you, old boy?"

Bale had been at the table making a drawing; quite a wonderful piece of colored pencil work primitive in style—rather like a Bombois.

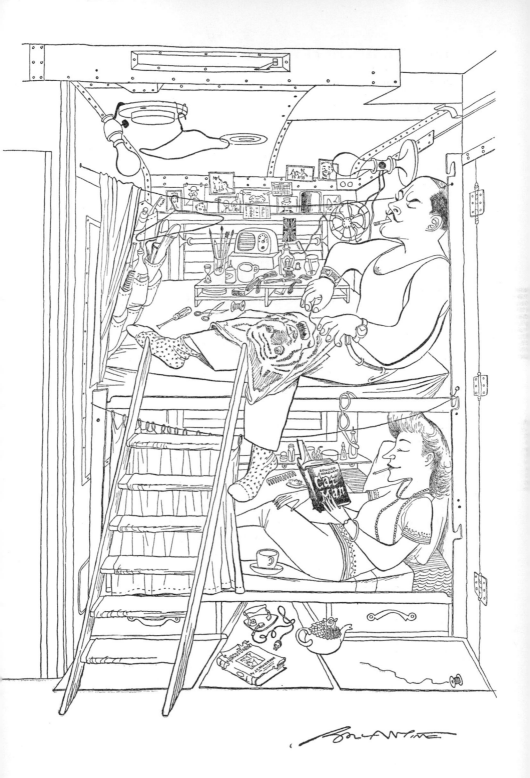

"It's me old act, like the one me father did," he explained, "I'll photograph it so we can get some bookings."

Up one side of the paper was a tall, tall unicycle on which a hobo rode. ("That's me when I was 'Len Rover,' the tramp.") Alongside was a motorcycle, and bent way over it's handlebars was a determined rider, looking somewhat like a man about to be shot into outer space. "It's me, too," Trevor pointed out. "I change costumes. *Zup-p-p-p!* you never see the rags come off." On this fellow's flattened back was an upended cyclinder with a diameter of approximately six feet. On its broad inside surface rode a girl (upside down at that moment) on a small motor bike. "That'll be Gloria," said papa. Gloria beamed from the couch.

Then came the photo albums. Trevor at three with a "stretching pig." Trevor's first animal act, three dogs and a pony ("Me mother used to assist me; I made me own clown dress"). Harder, the half brother, a huge hulk of man with chest almost a yard across, standing with a lion whose head reached from shoulder to shoulder ("Simba, that one is; fifty-seven stone he weighed—that's about eight hundred pounds"). There was a photo of Trevor poised on a rola-bola cylinder, balancing on his head a tea service for six plus a shower of four Union Jacks; and one of him executing that especially difficult Lippezanner trick, the Cabriolle, on a mule.

It wasn't long after that pleasant evening with the Bales that Trevor had his first real trouble with North's new tigers. Vicki, one of the Siberians, was the culprit. The moment of truth came while Bale was working the big cats in the outdoor arena for a crowd of Sunday visitors. The she-devil knocked both the stick and whip from the trainer's hand, crashed the chair also, then in a swift shift jumped the man from the back. Bale found himself, his right arm pinned to the ground, looking into a set of gleaming evil ivories, his shoulder and hip bleeding from claw rips.

He told us all about it that evening when he returned from being patched up at the hospital. He had suffered a badly lacerated back, a twisted knee, badly bruised shin, a ripped thigh and shoulder mangled.

"The bloody people screamed," he recounted, "and then I couldn't see nothing but Vicki's face against mine. Her eyes were narrow, greedy and burning like they was on fire. Her ears were slick back; her muscles tensed. Her breath was hot, moist and foul, and she lapped her rough tongue across my cheek—like sandpaper it was. I cussed her out good, then I got up all my strength and yelled

'VICKI!' just as good and loud as I could right into her open mouth. It either startled her or maybe just tickled her throat, but irregardless she jumped back a mite, just enough to release me arm and I rolled out from under. Cripes me back was raw! I got hold of the hickory, grabbed Vicki by the throat hard as I could and whaled the bloomin' daylights out of her. I hit her again and again and again, finally driving her back to the pedestal. I guess I yelled everything in the book and some special chapters of me own. The old girl must have thought I was gone barmcy. I guess I forgot to say my prayer today. 'Dear God, I'm as much your creature as they are. Look after us both.' "

The injuries didn't keep the great Dane down for long. In a few days he was back in the ring barn. The act was shaping up fine. John Ringling North was more pleased with it than by the results of his annual winter-quarters reducing diet (total abstinence and 250 calories daily).

Bale had managed to work out a new gimmick for the tried-and-true standard-finish pyramid. On an arched bridge between the two highest pedestals he had affixed a shower of large American flags and underneath hung a small trapeze. When the six cats were all in position, the two on either side of the bridge sitting erect on their hunkers, the trainer took his place on the trapeze bar for a gay little swinging bee. It was an old-fashioned flag-waving finale, but this fillip of childhood innocence made it most effective.

Among the individual tricks there were a plank walk and two rather out-of-the-ordinary leaps—one through an extremely small hand-held hoop, little more than the diameter of the beast; the other through a long canvas sleeve. Both stunts took advantage of the tiger's great leaping ability; the big cats can shoot through the air from nine to twelve feet, the record.

One rainy morning not long after the Sunday-afternoon attack, I sauntered into the ring barn to see what the energetic Bale was up to. He was beginning to break a tiger to ride a horse.

Animal men consider the tiger-horse pair one of the most dangerous and difficult of wild-animal tricks. "Elephant and tiger is worse," said Bale. "They hate each other and both hates you. Besides teeth and claws to worry about, there is the elephant's trunk—nothing but muscle. And those four pile-driver legs that can tromp you or the tiger into bloody porridge."

Teacher and pupil had already gone through the preliminaries of pedestal leaping and now in the arena, sans tiger, the horse was being walked about gently so that he would become accustomed to the very pungent smell of the striped beast, which is powerful enough to set most horses (and humans) rearing and plunging. After the horse has become accustomed to being within the acrid arena, he is stationed, under a strong hand, just outside the bars while the big cat gets used to seeing that much fine horse flesh on the hoof. After the tiger-rushes and horse-panic ease off the two animals are finally brought together inside the arena. The tiger is restrained by a neck chain attached to a lunge line of strong rope held by the trainer. The horse wears blinders and checkrein, and the body is protected from his natural enemy by a heavy canvas blanket padded on top. The neck carries a heavy leather and wood collar, studded with spike points to discourage tiger bites. Sometimes canvas leggings are also worn as a big cat finds shank nips very soul-satisfying. The cat rides on a flat platform saddle made of wood with rope nailed to it for more secure footing. The most difficult part of the training comes at the moment of meeting. The horse must be trained to stand absolutely motionless as the big cat enters the arena. If the horse so much as twitches a muscle, the cat is apt to attack.

"I wish I could get my tiger to leap at me like that lion an old-timer named Bob Thornton had," Bale said. "The cat with a chain about its neck would leap off the cantering horse and Thornton would whip the chain around a stake in the middle of the ring, take a couple of turns and hold the beast. Very spectacular act that. But there's not time; I'll be lucky to have this bloody tiger just riding with no fancy extras."

It did seem to me that Bale was starting this virtuoso showpiece just a bit late, since in less than ten days the circus train would be packing up to leave town for its New York grand opening.

"Tommyrot," he said. "It'll be ready."

I wished him good luck, but this time the invincible was wrong. He had to leave town without accomplishing the tour de force.

The little railroad-car apartment was lonesome and empty after the Bale family had gone. I missed those five-o'clock blasts of ELV-VIN-N-N! DAWN-NITA! and GLO-O-O-O-RIA!, and our bedroom was so quiet that Whiskers and I had a hard time getting to sleep at nights.

According to all reports from the North, the tiger display was not perfect, but under the lights and with the distraction of colored saw-dust, and spangles and the blaring band, it was a passable act to all but the more discerning circus buffs.

Trevor Bale himself took New York by storm, by displaying the gracious style of a storybook animal trainer, very much in contrast to the usual rip-snorting gun-banging native American variety. The public was completely entranced by this flamboyant fellow, who brought such an air of gentlemanly European elegance to the barred arena. Here was a performer stamped from the mold of the historic Isaac Van Amburgh, that first beast subjugator to reach America from England in 1833, the man who made a lion and lamb lie down together, and whose heralds proclaimed his fame as being "contemporaneous and extensive with the Universe itself." Bale was an old-fangled tiger trainer in the perfectionist manner of the 'nineties, a courtier who could have graced the banquets of any king, who could have bowed to the bidding of Victoria Regina or performed on the same bill with Jenny Lind. He was "real circus" to a public hungry for it.

John Ringling North, immensely pleased, went off his diet.

One Sarasota evening, when I came from the paint shop home to our railroad flat, Whiskers was waiting with more than the usual excitement.

"Look," she said, handing me a *New York World-Telegram* folded to a story about our erstwhile neighbor. He had submitted to an electrocardiograph test given by a covey of scientists to tap "anxiety palpitation" of the heart during the screening of an Alfred Hitchcock movie thriller. Bale's partners in the experiment had been a female trapeze flyer, a skyscraper window-washer whose bailiwick was the Empire State building, and a lady private-eye. The victims, while they watched the picture, had been plied with Freudian questions by a heart specialist, a psychiatrist and a psychologist.

"The aerialist went into a mild psychological freeze during the movie," stated the doctors, "a bit more scared than the average person in the average job."

The lady detective was barely affected. "Real corn," she was quoted as saying. "Bad sleuthing methods; amateur shadowing."

The high-altitude wiper of glass surfaces, a mild fellow who had once dangled by safety belt 102 stories above the street, indicated severe trauma.

Our tiger-training neighbor, according to the test results, was the most scared. The heart specialist said that Bale's ticker had pounded like a trip hammer. The physiologist was amazed by Trevor's jittery responses. The psychiatrist said that for a "tiger tamer" Mr. Bale had "unusual readiness for panic," and that his "perturbation" was considered very surprising for a man living close to the jaws of death.

Whereupon, so the story said, Trevor Bale twirled his exquisite waxed mustache, shrugged and said, "You must please excuse me now. I'm in a hurry to get back to those damned cats."

"Gee whiz," I said to Whiskers, "do you think Johnny North should start looking around for another tiger trainer?"

"Pish tush," my wife said. "Psychiatrists are not usually God Almighty and I *never* trust machines." And my lady flung a long arm into a beautiful center-ring "style."

"Down psychiatrist!" she exclaimed. "Up tiger man."

NAYCHEZ MISS.

Lions Hate Tagers

There are few places more miserable than a circus on a rainy day, and the agony is compounded if the circus happens to be in Southern boondocks. This circus I had come south to visit—one of the few larger ones still under canvas—was set up in a dismal field a short haul from the edge of a town with a streak of railroad down its middle and not much else. The show had been canceled out of yesterday's town when the first wagons on the gumbo lot sank to their hubs. Today was not exactly what you could call a winner. Asian flu had all but closed the schools. Hurricane Esther, buffeting the Gulf coast, was sending a backlash of stiff wind and heavy downpour against the spread of dirty canvas, giving it the beating of its wearisome life.

I had come to this wretched devil-begotten place at the bidding of a magazine to get a by-line story from the show's star performer, the great lion'n' tiger expert, Clyde Beatty, who hadn't been seen in the East for a couple of decades.

The matinee had just started as I picked my oozing way across the sloppy backyard to the Big Top's side entrance alongside the

||||| 115

bandstand. There were more seats than people in the grandstands, but Beatty was giving his all just the same.

The act was almost over. The great trainer had just coaxed his famous spinning tiger, Sleika, off her pedestal. The trick is one of the act's more fearful features, for as the tiger crouches, belly to the ground, facing Beatty, the trainer's eyes must be strictly on her, leaving both man and animal wide open to attack by the lions. But the real balance of terror, the act's most perilous moment, comes when the big cat spins like a puppy chasing its tail, for this movement greatly excites the lions. Sleika was just going into her wind-up crouch when the old lion-tiger jungle hatred flared. A lion sprang from his high pedestal and landed within inches of the tiger. The two locked together, kicking up shavings and mud on the slippery ground, struggling fiercely for tooth-and-claw advantage.

Beatty grabbed the heavy hickory stick that his Negro cage boy, Junior, was quick to push through the bars. Brandishing it, he rushed the flailing gladiators, blanking them (firing his gun) square in their snarling faces. Declaring the act unofficially over, Beatty yelled to Junior to rattle the exit chute's iron bars, standard cue for animals to leave an arena.

As the cats skedaddled out, helped along by prods from Junior, Beatty gave his troublemaker a whale of a clout on top of his murderous head, which made the lion let go the tiger's neck long enough for the trainer to thrust his trusty chair between the two writhing beasts. The lion turned on him, which was exactly what he expected it to do, and the tiger, bleeding slightly from the shoulder, scampered to the chute. Leo, plenty mad, clawed and bit the chair away from Beatty once before the trainer was able to drive the beast through the exit.

As the wild-animal man passed alongside the seats on his way out of the tent, a grizzled, highly satisfied old man seated in the front row said to him, "Bet yo'all glad, sir, to get out of there."

"You bet I am, boy," said Beatty. "I was afraid that packing the dentist put in my tooth this morning was gonna shake loose, and I'd start to hurt all over again."

I had never met the great Beatty, for, since I had come of circus age, he had done most of his performing west of the Rockies. Beatty has the liveliest "fighting act" in the business today (action as opposed to a "still" or tableau act). There are few American boys who haven't thrilled to the magic words "Clyde Beatty," for he has starred in many movies, had his own radio and television shows, and for more than thirty-five years has handled almost every species of wild beast in the big cages of such stellar outfits as Hagenbeck-Wallace, Al G. Barnes, Cole Bros, Hamid-Morton, his own Clyde Beatty Circus, and Ringling Bros and Barnum & Bailey, where he was the first, and practically only, performer to have his name in lights on the marquee of Madison Square Garden in New York City.

Beatty had been touted to me by circus-wise friends as a laconic, ornery crosspatch. I braced for the worst. But the king of beast trainers didn't chew me up when I spoke to him as he came alongside his animal chute, bundled in a heavy bathrobe with a thick towel wrapped around his neck. He was running a heavy sweat, was tense and extremely nervous. (I hadn't been told that after the act is the worst time to catch Beatty.) He was abrupt but not sharp, and we made a date for dinner before he disappeared into his trailer to take a nap to smooth his raw nerves.

An usher said, "You'll just get the old iggy brusheroo." (Iggy describes the typical know-nothing attitude circus people usually reserve for towners.)

I found this not to be true. Being one of the great legendary characters of the circus and somewhat a loner, as are all men close to animals, has made Clyde Beatty greatly misunderstood. In the time I spent with him bucking that miserable hurricane weather, I found him honestly affable and never once the least bit unpleasant—and those stormy days it was easy to be nasty. He was impatient only directly after the act. Then he was often on razor edge, almost impossible to speak to, as you might expect of a man who has been jousting against fangs and claws.

There were twenty big cats in Mr. Beatty's act that stormy day, but for many seasons his huge steel cage held forty lions and tigers— a few more than any Roman Colosseum martyr ever had to face alone.

Clyde Beatty is not the first man to mix lions and tigers in the same arena, but he is the only one today able successfully to bring together the traditional enemies of jungle and veldt, both male and female, on so large a scale. A great European trainer named Herman Weedon, along about 1898, was one of the first to put a tiger in with lions in a nine-animal act that included three bears (brown, sloth and Tibetan), a hyena and a Silesian boarhound. Pete Taylor, whom Miss Stark regards so highly, was one of the pioneer lion-and-tiger mixers in the the American circus. It was Taylor who encouraged Beatty to inaugurate lion-tiger displays to a grander degree than the circus world had ever seen.

Aside from being the most famous wild-animal trainer of our time, Clyde Beatty is the most durable—only Mabel Stark surpassing him. Beatty has been around wild beasts since 1919 when, as a circus-happy kid of almost fifteen, he left his small Ohio home town to join the Howe's Great London Circus. He didn't intend to be an animal trainer but had in mind something in muscles and tights like an acrobat or wire-walker. However, the only job for which he could qualify was that of raking cruddy shavings out of cages, chambermaid to big cats. He became cage boy to the great Louie Roth. The next year he moved to another circus, the old Gollmar Bros–Yankee Robinson show. One morning, after cage boy Clyde turned an ankle trying for a round-off flip-flap from an elephant tub, Danny Odom, the circus manager, took him out behind the donnicker for some fatherly advice.

"Forget the tumbling, kid," he said. "I been watching you. You belong with them animals."

At the winter quarters of the circus in Montgomery, Alabama, in 1923, the kid, then just past seventeen, got his first crack at handling a wild-animal act on his own—a mixed group of lions, leopards and bears. The cocky Clyde, also careless, was promptly picked off the arena floor with some pretty lion-tooth embroidery in his shoulder. But this first brief encounter with *Felis leo* didn't douse the fire Odom had sparked.

During that summer season the trainer for whom Beatty was cage boy, Chubby Gilfoyle, collapsed one night in the arena. After Mr. Gilfoyle had been hauled out, Clyde continued the act, giving such a stylish performance that the audience rose to its feet and cheered. Great style is still Clyde Beatty's greatest asset. Even those who find Beatty a little hard to take personally admit that as a performer he is absolutely first-class. That feeling of professional admiration is epitomized in an unpolished remark that I heard many times during my stay with the Clyde Beatty Circus during its mucky trek across the South. "After ya seen Beatty the rest of them stinks."

There is, I'm sure, a deep, almost Neanderthal, thrill in close communion with wild beasts. You sense this in Beatty. Full face, he has a strong resemblance to his handsome tigers, just as Mabel Stark does. His large nose hooks and flattens a bit, the nostrils flare high.

His cold blue eyes are ·penetrating; they seem, like a cat's eyes, to look through, rather than at, you. His hair is thick and wire-curly, only slightly peppered with grey. He has the East-European look that the Irish often have, though he says the name is English. "Bay-tee" is the way the master of tigers pronounces it; everyone else in circus business calls him "Bee-tee."

Beatty's voice is as gravelly as the Ohio River bottom, but it does not slide into the usual "dese, dem and dose" circus grammar. He calls tigers, "tagers"; Hagenbeck as Hagen*back*. He curses only in anger, which is seldom, and has a ready, musical laugh. Beatty is a stocky five-foot-six, hairy-chested, his torso scarred only on the back. His arms dangle clear of his body, cocky and ready, like those of a boxer or an acrobat.

At dinner that evening, Beatty was a one-beer man and ordered Mississippi river catfish.

"I like it, but I won't eat that again for maybe a year," he said. "I can eat everything and anything; have the digestion and appetite of a twenty-year-old."

In the short time between shows, on that rainy evening, Clyde Beatty told me many things I never knew about tigers, and by the time I left the soggy show three days later I considered myself a graduate of tiger university. I learned just about all there is to know about the big striped tomcat except how many teeth it has. Clyde Beatty didn't know.

"Lions hate tagers," he told me that first evening over coffee. "That extra hazard is what has kept my act on top all these years. Pete Taylor, one of my first teachers, put me on to that years ago. I've only met two cats in my life who were exceptions to the lion-hate-tager rule. One was Trudi, a Sumatran female, who made a practice of attacking lions, and there was my roughneck lion, Duke, who mashed around with two lady tagers, Venus and Ruth, after he had tore up almost every other tager in sight—male or female."

I asked Clyde the names of his tigers and lions and he gave them to me—as many as he could remember. "Saber (he's the roll-over), Singapore, Frisco, Princess, Sleika (my spinner). Those are the tagers. And my lions—let's see—there's Rajah, Brutus, Ceasar, Nero, Simba, and that last one—tough little guy. What's his name again? He's one of the oldest lions in my act; I'm gonna retire him soon. Oh, yeah—Sultan." ·

A menagerie man had once told me that the big cats hear only vowel sounds: therefore the names must have plenty of a, e, i, o and u.

"To me," said Beatty, "names don't mean nothing. They're only so's I can direct my cage boy. My animals know me by smell; they can pick me right out of a crowd. I don't even bother calling my cats by name, because they don't know them anyhow. Besides I believe my voice irritates lions and tagers, so I whistle to them instead. I'm the world's only whistling tager trainer." He gave me a few sample calliope tremolos, then continued, "You don't have to say anything to a cat. Footwork and hand gestures are all the commands you need if you break them in right.

"I don't believe in breaking by force like I hear they do in Europe. If you have to knock a cat up on the seat, that's not training. I don't ever shout at my cats. The animal's dignity has to be respected; you shouldn't humiliate any animal, but especially not a wild one."

Beatty prefers jungle-bred cats; years ago he gave up working so-called "tame" or captivity-bred lions and tigers. He believes that, once man marks a wild animal as a pet, it is forever ruined for the big cage. A pampered indulged and fondled young cat becomes a sullen, obstinate, unmanageable adult monster, completely lacking in character.

"Give me the wild imports every time," he said. "They're stronger, more ferocious, and usually smarter than their civilized cousins."

The greatest advantage of the cat fresh from the wilds is that it is bluffable, man being an unknown quantity—something to be carefully studied. If the trainer takes immediate command and handles the cat with authority, he will be feared. This fear of man, Beatty feels, is what a cat-teacher wants most of all in his classroom. The trainer, in knowing his arena by heart, its floor plan engraved in his memory, has further edge over the greenhorn big cat, to whom the big cage is an unfamiliar frightening place. The best trainer has an expert poker player's instinctive ability to dominate a situation. Women, though they are able to put men over hurdles and through quite complicated tricks, seldom have enough commanding authority successfully to handle other wild animals. No trainer in the world can survive in an arena with a lion or tiger unless the beast is over-awed by the man and completely unaware of his relative power.

The big cats weigh up to 750 pounds, and an average tiger on hind legs towers over seven feet (inside the steel cage this can seem like fourteen). A tiger's sharp molars can crunch the bones of a water buffalo; its strong jaws break a horse's back. With forepaws, the striped demon can gash, squeeze and deliver a haymaker that could drop Floyd Patterson.

Having lions and tigers in the same arena is extremely dangerous, but the mixing has the advantage of being practically the only life insurance a trainer can carry. A lion, intent on killing a tiger, is less liable to have his murderous mind on the man.

"I've never come across one insurance peddler yet who considered wild-animal trainers a good risk," said Clyde. "Lloyd's would probably cover me, but although I do pretty good, I still couldn't meet the premiums."

Beatty's life has been saved more than once because a lion hated a tiger more. There was that time out in Kokomo, Indiana, during a press preview before the Hagenbeck-Wallace show hit the road. A new tigress in the forty-cat act had never performed with a band. The loud brasses rattled her some, and just when Beatty calculated that she had calmed down, the tiger sprang. He swung up a chair but it went spinning. The cat got reset and lunged again.

"I blanked her *good*," he recalled, "but she was out to get me. A tager is not usually a try-try-againer, but that one sure was. Her third leap hit me full chest, and I went down between two pedestals. She pounced and clamped her jaws on my right arm. Boxed in by the furniture, she couldn't chomp down full force, otherwise my arm would have snapped like a dried wishbone. I'm gone, I thought, not a chance. Then, twisting my head, I see a lion rushing at us—Nero, the arena boss. He grabbed the tager's rump. She screeched and let go my arm, boy—right quick! When I sat up, those tagers on the pedestals began to swipe at me. In the excitement I'd forgotten all about them being there. One ripped my shirt, shoulder to belly, the other grazed my scalp."

Beatty ducked to the floor, and someone pushed him a heavy stick through the bars. By then all the tigers were off their pedestals with most of the lions raging around them. The only way to avoid a donnybrook was to get Nero, the head lion, back onto his perch. He was dragging the tiger around the arena, digging deeper and deeper into her hindquarters. Beatty, his arm badly chewed, managed to pry Nero loose and drive him back to his seat. Once the other lions saw him on the throne, the melee broke up. The tigers skittered through the chute and the lions were soon rounded up and sent packing.

"Well," said Beatty at the end of the story, "cripes, you should have seen the papers the next day! 'Faithful Lion Saves Beloved Master' was the general theme. Good publicity, but what a dream-up! Why, hell, Nero was not one bit interested in saving my life. He just saw a good chance to rip up a tager and took it."

One of Beatty's leopards once dragged a balky hyena from the animal chute into the performing arena. Cute, murmured the audience. Look—the spotted kitty helping its master. Nonsense! The cat was just after a little wild hyena on the half shell. Her jaws had to be pried loose to release the smaller animal.

Gratitude or sentiment never enters the one-track minds of the big cats. They are as heartless as a banker turning down a supplicant with no visible assets. Beatty feels that love cannot be a part of the relationship between him and his beasts. Mutual respect and understanding, yes; but no hearts and flowers. When he visits the cats' traveling cages after the act, it is not to bill-and-coo them but to check for injuries and to see that each beast is in its proper stall.

The misconceptions of the general public concerning the big cats sometimes vex Beatty.

"So many people," he said, "think that my cats never attack me because I feed them just before the act. (I wonder where they think I got all my scars.) Nothing could be more wrong. In the first place, my animals are fed once a day, *after* the matinee. And I never personally feed them; my handlers take care of that chore. And wild animals in captivity don't attack because they're hungry; a hungry cat is a weak cat. When lions and tagers jump you, they're expressing a primitive urge to kill. I've *seen* lions and tagers kill human beings; they don't eat them. When the victim stops quivering, the cat drops the body and leaves it alone."

Circus-goers sometimes believe that performing lions and tigers are doped (what a slow act *that* would be), have their claws filed, their teeth pulled or wear dentures. All sheer nonsense. There are those who think that Beatty has a hypnotic eye because of his act's finish trick in which he casts aside his whip, chair and gun to stare down a lion until it turns and slinks away. Rubbish! The outstaring bit is just a clever stunt taught that particular lion—nothing but skillful showmanship. The eyes of lion and man do not even meet.

Of course, a risk is involved with Beatty down on one knee, his face within two feet of the mighty jaws—but it's a carefully calculated risk.

Show people have their own folklore concerning wild animals. A cross-eyed candy butcher or horse trainer is supposed to bring the curse of disaster down on a cat act.

"When a tiger gets skinny," a cookhouse waiter once told me, "that means its nourishment is all goin' into its tail. You just snip a piece off the end and she's cured."

Sometimes circus people misinterpret dangerous things that happen to Beatty in the barred arena. While I was on the Clyde Beatty Circus, in Mississippi, a tiger, raring at the famous trainer, came down with its claws out and skinned off both his leather gloves without leaving a scratch. After the act, Boom-boom, the drummer in the band, said, "Great trick, Clyde. If I'd 'a' knowed you was gonna do it, I'd 'a' give you a roll on the snare drum."

Amateur do-gooder humanitarians are the worst nuisance of the wild-animal trainer's profession. "Someone is always picking on my whips," said Beatty. "Now anyone who has ever handled a whip knows that the snap proves it hasn't hit anything. Why I can practically snap a cigarette out of your mouth without touching your nose. The only noise a whip makes lashing into an animal is a dull cutting sound, and you'd have to be right up against the bars to hear it. But even a stray flick that connects doesn't hurt a lion or a tager—their hides are so loose and tough. You crack a whip at a wild animal to get its attention, to keep the lazy bums on their toes. If the idea was to inflict pain, I'd take me a nail-studded ball bat into the arena instead of a lash whip."

Beatty claims that the tall tales about cruelty in training wild animals are completely untrue, including the one about intimidation with a hot poker. "Hell," he said, "burned patches would only spoil an animal for exhibition. How that one got started: someone in the old days saw irons being heated in a coke fire to mull the chill out of a lion's drinking water. One old-time trainer named Frank Bostock even figured that the hot metal changed the water into an iron tonic. Why even today trapeze flyers heat the water for their dressing-room bucket baths with hot metal rods, only now they're electric."

About poking lions and tigers with pointed lances to gain obedience, Beatty had this to say: "No one who wants to live long ever pokes a big cat with a pointed lance. No jungle animal can be trained successfully by cruelty. It'll take the maltreatment for a while, then whammy! One day the cat explodes into a raving maniac, and you're done for."

Most big jungle cats are already "cage-broken" when they arrive in this country; that is, they are accustomed to confinement and can be approached with caution when they are given the liberty of the large arena. Occasionally an especially wild or unmanageable beast is restrained, for the safety of both animal and trainer, by a strong leather training collar (sometimes augmented by harness) to which is attached a non-chewable short length of chain, joined in turn to a heavy rope, which threads through a floor eyelet and passes between the bars to handlers outside the arena, who use this lunge line to control the beast. The collar is put on the wild animal while it is held in a "squeeze cage"—one whose sides have been moved in to pressure the animal securely. The method is superior to that of roping the cat into a four-legged spread-eagle as the danger of rope burns is eliminated. A block of wood is placed in the compressed cat's jaws to prevent biting.

According to Beatty there is no standard method of wild-animal training. No two trainers are alike. Each has his own system, except for a few basic truths that apply to the handling of all mammals.

"I had good teachers," said this foremost lion-tiger handler, "Bobby McPherson, Chubby Gilfoyle and Pete Taylor. They were the men taught me the most when I was a green punk."

Our homespun animal trainers—Clyde Beatty's teachers and others of the same early American period, such as Louie Roth and Al G. Barnes—brought to our native circus a wilder kind of animal training than that which had developed in the great arenas of Europe. These American trainers were all unscholarly men who, as sprouts of boys, had run away from small towns to the circus, knowing little or nothing of the effete, polished performances abroad. They had jumped into the arena with a crude, wild spirit of trial and error and as a result, the U.S.A. wild-animal act has always had a very exciting primitive quality quite different from that of its foreign sisters. The American wild-animal arena, with its emphasis on "fighting acts," displays the beasts as dangerous jungle killers; the European tendency is toward the great élan of the stylish "still act," the posing tableaus with complete and very calm control.

Of all the modern wild-animal men, Clyde Beatty presents the purest version of the all-American "fighting-act," but with excep-

tional style which comes from a marvelous rapport of the man with his beasts that few others have achieved. The showy hypnotism bit of the act's finish trick, mentioned earlier, is nothing but a carefully trained stunt. However, in *training* a big cat, Clyde Beatty somehow manages, like Mabel Stark, to get inside the animal's skull.

"I don't know for sure," he said, "how I get the big cats to obey me. Personally, I believe you can teach an animal nothing. They show *you* what they can do and then you develop it."

Natural balancers, by this token, are taught to walk the tightrope or do sit-ups; exceptional leapers to jump through hoops. An extremely nervous cat will never walk the rolling cylinder or globe. For him there are other stunts, such as hurdle leaping, in which flightiness is no handicap.

"You take my first spinning tiger," said Beatty. "She just had that spin trick in her. I was breaking her to do hurdles after nine days of getting nowhere on the roll-over. Now even the dumbest cat has a fundamental, protective cunning, and it is hard to get them to leap a blind hurdle. They like to gauge the possibilities of any unfamiliar action. To get this cat over the barrier, I got to squatting alongside it so that the animal, in leaping at me, would go over. But this baby somehow got to balking at my sight, whirling and going back without jumping. That gave me an idea. I sloughed the hurdle and from then on fixed on establishing that balking spin.

"She became an expert. I could get her going so fast that the spin would rare her up almost into a standing position. None of my spinners since have come up to that one."

Each lion and tiger is an individual, no two alike. Beatty once had a tiger who wouldn't obey unless the whip was held in his left hand; a lion who was no good unless he could wear his training collar with a short dangle of chain.

"One of my lions," laughed Beatty, "ate nothing but hamburger; another one was fond of strawberries and sour cream."

He once had a pair of wacky lioness sisters, Topsy and Mary, who were overly fond of their mother. They ate her—the only case of cat matricide ever known.

Beatty has worked with cowardly lions, sneaky tigers and chip-on-shoulder beasts who did nothing but start scraps. And he has had furious fighters who have kept the peace unless attacked. In his act there have been gorgeous hussies, too knuckle-headed to learn anything beyond mounting a pedestal; dismounting required a large push.

Besides lions and tigers Beatty has worked other combinations. One of his earliest mixed acts contained a black leopard, 2 common leopards, 2 jaguars, 2 pumas, 2 tigers, 2 lions, 3 hyenas, and 5 bears (2 polar, 2 Russian, 1 Himalayan). That was more than thirty years ago, and people still ask him about that black leopard.

"He was," Beatty recalled, "without a doubt the most truculent animal I ever worked with—the most treacherous cat I ever had—practically untrainable. I never wanted to tackle another."

The tiger man doesn't cotton up to house cats at all, not even the wilder Siamese, and has taught only one trick to one domestic animal, a German shepherd dog named Timber that Beatty had when he was a young man. Timber was broken to balance a lump of sugar on his nose. Considered savage and hopelessly untrainable, he had been found in a Western Germany dog compound, securely chained and slathering through a heavy muzzle. To the amazement of the attendants Beatty had the restraints removed and was able to go to the animal and wipe the slather from its mouth. The two became inseparable companions, and that dog, Timber, was the only domestic animal Beatty has ever really cared for.

The tiger man has never found a "born performer." According to him there is no such animal—and not many that have the spark of arena genius, a built-in responsiveness that can be developed to make a good circus performer. Nor has the great trainer ever found a really dependable animal; one that could be completely trusted.

"You never can trust a cat," explained Beatty, "even one that has been a sweetie-pie for a long time. And you are never careless with a wild animal. When a tiger takes a swipe, even a little one, at you or another cat, you must stop him right away. Otherwise he'll keep it up, a little more each time, until finally he pounces. A trainer's life depends on how well he knows his animals. I learned these lessons early and I never forgot them."

One rainy evening, standing just inside the Big Top behind the bandstand of the Clyde Beatty Circus just before the wild-animal act, the lion'n' tiger authority turned to me and said, "I shore hate rainy days. It's so easy to lose your footing in there and then you're apt to get clobbered. The cats hate thunder and lightning, too. Did I ever tell you about that time in Greensburg, Pennsylvania? That was the worst circus storm I was *ever* in."

A gale had come up without warning that memorable afternoon when Beatty was about halfway through his act. It got dark outside; wind ballooned the big tent alarmingly.

"I couldn't take in all the details," said Clyde, "because I had to keep my eyes riveted to the cats, but I knew some of the quarter poles were dancing, for I could hear them thwacking into the grandstands."

When the lights started to flicker queerly and dim, all the cats became extremely jittery, half of them leaning forward on their pedestals, ready to leap at the first opportunity.

"I was just beginning to coax my rollover cat, Venus, down off her pedestal to the arena floor," continued Beatty. "I thought if the lights really go out, Clydey old boy, you'll be in a pickle. I didn't figure they would—we had a pretty good 'shandy' on our light plant—but they did. Three drops of cold sweat hit the base of my spine. I remember counting them."

After what seemed like an hour of darkness—really only a few seconds—the lights crawled back on. The rumbling roars of thunder were coming closer.

"I knew I had better get out soon," said Beatty, "but I didn't want to panic the audience, so I decided to complete the rollover."

For several long tortured minutes the trainer shot Venus some of his most persuasive thoughts. Finally with great reluctance the big cat scrambled down and sullenly went into her low-bellied stalk. One halfhearted rollover seemed like a good enough finish trick that day.

Beatty yelled, "Let 'em out!" The cage boy rattled the exit-tunnel bars, and the band struck a big fat G-chord, which the cats recognized as the end of the act. The last striped tail had barely cleared the chute when, with a tremendous clap of scalp-raising thunder, the heavens were split by a bolt of lightning. The steel-blue streak found the arena, and Clyde, who had just left his safety door exit, could hardly believe what he saw in the next awful moment. The big cage seemed to be on fire, with jagged flames shooting from every bar. Then just as suddenly the flash was over. Later I asked old-time circus hands about that Greensburg bolt, and everyone said that in all their years they had never experienced anything like it. It was Beatty's closest direct person-to-person call from Gabriel. If he hadn't gotten the act out of the arena when he did, likely he would have been either burned to a crisp or torn to shreds.

While bad weather is one of the greatest hazards of a tented circus, the most dangerous situation for a wild-animal act is a fight within the arena. One sure way to break up one of these barneys is by directing a heavy stream from a fire hose between the bars. It knocks the breath out of the animals and in opening their mouths to gasp for air, they release their murderous grips. Squirted ammonia is good also. The pungent stuff will send quarrelsome cats spewing and coughing to the exit. The accepted way to unlatch a cat once it has bitten into another animal or person is to shove an iron bar down the beast's throat.

The chair, pole and blanking gun will stop most single-cat attacks. In a real serious situation a clout on top of the head is recommended, or a punch in the nose. Nothing makes a cat madder than a nose poke. A lady lion trainer named Gladys Cote had an unusual wild-animal act in which she did a veil dance around a lion named George (many lions two decades ago were named for King George V of England). Miss Cote had little lead weights sewn into the veil's hem so that, in passing, she could flick the lion's nose to make him roar. George took just so much of this indignity and one day he removed the veil—*and* poor Miss Cote.

Beatty considers the sturdy lion-trainer's chair one of his most important tools and his best protector. Its four legs are confusing prongs, and something for the cat to chew on instead of the trainer; the seat makes an excellent shield. Beatty's press agents used to say that his cats consumed as many as seventy of these bent-wood chairs a season. But the unvarnished truth is that he's had the same half dozen or so for years and years. They are well reinforced with steel bars, studded with bolts and kept in good repair. Replacements when needed are found in cheap hash houses and barrooms.

Anything strange will invite a big cat attack. Shock or surprise will spring the beast. But Beatty believes that behind most lion-tiger assaults is sex, in one of its two most manifest forms—desire and jealousy. In a large mixed group of animals the majority are females, and there is always one in heat.

Sex once saved Beatty's much-threatened life when he was attacked by a big lion named Bredo, who knocked him flat and started right in on his mid-section. Fortunately Clyde was wearing a heavy, wide leather belt, and Bredo got that hooked in his teeth instead of flesh. The lion lifted the man off the ground and carried him once around the arena. The audience applauded wildly, mistaking Beatty's dilemma for a new trick. Then Bredo opened his mouth, dropping the trainer, and straddled over his body ready to try for a more satisfying bite. A lioness on whom Bredo was sweet trotted over and rubbed her chops on his. Bredo immediately lost all interest in food. Decently moving over a few paces, he applied himself to his lady love. Surprisingly, the audience failed to applaud that trick.

Clyde Beatty's worst lion-and-tiger mix-up, and likely the classic wild-animal battle of all modern circus times, was a free-for-all that happened at Connellsville, Pa.—a battle that has never been forgotten or, fortunately, repeated. It was awful, a nightmare's nightmare.

At that time the three top-mounting tigers in the act were run into the arena first for the opening pyramid. When they were safely seated on their high perches, all twenty lions were let in. Those tawny ladies and gentlemen would mill around visiting each other, stretching their legs, indulging in minor sex violations, until Beatty fought his way through the mob from the safety-cage entrance. After the lions were properly mounted on their pedestals the rest of the tigers would be admitted.

On the grisly evening of the big clem (circus talk for "fight"), before Beatty had a chance to get into the big cage, one of the lions leaped from the floor and dragged a high-perched tigress named Rosie from her pedestal. She quickly shook herself loose and scrambled back upstairs just as the trainer entered the barred arena, cracking his whip and blazing away with blank pistol.

All was quiet on the lion front until the pyramid was formed. Then Snip, a flighty tigress, jumped from her perch and started running under the long-legged pedestals of the lions. Naturally, one jumped her. Whereupon Duke, the original trouble starter, jumped off his pedestal and fastened onto a nearby tiger. And the melee was on! All the other tigers except the three top-mounters left their seats— not so much to get into the skirmish, because tigers usually avoid gang fights, but just to get the hell out while the getting was good. The bunch of striped cats didn't get even close to the escape chute before every single lion in the arena was after them—twenty lions tangling with nine tigers! Chester, a fair-sized Sumatran, but no giant, soon had ten lions tearing at him, chewing on every available part. The arena shook and trembled in the uproar.

Only a fool would have tried to stop such a battle royal. Beatty, even then one of the sanest men in show business, edged his way with agonizing slowness to the safety door. "That steel jungle was no place for me, boy," he told me.

At any moment the snarling pack might have spotted him and turned their deadly wrath his way. He had just about made the door when Big Chester saw him. With a herculean effort he shook loose his tormentors and came at the trainer, hate boiling in his eyes, somehow blaming the man for his troubles. He had gained only one yard before the lion tacklers dropped him. The mob was now right at Beatty's boots. The bars bit his back as he carefully inched away from the scrimmage, with Chester straining to get out from under his maulers to nail the trainer.

Then the unexpected happened. Theba, a really gigantic tiger, freed himself and dashed for his regular seat alongside the exit door. To make things worse, Hilda, a lioness, deciding also to quit the fracas, leaped to the stool on the door's other side. To leave the arena now, Beatty would have to pass between lion and tiger. He stood rooted.

Then Chester made the decision for him. With super-tiger strength the beast tore loose and lunged, face distorted with rage. Beatty shot between the two feline door guards into the safety cage before they knew what was happening. His shirt sleeve was torn; his arm got a scratch—no more. Both cats had been taken by surprise. The lions ganged up on poor Chester again and the cage-hands, their boss safely out of the way, began to shoot the ammonia through the bars. The biting fumes sent all but nine cats retching to the exit. Two of the remaining looked quite dead.

As soon as the ammonia cleared, Beatty re-entered the arena and with chair, pole and blank gun drove the last battlers from the slaughter ground. Then he went over and waked Rajah, the chief top-mounter, who had dozed through the whole ruckus. Amazingly Chester, the much-put-upon tiger, came out of the scramble with no crippling injuries and within a few weeks was as good as new.

"All of my tight squeaks didn't happen in the big cage," said Beatty one night after the show as we sat in his trailer. "I've had some rough times in the wilds of Hollywood. The director I remember best is 'Breezy' Easton, finest serial man in the business. I made three movies with him, and he tried to kill me in two of them." Beatty chuckled. "Not intentionally, of course. He was just an all-out guy for realism. Once he had me tossed into a deep pit with a strange tiger I had never seen before. He thought I could rassle her better than a stand-in. That baby didn't know the Equity rules; on the first clinch she closed her jaws on my shoulder and wouldn't let go. An old hand like me should've known better than to take on a strange cat. But 'Breezy' was like that; could talk you into anything."

The rain beat down on the trailer roof almost drowning out a timid knock on the door. Clyde opened it and found two drenched small boys who wanted to meet the "tiger tamer" and get his autograph. He gave them each a glossy eight-by-ten from a stack in a cardboard box under the table. When they had gone their enthralled way Beatty continued his celluloid ramble.

"Had a lot of laughs out there, too," he said. "I remember Lou Costello bringing twenty custard pies to the studio every day along with a little Italian stooge to push them in the faces of the cast, which included those muscle-men, Max and Buddy Baer. I was the only one didn't get a pie in the puss; the little bum didn't dare. And Andy Devine, once he decked himself out in a tiger skin and scared the chief cameraman so bad he quit. One of the Three Stooges (do you remember them?)—that one with the straight-across hair (Moe, I guess he is)—got pea-green seasick on a raft in a studio tank that wasn't more'n two feet deep."

Beatty laughed merrily, remembering his old buddies. He said the scaredest he's ever been outside his big cage was when he rode a dynamite crash-car with the famous Hollywood stunt man, Lucky Teeter ("But he was chicken when I took him in with my tigers"). And that his silliest accident was when a blank gun fired unexpectedly in its holster searing his thigh and setting his pants on fire.

As Beatty and I talked, the rain whipped against the windows of his home on wheels. "Do you think it'll ever stop?" asked the tiger man. "This is like a tropical monsoon."

He pulled up the slats of the trailer window and looked out at the splashy wet street, its gutters running with torrents.

"It's hard to like canvas trouping, boy, under these conditions, but I still think it's the best for me. Ball parks and stadiums are no good for my act. Under the open sky there is no sense of close-in danger. All things considered, I'd rather perform in arenas indoors. Before I'm finished I want to take my act to Europe; they've never seen a real American 'fighting act' over there. I believe we'd be a sensation. Also I'd like to show my big cage in one of the big Las Vegas gambling clubs. A night-club engagement, however, has its problems. Enough space is one; you need plenty room to house and show twenty lions and tagers. And the slick floors are bad. Of course, we could put down floor mats, but I haven't found anything yet that a cat couldn't tear up in no time at all. But the biggest drawback to a club-date is one you'd just have to beat—that old tager stink. It is strong, boy; it is strong. In a circus it's different; nobody sits around in evening clothes eating their supper."

I had seen Beatty's act recently on television and was curious why so little of it had been shown.

"Oh, that," smiled the tiger master. "Well, I'll tell you. One of my tagers got scared of the strange floor and the lights and tried to climb out over the top of the cage. So they cut us off the cameras. Tagers are always unpredictable indoors; it's not a natural element for them. Some of the scariest tager escapes I've ever had took place in buildings."

One of the most dreadful, he told me, happened one winter night in Detroit. Beatty had hauled his big cats into town for a private performance at a salesmen's convention. The tigers and their paraphernalia were stashed in the basement under the auditorium of a partly finished Masonic club-hotel. The quarters were so cramped that the cages had to be spotted along a narrow corridor leading to a service stairway. At midnight Clyde had retired to his own hotel just down the street and along about 3 A.M. the night clerk woke him with a phone call.

"All hell's broke loose over at the Temple!" he shrilled. "Your watchman just phoned. All of your tigers are out!"

Beatty knew this was hardly likely but, as even one could mean plenty trouble, he grabbed pants, shoes, shirt and topcoat and headed for the elevator. By the time the lift had crawled up to him, he was dressed and ready for anything. About half the rooms and suites above the Temple's auditorium were finished and occupied that night by over a hundred convention delegates and their wives. It wouldn't have taken an invading tiger long to slit a few throats.

When Beatty got to the Temple, he discovered that only one tiger was loose—Gracie, a big devil. She had worked a cage bar loose from its wooden frame and bent the adjacent ones enough to squeeze through (Gracie was big, but lean).

Escaped big cats seldom know what to do with their stolen freedom. Usually they make for the first avenue open and skulk into some dark corner. Beatty figured that Gracie had done just that and, not wasting time to unlock his trunk for blank gun and flashlight, grabbed up the watchman's folding chair and headed up the service stairs, three at a time.

No sign of Gracie—no snarl, no bloody trail—until the fifth floor landing was reached. Here a staircase door was ajar. Beatty kicked it wide and, with flimsy chair in front, moved into a velvety black room. In the dim light from the landing he could make out it was an unfinished swimming-pool room, cluttered with planks, scaffolding, piles of tiles, sacks of cement. There were towel closets, shower cubicles and locker rooms—all wonderful hiding places for an escaped tiger—a custom-made jungle. Beatty knew Gracie had to be there and she was, but he had a dickens of a time flushing her out.

"She slinked out from behind a pile of sandbags and leaped at me in the dark," Clyde said, "and disappeared under a crash of building material. In trying to find her again, I tipped over a keg of nails and a gallon of paint and they didn't help my footing none, boy.

"I finally got her out into the corridor by using a chunk of timber about the size of a ball bat, both of us slopping around in the paint and skidding on the nails. In the doorway I had to lam her on the head, and that knocked some of the fight out so I was able to force her down the hall and then step by step down the stairs."

Two flights down the tiger turned on Beatty, baring her wicked teeth, curling her upper lip, but before she could strike, Gracie lost her balance and crashed against the landing door. It burst open and the tiger took it on the lam down the carpeted corridor. A sleeping floor! But was it occupied? Beatty took off after the cat and was only a few yards behind her when she wheeled into a bedroom.

"Oh, lordy, I thought," continued Beatty in telling me of that eerie night, "don't let anybody be sleeping in there."

He hit the wall switch. Empty—except for Gracie snarling from the far side of the bed. Beatty bounced out and closed the door against her. He needed a breather.

"But she got one, too," he said. "And I needed mine more."

Beatty realized that his greatest advantage was psychological. As long as he could keep the big cat puzzled he was on top. So far that night he had her bluffed. It was *he* who closed the door on her, and *he* who gave her that thumping headache. While Gracie worried over his next move Clyde barricaded—with an assortment of sawbucks, sacks of cement, kegs and boards dragged from the top-floor swimming-pool room—the stairs leading to the upstairs hideout. Then, with a painter's drop cloth, he constructed a baffle across the narrow hall beyond the bedroom. Gracie would believe that this canvas wall was solid; the trick will fool any big cat. Then Beatty took a couple of deep oxygen-charging breaths and re-entered the tiger lady's boudoir.

The cat was scrapping-ready for him. She charged Beatty all over the little room, ripping the mattress with great clawing bounds, scarring the wallpaper, slashing the drapes. She smashed the mirror on the bathroom door, gnashed a chunk out of the toilet seat, pulled the shower curtain rod from the plaster. She splintered Beatty's frail chair, shattered a sedate red-plush replacement. He snatched up the telephone table, parrying the tiger's thrusts with its skinny legs. He still had the chunk of studding and soon got a chance to use it again, whamming another stunner down on Gracie's cranium. She winced, retreated and backed down the corridor, completely duped by the curtain hanging across it. On the landing Beatty got ready to deliver a third smasher, but the huge beast rose on her hind legs, balanced almost completely erect. Her deep chest was at the man's eye level. The tiger swiped a tremendous one-two punch with both forepaws, knocking the timber and what was left of the telephone table completely out of Beatty's hands. He was now unarmed, facing the raging animal barehanded.

"Scared?" he said. "What do you think? But I didn't dare let that fiend know it. I didn't move a muscle, boy, but my nerves were screeching."

It seemed like eternity to Beatty but in just a second or two Gracie suddenly dropped to all fours, whirled and bounded off down the stairs to the cellar and back into her broken cage. She didn't realize how close her jaws had been to sweet revenge.

Beatty found a towel, stripped and dried off. The hour-long battle had drenched him with perspiration and left him completely knocked out; he said it was the toughest tilt he'd ever had with any animal.

The big cats, contrary to popular opinion, are not constantly plotting ways to escape confinement. Tigers fuss with their bars a bit more than lions, but as a rule both jungle beasts adjust surprisingly well to cage life. Another widespread belief is that a big cat at liberty turns into a vicious man-eater, out to devour all comers. Even in country abounding in wild mountain lions, people lose their heads in fear of an escaped circus animal. An escaped wild animal is invariably pretty well frightened himself. The only idea in his single-track mind is to get away, far away. He will attack only those who try to stop or molest him.

Outdoors it is fairly simple to recapture an escaped big cat. The regular circus method is to surround the animal with a long piece of canvas, usually a stretch of tent sidewall, held erect by a crew of workhands. Once the cat is enclosed by this seemingly solid barrier, an open-doored cage is quickly wheeled into the space where the ends of canvas wall meet. Then the trainer slips into the enclosure and with the usual tools (gun, chair, pole) forces the by now thoroughly bewildered beast into the den.

"We had a bad escape once in Cleveland, too," Beatty said. "We'd all had a little layoff and were feeling good, having a lot of laughs backstage because the management had established a protective armed guard around my arena to make the act look more dangerous. It was just a Kraut teeterboard act in fancy uniforms and shiny tin helmets. The ringmaster used to always announce, 'The rifle bearers are for your protection; the trainer will protect himself.' Pure hokum. Not one of them could've hit the side of a barn with a cantaloupe. Besides there were no bullets in the guns, not even blanks, for you can't shoot at an escaped animal in a crowd; you'd wound more people than animals."

On indoor dates away from his Big Top, Beatty continued, they didn't use his regular chute but had one fashioned by local carpenters to fit the conditions of the building. This time somebody had goofed. Midway in the chute is a safety door, made to swing one way only so that a cat departing the arena cannot return once he passes that point. Someone had built this door to swing the wrong way, and at the finish of the act the tigers couldn't get out. Six of them jammed in the narrow runway, and the other fourteen tried to force their way past. The box was rocking—the cats getting madder and madder. Prodding did no good at all.

Then with a ripping cracking of timber the top of the chute shot up like a jack-in-box, and three big, mighty angry tigers whipped out onto the hippodrome track.

"The equestrian director, named Hauser," said Clyde, "jammed the lid back on and sat on it. The tin helmets scattered in all directions, mostly up into the riggings."

Quick-working animal men managed to get the menagerie giraffes from their big wire pen into their underslung wagon, and Beatty cued the three escapees backward toward the vacated enclosure, trying to keep them focused on him instead of the panicking audience. Two behaved beautifully and leaped right into the corral. The third fugitive, a tigress named Snip who had always despised Beatty, turned and began to circle. An ominous maneuver—she was getting ready for a heavy spring. Inside the barred arena she had a scant 32 feet in which to develop attacks. Out on the track she had jungle-like freedom and could easily get a long running start for an *accurate* leap that would smash in like a freight train out West.

"This was good," Beatty said. "If I could just keep her mad at me, she'd lay off the audience. Out of the corner of my eye I could see the boys bringing up the canvas to make a funnel from the track to the cage runway. I started to force her towards the canvas trap. And then I saw that an old geezer they called Dad was right in line. He hadn't been able to climb out of the way. I yelled to him not to move a muscle and boy, you'd 'a' thought he was a living statue. I forced Snip to charge me again to give the old guy a chance to edge out of no-man's-land, and then inch by inch I backed up that hell-cat until I had her through the funnel and behind bars again.

"Telling it now," he added, "it doesn't seem like much but that night, boy, every muscle in my body ached, and my legs felt like they had been beaten by chains. Handling a wild animal outside the arena is a hundred times more difficult than it is inside the cage."

With circuses becoming more and more modern there aren't as many escapes of big cats as there were in the old free-wheeling days. (There aren't so many animals to escape any more, either.) Beatty said he had never met a tiger or lion yet who couldn't loosen the finest, strongest bars by working and gnawing at them through the long quiet hours of the night.

"But don't worry," he said, "you're fairly safe. Most lions and tigers are too damned lazy to bother escaping."

He was quiet for quite a while.

"I expect one day I'll get chopped down," Beatty finally said. "To go quick, that wouldn't be too bad. But I'd shore hate to linger on with what we call 'arena shock,' a mysterious breakdown that sometimes ends a trainer's career. You wake up one night in a cold sweat, fighting off nightmare lions and tagers. Something has snapped; your courage is just as strong but your confidence wavers. The spark between you and the cats is gone; you start looking for excuses, ways out; and one day the collapse is complete. You never dominate an animal again. Old Pete Taylor, one of the men who broke me in, he went that way. I hope it never happens to me.

"I once said if I had a son who wanted to be a wild-animal trainer I'd wallop him good. Well, I have Clydey now. He's five and if he wants, when he's old enough, he can come into the business, but I'll do all in my power to persuade him not to. Maybe he wouldn't be as lucky as me. Wild-animal training is a rough trail. I wouldn't advise anybody to set off on it, especially these days when the circuses are dying out. Why there are less than a dozen animal-training jobs in America today worth their salt."

I asked Beatty if he ever thought about training a protégé.

"I'd like nothing better," he answered, "than to turn over my years of experience to some kid. I'll never stop looking, but I don't think I'll ever find one with what it takes; raw guts, steady nerve, real endurance, a feeling for animals—and he's gotta be just plain cussed crazy about circuses.

"The boys I get all want to be tiger professors the very first week. They don't want to study and learn the animals, which is the only important thing. To train any beast you have to know it thoroughly. Anyhow, these days the kids all want to make money crazy quick, like Elvis Presley—or else they want to be scientists, engineers or rocket men—fly to the moon."

Beatty looked through his trailer window and added: "But don't forget. Maybe in outer space there are wild animals, too. The scientists don't know everything yet."

Sea Lions in the Garden

🎵 When circuses were glorious strung-out affairs of three rings and four stages, requiring seven eyes to take in all the wonders, the most magical time in the day's spangled occupation was that pause while the sea lions rendered "My Country 'tis Of Thee." (We kids never referred to it as "America.") For this precious moment even the band stopped its headlong brass stampede, and the only sound was that of summer breezes whispering to sky-flung canvas, a happy sweeping murmur of anticipation, and the soft flapping of limp cardboard fans.

First a seal (we didn't know then they were sea lions) in the center ring would play the patriotic aria sedately and properly; then seal on Stage Number Two alongside would give it a lightning quick ham-up that never failed to bring down the house. I can hear them yet. First the virtuoso: *Barp, barp, ba barp barp-pah-h-h . . . pah-pah parh, pahp pah pah . . . bah barp pah par-r-r-p.* Then the ruff-necked comedian, after much mad neck weaving and tossing of shiny black head: *Barp-barp-ba-barp-bar-pah . . . pahpah parhpah pah pah, bahbarpbahparp.*

The musical sea lions that you and I saw were undoubtedly those of the famous Tiebor brothers (John, Roland, Ed and Roy), most accomplished trainers of sea lions in America. In those days, the Tiebor family operated four acts, exhibiting thirty-three sea lions. Tiebor sea lion displays graced the Sells-Floto, Sparks and Hagenbeck-Wallace circuses; and from the early 'twenties on through 1935, Ringling Bros and Barnum & Bailey featured on all four stages and the center ring, Captain John and Captain Roland Tiebor (neither landlubber captain ever closer to the sea than Niagara Falls). After those triumphant years, Roland Tiebor disappeared from the American circus scene and went to Europe where he remained until just before the outbreak of the Second World War. He performed in the arena of the great Bertram Mills circus in England; on the stages of the Apollo Theater in Dusseldorf, Germany; La Scala and the Winter Garden in Berlin; and with the heated, tented circus of Amer Frères in France and North Africa. Roland's youngest kid, Johnny, learned to walk on the boat going over and the other youngsters, Roly and a daughter Gloria, were old enough to begin their education in private schools in the English provinces.

The notable sea-lion-training family has now gone into its third generation, with Roly, the older son, carrying on the tradition—again with the Ringling show.

I called around one afternoon to see the third generation Tiebor and his talented sea lions when that organization was opening its season in Madison Square Garden, New York City's mammoth midtown arena. It was Saturday. A drenching April downpour had come just as the matinee began. The ordinarily serene dignity of the circus was being violated by a pay load of sticky, screeching kids, greatly outnumbering and overrunning a determined regiment of harassed adults. To avoid this unholy mob I cut into the Garden through the Press Entrance on the Forty-ninth Street side and went along the narrow backstage corridor, deftly skirting small islands of performers awaiting their cues, receiving from old friends among them a variety of greetings: an upside-down smile from a

twinkly-eyed Eurasian acrobat; a quick but friendly nod from a busy
Indian-club juggler; a gloomy hello from inside the false gauze-fronted
bosom of a lady clown, who was masquerading as a cigarette-puffing
pinhead and suffering the miseries of springtime grippe.

At the center entrance to the arena I turned and descended to
the building's basement where the sideshow, menagerie and performing animals are housed. Roly Tiebor's small caravan truck was
parked just beyond the bottom of the long L-shaped staircase, and
he was inside his little blue and yellow home on wheels getting the
sea lions ready for their matinee wing-ding. Roly was surprised to
learn that it was raining outside.

"Down here," he said, "you don't know what's happening upstairs. Can't see nothing, can't hear a thing except those Hungarian
dogs back of me and those braying jackasses. I'd rather be outside—
rain or no rain. It gets pretty darned stuffy down here sometimes.
Come in and sit down." Roly had just finished applying a light stage
make-up to his lean, large-boned face. He lifted his costume from a
hanger. "Some colors," he said. "Who ever heard of putting orange,
bright red, purple and pink together on a blonde?"

After he had climbed into the garish outfit he said, "I've got
to run upstairs soon to see what's on. I think there's still the wire-
act, the acrobats and the Chinese number, but I want to be sure.
We go on before 'Spec,' and I put them in the water when the wire-
act starts. They're prettier dry—these two have especially beautiful
markings—but the public is used to a sea lion being all black and
shiny. Seals are supposed to look like they're made of black oilcloth."

I climbed inside the truck and found it a cozy one-room bachelor
apartment, paneled with plyboard, oak-stained and varnished. Crossways at one end was a high bunk above a built-in chest of drawers.
Alongside it was a small window and under that a low kneehole pine
desk, its top cluttered with a lamp, a rumple of shaving things, portable typewriter, stationery, letters from home, photo albums, an
electric fan, a coffee can full of odds ends and match books. Against
the walls on one side of the door stood a tall narrow electric heater;
on the other side a deep-freeze full of fish.

"It holds a week's supply," explained Roly and when I commented upon the compact arrangement of his quarters, he added,
"I like it. This way I can be all by myself. I'm with the animals practically all the time, anyhow. I get up early to cut up their fish. I give
them their first feeding at nine thirty in the morning, and I feed

after each show. Different fish, mostly mackerel, but we feed her-
ring, black cod, and trout when we can get it. Mackerel is high
now, thirty-four cents a pound; I never paid more'n twenty or
twenty-two before. The weather has been so bad, the boats haven't
been going out. Each animal eats about fifteen to twenty pounds a
day—no heads, tails or bones, of course. You'd think we'd get tired
of fish, cutting it up every day like that, but my dad is very fond of
fish and so am I." He opened the freezer and took out a metal bowl
of fish chunks. "I change the water in the tank every morning, and
by the time I write Dad and do a few other things it's time for the
matinee and we're on again."

He climbed down the waist-high steps and went up to the arena
to check on the program.

The two sea lions were enclosed at the end of the room opposite
the bed behind a wire-mesh screen on a raised platform divided di-
agonally by a framed screen, a device which gave both compartments
three long sides each the length of the animal. The pair were as
beautiful as Roly had said and had long thick white whiskers curving
downward. Every once in a while one would dip its head into a
bucket of water and whip it out splashing or let go with a quiet
awr-r-r-k. They didn't bark at me or take notice of my presence in
any way. Anticipating their appearance before the public, they constantly swayed back and forth excitedly, causing the truck to creak
and rock slightly, making it seem like a subway train in motion.

Sea lions are aquatic carnivores and members of the seal family,
which includes the fur seal, true seal, walrus and elephant seal, that
large-nosed monster commonly known as the sea elephant. Sea lions
are really eared seals with no under-fur. Besides having external ears,
they differ from true seals in having necks which are longer and
more flexible, and in their ability to use their rear flippers for walking.

There are several species of sea lion. Steller's or the Northern
sea lion, ranging from the Bering Straits south to the Farallon Islands off the coast of California is the largest, males occasionally
reaching a length of thirteen feet and weighing up to two thousand
pounds. There are South American sea lions, small pug-nosed fellows
usually weighing, in the wild state, less than two hundred pounds,
which is about the weight in captivity of the common circus sea
lion (*Zalophus californianus*); in their native habitat Z.c. males often
attain a weight of as much as 600 pounds, females being half that

size. There is an Australian sea lion, and Hooker's sea lion is found in the South Pacific, principally around the Auckland Islands.

When Roly returned from his jaunt to the upper regions he said, "Wire-act's on," and then removed the partition between the sea-lion compartments and lifted the floor panel covering the tank. He sloshed it and the section of remaining floor with a wet broom and the sea lions slid happily into the water. I asked about the temperature of the small pool.

"I keep it about sixty degrees," said Roly. "Not with a thermometer; I just feel it with my hands—like you would a baby's bath. Have to carry the hot water over from the bull department; that's the only hot spigot down here. In the Garden you can't use the water right out of the tap; it's so cold sometimes you just put your hand in and pull it out, it's *blue*."

Roly told me he also adds salt to the fresh water about once a week, this being necessary to remove scaling from the eyeballs caused by fresh water; sea lions will eventually go blind if this is allowed to accumulate.

"I got the tank too full this morning," Roly said philosophically, surveying the huge splashes that were beginning to make the floor of the little room awash.

Roly's pair of sea lions, named Penny and Tommy, were captured, he told me, off the California coast and furnished to his dad by the same outfit that has supplied the family ever since Grandfather John W., Sr. (then City Engineer at the Tonawanda, N.Y., Water Works), bought his initial sea lion in the late 1880's, having become intrigued by the first one he had ever seen, a new resident at the nearby Buffalo Zoo. The original procurer, a hardy seafarer named George McGuire of Santa Barbara, California, is no longer living. His nephew, George Howe, is now operating the business of fetching desirable creatures from the roaring ocean.

"Old George must have lived to be over a hundred," said Roly. "Dad saw him only a few years ago—and he was ninety-seven or ninety-eight then."

The Tiebors liked to do business with McGuire because he knew exactly the kind of animal they wanted for training. The job called for implicit trust.

"Sometimes McGuire, he'd throw back twenty or thirty seals before he'd find the kind he knew my grandad, dad or my uncles wanted," said young Tiebor. "Sometimes it'd take a whole month of netting to get just the right one. This would run the price up, but we just took old George's word for it; he never cheated us. Some of our sea lions cost as much as fifteen hundred dollars. But then sometimes we was lucky and got a jim-dandy for only a hundred and fifty or two hundred." The prices have gone up a little since those days; the same sea lions now would run from five hundred dollars to as high as over two thousand.

The Tiebor standards call for a sea lion about one and one-half years old, ideal size about sixty pounds. It makes little difference whether the animal is male or female; what matters is the intelligence of the mammal, which is judged by the width between the eyes.

"Dad doesn't measure it," said Roly. "He just looks and decides if it's right or not. After all, he was raised on sea lions."

With wing nuts young Roly Tiebor assembled a small folding wooden ramp down which the sea lions would descend from their enclosure. Then he stood quietly in the doorway of his cabaña waiting. After a long silence he asked, "Did you hear about Tell Tiegen? He was killed yesterday—out in Ventura, California. Fell from eighty feet the papers said, but it was more likely probably only sixty."

"That's still plenty high," I said. I had heard the tragic news of Tell's final finish trick. A twenty-nine-year-old acrobat, worried about his future, had told me in the Belvedere Hotel across the street just before I came into the building. Tell was an old friend, a young Dane who balanced on a precarious pile-up of chairs atop a high pedestal. Six years before when I was with him on the Ringling show in Montana, he had fallen forty feet, landing on his head, when a drunken workhand allegedly lurched into one of his guy-lines.

"Seems like every year it's one more," Roly said, continuing to stare across the ringstock department, now empty but for three quietly nibbling burros. "They don't ever quit soon enough." He added, "Even in what you'd think is a safe act like ours there is always some danger. Not to us so much, but to the animals. Did dad tell you that our Sadie was almost killed at that TV show he was on last week? You know the trick where Sadie stands on her front flipper on the piano stool and Dad whirls her around? Well, some gazooney (Dad thinks it was the guy who had the dogs for the commercial) monkeyed with the stool—probably sat the dogs on it not knowing what he was doing. It's always turned up eight turns before the trick, but just before Sadie went on, Dad noticed that it was turned right down tight. If he had put Sadie on and pushed she'd have flopped right off and probably been killed or at least broke her flipper." He swung down the steep stairs. "Some of the band guys hooked some of Dad's special music, too. I don't think dad likes TV too well; the money ain't *that* good. He drove all the way down from Tonawanda and back on the same day with the sea lions just for seven minutes on the air. . . . I'm going upstairs again to check; be right back."

When he returned he said, "We'll go up in about a minute." Then he set up the ramp against the sea-lion compartment and opened its door. He talked to his performers, patting their sleek necks. "You're going up there and do a good show, now aren't you, baby? Sure you are; that's a *good* fellow. Yes-siree, he's a *good* baby." And more of the same flattering palaver.

The sea lions edged down the truck steps backwards with no assist from their boss, then followed him as he strode off, a bowl of fish cuttings in hand, to the main staircase. They hopped as fast as I could go up the steps; I counted thirty-three of them.

In the backstage passageway, a sturdy flat-bed coaster wagon was waiting with an assistant at its helm. The sea lions hopped onto it without being cued or coaxed, staying only long enough to have their weaving necks costumed—one by a pink clown ruff, the other by a white bow tie. Then they dismounted and the wagon was lifted through the entrance curtains and up the five steps to arena level. The sea lions followed on their flippers and got back onto the wagon for their journey into the ring. In a moment the music of the band changed, the ringmaster's whistle blew, and they were on. I ducked around to the seats to catch the act.

Roly had Number One Ring, his Hungarian dog neighbors held down the center, and a lively troupe of boxer dogs were in the other end ring. Young Roly had a smooth-working act and included were two new, exclusively Tiebor, tricks that Roland, Sr., had told me about: the sea-lion muscle grind, in which the animal, holding by front flippers crossed on its chest, throws its body around and around a horizontal aerial bar; and a blindfold stunt in which the sea lion, wearing a sack over its head, balances a ball on its nose while ascending and descending a stepladder.

Roly, in the family tradition, held the big arena all alone for his finish trick, the famous horn solo. Embellishments had been added: a pair of cymbals struck by the sea lion's rear flippers and a bell rung by one of the front ones. The horns as usual played "America" without, however, the comic speed-up, which I for one greatly missed.

As the sea lions exited, they were met by a newspaper man, Fred Woltman, an old friend of Roly's dad. He was anxious to talk to Roly and followed along with us. He pulled a newspaper clipping from a small leather case he was carrying, opened the circus program to a picture of Roland Tiebor, Sr., and compared it to one in the clip. They were identical. (Young Roly's picture is not used in the circus playbill.) "Look," said Fred, "the same picture that was with my story on your dad thirteen years ago—the seal playing the horns."

We went down the stairs again and re-entered the truck, the sea lions climbing in first and scurrying back into their water after a little loving praise from their handler and a few self-satisfied *awr-r-rks*.

"That's always been one of my favorite stories," said Woltman. "I came here to see your dad on the day that Roosevelt died, and the circus had closed out of respect for him. The place was unearthly quiet. Then I heard the sea lions barking and I looked into the arena, and there, playing to the thousands of empty seats, was your dad and his act. When the sea lions played America on the horns that day—well, to me it was the saddest thing I'd ever heard. Even the comic speed-up just about broke my heart."

Roly, Jr., explained that the sea lions had performed on that sad day because, during the run of a show, if they are not worked on schedule at their regular time, they go wild and are apt to fight in their den. There is danger that they will hurt each other by biting. "The eyes especially are vulnerable," he said. "They stick out so."

When there is a *normal* day off, a Sunday or a traveling day, the animals invariably sense it and are peaceful. "You just can't figure them; it's funny how they react," added the young sea-lion man. "Dad always said they could even tell when he had even just one little drink. He said they can see it in your eyes; they always watch the trainer's eyes during the act. Dad said they actually disapproved of drinking, but I don't really believe that. I think he was just pulling my leg."

I'm not so sure that he wasn't serious, for if anybody is Mr. Sea Lion, it is Roland Tiebor, Sr. When I trouped with him back in 1947, with the Ringling Bros Circus, I never tired of listening to his talk

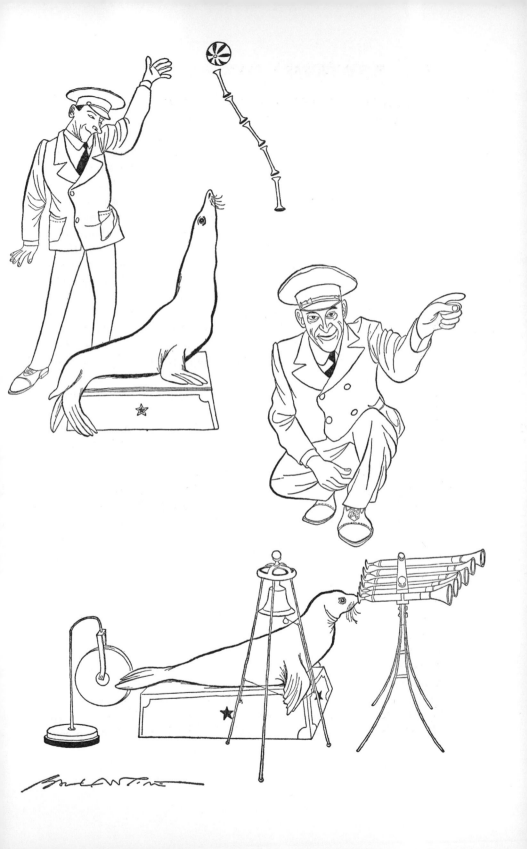

about sea lions. He told me that his earliest memory is of being chased around the backyard at home by sea lions.

"I started in with my father," said the elder Tiebor one summer day as I sat on the fishy steps of his sea-lion caravan, watching him cut up mackerel, "in 1915 when I was a kid of fourteen— Latino's Wild Animal Circus. My main job was to ride in parade in the tank wagon with the seals (Dad always called them seals). You know how they used to parade—lions, tigers, snakes and every other thing with their trainers sittin' in the wagons with them. That was the happiest year of my life in show business. Down South I'd listen to the people along the curbs. They never seen a sea lion and didn't know what they were. You should hear the names they give them: eels, snails, Oregon weasels; half of them couldn't even read the signs on the wagons."

(It is noteworthy that in one Dixie version of a popular English ballad, "Lord Randal," a sad tale of a young nobleman poisoned by his true love, the phrase, "I had eels boiled in broth" is sung as "seals boiled in broth.")

Grandfather Tiebor didn't have the only trained sea lions in America at that time. There were several contemporaries, notably the Webbs, Albert Stonehouse (brother of Al G. Barnes) and the Huling brothers (Max, Frank and Ray), who lived in Grand Island just across the river from the Tiebors. (Mark, a son, carries on the Huling tradition with water-hurdle-leaping sea lions, appearing today mainly at sports shows.)

Roland Tiebor, Sr., has always claimed that he hasn't the slightest idea how sea lions are trained. "If you was to ask me how to train a sea lion," he used to tell me back in my circus days, "I couldn't tell you how. You have to be brought up in it; go from one thing to another. Sometimes just one half-minute too long is enough to ruin the animal in training; you have to sense when to stop. You do everything by instinct."

This Neptune-given instinct has enabled the Tiebors to originate more tricks than any other sea-lion trainers in the business. Their sea-lion tightrope walker had a four-year lead on all the others. The Tiebor family, besides having the first sea-lion musicians, was the innovator of ladder-climbing and cakewalk-dancing sea lions. A Tiebor sea lion did the first hand-to-flipper balancing and the pioneer one-flipper stand. Roland Tiebor exhibited the first sea lion able to applaud with its tail flippers. "And we've had sea lions that rode ponies and elephants, too," said Roland, Sr., "but that don't amount to much. It's just a novelty." He has had sea lions that stood erect on their back flippers also. "But I don't do that any more," he says. "I found out it's hard on their spines."

How this gift of handling sea lions came to the Tiebors is a mystery. Nothing is known of the family beyond the fact that it is of Scandinavian origin—Norwegian, Roland thinks, though he is not positive of this, since after diligent personal search in that country he has been unable to find any trace of the clan Tiebor and only one person by that name in all of Sweden, definitely no relation.

Besides an inherent rapport with sea lions, the greatest fortitude and singleness of purpose is needed to train the animals. Very often a sea lion, after capture, will not eat for as long as sixty days. Being used to catching its own fish live, the animal is extremely slow to adapt to a change in environment.

"There is very little you can do about it," says Roland Tiebor, Sr., "except to wait and to try everything all ways—except forcing; you can't drive a seal. You try to tempt them with minnows, different feeding pans, and so on. I never lost one by starvation yet." Some sea-lion trainers tie threads about fresh dead fish and jiggle them in the feeding pens to deceive the newly captured animals. Roland Tiebor just waits.

After the captive sea lions begin to eat well, they are turned into a shallow corral and the trainer wades in among them wearing leggings of metal or heavy leather. A green sea lion is about as fighting and biting a creature as you can meet up with. It is not a dangerous animal, but the bite is vicious. Sea lions have a terrifically strong head shake, being able to rip a good-sized fish in two with one brisk jerk. Head and neck patting begun at this stage of training must be very cautiously done; that same shake that tears apart a fish can break all the bones in a man's hand. A favorite aggression of the sea lion is to hold the trainer at bay by leaning heavily against his thigh or stomach with head held high and jaws wide open ready for biting. One false move from the man and he's had a rough bite in the leg or neck—perhaps even in the jugular vein. Sometimes this threat will be held for as long as ten minutes. Tiebor has had his sea lions gang up in an attack on him. Three once jumped him when they came to the rescue of a female, protesting the application of a light wooden splint to her broken flipper.

By soothing words and kind treatment the frisky sea mammals are soon quieted down and no longer try to snap and bite. They are then introduced to the training platform and accustomed to their seat; home base from which all tricks will be launched. Sea-lion training begins in the Tiebor household one and one-half to two months after the animal is delivered.

Unlike other wild creatures, the sea lion does not first show the trainer what it is capable of doing. The man decides on the routine, and teaches it slowly and carefully to the animal.

"Everything is done by coaxing," says Roland, Sr. "You just can't pick up the seal and put it on the seat; they won't stand for it. It's a good long time before you can pick up a seal in your arms. You can't use a harness or support the seal in any way; they just got to be coaxed along slow and easy. They're very shy and timid; even one tiny slap in training is apt to upset a sea lion for weeks. They're skittish of every little thing—strange sights or sounds. But mainly sea lions got to like what they're doing and to trust you."

Everything about sea-lion training is terribly difficult and requires the patience of a lighthouse. The animal has no keen sense of smell; its hearing is poor. And although it can focus on a moving object quite well, it seldom notices one that is stationary.

"Nothing is easy, if you ask me," said Roland. "Sometimes it is six months before they can take a ball on their noses. Seals are not natural balancers; they have to be taught. Their necks are strong, thicker and bigger around than their heads; with one shake they can ruin a beach ball."

It takes one entire year to teach a sea lion to do a one-flipper stand; about two years to play the horns. Albert Rix, who has trained all sorts of animals under the banners of the famous Hagenbecks in Germany, once spent three years teaching a sea lion to stand on one flipper and simultaneously play the opening phrases of "Tannenbaum" on the horns. The accomplishment which required forty seconds in performance had, in training, swallowed up 78,000 precious minutes of Albert's life. His horns were the pinch-bulb types, tooted by light bites by the sea lions; Tiebor's are actually blown—by *nose*, not by mouth, for sea lions can readily open and close tight their nostrils (a necessity in swimming); the mouthpieces are not rubbed with fish to make them attractive to the sea lions. Usually the first sniff into a horn scares the very dickens out of a sea lion, and he must be carefully coaxed back again.

Tiebor, Sr. considers the muscle-grind the most difficult sea-lion trick of his career.

"You know inside of you whether the animal can hang on to the bar or not," said Roland when I asked how he chose his aerialist. "We don't start low and gradually go up like people do; we start high right away. The seal holds to the bar with its front flippers, crossing them and pressing them to his chest. Then *he* decides whether he can turn himself over around the bar or not. I've been working on one animal now for two years just to get him to turn over once. He hasn't done it yet, and I can't push him over. You scare the animal just one time, and he's finished. You can never use the same seal again for the trick."

Penny, one of young Roly's sea lions, revolves ten times around the bar—a most spectacular stunt. It looks so simple it's hard to realize the real grind that made it possible.

Just as in the training of other animals, sometimes in the sea-lion business a good trick is stumbled upon. The blindfolded sea lion came about when Roland Tiebor, Sr. was asked a few seasons back by Pat Valdo, performance director of Ringling Bros, if sea lions could be accustomed to wear masks. The director and the costumer of the big show that year, Richard Barstow and Miles White, had bumped their clever heads together and sparked an idea of a grand aquatic carnival finale for the circus, a mad melange of diving girls, clown fishermen, showgirl mermaids, elephants squirting on cue, sparkling fountains and sea lions costumed and masked to represent curvaceous movie queens—principally Marilyn Monroe, Ava Gardner and Rita Hayworth.

When Tiebor recovered from the initial shock of this inspired flash, he said no, absolutely no, a sea lion wouldn't submit to having its head covered or to wearing false bosoms. But he didn't discard the idea entirely; the more he thought of it the more of a challenge it became. First he tried a blindfold mask on a sea lion to cover the eyes only. The animal objected some, but after a few months' game of patience, the blind was tolerated and Tiebor was able to guide the animal by vocal cues alone. However, the eye-shields didn't show up too well, and Roland, feeling that the difficulty of the trick would not be readily perceived, devised something large enough to be seen by the audience; a sack that covered the entire head of the sea lion.

Nobody except the trainer knows just how the flighty animal was induced to wear this claustrophobic device, but doubtless he was conned into believing it a gay springtime bonnet, for Tiebor believes implicitly that sea lions dig man talk. He claims that the aquatic beasts understand the language of humans, not just cues and sounds, but actual run-of-the-mill conversation. When I asked the great trainer just how many words he calculated that a sea lion comprehends, he said, "They understand *every* word we say; no special words or just cues—all ordinary conversation in a normal tone of voice. I've tested this out many times. I'll walk into the training barn and say, 'Okay, boys, everyone in the water'; and they'll all jump in. Then I'll putter around a little and just say, quiet like, without even lookin' at them, 'All right, fellows, let's all get out,' or some such thing; and they all jump out again. It doesn't matter what words I use—they're never the same ones—and I don't just do this at the same time every day either."

Roland said that he used to test his sea lions' powers of comprehension often when he worked them in vaudeville. In fact, one of his best stunts was based on this supposed faculty of the animal. The sea lions perched downstage on pedestal boxes, each lettered with the animal's name, and Roland, facing the audience, would ask the spectators to call for whichever sea lion they wished to come forward. Roland would then summon the animal by name and it would respond. This trick had several variations which seemed to indicate that the animals were not simply answering to their own names or to pre-arranged cues. Tiebor would sometimes say such things as, "Everyone come forward except Frenchy," or "Everyone stay back but Sparky and Frisco," and the sea lions would obey whatever command was given.

So far as I know no exhaustive scientifically controlled tests have ever been made to learn the extent of vocabulary-understanding by sea lions. Animal psychologists tell us that, by including variations of the basic form, any list of understood words can be endlessly lengthened. Adolf Frohn, the Miami Seaquarium's porpoise trainer, told me that it is possible to induce his sea lions' tricks by simply using words that *sound* the same as the cue words. For example, if the cue word is "stick" the animal will perform just as well if the trainer says "click," "wick," "brick" or "tick"; the sound rather than the actual meaning of the word instigates the action. Also almost any number of related words can be built around a cue word, but there is no proof that the animal understands more than the one key word or phrase. Other factors should be considered in judging the extent of an animal's understanding of words. Often a situation or the time of day gives the animal its clue. Then too, gesture, inflection, facial expression, pitch and tone of the trainer's voice are all associated with the words, so that it is difficult to be certain exactly to what the animal is responding.

Frohn tells me that it is best to use the same words, unembroidered. "The shortest way to the trick is best," he avers. On his sea lions he uses German because his father before him employed that language. (Adolf trains porpoises in English.) Frohn's words do not always suit the action of the animal. To get his sea lions to balance Frohn says "SCHÖN" (beautiful); the word "brav" is given as praise. He contends that the emotion expressed by the word is what really counts and that with a sea lion it must not only always carry the authority of command, but love as well. Frohn has had at least one puzzling experience with sea-lion intelligence. His father, in a training session, once called for a stick; there was none available, and the ingenious sea lion pupil fetched instead, a broom.

While it is certainly presumptive to place too much credence on claims regarding the understanding of human language by an animal, the creature man is very likely comprehended by the sea lion to a high degree, because the nature of the animal's training exposes it so closely to the human for prolonged periods (in this respect it is akin to dog, horse and elephant), whereas another wild animal, such as the lion or tiger, caged away from its trainer the greater part of its captive life and trained principally by force, has little opportunity to study and absorb man's normal ways or his oral communication.

An extra bright sea lion in the Tiebor stable was Frisco, a female, fifteen years in the limelight. Tiebor claims that he could carry on right sensible one-sided conversations with Frisco. She died enroute with the Polack Bros Circus Western Unit coming out of Eureka, California—lost to an intestinal parasite.

"I had fed her raw salmon," said Roland, "and the vet that did the post-mortem told me that one salmon in a thousand has a parasite that causes internal hemorrhages in a sea lion. Frisco just happened to get that one. That's one thing I never feed any more—raw salmon. I haven't taken a bite of salmon myself either ever since that day."

Tiebor, Sr. does most of his own sea-lion doctoring, having discovered that veterinarians get so few calls to ailing sea lions that they know next to nothing about the animal.

"You have to be the most careful of worming a sea lion," contends Roland. "Worm medicines cause them to go into fits. There is hardly anything you can give a sea lion in the medicine line. And by all means nothing with calomel in it. It 'solvates' in the stomach, and when the seal goes into water, it'll kill it right away." (Calomel—mercurous chloride—used to be a popular anthelmintic remedy.)

Roland said he has found, by long study of the sea lion, a regurgitant that can be safely used to expel intestinal worms; he doesn't care to disclose its identity. "There are certain things we spend a lifetime learning to find out," he says sensibly, "and we don't want to give them away to competitors."

One of Roland's most proficient sea-lion pupils and his best-remembered friend was Sparky, a male, eighteen years a performer. "He was very faithful," says the nation's premier sea-lion trainer, a far-away, most kindly look lighting his broad, appealingly honest face. "Sparky knew just what to do, exactly what time he went on. His specialty was the tightrope walk; if any other animal tried to do the trick, Sparky'd push it right off the rope. Sparky was stone-blind his last five years, but he worked right to the end—a perfect performer. He died in England in the training quarters of Bertram-Mills at Ascot. I sure hated to see him go. And I know for sure—no matter what the psychologist professors say—that he understood every word I said that night when I kissed him good-bye."

The Camels
Are Going

The camel has changed hardly at all since its first domestication about five thousand years ago. It remains God's most cantankerous creature, a perpetually discontented, grievously outraged, melancholy beast with tartarous yellow teeth, a harelip, an outlandish hump and ridiculous neck, corns, halitosis and four stomachs with dreadful names: rumen, reticulum, omasum and abomasum. Camels are idiotic cud-chewers, given to bilious hiccups, and they dribble.

Camels hate being camels but would loathe being anything else, regarding all living things utterly beneath contempt—especially man; the very sight of man is enough to turn a camel's entire complement of stomachs.

The camel is gloomy and bitter-hearted, full of plaints and objections, a beast burdened by a blanket of grievance against everything, an animal constantly seething in a gentle fervor of hatred.

Its long days and nights are irksome and endured without hope. The camel asks for neither love nor pity. And it gets none. People who cuddle puppies, stroke cats, pat elephants' trunks and horses' foreheads and scatter crumbs for slovenly pigeons never even approach a camel. If such blandishments were offered, the camel would—depending on how nasty it was feeling—either make a halfhearted effort to bite the bearer of these gross insults, or affix him with jaundiced eye and spit on him (the aim is deadly; the spittle outrageously vile), or it would simply not deign to respond at all in any way, deeming such sentimentality very much beneath its dignity.

An Arabian legend professes that the camel is so grandly and smugly aloof because it knows the one-hundredth name of God, whereas even the most pious of men are aware of only ninety-nine.

The word "camel" is Anglo-Saxon and Old North French, deriving from the Latin *camelus* and from the Greek *Kamelos* of Semitic origin (the word in that culture being *Gamal*). There are two types of camel: the *dromedarius* or Arabian, and *bactrianus*, the two-hunched Asian, or Bactrian, which is shorter-legged than the Arabian, more hardy, a better foothill climber and able to feed on thorny bitter plants and to drink brackish water without harm. It is found throughout central Asia, in Siberia and Mongolia, and it is able to endure bitter cold under a coat of long shaggy hair, which it sheds in springtime in great clumps. The Bactrian is so called from the ancient name of a satrapy of ancient Persia, Bactria, now called Balkh (appropriate name for a place of camel origin).

Camels were unknown in the Nile valley until the Roman times, when they were brought in from Arabia and Syria. Today the beast is more typical of Egypt than any other animal. The South American llama, alpaca, guanaco and vicuña are also members of the camel family. The first two are domestic; the others, truly wild species, live high in the crags of the Andes.

Zoologically speaking, the beast is of the family *Camelidae* in the suborder *Tylopoda* of the order *Artiodactyla* (from the Greek meaning even-toed). These are the so-called cloven-hoofed mammals, which are really paired-hoofed, since they do not have a single hoof—such as that of a horse—cleft down the middle; each half of the supposed cloven hoof is really a completely independent toe on its own. Some *Artiodactyla*, such as the camel, have only two toes; others have more. The hippopotamus has four of equal breadth; the pig has a supplementary one on each side of the main toes. Cows and sheep have only vestiges of these little side hoofs, so small they are often called "dew claws." The *Artiodactyla* genealogical tree indicates that the family Camel is one of three main limbs that have grown into the present time from the inception of placental mammals on earth (Eocene epoch of the Cenozoic era, beginning sixty million years ago). The other two are the *Suina* (pigs, peccaries and hippopotamuses) and the *Ruminantia* (deer, giraffes, tragulids, pronghorns and bovids). Ten other multi-syllabic genealogical tree limbs were lopped off before the Pliocene period was entered.

Asked to select the wild animal least likely to succed as a circus performer, most animal trainers chose the miserable camel. It is the least tractable of beasts and, according to some reports, the most stupid. The camels that were trapped in the disastrous menagerie fire of the Ringling Bros and Barnum & Bailey Circus in 1942, unlike all the other animals, made no attempt to save themselves and resisted all efforts to lead them from the burning tent. They just stood placidly, refusing to move. In his book *Circus Doctor*, Dr. J. Y. Henderson, the famous circus veterinarian, in describing this camel reaction to catastrophe says: "They lay down, staring out off into space like old men looking out of a club window, and died." The entire herd of thirteen was lost.

Sir Francis Turner Palgrave, the eminent British poet and critic of the late 1880's, in reviewing the camel has said:

> He is from first to last an undomesticated and savage animal, rendered serviceable by stupidity alone, without much skill on his master's part or any co-operation on his own, save that of extreme passiveness. Neither attachment nor even habit impress him; never tame though not wide-awake enough to be exactly wild.

In the old lush days of the circus camels were very serviceable street-parade animals and every circus worthy of the name carried as many as it could afford. Camels also made very spectacular and educational additions to the menageries. The yokels and crackers of the cotton-South, Middle West corn shuckers and wheat-reapers, pinetops from the Appalachians, and Mississippi flat-boaters—all likely saw their first live camel when the circus came to town.

Early American circus impresarios were quick to recognize the value of the immense appeal of the camel to simple God-fearing audiences, even the most agnostic stogie-chewers being shrewdly aware of the camel's impressive "write-up" in the very first book of the Bible with fourteen mentions in one Chapter (Genesis XXIV). In the entire volume, camel references total twenty-seven, in nine different books. The lion, which is the wild animal most spoken of in the Scriptures (slightly nosing out the serpent, which is awfully popular), gets only thirty-seven nods in eighteen books; the bear has eight. (Other wild animals with brief Biblical recognition are the ape, antelope, deer, fox and ostrich; absent are the tiger, giraffe, zebra, rhino, hippo and elephant—although ivory is spoken of.)

The first camel to be shown in this country came in 1721, five years after our first imported lion. Several generations later, in 1787, a pair of camels on exhibit in New York City were proclaimed with an abridged version of the camel-loaded chapter of Genesis printed on a herald under the line stating the "Price of Admittance (Gentleman or Lady Nine-pence each)." The animal is depicted by woodcut on this handbill as a rather snobbish long-legged dinosaur.

The chief use of the humped beast in early circus days was in the traditional colossal pageant, the Spectacle, pronounced Speck-tack'-le by inmates of the tented world (and affectionately dubbed "Spec" by all but the late Mrs. Charlie Ringling, who insisted to her dying day that it was the "Tournament"). The theme of the earliest of these gaudy conglomerate cheesecloth productions was usually Oriental or Biblical, and camels were a natural for either subject. They added their doleful groanings to the Pomp, Ceremony, Life and Wisdom of a Period 1,000 Years Before the Christ, woefully chewing their cuds as The Most Interesting Woman of Her Day, Balki, Queen of Sheba, tossed her mildly undulating, decently covered hips at Solomon in All His Glory. Camel backs carried the oil jars of the Forty—count'em—Fourteen Thieves of Ali Babi, and waspish camels disdainfully waited while Aladdin (top-mounter of a Hungarian acrobatic troupe) dutifully rubbed His Wonderful Lamp. Camels brooded through The Return of Marco Polo; unwillingly helped Nero (cookhouse griddleman) get on with The Destruction of Rome; and suffered themselves to plod through that most famous "Spec" of all, The Durbar of Delhi, the churlish beasts grandly ignoring The Opulence of Oriental Rajahs, the Sacred Cattle and Sacrificial Animals, and the Sublime (albeit tacky) Array of Ameers, Pashas, Caliphs, Sheiks, Mikados, Mufti, Barbaric Tribal Chiefs, Savage Despots, Kaisers, Czars, Queens, Princes, Viceroys and Grand Dukes plus a Wonderful Representation of Strange Odd Remarkable People whose Duplicates are not on Earth; representing the Whims and Vagaries of Nature while in her Most Eccentric Mood.

The animal popularized to the American public by the famous cigarette is a dromedary camel, the type usually used as a racer, known to the Arabians as a "heirie." It is a rough rider, and in the desert the three kinds are classified in an odd way. It is said the Talatayee can go three days' distance in one; the Sebayee can do seven days' traveling in one; and the Tasayee, a very rare type, can travel a nine days' course in one. Allowance must certainly be made in these figures for what is likely a used-camel dealer's normal exaggeration. A day's traveling distance is usually reckoned as being between ten to twelve leagues (thirty to thirty-six miles), the daily travel of an average caravan. Using this figure, the Tasayee camel would be making a minimum of almost three hundred miles a day, which I think is somewhat incredible, since a mighty good cross-country horse can *possibly* make one hundred miles in one day, but will then need to be rested the following three or four days.

The Arabs have a parable concerning the swiftness of the heirie: "When thou shalt meet a heirie and say to the rider, 'Salem aliek' [Peace be between us], 'ere he shall have answered thee, 'Aliek salem' [There is peace between us], he will be far off, and nearly out of sight; for this swiftness is like the wind." In other words, quicker than you can say "Yankee Robinson."

There are three principal drawbacks to the popularity of racing camels on circuses: mounting, dismounting and kicking. Also it is not easy to get a circus camel, spoiled by a life of menagerie indolence, to wear anything, most especially a saddle. An unorthodox genius in wire-construction named Paul Wenzel (an ex-tailor, who takes his measurements by knots tied in string) once was able to cover a camel almost entirely with a silk and wire contraption, transforming it into a gigantic Mother Goose, but his feat has never been duplicated. Camels simply do not like things on their backs—especially men things.

The noise that is used to get a camel down onto its knees is an unholy mixture of rolling r's, gargling, tongue clicking and clearing of the throat. It is rather trying, and I'm told that one never gets accustomed to it. Mounting a camel is quite an acrobatic operation. The humped beast, crouching with forelegs bent inwards under him, can be held in this position by placing a foot on one bent joint. To mount without this kind of foot help, the rider faces Mecca, spits into the wind, flips hastily through the Boy Scout oath and takes a deep breath. First a foot must be lifted to saddle height, which is about four feet off the ground. With foot resting on top of saddle, the pommel is grasped, and the rider springs like a gazelle for the seat. Now if the camel is not restrained by foot on leg joint, it is

apt to skitter to its feet at first contact, either leaving the would-be
jockey hanging by pommel, head down with one foot skyward, or flat
on his back on the ground. The adjustment to seat is no cinch either.
The camel's back legs rise first, lurching the rider forward over the
neck; then the front legs straighten sending the luckless fellow sailing
back toward the tail. Same rock and roll on descent.

Kicking, however, is the worst problem. The camel can kick
around 180 degrees with a radius of six feet. There is a saying around
the circus: "Beware of the back and front of horse and elephant, but
all four sides of a camel." Camels, too, have a nasty habit of suddenly
dropping their heads, using them like a pile driver on the noggin of
whoever happens to be in their disfavor at the time.

As well as being used in the "Spec" and occasionally in hippodrome track races (they can hit 35 mph) camels were sometimes employed by the clowns. These occasions were not numerous, a double
barrier of misunderstanding keeping the two crusty species from ever
becoming chummy. Clowns instinctively dislike and distrust camels
just as they do boxing kangaroos.

Eventually someone got around to framing a ring-act using
camels, but in these early displays the animals didn't do much else
but stand immobile around the ring-curb or in a front-leg mount to
pedestal while zebras or ponies performed a simple drill about them.
One of the earliest maestros of these elementary camel acts was a
fellow named Jack Joyce, son of the same Buffalo Jack Joyce whose
Norwegian Cowboy trup is the earliest circus memory of Trevor Bale,
the tiger trainer. Mr. Joyce's first brush with performing camels was
on the old Al G. Barnes Circus in 1934, after John Ringling had
tucked it into his expansive vest. In the same performance Joyce had
an act of liberty horses (a group of drill horses), six high-school
prancers, jumpers and racers. He furnished the horses as well for the
Living Statue tableaux and presented the revolving-table and bucking
mules. He had high-jumping greyhounds, racing whippets and collies.
He worked six zebras in the center ring, sea lions on one of the stages,
and drove around the hippodrome track a team of clown pigs bearing
a sign "Pike's Pig or Bust." For this effortful outlay Joyce received
the sum of thirty-five dollars a week. "My contract specified that I
was to be 'generally useful,'" Jack says today, "and I guess I was."

Joyce broke into circus business with his dad, a horse trainer for
the old Buffalo Bill's Wild West Show, who was with the outfit when
it went bust in Europe in 1907. Joyce, Sr., and his family stayed on

the other side of the Atlantic for eighteen years, returning to the States at the end of 1924, bringing liberty horses and high-school units to play vaudeville. In 1927, the elder Joyce received a wire from Ringling Bros and Barnum & Bailey Circus to join out and take over the training of its horses. The father was not interested, and young Jack, hearing the tap of opportunity, answered the telegram signing it Jack Joyce, conveniently forgetting to add "Jr." When the kid turned up to sign a contract, old John Ringling was astounded, huffed a bit, but gave young Jack the job.

He stayed with the big show until 1931, then trouped with various other circuses for several years. From 1938 through 1944, Joyce worked as animal trainer and handler in Hollywood, best stomping grounds in America for camels. The big humpers have been drudging across studio sands and bleating in the noisy, but antiseptic, Oriental bazaars and markets, stocked by ingenious prop-men, ever since the early days of the silents when Sheikish tales of lust and intrigue were standard stock in trade. During this celluloid sojourn of five years, Joyce drew pay principally from Metro-Goldwyn-Mayer, while he observed well the stupendous idiosyncrasies of the doleful dromedaries and baleful bactrians.

Then he did a bit of free-lance animal exhibiting, finally operating his own small circus, which he sold to Russell Bros Circus, staying on for a time as partner to the famous Arthur M. Concello when that shrewd operator acquired it. (In recent years Concello has been the leading, and most controversial, kingpin of Ringling Bros hectic affairs.)

After a hitch with Clyde Beatty, plus a short one with the U.S. Army, Joyce went to Australia to join the Wirth Circus. On returning, he brought back fifty camels to the Fox Studios for use in the Biblical colossus, "David and Bathsheba."

Like a wise desert trader, Joyce had seen to it that eleven of the camel cows he purchased for Fox were pregnant.

"I had to pay a little more for the expectant mamas," he told me, "but at least I saved the boat fare of about fifty-five hundred dollars. We only lost one. On the way over one cow had a miscarriage, and we had to shoot her in Pago Pago. We used all the penicillin the Naval Hospital there had, but we just couldn't save her."

It wasn't long before Joyce was tending a good-sized herd of baby camels, and it was then that he devised a new type of camel act for the circus, framing with three camels, two llamas, a zebra and a pony with monkey-jockey, a mixed display that would perform an active routine similar to that of a liberty horse act. The act has had phenomenal success, being the only trained animal display to date to appear on the Ed Sullivan television show five times.

"My camels do things no circus camels ever did before," says Jack, explaining his contribution to circus business. "Single-file, waltzes, go-by-twos, wheels-of-four. I even got one camel that walks on its knees, and they not only all mount pedestals but turn spindles, too. That's really difficult because with such a long neck extending way out over the spindle the camel can't see where he's putting his feet. The zebra does figure eights with the camels, marches and the Spanish trot; the llamas leap over the camels lying down and do thread-the-needle with them. Then the whole company, including the pony and monkey-rider, does high hurdles. I had three inflatable rubber Arabs made to ride the camels; they cost me five hundred dollars apiece. It's a real lively display."

Besides this variegated act, Joyce, in association with a chap named Jack Kochman, operated for some time a Jungle Racing outfit geared as a grandstand show for county and state fairs. Besides the Joyce mixed act, the program included only three more or less standard turns: performing elephants, a dancing horse and trained pigs.

The other eleven numbers were all in the nature of competitions, most of them counting on getting their laughs and some of their thrills from audience participation: there was an old-fashioned bucking-mule act, Florida greyhound racing, and a bareback riding school for local volunteers. There were races with llamas drawing sulkies; with razorback pigs pulling Conestoga wagons; camel, Shetland pony and goat races; a mixed animal race, each contestant driving a different team; and racing elephants—*not* with local riders. (The show carried its own bosomy lovelies able to stand the rough jouncing.)

Though Joyce enjoyed the variety of such a heterogeneous collection, he much prefers his own mixed group and has gotten right fond of the cantankerous camel. "They have such wonderfully sad eyes," he says, "really beautiful—with long sweeping lashes. And when they whimper, they like to break your heart." Joyce is the only man known to speak of the surly soured devil, the camel, as though it were a ravishing, captivating, veiled princess of Medina.

Jack's interest in this most unusual of circus wild-animal performers is genuine. He likely knows more about camels than most Arabs and has a very high regard for the ungainly beast.

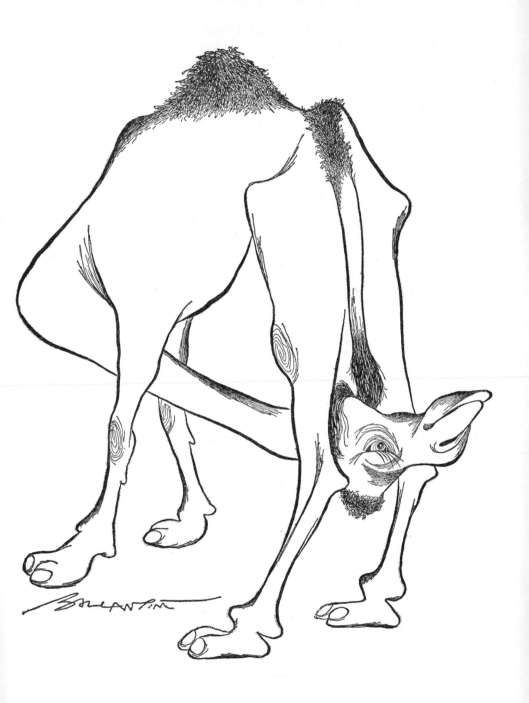

"Without the camel, civilization would be further behind than it is," he reasons. "Camels made communication possible between countries and peoples that never would have gotten together otherwise. Camels are, I'd say, the most useful of all the animals in Asia and Africa, including the elephant, which after all is mainly used as cheap labor."

While motor vehicles have been introduced to the desert, the camel is still the most reliable year-round means of traveling the scorching dunes.

Camels have been known to go ten days without water, but the dry spell for a normally healthy camel is three days and a distance of about ninety miles; with forage, water can be dispensed with indefinitely. Camels have one super advantage over the machine. Their scimitar-keen sense of smell can always locate water. Water is stored in the cells of two of the parts of the compartmented stomach; in the desert water taken from the stomach of a dead camel is potable —not like a drink at the Biltmore Men's Bar, but passable. A hauling camel will carry a load of 500 pounds for three days at 25 miles per day without drinking. If a camel goes too long without drinking, however, his chronic halitosis becomes almost unbearable even to himself, and the water reserve in the stomach periodically comes rumbling and gurgling into its throat embarrassing inexperienced riders, who are at a loss to tell from just where these liquidy burbles and bubblings are coming. It's the sort of thing that can scar sensitive people for life.

Camels are not called the "ships of the desert" without reason. A camel's wide, soft, padded feet, with only the tips of the toes hoofed, are very adaptable to walking in sand. The beast walks with a digitigrade rather than an unguligrade gait—that is on tiptoe, rather than on the tocnail of its foot as does a horse, cow or deer. Muscles in the nostrils can close them tightly in a sandstorm. The hump is a store of fatty flesh which is reabsorbed when necessary into the general system. A well-fed camel's hump is large and firm; when food is scarce it sags and flops emptily. The usual meal of a camel is a smidgin of beans once a day, a few balls of barley meal, some dates and whatever meager shrubbery the beast can find for itself.

The average camel, loaded only with a rider, can make 8 to 10 mph for the first six or eight hours without water during a three- or four-day junket. Properly watered, a good speed-camel can do 100 miles a day, although only the most hardy riders care to go more than 60. The quick jog trot of a camel gives its jockey a thorough bone-shaking, and the gallop is something no man should attempt unless in fine physical condition. If he isn't, he soon will be; the gallop is a great muscle-toner and weight-reducer. Walking a camel meant for trotting and running results in a nauseating seasicky rolling and lurching, very unpleasant for the rider. Camels often trip, but their marvelous four-way shift legs keep them ever from falling.

Camels have been imported to Italy, Spain, South Africa, the Canary Islands and on to Australia but have never had much success in the American deserts, although an attempt was made in 1856 by the United States Army, on the approval of Jefferson Davis, then Secretary of War, to use camels for communications and freight hauling in the Southwest. A herd of seventy-four camels was landed at Indianola, Texas, an Arabian named Hadji Ali in charge. The United States Army made absolutely no impression on a single one of the beasts. It is not recorded how many of the officers were spat upon, but a summary order was issued through channels for the abandonment of the project. The War Department typically left the iracundulous recruits to shift for themselves, and a report of the period states that they "survived many years, creating interest and excitement." I'll bet.

It is odd that the camels didn't like our Southwest, for this was their last ancestral home in North America, some surviving in Nevada almost until recent times, at the end of the Pleistocene epoch of the earth's Cenozoic era.

Hadji Ali adapted more readily to the land that adopted him. Driving through Quartzsite, Arizona, once I came upon a monument erected to Hadji. It is a small squat pyramid of native stone, and fastened to its side is a metal plate, with lettering that appears to have been crudely tooled in some primitive manner by a blacksmith, telling the story of the ill-fated clash of the army vs. camel id. Atop the stone pile is a cut-out metal camel inscribed with the driver's name, affectionately Americanized to Hi Jolly. This tribute to America's first camel trainer is in a small graveyard (hardly grand enough to be called a cemetery) in which there are only a few fancy marble stones in the accepted mortician tradition. The majority of the graves are marked by skinny, rough wooden slabs, mainly dateless, the names of the dead stenciled on in black—long names split any old way to make them fit. For instance:

John
J. Cummi
ngs

One unmarked mound was strewn with colorful bits of broken crockery: "Probably the Company dishwasher," commented my wife.

The humped creatures are excellent burden bearers, but they don't thrive on other kinds of work. Camels have been induced to plow fields—a task which they regard with superfine disdain—and under heinous protest they have been hitched to water wheels but this only makes them terribly giddy. In Egypt, at harvest time, camels are so loaded with green fodder that they often become top-heavy and topple over, sometimes covering in the ensuing avalanche some luckless motorist cursing his way past the road-filling obstacle.

There is a notion abroad that horses as well as motorists hate the very sight of camels, supposedly not liking the smell of the beast. This is a fallacy. Horses regard the camel with great suspicion and distrust possibly because they are forever startled and mystified by the queer untoward antics of the animal. Camels can get into more peculiar positions than a preening pelican. A camel can turn its head completely around and stare a rider full in the face. This is *very* disconcerting. A camel can stretch its neck to nibble its own tail; can rest its chin on the saddle; scratch its ear with a hind leg. (It's like the flamingo in *Alice in Wonderland*.) It can bite itself in the stomach and often does. And it can drop its neck downwards and inwards back between its forelegs to look out between back legs with an upside-down face. It's enough to drive a Mohammedan to drink.

From the foregoing it is not difficult to undertsand why the camel is considered the worst wild animal to train for circus performance. A camel gives a trainer very little, if any, co-operation, and constantly tries its best to make the man feel like a worthless cad. While camels have a good memory, they are not creatures that adjust well to habit, and they seem to hold their teacher in absolute abomination, utterly detesting his every move. Jack Joyce, the greatest camel trainer in the Western world today, has never found them diligent or willing pupils.

"They are most stubborn," he told me. "And they're not only resentful of being taught anything, but they naturally hate whatever they've been forced to lcarn. They're the most perverse animal I know of—and I've known them all. However, while they like to get revenge, once they get even, they don't hold grudges. And they're not so flighty as a horse, but they're lazy, and if you force them too much they sulk."

Jack is not much concerned by the camel's ugliest habit, that of spitting to register displeasure. "First of all I don't aggravate them too much," he says. "The spitting is only to get rid of the annoyance of man. If you got the guts and the nose to stand your ground, they'll eventually stop spitting on you."

I asked Jack to describe the horrid smell.

"Well," he said, "it's just like an old show-hand who hasn't been able to take a bath for about six months—a strong b.o. smell, sour and very obnoxious."

To get action out of these creatures, Joyce stresses respect. "You can't hit camels," he says, "and expect them to respect you. If they're hit, they just stop, close their liquid eyes and shudder; a llama will shake even more."

Some of Joyce's camel tricks have had adventitious beginnings. The comic way in which a runaway camel leaped a low fence, never taking more than one of its knobby legs off the ground at the same time, was the inspiration of the hurdles. A camel trying to crawl quietly away out of sight to escape its turn in training was the basis of the knee-crawl stunt.

"I'm thinking of breaking a camel to do a hind-leg stand," says Jack Joyce. "I know they can do it because I've seen a picture of one. The zebra ordinarily can't do the hind-leg because it's so long-vertebraed. In the old days they did hind-leg zebras a lot because then they weren't expensive; as soon as one got ruined, they'd toss it out and break in another one."

Jack Joyce has never bred camels, and his act is composed entirely of females, since they have whatever better disposition a camel is capable of. Joyce will have no part of male camels, finding them rather disgusting during rutting season. The male camel in love masturbates, stinks fearfully, and tries to attract his lady by making gurgling noises sounding like the last water running from a bathtub, and it inflates its tongue until it hangs from its mouth like a pink bubble-gum balloon.

Camel mothers carry their young, hating every minute of the period, from eleven to twelve months, giving birth to only one baby at a time. The newborn stands about three feet high when it is one week old. A camel is full grown at age fifteen and lives a long life—forty to fifty years. Camel milk is rich, thick and creamy but—naturally—it curdles tea and coffee and makes lousy butter. According to a man who should know, Arthur Weigall, one-time Inspector-General of Antiquities of the Egyptian Government, camels *teach* their foals to grumble. He had a ludicrous camel named Laura who would start bleating and bubbling on his approach, putting her head close to her infant's as she did so, so that the sounds might be imitated.

Jack Joyce believes that he has had such good luck with his testy beasts because he takes good care of them. "How you provide for any animal is the key to any good act," he says. "But especially the camel —it's so persnickety." In this respect the help employed is mighty important. One wrong move by an attendant during the night can undo everything the trainer has been drumming into his animal with love and kindness all day.

Joyce says, "On circuses I've had horses go head-shy on me overnight, and when I investigate it's usually been because some wino stumblebum got lushed up and took out his grudges on the animal during the night, or some mean ignorant hostler smacked it in the head with his fist or an iron stake. That's why I don't ever want to hire out any more to work company-owned animals on a circus. With a private act like mine, where I own the animals, I can control the help: I don't hire anyone who doesn't genuinely love animals."

Contradicting a remark of mine, Jack said, "No, the *quality* of animal acts hasn't deteriorated, but the quantity has. Shucks, what we have today in the ring are better trained animals than there ever was back in the good old days that everybody raves about. Look at Sciplini's Chimps and Victor Julian's Dogs. Marvelous! And all those wonderful animal acts on the other side, especially in the Russian circus (the small stuff—weasels, penguins, rabbits; those bears that ride bicycles piggy-back; the tiger that swims with the lady). Sure, we did stuff like that over here years ago—*when* there was plenty of animal-act competition. But nobody's going in for animal training in America any more; there's very little incentive for a kid in that line. What happens when all us old-timers die off?—because we will. Where are the young trainers?"

Joyce finds it sad, as I do, to see that matriarch of present-day American circuses, Ringling Bros and Barnum & Bailey, slipping more and more away from the original idea of circus, which is a display of animals—both wild and trained, human and four-footed. The Ringling show has three arenas of wild animals for its New York and Boston runs, a matter of approximately seven weeks, but they hit the road with only one for the balance of the nine-to-ten-month season beyond these two metropolitan centers. I remember when a giraffe and a pygmy hippo were an amusing part of the "Spec"; once upon a time there was even a monumental sea elephant named Goliath pulled around the hippodrome track on a big flat-bed wagon. The gorillas, Gargantua and Mme. Toto, were toted along the same course in their mammoth glass-enclosed, air-conditioned cage wagon. When the big show was a canvas-covered circus, it housed over eighty head of horses, and one season there were more than fifty elephants. There are about fifteen now, and around the same number of steeds. There used to be three stirring rings of spirited, blooded liberty-drill horses; this year's program lists not one.

"Where will you find a better horse trainer in the world," asked Jack Joyce, "than Charlie Mroczkowski? And look at what they got him doing—simple kid-trainer tricks. He's wasted on a few single horse tricks that any just ordinary trainer can do. In Europe I've seen a trainer walk *six* raring horses across the ring; Charlie can do that, too, but first you have to have the six horses."

Ringling Bros protests that its difficulty in being able to present the old-time savage razzle-dazzle of the animal kingdom lies mainly in the increased cost of animal upkeep, although because of the big show's new style of presentation—performing in arenas, ball parks and fairgrounds—other factors bear on this decline of performing and menagerie animals. (Seat prices, incidentally, have not declined.) Transportation is one, it being more awkward now to carry large groups of animals, since the circus train is no longer operating. Adequate housing is another, most arena buildings simply not having large enough backstage quarters for the beasts. Back in the expansive tented days space was not much of a problem; usually there were acres left over. Then, the Greatest Show on Earth was a self-sufficient integrated community, performing seven days of the week most weeks. Now, America's biggest circus, having relinquished its uniqueness, is operating like any other traveling theatrical enterprise—such as an ice show or a road-company musical—with intermittent layoffs and with performers looking after their own transportation and room and board. Animals have become a large financial headache with which the management does not care to cope. When animals lay off they must still be paid in the coin of their realm—food and care. They cannot exist on pro-rata, and there is the rub. Animals cost money the entire fifty-two weeks of the year, whether they appear before the public or not. Two-legged troupers can be easily put out of sight, out of mind. If animals in captivity are treated in that cavalier fashion, they perish. Therefore in the new-style arena circuses the tougher two-legged animals are preferred.

Although wild animals, in this mechanized period of mankind, face, in this country, a somewhat bleak future in the circus, in other facets of show business all four-leggers except the camel are still doing all right—in fact enjoying a healthy revival. The musical, "Li'l Abner," has brought pigs, hounds and donkeys back to Broadway. Horse operas are more popular than ever before as television reverberates with clopping hoofbeats. Even the real opera, the Metropolitan, is again employing live animals to supplement its arias (only elephants being barred from the creaking old stage). The perennial jungle movies keep the big cats, pachyderms and apes occupied.

But the camel is losing out all around. The hardy beast that has bleated and beat its way up from earliest mammalian times by sheer asperity is not doing so well today. In Hollywood camels have become a drug on the market. DeMille's second "Ten Commandments" and Billy Graham have pretty well sated that large segment of American public that seeks entertaining religion. Arabians have become too controversial to be amusing to the celluloid peddlers and have been replaced by the more acceptable, more exotic Japanese, whose kimonos and communal steam baths are considered sexier than a plethora of pointy black beards and Oriental rugs in smelly old tents heavy with frankincense, myrrh, and spitting camels. No Arabs, no camels—cut! Whatever camels *are* being packed into the flat round cans today are being photographed in the new style of Hollywood—in their native habitat by location companies.

In circus business there are only a few animal men who are grandiose operators like Jack Joyce, able to sink thirty thousand dollars or so into the equipment and rolling stock necessary for operating independently a large wild-animal display in which camels can be used. That leaves to the camel only the mud-show circuses whose small, already operating menageries might absorb the humped malcontent. While a notable few of these truck circuses have grown considerably since the mammoth Ringling outfit bowed out of the tented field, not many are grand enough yet to afford the perpetual nuisance of camels. Eventually camels will enjoy (as much as a camel can enjoy anything) their circus business revival in the small tented shows.

That is where they will be—your children and their children to marvel at—chewing their cuds, turning their gloomy heads upside down. No animal, except perhaps the elephant or giraffe, is so curious and exotic.

"The camel has seen them come and go," says Jack Joyce. "It will survive this down-beat generation, and so will the circus. They're both tough. You can't keep a good animal down."

Home Is Where the Snake Is

One February evening in Sarasota, Florida, which is the winter quarters of the Ringling Bros and Barnum & Bailey Circus, my wife and I took some Northern visitors to the Orange Blossom Hotel for dinner. Our waitress came to the table red-eyed from crying.

"I've just lost my best boa," she said and broke down, weeping dismally.

Our friends were perplexed.

"Do people still wear boas down here?" asked the wife.

"And why does she carry on so about a little old feather neck-piece?" asked the husband.

We carefully explained that the weeping waitress was an old circus friend, Josephine, wintertime hash-slinger by necessity, but summertime Snake Enchantress by choice; known to circus midways all over the nation as Señorita Carmen. The boa over which she had become so disconsolate was the very best boa constrictor of her collection—her beloved Sully, who had just died.

While that tragic picture of Miss Josephine is rooted in my mind, it is not the way I want to remember one of America's greatest snake charmers. The memory that I treasure is of Señorita Carmen standing boldly on the bally stage (the outside platform) of a side-show squinting into the noonday sun of summer, a big fat constrictor coiling lasciviously about her silken-draped thighs; the banner line behind stretches to right and left in all its ferocious sunburst splendor while the calliope wheezes "Visions of Salome" and the Outside Talker gives a flamboyant raspy-throated résumé of the delights to be found within, while over all drift the delightful smells of warm, dirty canvas, black coffee, wood shavings and warmed-over hot dogs. It is a picture we will never see alive again, for the greatest American side-show has gone forever—one of the major casualties of the closing, in July, 1956, of the world's greatest tented circus, Ringling Bros and Barnum & Bailey Combined Shows, Inc. (Josephine must have wept that day, too.)

I recall a happier day of another year. I was driving through West Virginia and saw by posters that the Ringling Circus was to show Huntington on the Fourth of July. My wife and I had been in South America that past winter, returning too late in the spring for the New York opening of the big circus and had been unable to fol low it to any of its spring and early summer stands. I was happy to have this chance to see the new edition of the Greatest Show on Earth.

July Fourth that year started out a real scorcher. It was plenty hot when I got to the lot late that morning, and the Midway was already jammed with a jostling mob. The Outside Talker was blatting into a hand microphone, trying to stop the surging flow of holiday makers.

"Well, look here now. Look here now. Watch the door. I'm going to let you see a great big snake. We're going to bring out a lady with a great big snake."

Josephine appeared in the little canvas runway that leads from the sideshow tent along the length of the calliope wagon to the bally stage. This was not Josephine the anonymous servitor of the Orange Blossom, but Señorita Carmen, a queen of the steaming tropics, bedizened, glamorous and bare-midriffed. Her tight-fitting skirt of pink and seafoam green, a pastel salute to her Mexican homeland, was gathered to one side of her saucy hips. Her bosoms were cradled in a hammock of crepe and spangles. Gold hoops swung from her ears. Eyebrows were painted sharp and black, and Josephine's wide mouth was a lurid slash of carmine. Her open-toed snakeskin pumps had spike heels, and around her muscular shoulders, the color of a creamy young palomino, was draped a thick shimmering rock python. A skinny man in lurid blue uniform pants and peaked cap helped the flashing Señorita climb a set of wooden steps propped against the back of the bally stage.

"*Here's* the lady with the great big snake! *Now* will you look? Now *will* you look? PAY ATTENTION!" The crowd paused and turned its eyes and feet in toward the stage. The Talker launched his spiel.

"Ringling Bros and Barnum & Bailey proudly presents on the outer stage at this time, Señorita (pause) *Car*-men! The world's premier reptile subjugator—or snake trainer if you prefer it that way. The world's premier *exponent* of the art of herpet-tology. The snake the little lady is carrying *is* one of the smallest in her collection. This snake was born just four weeks ago. As you know snakes are not born from eggs but from membranes. The mother of this snake you will see on the inside on platform seventeen. She is twenty-three feet in length and weighs one *hundred* and *twenty*-two pounds.

"Now these aren't the ordinary kind of snakes you find in your backyard here in Huntington. Señorita Carmen will handle snakes that measure up to nineteen feet in length and weigh well over one hundred and twenty pounds. Poisonous? No. Dangerous? Of course. And deadly? Yes, indeed. Why? Because as they *do* kill their prey there is constrictive power in their muscular coils, crushing power within those muscular coils, to sque-e-e-e-eze the daring young lady to death in less time than it takes to tell—in fifteen or twenty seconds.

"Señorita Carmen *will* enter the steel-bound arena. Those snakes will strike and bite at her and then at a word of command they will leave their moss-bound beds. They will come twisting and curling, entwining about her lovely body until that girl, *that* daredevil, stands before you a hissing monument of reptilian flesh! Her highly educational lecture on snakes and herpet-tology is one you will remember the longest day you live."

Josephine's cool eyes, scanning the crowd with that go-to-hell look of the experienced show-hand, caught mine and gave an ever-so-slight flicker of recognition. As the Talker wound up his "opening" by calling attention to the flamboyant banner pictures of the fourteen other attractions to be found inside the tent, I wormed my way to the ticket box and noisily smacked down a half dollar. The ticket seller, who was my old friend Scott, true to the code, gave no sign of recognition but ostentatiously handed back two quarters, saying loudly, "Your change, sir. *Don't* forget *your* change."

Clare, the doorman, whom I knew from my clowning days, pretended to take a ticket from me, and I passed into the low canvas corral of the World's Strange Exotic and Curious People.

The paying customers were knotted down at one end of the canvased cloister before the platform of Mossa Kutty Singhalee, India's Fireproof Wonder, who was demonstrating his Mahomet-given ability to travel the flame of a blowtorch across his eyeballs and bare chest, to lay his tongue along a cherry-red iron, to press his bare foot to a white-hot bar. The flames of the torch were not the three-alarm bonfire depicted on the outside banner painting nor was the Mossa himself the promised firm-bellied, sexy green-eyed devil, but the act from where I stood seemed effective enough.

Josephine's platform was identical with the others and had at its rear a large, white-painted box the size of a maiden's hope chest. The lid, lined with mirror, was propped open so that the undulating snakes could be seen from ground level.

Josephine was glad to see me again and anxious to show off her reptilian family.

"You already know Sully," she said, once we had dispensed, with a quick rake-through, our recent pasts. "He's the one I named for Father Sullivan—you know that Boston-priest circus fan." Sully was a 6-foot boa constrictor. "And here's my favorite baby, Frieda, another boa. I named her in honor of the Armless-Legless Girl." Frieda was a small one, only 5 feet in length, weighing, Jo said, about 10 pounds. "This one is Woody. He's an African rock python, fat and sassy, just like that Woody on the front door." Woody was a good 14 feet long and weighed 75 pounds—a heap of snake. "And Storky—55 pounds and 15 feet long. He's tall and thin like a stork—like a circus fan I know up in Beloit, Wisconsin, named Starkington.

"These four," said Josephine, "came originally from the Joe Chase Animal Farm in Egypt, Massachusetts. I got them from Tanit Ikaou, the only woman in the world that works crocodiles and alligators. I paid a thousand dollars for the lot. The show put up the money, and I'm paying them back a little each week; they take it out of my pay."

She returned Storky to his playmates.

"The two pythons were already broken in. I had to do the boas myself, but they weren't so wild. Didn't have to muzzle them even the first couple of weeks."

They were handsome reptiles and I said as much to my snake-twisting friend.

"Not one is as good as my old favorite, Youngblood," said Josephine. "I named him for a Negro helper I had who wasn't afraid of snakes—most of them are, I find. Youngblood would sink his teeth deep into this boy's bare shoulder, but he'd just laugh him off. The snake was twelve feet long, weighed one hundred and fifteen pounds and was real mean and jealous of my other snakes. He died of a twitch in Minneapolis after I left him there with a herpat-tologist friend."

She reached back into the box and lifted out another good-sized boa. "And here is my sweetheart, Cookie," she said. "At the end of last season he was the only one I had. Down in the Carolinas and Georgia we had so much rain and cold even the water pipes froze one night in the cars (Valdosta, that was), and I lost all four of my snakes within two weeks, and then the three more I bought to replace them. I finally run out of money. So the boys on the midway and from the cookhouse, they all pitched in, took up a collection and bought me a snake. I named him Cookie, the Butcher Boy."

Boa constrictors are favored by most circus snake handlers because they domesticate easily and are fairly docile in captivity. However, Josephine prefers the Indian rock, or black-tailed, python for exhibition since it acclimates so easily.

"But you can't get them too dark," she says, "else they just look like eels. They're especially beautiful in the sun; they have that deep purple irridescent color."

She does not care for the regal python because it is yellow; she prefers the South American boas to all other species of boa and finds Mexican boas no good at all. "You cannot tame a Mexican," Josephine says, "either human or snake." The anacondas are too vicious for show work and as far as Señorita Carmen is concerned, "cobra" is a dirty word.

The beauty of the boa constrictor and rock python is an important factor in their selection as Thespians. The boa is a handsome creature of dark brown and black with pale, boldly defined, elongated saddles of tan along its back. Toward its tail the monster snake becomes brick red, and crimson, marbled with paler and darker hues.

The Indian rock python, the species most seen in circuses, is strikingly patterned in pale hues of brown and yellow, resembling an Oriental rug.

Both boas and pythons are of the zoological family *Boidae*, though the latter are now considered a separate branch known as *Pythonidae*. The South American anaconda, the Americas' number one snake behemoth is a water boa, found in the swamps of Brazil, the Guianas, and the jungles of northwestern Peru. Its maximum size has long been a point of dispute between experienced jungle travelers and zoologists, who are not inclined to stick their (and the anaconda's) necks out beyond 26 feet. A snake of that length would have the girth of a small barrel and appear enormous to an excited observer, who might wrongly estimate length in proportion to thickness of body, a method which cannot apply to the anaconda since, being a water snake, it can grow exceedingly fat and remain extremely mobile, unlike its bush-tangle brother who must stay slim to travel swiftly. The jungle giants have been *estimated* by accredited observers to be from 55 to 90 feet long, the latter dimension vouched for by the official Brazilian Boundary Commission. The largest anaconda ever exhibited alive in New York's Bronx Zoo was 19 feet long, 36 inches in circumference and weighed 236 pounds. It gave birth to a clutch of seventy-two, each 38 inches in length.

However, authenticated records be damned! A reliable Amazonian hunter named Algot Lange once encountered a veritable monster of an anaconda coiled in a cone-shaped mass 7 feet high, its head lying on the ground. Lange shot its crown to pieces and when the beast was stretched out full length, it measured 56 feet, with a diameter of 2 feet, 1 inch. Lange told his Indian companion that no one in the states would believe there was such a snake. Whereupon the Indian shrugged and said he himself did not believe the Norteamericano's tales of houses of forty layers, one on top of the other.

The adventurer Willard Price, in his book *The Amazing Amazon*, gives an eyewitness description of the capture of an anaconda whose gyrating body filled a 22-foot long cage, leaving a 12-foot length of snake still writhing outside.

You will never see one of these gargantuan reptiles in a traveling exhibition, no matter what the promises of banner paintings and the man with the snaggle gold tooth. Its unwieldiness alone does not prevent the anaconda from becoming a sideshow star. The shiny olive-green monster is considered by many the meanest serpent in existence, a miserable, bitter-end unrepentant villain. I have heard of only one case of an anaconda's domestication. The story was told to me by a brother of Hector Acebes (the man who discovered the source of the Orinoco River), as we cruised by mahogany-burning stern-wheeler down the upper third of the immense Amazon. The tale concerned the 15-foot-long anaconda, pet of a Barranquilla, Colombia, shopkeeper who used the reptile as a cash-drawer guard. When the merchant fell ill, the snake is credited with becoming concerned enough to slither off for the help of a neighbor's wife, bringing her back by tugs at her apron strings. The man recovered, courted the lady, and married her away from her husband. The snake, succumbing either to outraged moral standards or to an unreasoning jealousy, eventually strangled the unfaithful squaw while her new husband was off on a business trip. The gentleman, upon his return, shot his erstwhile pal dead through the head with a revolver. The only authentication of this story came from a good many cans of warm Brazilian beer, so you can take it or leave it.

Amazonian Indians frequently make pets of the ordinary South American boa which pays its way by ridding the thatched premises of rats and other vermin. This smaller brother of the anaconda seldom grows longer than 15 feet. Zoologists call this boa Constrictor constrictor, which makes it sound more dangerous than it really is. When I asked Josephine what she would do if one of her constrictors started constricting, she said, "I'd bite down real hard on its tail."

It is an old Indian legend that if you bite the tail of a squeezing snake hard enough, it will uncoil.

Northern South America has the green tree boa, which grows to about six feet and is a vivid emerald green with cross bars so pristine white they appear to be enameled. This fellow coils symmetrically around a tree branch, forming a very difficult-to-spot green ball. Cuba has small ground boas no thicker than a man's finger and only two feet long. And the mountains of California conceal the rubber boa, a two-footer, one inch thick, tail as stumpy as head, silvery grey and very gentle. Elsewhere in that state is the rosy boa, which I can recommend as a children's pet (my wife had one when she was a little girl).

There are no true boas in Africa and Asia, pythons being the reptilian titans of those continents. A python is more slender than its New World relatives, otherwise there is little structural difference between the two species, except that the boa lacks a superorbital bone (head bone above eye sockets). Boas are born live, pythons from leathery-shelled eggs. Both have clawlike vestiges of back legs near the anal cleft. The only python native to this hemisphere is one found in Mexico (*Loxocemus*). Besides the beautiful Indian rocks most seen around circuses, the python family includes the African rock, just about as large as its Indian cousins; the ball python, a thick-bodied timid soul who coils into a ball and hides his head ostrichlike; the amethystine python of Australia, New Guinea and the Moluccas; and the reticulated or regal python, found in Burma and the Malay peninsula, including the Phillipines. This one, a rich brown and yellow beauty, occasionally reaches a length of 33 feet and a weight of three hundred pounds. The largest regal python ever exhibited at the St. Louis Zoo was a 21½-footer weighing 250 pounds. It had to be force-fed thirteen of its nineteen years in residence, due to atrophy of jaw muscles.

Snake charming, which is really nothing more than snake handling, has been an integral part of the American circus since its museum and moral entertainment days, but ladies were not admitted to the sinuous profession until 1870. In the 1880's, the snake-charming act with the very early version of the Greatest Show on Earth was worked by the wife of Albert Ringling, the oldest of the famous brother combo.

Reptiles have always appealed to the showman's highest standards of hyperbole. One of P. T. Barnum's finest poster creations depicts a modestly dressed bare-footed young lady standing in a den of thirty-one reptiles as calmly as though she were waiting for a streetcar. The caption: "Nearly a Mile of Writhing, Crushing, Hissing, Stupendous & Deadly Snakes. Huge Boa Constrictors, Gigantic Pythons, Dreadful Cobras and Poison-saturated Vipers, the Defiant Hindoo Snake Charmer Seen Wreathed and Festooned in Their Awful Coils."

The general public is more curious about snakes than about any other type of exhibition animal. It is not surprising that the St. Louis Zoo receives more inquiries concerning snakes than it does for any other group of inmates. At that famed zoological garden an audience of four thousand once gathered to witness the force-feeding of a hunger-striking python on a Monday—the traditional rock-bottom day for show-business attendance.

This extraordinary attraction to snakes undoubtedly has deep phallic roots. The cult of the serpent is universal, and the snake deity crawls through the culture of mankind. Snake worship has taken firm hold in many enlightened countries, including our own in some of its benighted backwoods areas.

During an earlier age of outdoor show business every tent show had its lady "snake charmer." In the new era of entertainment, following the Second World War, the number of active practitioners dwindled to a handful of less than a dozen. At present it is doubtful that there are half that number of big snake manipulators in this country—this estimate not including the various snake dancers and strip teasers of the honky-tonk night-club circuits and a few of the more rabid Southern evangelists who employ harmless native seducers such as black and striped chicken snakes. My snake-charming friend, Josephine, could name only five reptile colleagues that she knew personally.

"There's Miss Ida (Ida Mae Sabo), who was on the Cole show," she said, "and Myrna Carson; Mrs. Cliff Wilson of Cliff Wilson, famous for jungle shows on carnies; Barbara White—she's a newcomer; and Tanit Ikaou—the crocodile hypnotist. Her real name is Joanna Pories."

Señorita Carmen started life as Josefina Maria del Carmen Martinez Escalante in the Mexico City district of El Carmen or San Juan de la Tran. Her father was a King Alfonso refugee, who earned his family's living as a translator. Josephine saw her first monster snakes at the age of nine on a family visit to the Argentine. She first handled reptiles professionally in 1933 on the Beers-Barnes outfit, a tented repertoire show that turned into a circus. She broke into the business being chief cook and snake-washer for that show's official charmer, Monya Podres. In 1936 Monya sold out to Josephine for $300. ("Everything was cheap then," Jo says, "even snakes.")

Señorita Carmen has been flaunting snakes before the public for a total of fourteen of the twenty circus seasons since that time. During the other six she danced and supered in the Big Top performances of two truck circuses (Russell Bros and Sparks) and swayed and wiggled as a "Genuine Hawaiian" for the Ringling Bros Sideshow.

During all that time the most money Josephine was able to carry away from the pay wagon was $75 a week (meals and accommodations furnished outside New York). In the Ringling sideshow she was considered an average act, falling between the highest paid (the Giant—$125) and the lowest (the Fireproof Man—$45). She earned less than the calliope player banging his pipes for union scale ($109.10), more than the ticket taker ($60); and $25 a week less than either the Monkey Girl or the Alligator Skin Boy.

To eke out her meager income, Señorita Carmen sold photos of herself, and "bugs"—chameleons.

"I make my real money on the bugs," she told me between appearances, carefully tying strings to the brittle tails of the wiggly green lizards, "at fifty cents a pop (each one) and the food goes for a quarter a box."

And now it was Señorita Carmen's turn for a go at the gawking gillies.

"Presenting at this time," mumbled the elderly Inside Lecturer, "the charming enchantress of jungle reptiles, Señorita Carmen an' her pets 'a' the jungle. Kindly give her your attention."

Josephine stood before her open snake box. "Thank you, sir. . . . Ladies and gentlemen, now before I introduce my snakes I want you to know I have here for sale the live chameleons and baby turtles. They're all alive; they're fifty cents apiece. They make wonderful pets, especially for little children. On each individual box there is instructions how to take care of them. If you will follow them, they will live for many many years. I also sell the scientific food which is prepared especially for them, twenty-five cents each. Each chameleon and turtle has attached to its neck a little chain and a safety pin so you can pin them to your lapel. As you know, the chameleons change color. Anytime you desire to buy one when you're visiting the Sideshow step right over, and I will try to wait on you. I'll be glad to do it." She bent over her snake box and proceeded carefully to heave out the monsters one by one. When Storky the 15-foot python appeared, he got quite a rise out of the audience—an audible sucking in of breath.

"As you know," Jo continued, "boas, pythons and anacondas are the three largest reptiles in the world and are found in all the equatorial zones of the world—Africa, India and South America. When they fulfill maturity they get to grow twenty and thirty feet in length, weighing three hundred to five hundred pounds. So you can readily see any snake I exhibit here is a mere youngster."

She paused to push back the sassy Woody, quietly slithering out over the edge of the box.

"Most people have the impression that the fork-ed tongue that

protrudes from the snake quite frequently is the fangs or stinger of
the snake, but on the contrary it's only the snake's ears, as they have
no external ears whatsoever. They catch vibrations, sounds, sense
danger. During the shedding period, which is five times a year, they
go completely blind about one week out of each shedding period.
They have no eyelids, and the dead skin forms a film over their eyes
and the fork-ed tongue, which is called a feeler, is used in the same
manner as a blind man would use a walking cane in the city. After
they shed they regain their sight, starting from head to tail. The
snakes have three rows of teeth slanting inwardly. They use them
only as a leverage to hold onto their prey. Even in captivity snakes
must have live food. As they strike at the animal or prey, they hold
the animal with their mouths, coil around it, crush it to death and
they dislocate the lower part of their jaw which expands about four
times larger than their normal head. They are able to swallow a large
object. They push the food down their throats with their teeth. It
takes them eight or nine days to digest whatever they eat. They have
strong gastric juices and can digest—for instance, if a snake eats four
or six guinea pigs they can digest fur, bones and meat."

The audience collectively paled.

"Being tropical snakes, they require a lot of care. Most people
have the impression that snakes are frozen or doped or teeth are
pulled out, but on the contrary they're like babies. On cold nights
you have to use hot-water bottles, electric pads and quite a few
blankets as they are susceptible to colds and pneumonia. On warm
days you have to bathe them every day as they absorb quite a bit of
water through their skins as nature has provided them to be the
cleanest animal on earth. They won't eat anything that is dead or
sick." (The audience gulped as one man.) "Their shiny skin does not
make them slimy. On the contrary, it means they are healthy. Now
there might be other questions you people might like to ask in
regards to my snakes. If so come over any time while you are visiting
in the sideshows, and I will try to answer them. Now if you will
kindly pass on to the next platform. . . ." She waved vaguely to her
left, deposited her python in the box and abruptly sat down.

"Ladies and Gennlemen," said the tired Inside Lecturer, "Sealo,
the body of a seal, the head of a man and he's alive. . . ."

Most of the crowd dutifully ambled on to gawk before the next
platform.

Hanging back was a lady in a rose-printed housedress, who

wanted to know could the chameleons change color—any color?—and a few kids unable to take their popeyes off the fascinating snakes. A buck-toothed towhead, fingering his front incisors, asked Josephine, "Did you take the stingers out, lady?"

Jo smiled and explained.

A boy asked his big sister, "Whyn't they bite nobody?"

"She trains them," said the girl, "but they could try to squeeze you to death."

"Someone would save you before he got through," said the youngster, with a small boy's supreme confidence in mankind.

A skinny dirty-faced urchin looking longingly at the chameleons asked, "Is them things real?"

"Yes, sweet, they are," answered Josephine.

"If I had money, I'd buy one."

"Chameleons are from Cuba," said Jo kindly.

"Is that in Canada?" asked the kid.

"Nah," interjected another kid, "inna desert. It's a humid country. They got them down in Mississippi, too—crawlin' on the trees. Them is from Mississippi."

The stragglers left when Sealo, the Seal Boy, singing casual excerpts from the "Barber of Seville" began to shave with a simulated straight razor made of wood, held in one of the flipper hands that grew directly from his shoulders. The other hand held a stump of cigar. Sealo was quite rotund and wore a sailor's middy blouse of pale blue satin.

"I only mind silly or stupid questions from grownups," said Josephine. "The kids, they don't know any better. I hate to see them get out their pennies to buy bugs. I don't ever let them buy the food. I tell them to let the chameleons out on a screened porch to catch flies for themselves."

A little black dog came running across the tent floor and climbed Jo's almost vertical ladder to be petted. It was Negus, the menagerie watchdog.

"Good thing I ain't got that boa any more that liked to eat dogs," Jo said, unfolding a newspaper clipping dug from her purse.

"Did you see this?" she asked. The headline said: Box Taken from Youth Holds Lesson for Thief. The story related how in a New York subway train a box containing eleven iguana lizards and a boa constrictor four feet long had been snatched from a young man on his way to a pet show. "Imagine when the crook opens that box," laughed Jo. "What a surprise! A kid from up in Virginia, who always comes around to see me and the snakes, sent it. He's interested in snakes. I'm sorta' looking for him to show up here today. It's a holiday." She sighed. "The Glorious Fourth. Independence Day. We'll only have to grind out about thirty-two more shows if the tip (customers) keeps comin' the way it's been."

Josephine started to string a new batch of lizards. "Once when I wintered in Los Angeles," she observed, "I stayed in an apartment house on west Seventh Street. The landlady found out I kept snakes and said I'd have to move. She said she lost three tenants because of my snakes. She said I kept a filthy snake den, so I invited her to come in and have a look. 'My God,' she said, 'you have a beautiful place.' I showed her how I kept the snakes out on the screened porch and only let them in on the carpet sometimes for a little run when I was at home. After that I had no trouble. She said she was sorry she called the S.P.C.A., and after that she never rented to anyone who said they didn't like snakes. She'd bring people in to see the snakes even when I wasn't there. And at Christmas she sent my babies a half-dozen live white mice."

People are usually afraid of the big snakes even though they are only mildly dangerous and will not squeeze if well broken in for exhibition and reasonably well fed. They seldom bite with their formidable array of teeth. Jo showed them to me—sharp as needles, about two hundred in three sets, two upper and one lower.

Boas and pythons are not poisonous; constrictors have no fangs. Josephine contends that the public wouldn't fear snakes so if they became better acquainted with the crawling creatures.

On at least one occasion this inherent fear of snakes was a big help to Josephine. During a winter layoff, while working as a night-owl waitress, Jo usually stopped in a nearby bar on her way home to unwind with a few nightcaps, sometimes staying until closing. After one of these early A.M. sessions, the bartender offered to escort Miss Josephine home. He pushed his way into her apartment and, pretending to be drunk, flopped down on the bed. Routing by ordinary means proved impossible.

"Okay, big boy," Jo finally said, and went to the screened porch. "I brought back—I forget if it was Chunga Hula or Madame X," she told me, "and laid the big snake gently down beside this big hulk. 'My friend here,' I said sweetly, 'always sleeps with me.' The guy turned sixteen shades of white, and he couldn't get out fast enough. And I had to find me another nightcap joint."

A young boy walking past Jo's platform tossed her a rosy peach and called to her, "The flag just went up, Jo. You don't wanta miss that Fourth 'a' July dinner." (The circus dining tent hoists a pennant to announce that a meal is being served.)

"That's Joe, another one of our summer tourists," said the snake enchantress. "Betty Broadbent's son; she's the tattooed lady. He's one sweet kid." She pushed back a couple of exploring snake heads and closed the heavy lid of the big white box. "Let's go to cuckoo-house and see what they dreamed up for our holiday."

The Fourth of July is the only holiday officially observed by the circus world. In early canvas times the day was an occasion for happy reunion when, with the route finally laid out to season's end, the advance men returned to the fold. On the Fourth, every acrobat, by canvas-bound tradition, must "turn over" once, no matter his age or present debility. On small mud-shows, the young vigorous acrobats creak the oldsters through their one obligatory "somerset" with the help of a "mechanic," a leather belt which supports the somersaulter by ropes held on either side by assistants. Between shows in the Big Top, performers celebrate the Grand-and-Clorious by producing a brief show which parodies the most temperamental star-turns. The acts are sketchily rehearsed but professionally presented with full band, lights and ringmaster—and no quarter is given. The program is for showfolks only, but especially the roughnecks whose working schedules prevent them from ever seeing the regular circus performance. After this hilarity, all hands join in a rash of contests and races that rival in boisterous brutishness the bloodthirsty feats of the Roman games, with dog-eat-dog competition for cash prizes handed the winners of foot races (midgets', childrens', mens' and girls'); a rowdy, muscular tug-of-war; wheelbarrow, sack and three-legged races; stake-driving and web-climbing contests, both against time.

The cookhouse does its level best to make the noonday dinner a festive one, decorating the drab canvas dining room with colored pennants and Old Glory sagging from the ridge rope. When Josephine and I arrived there, the canvas wall that separates the "long-side" (workingmen's) from the "short-side" (performer's) had already been dropped (according to tradition) and each group was studiously ignoring the other (also according to tradition). The de luxe meal included soup, fried capon, corn on the cob, mashed potatoes, salad and ice cream—plus nuts, olives, celery and scallions, rare delicacies that appear in the circus cookhouse only on this one special day.

The Sideshow people ate in two shifts, leaving some attractions always available to the paying customers. The tables were covered with the usual red and white bold-checkered tablecloths and on each of the three assigned to the Sideshow was a small pickle jar of red, white and blue wild flowers. A card leaning against each one was inscribed in the inimitable mouth-written Spencerian of Frieda Pushnik the Armless-Legless Girl: "Proud to be an American—4th July 1951." At Josephine's table were the midget Doll family; Sealo, the Seal Boy; Baby Bessie, the fat lady; Percilla, the Monkey Girl and Emmitt, her Alligator-Skin husband.

"Did you hear about the 'Globe of Death' guy?" asked Sealo. "He tried to come in the cookhouse in his undershirt and the waiter refused to serve him. They finally lent him a waiter's white coat."

"Imagine," said Baby Bessie disgustedly, "on the Fourth of July!"

"He thinks he's a big star," said the midget man, Harry, "but just the same him and his alligator, they sit at the wardrobe ladies' table." (Alligator meaning wife.)

"Half the time he can't get that rig of his in the air," said Sealo. "You watch, some night the boys they red-light it off the train. It's too heavy to bother lifting and loading and carry it every day." (Red-lighting is being dumped from the moving train.)

We were halfway through the meal when it began to rain.

"It's always hot on the Fourth of July," said Percilla, "and it always rains."

"It's just a shower," said Emmitt. "We can sit it out."

Through the gap between the sidewall and the scallopy suncurtain we could see the bear trainer's wife rush from the dressing room to gather in her laundry strung between the Big Top guy-lines and the high-wire's A-frame.

"I knew it was going to rain," said Josephine. "The snakes were all up all morning with their heads pointing in the direction of rain. They're good barometers."

One of the dwarf clowns came by peddling his weekly supply of *Billboards*. Emmitt bought one and as soon as the rain let up a bit we all went back to the Sideshow, Percilla wearing the thick show-business journal over her head as a rain tent.

"I wish we could get into the Big Top to see the show," she said wistfully, "but we'll be working."

"When we get back," the midget, Harry, skipping small puddles, said to me, "remind me to show you a menu I got in my trunk from a *real* Fourth of July dinner in the old days."

Harry Doll later went to the men's dressing room and brought back the cookhouse menu he had promised to show me. It was a carefully preserved, four-page book-fold, held together by a fancy twist cord of red, white and blue. It looked something like a dining-salon menu on a luxury ocean liner and was dated July 4, 1920. On the cover a golden embossed eagle screamed over a crossed pair of draped American flags. Underneath this resplendent double ensign was printed: Fourth of July . . . Ringling Bros and Barnum & Bailey Combined Shows . . . The World's Largest Amusement Institution . . . At Home . . . on the Nation's Birthday . . . Bridgeport, Conn. Nineteen twenty.

"Now look inside," the midget whispered reverently.

I scanned the menu. Appetizers: Green Onions, Queen Olives, Jerusalem Artichokes, Salted Almonds, Radishes, and Dill Pickles. Then Madrilene with Sour Cream and Herbs, or Mock Turtle Soup, followed by Boiled Salmon with Lemon Butter. Entrees: a choice of Chicken a la Maryland with French Fries and Corn Fritters, or Roast Lamb with Mint Sauce and Soufflé Potatoes Louis XIV. The vegetables were Creamed Broccoli with Mushroom Soup Sauce, Scalloped Cauliflower au Gratin, and Asparagus.

There was a dazzling array of desserts: Fruit Salad, Macaroons, French Pastry, Chocolate Eclairs, Ice Cream and Marble Cake. Beverages: Tea, Coffee or Iced Tea. And for the blow-off, Cigars and Assorted Chocolates.

"Them was the days," said Harry, running his finger over the embossed eagle as though it were a roast capon under glass. I'm not sure, but I believe a tiny tear appeared at the corner of one of his small eyes.

There remained more than an hour before the matinee would begin in the Big Top, and Josephine was kept busy dashing, boa-entwined, to the outside stage to "make a bally," alternating with the midgets, the India Fireproof Man, the Sword Swallower and the Cuban Dancers. Sideshow managers usually consider a big snake their strongest bally—the best means of stemming the Midway onrush. A monstrous reptile will always stop the mob of potentials if only for a second or two, which is enough for an experienced persuasive Outside Talker to wedge in his ticket-selling pitch. On a good day Josephine and her snake would make about ten ballys, during both matinee and evening "come-ins."

After the ringmaster's whistle started the show in the Big Top, visitors to the Sideshow became fewer and finally Josephine said, "This is as good a time as any to give my snakes their bath. C'mon out back."

It had stopped raining, and the sun was trying to shine. Jo called to a work-hand standing by one of the wagons to which the bannerline frames were attached. "Give me a hand, will you, Clay?"

This big, blubbery innocent, bare to his waist, had a string of tattoed, tailed-up elephants parading across the fat folds of his stomach. Under the nipple of one bosom was tattoed "Sweet milk," under the other "Buttermilk."

Clay carried out a tin washtub full of water and set it down in the grassy enclosure between the wagon and the sideshow tent.

"If it hadn't rained this would be a nice lot for them to run a little," said Jo, lifting a pulsing section of huge snake gently into the tub.

"I had me a thirty-cent bath last night," said Clay, "in a Japanese place down in the basement of that chop-suey joint Sanchez was talkin' about. I was in there more'n an hour. I bet it cost that Jap more'n the thirty cents just to heat up all the water I used. The drain was stopped up and the water was up to here running out under the door and he was bangin' on the door and hollerin'."

Josephine with Clay's help dried the snake in sections, using a towel once owned by the Antlers Hotel. The snake yawned. "That means he's hungry," said the reptile expert, "but he don't eat. I turn him loose in under the stage with the live guinea pigs and rabbits, but he don't even try to catch them. I have to force-feed this one."

From Jo I learned that the big snakes need a tremendous amount of care. On very hot days, the snake enchantress swabs her reptiles every half hour with warm water. During warm weather the creatures have a tendency to become lousy. Nits must be carefully removed from under the scales and sweet oil rubbed in to prevent further breeding. Stronger disinfectant would injure the snake. "Tanit," said

Jo, "she once used the stuff you put on human crabs (Cupidex I think it's called) and it killed the snake. It was too strong."

The monster reptiles need mouth wash constantly, and they are very susceptible to cold. On inclement days they get the sneezes, need nose drops and a warm place to snuggle into. For that purpose Josephine keeps a large supply of baby blankets, hot-water bottles and heating pads. In shipping her snakes one winter, a railroad delay caused the snake crate to linger too long on a station platform and Josephine, in one fell swoop, lost her entire troupe to pneumonia.

"In New York," she said, "when we play the Garden, I always take my snakes into the Belvedere Hotel for their baths. They don't mind there because they're used to show folks, but once when I stayed at the Capitol I forgot to tip off the maid and left one snake soaking in the bathtub while I took two others back to the show. The snake scared the livin' daylights outa the maid, and they asked me to move."

Josephine used to make these short jaunts through the city streets by taxicab with the snake casually draped over her shoulders, a satisfactory method though it shortened the lives of a considerable number of hackies. "But one day," she said, "one of my boas got feisty and slipped down into the spring coils under the seat. The driver turned white and left the cab right in the middle of Broadway. 'You can have the hack, too, lady,' he yelled. So now I carry them in a couple of old suitcases."

The snake lady has the muscles for this kind of heavy hauling. Constant serpent hefting has given her a formidable set of shoulders. During her mud-show days, Miss Josephine helped to put up and tear down the Sideshow tent, was able to lend a strong hand to the guying out (tightening of tent ropes), could make a double hitch to stakes, and wield a five-pound sledge hammer in driving them.

With Clay's help Josephine managed to bathe her entire company of snakes and while she was rearranging them in the snake box, I wandered onto the Midway for a cup of coffee. It was fairly empty of people now and a great lassitude had set in. There were no customers at the Sideshow ticket boxes and Scott, the Sideshow ticket seller, in the one next to the bally stage, was leaning on his elbows jawing to his fellow conspirator, Charlie, who was the husband of the sword swallower.

Behind the bally stage the nurse of the Sideshow's sound equipment, a gaunt, hollow-cheeked fellow named Brazil, was feeding corn to a pair of ring-neck doves, the Inside Lecturer listlessly watching him.

"I'm callin' them Patchy and Pidgcy," said Brazil, as I came along. "I'm a'hopin' they won't fly into the electric fan in my berth the way the parakeet did. I paid three bucks for them in yesterday's town."

Inside the low Sideshow tent the summer afternoon doldrums had set in. The sun beat down on the wet canvas and made the air heavy and muggy.

Nobody was present except the entertainers and at the moment they were not especially entertaining. I made a slow tour of the platforms. Baby Bessie was knitting an afghan, yellow with green stripes and enormous strawberries.

The Cuban top-spinner dozed.

The Human Pin-Cushion, a fellow nicknamed "Spider," sat behind his platform in a canvas sling-chair meticulously picking the woven names out of a pile of hotel towels. A pair of crutches leaned against the sidewall and one foot, broken by a fall from his upper berth a few nights back, was in a plaster cast. A small accumulation of empty beer cans lay behind the chair.

The Fireproof Man was killing flies. "You spread your fingers— wiggle them a little is the best way," he said to me. "Hyptonize— never miss. I keep score—seven thousand six hundred and eighty-three this season so far."

Josephine's helper, Clay, leaning against the platform of the Tattooed Lady, was regaling her with wild tales of his candy-butchering days.

Freddy, the magician, was talking to the Giant, who was sorting and marking boxes of shoes, the stock of his on-the-side shoe business.

The Doll family was being visited by a couple of big show midget clowns off duty for the moment.

On his platform Sealo the Seal Boy was talking in his loud out-of-doors voice across the gap to Josephine on her platform. At the same time he was exploring the outside world with binoculars over the top of the sidewall. He shouted a bawdy sally across to Josephine, then whooped and snorted, stamping his feet heavily on the platform, flopping his flipper hands.

"You win the cigar," said Jo. Then to me, "Stick around. Right after the big-show blowoff I'm going to force-feed that boa."

It wasn't long until we heard the Finale music coming from

the Big Top, and very soon clusters of customers began to wander into the Sideshow tent. Josephine answered her usual quota of inane questions.

"The one thing I like about this job," she said, "is I get to meet the public so close. They are more curious about snakes than anything else, except maybe the sex life of the giant or the midgets. I meet the same people year after year—regular visitors."

A wizened old lady carrying a large paper sack approached the snake platform. "I just been feeding the elephants," she told Jo, holding open the bag for an inspection of contents, marshmallow Easter crosses (seconds) and broken Christmas clear-toys. "My hobby is really squirrels; it started when my mother died. I have a squirrel ring with an opal acorn. I been waiting a long time for a squirrel to fall out of a tree, but none of them did, so I found a dead one and had it stuffed by a taxiderm-minist."

Jo said nothing but smiled sweetly. Then the lady asked what the snakes ate.

"Live guinea pigs and rabbits, dear," said Jo, without batting an eye.

The visitor blanched slightly, swallowed hard and said well she guessed she'd better be getting along home to get supper for her sister and good-bye, Miss Snake Charmer.

"What *else* can I say?" Josephine appealed to me. "I can't say I feed them chops and steaks or even horsemeat. Poor thing. I feel so sorry for people so often."

When almost the last home-going towner had left the tent, Josephine hauled her reluctant boa constrictor from the snake box and took it down to the grass alongside her platform. The helper, Clay, had laid out a piece of canvas covered by a spread of newspapers. "Now for your supper, pobrecito," Josephine said, placing her cheek affectionately against the snake's jaws. She lifted the heavy plastic sheeting that draped the platform, which had a stretch of chicken wire wrapped about its supports, making the underneath area into an impromptu pen for a dozen or so guinea pigs and white baby rabbits.

She disengaged a section of the wire, reached in and pulled out a wiggling, squealing guinea pig.

"I don't know if he'll eat today," Jo said to me, "on account of the rain. It's better to be a warm, really sunny day." She turned up the volume of her portable radio, then without ceremony whacked the little cavy over the head with a pliers. It sagged. She doused it quickly in a small tub of water and held it momentarily to the snake's nose. The reptile wouldn't accept it. Clay then took hold of the jaws of the undulating monster and pried them open. Josephine tried to force the warm furry mass into the yawning mouth. It wouldn't go, so she slipped a sharp knife along the fur, skinned the animal, broke its jawbone with one crunch of the pliers and by forceps rammed the meal into the boa's mouth being careful not to damage it. At the same time Clay choked his hands around the snake's neck. The pink and blue heart, inscribed "Mother," which was tattooed into his left biceps, swelled considerably.

"It's too bad he wouldn't take it alive," Jo said. "They need the bones and fur. He can eat four or five guinea pigs if we can get them down him—about twelve to fifteen pounds."

The little animal was entirely in the snake's throat now. "The menagerie boss buys them for me along with the regular animal feed." Josephine was choking the meal along now, with Clay holding the snake's enormous jaws tightly closed. "After he eats, the snake can't be handled for eight days, or he'll reject the food."

"She means he'll t'row up," explained Clay.

The dinner was well on its way. "They only feed every three weeks in summer, every five in winter," said Jo.

While Jo and Clay were engaged in the unsavory business of force-feeding, the Tattooed Lady's son, Joe, came along.

"You want anything from the Grease Joint?" he asked the snake lady.

"Well," said Jo, "it's very kind of you. If you're going over anyway, see if they got any of them special little steak sandwiches. Otherwise a cheeseburger and one all the way and a carton of buttermilk. That should hold me until the weenie roast tonight." To me she added, "We're having a little party down by the coaches tonight after the show. This morning Harry Doll found a water valve in the freight yards that we can turn on to go in in our bathing suits, and we'll have a fire and toast marshmallows and hot dogs. It's our own Sideshow Fourth of July celebration."

When the boy returned from the midway diner with Josephine's supper tucked into the lid of a doughnut box, he had with him a genial, rotund, mustachioed gentleman, who looked a bit like a small-town general practitioner, and a burly, blond young man, who looked like a college All-American. Josephine was pleased to see these newcomers and introduced them.

"This is Ben Key," she said of the younger man, "the boy that sent me that clipping about stealing the snakes in the subway. And this is an old friend Louie Pasteur, who handles cobras. And if there is one thing I'm afraid of it's cobras."

"How do you do, Mr. Pasteur," I said. "My name is Paul Muni."

"No, really," Jo said, "his name *is* Louie Pasteur. His father was the brother of Louie Pasteur, the French scientist."

Ben, who wore a string of animal teeth around his neck, was one of Josephine's regular callers, a telephone lineman whose hobby was snakes. "I've got them in cages all around my bedroom," he told me, in a soft Virginia drawl. "And the Negroes back home in Petersburg follow me around and call me Prince of Evil." He gave a big corn-fed smile and didn't seem a bit evil.

"I brought my new boa along for you to see," he said to Jo. "He's over in my car, lying on the shelf behind the seat. I got a new convertible. It's the color of snake venom."

"I'd love to see him, hon," said Josephine, "but first I've got to take a bucket bath. It's been such a sticky day."

"I've got a bushmaster and a fer-de-lance since I saw you last," said Louie to the snake siren. "I was hoping you could have dinner in town with me tonight but I see you're already fixed up from the Grease Joint." (Grease Joint is what show-hands call their private back-yard lunch wagon.)

"Look," said Jo to Louie, "you and Bill here have supper with Ben, and we'll visit when you get back. I've just *got* to have a bath. You can tell them all about those horrible cobras of yours."

So, bonded by circus camaraderie, we three who had just been strangers drove into town in the young man's venomous creamy convertible, a boa constrictor pulsing at our necks. And from the only man in America who trains and exhibits cobras I learned a few fascinating facts about that highly lethal reptile.

Louie told us that cobras are even less acceptable to civilization than are boas and pythons. He had been ordered out of a good many hotels with his cobras and once was jailed for parking them in a bus-station quarter-locker. He said that he could stand a cobra straight up on its tail but not by the music of a flageolet. Cobras, like all other snakes, have no external ears or eardrums, but hear through inner ears, receiving vibrations carried through solid objects with which the snake is in contact. Cobras are made to sway and rise by being induced to follow the body movements of the manipulator.

The hood, which is created by movable anterior ribs flattening and stretching the skin of the neck, causes the cobra to be called the snake with a cape, the cobra-de-capello. Africa is cobra headquarters, having more than a dozen varieties (more than are found in India), including the widely distributed black-necked, spitting cobra and the ringhal, of the South African Boer country, a couple of dastards that force venom through their fangs to a distance of 6 to 12 feet in a fine blinding spray aimed at their victims' eyes. (The Asiatic cobra, in its southeastern range, is also a spitter.) The king cobra, which feeds entirely on other snakes, is the largest species of the family, sometimes reaching a length of 18 feet, and averaging 12 to 14. It is found in Burma and the East Indies, and its bite injects such a large amount of venom that it can easily kill an elephant if it bites on the soft part of the animal's foot.

The first king cobras born in captivity, a clutch of ten 18-inchers, in 1955, at the New York Zoological Garden Park, familiarly known as the Bronx Zoo, died of starvation because they refused the wide range of food offered, including small live snakes. At that time the curator of reptiles, Dr. James A. Oliver, was unable to determine the factor that puts the baby cobra's feeding apparatus into gear. In the summer of 1957 another batch of cobras were hatched at the Bronx Zoo with forty-six of a possible fifty-six surviving. This time Dr. Oliver was able, by beginning with tiny still-born garter snakes, proceeding through larger dead snakes, eventually to persuade the babies to accept live snakes as food. The zoo has traded most of these young buckos, still keeping a half dozen which are growing into healthy adult snakes.

Mr. Pasteur said that while the cobra is extremely dangerous (believed to cause upwards of five thousand deaths annually in India), it is not the most deadly snake in existence. His choice for Public Enemy No. 1 of the snake world was the African mamba, a whiplike snake whose bite is a grave matter—*one* drop of its venom is absolutely fatal. Other snake baddies, he said, are the banded krait, a dread devil as large as the cobra, found in India, South China and the larger Malay Islands, a sluggard unless stepped on, then a biter more tenacious than a bulldog; the bushmaster, the largest known pit viper (snakes with a deep pit on either side of their heads between eye and nostril); and the fer-de-lance of the American tropics, which fortunately for man has an enemy called the mussurana, a black, cannibalistic snake immune to snake poisons. It kills the fer-de-lance by constriction then swallows it intact. The gaboon viper, I learned, as well as being one of the ugliest snakes extant, is also one of the most poisonous, for its venom attacks *both* the blood stream and the nervous system, whereas the venom of other snakes attacks one or the other.

Louie cautioned me not to be fooled by the idea that only snakes with flat, triangular or heart-shaped heads are poisonous, since the cobra, mamba and coral have the ordinary narrow, supposedly harmless, heads. And he dispensed with the myths of the snake with a stinger in its tail and the glass snake that breaks itself into pieces when in danger. The first is a red-bellied snake of the Mississippi valley, which pricks harmlessly with its sharp tail when restrained. And the second is not a snake at all, but a legless lizard which, like all lizards, can detach its tail any old time it feels like it and grow another. The cobra authority also told me that, with twenty-four hundred kinds of snakes in the world, only in Australia do the venomous exceed the harmless, that only Madagascar has no poisonous species, and only the islands of Ireland and New Zealand are completely free of any kind of reptiles.

When we got back to the lot, it was evening, and the banner-line lights had transformed the Midway into a magic lane of make-believe. I had had my fill of snakes for a while so I left Dr. Pasteur visiting with a bathed and shining Señorita Carmen and wandered around to the circus backyard to look up some of my old clown cronies and to catch part of the show. I sat in the Big Top until the Spec was over and when I returned to the Midway, the Sideshow had begun to slough.

Its last performance of the evening was about to begin. Outside the ticket sellers were still earnestly trying to inveigle a few half dollars from the left-behinds lingering on the Midway. The sword swallower was working—very slowly—with one eye cocked over the sidewall at her husband, the head ticket seller. She was stretching her routine so that she would be the lead-off act on the go-round for the last "tip."

"This is my sword sandwich," she droned laboriously, exhibiting two swords which she planned to shove down her gullet together. As the last ticket for the night was sold, Charlie gave her the office (signal), and soon as the final customer set foot in the top, she hustled into a fast finish dropped the swords down her throat swiftly slid them out ("and thank you very much ladies 'n' gen'elmen") packed her cutlery with whirlwind speed and hustled off to the dressing room.

A work-hand stood by the drop-rope at each center pole. One was drunk and, as I went by, he muttered in an effort to prove he was still in the good graces of humanity, "You seen everybody shakin' my hand this mornin', di'n' you, di'n' you?"

The Human Pin Cushion, after a few swift jabs of a hatpin into his cheek, hobbled on his crutches across the trampled grass to his trunk in the men's side of the dressing room. The Big Top vocalist was rhyming "moonlight" with "June night" over the earth-shaking rumble of tractors, whistle shrills from the menagerie tent and clanking cage wagons leaving the lot.

Señorita Carmen hastily lifted the two small boas from her box, smiled pleasantly, slammed the lid, locked it, and pulling up her satin hobble, descended the steep ladder steps.

"Let's go," she said to me, "or we won't get a good seat in the bus. I'll be right out."

She kicked off her spiked heels and dashed madly to the dressing room.

The last-dog customers were hustled into the night through a lifted section of sidewall; a voice barked, and the big light on the center pole dropped, scattering a cloud of displaced moths. Curtains were quickly stripped from the platforms, which were then flopped, raising spasms of dust, and collapsed like so many bridge tables. Outside the folding banner line was being slammed shut with great metallic clangs. The Wonders and Curiosities from All Over the World were running, scampering, hobbling and feeling their careful way to their bus, standing alongside the stake line. The first seat by the door was reserved for the fat lady; the one across the aisle, for the giant. Sealo came running across the field, screaming and chortling, "Hey, wait for me. I'm afraid in the dark. Someone'll get my chair-ry." The snake charmer and I stumbled deep into the bus and sat behind Emmitt, the Alligator-Skin Boy, and his wife, the Monkey Girl, who had her black beard wrapped in a pink silk scarf. As the bus pulled off the lot, the Sideshow dropped its canvas, kicking up a cloud of tan dust.

The night had become very hot. As we left the bus at the Sideshow car, Scott, the ticket seller, said to me, "I got two pairs of trunks. You can use one. Just change in the donnicker; your duds will be safe on my berth. I'll get the fire goin'."

I had a beer with the car porter and when I came back out onto the tracks, The World's Most Unusual People were ranged along the side of the car facing the railroad switch yards. Most of them sat on canvas or wooden folding chairs, but some hunkered down on the rails, a thickness of cardboard carton between them and the hard steel.

Just down the track, the water-valve discovery of the midget Harry was shooting skyward a small geyser. No one had yet dared its cool spray.

The midgets were searing frankfurters, using untwisted wire coat-hangers as skewers. Percilla, the Monkey Girl, was trying to get a toasted marshmallow through her fuzzy beard. Emmitt was introducing the mysteries of the strange American confection to the Cuban top-spinner, who was fingering and lightly pumping a small concertina.

"Even if nobody goes in the shower," remarked the Alligator-Skin Boy, "it'll sure cool things off down here. No use going to bed now. You can't sleep anyhow. Them cars been sittin' here bakin' in the sun all day."

"I'd go in, if I hadn't taken that bucket bath," said Josephine.

"I'm a'goin' in," said Scott, appearing suddenly behind us, "and so are you." He grabbed Jo by the wrists, but she was too strong for him, so he gave me a large shove, and I had no choice but to get wet. Through the spray I could see across the yards the second section of the circus train, sending into the darkness a Morse code message of lighted and darkened windows. A bright white glare beckoned from the site of the crap game. After the muggy day on the lot, the water running down my chest and back felt good. Scott leaped in and soon we were joined by the Tattoed Lady's son and the treasurer's nephew.

Suddenly there was a great whoop and holler from the tracks and into our upside-down Niagara flapped Baby Bessie, the Fat Lady, clad only in a thin pink slip which, becoming immediately soaked, fit better than her voluminous skin, and enchantingly displayed the great lady's amplitudinous specialities.

As she dashed out, scampering gingerly across the sharp cinders in her bare feet, Harry Doll, the midget, flashed his camera at her. "I got it," he squeaked, "I got it. Oh, boys! I got it!"

Down the track, sitting by the concertina player, Josephine swung into a raucous song. "Ah doan wanna go to . . . Mex . . ico

. . . All I want is some. . . . good old dough . . . When ah get that *in* mah hand . . . You can have your *one* night stand . . . Ah'm gonna *hop* me on*to* a train . . . You won't see me around here again . . . Did some-BAH-dy mention N.Y.C.? . . . Wel-l-l-l . . . that's Home Sweet Home to ME-E-E-e-e-e-e."

Way off over the town a sky rocket split the inky sky with a shower of red, white and blue balls. "It's sure gonna rain tonight yet," observed Jo. "My snakes told me it was."

A very large Negro in dark bathrobe and slippers came ambling alongside the coaches, talking strictly to himself but loud enough so that anyone interested could hear the news he was carrying. "She done set a trap in the aisle for him with a pile of beer cans and when he sneak in to see his sweetie, she had him. Man, she run him into the weeds and light into him sumthin fierce with the heel of her shoe. She fetched blood."

When he had passed, the Monkey Girl said, "That's a part of the circus that I'd rather not know about."

"I think I know who it was," said her husband. "That flyer and one of them Spanish broads."

"Hot rail!" someone shouted. "Here comes the Squadron!" Everybody grabbed up his cardboard butt slab from the track and stood back for the approaching train, the first section of the circus on its way out of town—the section that carries the cookhouse, menagerie and Sideshow equipment. The huge black engine snorted by, spitting fire and sparks, belching acrid smoke, making a great iron clatter. It was followed by a long silver length of clickety-clacking flats and coaches. As the sleepers rattled past, the distinguished company assembled hooted and cheered. Sealo appeared on the platform of the Sideshow car, waving a sparkler in each of his flippers, barking like a sea lion. Josephine hooted, "Yeeeea-a-a-a-a Squadron! Yeee-a-a-a-a-a-a! Cookie, the Butcher!" The metal slats of several windows flashed in salute and the Squadron hooted back, "Yeee-e-e-a-a-a, Josephine! Yee-a-a-a-a snake charmer! Yeee-a-a-a-a-a-a-a!"

Through the Looking Glass

"To get revenge. That's how I come to be a chimp trainer." The skinny little guy's eyes flashed directly into mine for an instant. "A chimp bit me one day when I was working cats." He had a face weathered like soft leather and spoke with a dusty, Texas drawl. "Well, you asked me and I told you," the spare, relaxed man continued, using a favorite circus rejoinder.

He was leaning against a tall Florida pine, and overhead four chimpanzees were having themselves a free-swinging skylark in the moss-hung branches. He was late-thirties, maybe—could be older; hard to tell with circus people. "Name's Henry," he said. "Jus' call me Hank, and the wife is Thelma. You met her when she was lion-sitting for Pat Anthony. I know you, but you don't know me."

Hank Craig was the first chimpanzee trainer I'd ever met. I've come onto a great many more since but never another as interesting.

I had come, for some reason or other which now escapes me, to this casual little trailer encampment on the country outskirts of Sarasota, the Granada Machino, operated by a family of circus acrobats, and had been astounded by the sight of chimpanzees frolicking high in the trees. The first person I encountered as I drove into the shady grove over the man-made slow-down dips that are typical of Florida trailer parks, was an acrobat friend I know only as Muscles. I asked him about the high-altitude apes. "See that man ofer there," he said. "He's their fadder."

And that was how I happened to meet Hank Craig, chimp impresario extraordinary and sole proprietor of Craig's Chimpanzees, the man who trained the Great Bonzo for the Jungle Jim serial movies and Joe, the celluloid Tarzan's simian sidekick—and about 164 other chimpanzees, Hank figures, in the twenty years he's been at the trade.

Before that Craig trained big cats, but he has a more healthy respect for the big apes. "They're more dangerous than cats," he told me. "You can hold off a lion or a tiger with a chair, but you poke a chair at a chimp, he'll take it from you and beat you to death with it. They're a *little* afraid of anything with four legs except a dog (they ain't afraid of dogs). Horses, cows, elephants. It takes me three months to teach a chimp to ride an elephant. But they's only one thing they're *really* a'scared of—that's a blank gun."

Hank never worries about letting his chimps loose in the trees. He specializes in performing them outdoors at parks and fairs, though he has worked in the canvas confines of almost every large circus except Ringling Bros.

"I won't say I can understand them," he said when I asked how he achieved such remarkable control over his apes, "but generally I know what they want. They're very bright chimps. Bobby—that's him highest in the trees—he had the I.Q. test at the University of Baltimore, Maryland, and they reckoned he's as smart as a five an' a half year old. The others—well, Buddy maybe two an' a half, Bucky three an' a half. Don't know about Chipper yet; I only got him last April."

The last named, Chipper, had been acquired for the low price of $350 from a Chicago friend, who had gotten him in a pretty well beat-up state from an animal farm, where the ape had been unloaded by an inept trainer who had been unsuccessful in breaking the animal.

"He was a fright," said Hank Craig. "He's only just now coming around. You should have seen him then—no hair, covered with bruises, bumps and scars. That trainer didn't know beans when the bag was open. But by care and kindness we're bringing Chipper around and he's a'going to be a first-class performer one of these days."

Craig's strong sympathy for the runty, scarred and underprivileged Chipper was understandable. Hank was an orphan himself, his childhood anything but idyllic.

"My father," he told me, "was a full-blooded Cherokee, a Civil War vet, sixty years old when I was born. He was an outlaw, a train-robber confederate of Jesse James and Belle Starr. He was killed when I was three months old by a sheriff's deputy with a twelve-gauge shotgun from behind a tree. Ma gave me to Grandma when I was eight years old and lit out to marry a holiness preacher—the Pentecost holy-rollers—and when I was nine, Grandma died and I joined a circus."

Craig's chimps include in their repertoire a number of high aerial feats, including a cloud-swing and high-trapeze toe-hold. They also work on a tight-wire twelve feet off the ground on a twenty-foot spread. Besides the simple crossovers with and without parasol, the chimps walk the strand blindfolded and do somersaults upon it. On the ground they perform on balancing ladders, rolling barrels and globes, bicycles and unicycles and do a comical upside-down knuckle walk. Craig has often cued his chimp aerialists from a distance of 500 feet with hand signals alone, and he showed me photos of his apes performing alone aloft on a 135-foot sway pole with himself on the ground below.

"I copy nothing from other chimp acts," Hank Craig said, explaining his most unusual chimpanzees. "I watch the people-acts, and I copy them."

At the time, that seemed to me an excellent approach to chimpanzee training, and it still does. People look more into mirrors than at pictures, always much more interested in themselves than in other living creatures. In the chimpanzee, man sees an amusing caricature of himself. The hairy carbon copy of Homo sapiens is extremely popular with the public and therefore a splendid money-maker. (Very few chimp trainers enter the business for revenge as Hank Craig says he did, cash money being the usual motivation.)

Chimpanzee is the popular name for the commonest and most adaptable of all the great apes in captivity, more plentiful in America than any of the others (orangutan, gorilla and gibbon).

The orangutan is almost entirely an arboreal animal, while the gorilla is more earth-bound. The chimpanzee lies somewhere between the two, moving sometimes by brachiation (a name given by a British anthropologist, Sir Arthur Keith, to locomotion while suspended by the arms from trees) and sometimes on all fours on the earth, using the knuckles of its front feet. It is difficult for the chimpanzee to stand erect principally because of the disproportion of its limbs and the weight of its long arms. The peculiar balance of head on neck is another deterrent to an upright position, as is also the form of the pelvis and weak buttocks and calf muscles.

The word "chimpanzee" derives from Congo dialect, *ki penzi* or *chi penzi*. The chimp's proper scientific name is *Pan troglodyte* (cave-dwelling Pan; Pliny the Elder, Roman naturalist, described chimps as "satyrs").

Chimps are of the family *Pongidae* in the order of Primates, which also includes monkeys, marmosets, lemurs and man. Zoologists disagree on the number of chimpanzee varieties; there appear to be at least five: the white- and black-faced; the koolokamba; the bald-headed of the Gaboon region; and the bushy-haired Schweinfurth's chimpanzee of central tropical Africa, named for its discoverer, Herr Georg August Schweinfurth, noted ethnologist and tropical traveler, the man who established the existence of the African Pygmies.

The animals have intrigued man since remote antiquity. In 470 B.C. an expedition led by a Carthaginian named Hanno reported a meeting on the west coast of Africa with "gorillai" which later were indicated to be chimps. Spanish sailors before the end of the sixteenth century, returning from voyages to Africa, brought hair-raising tales of the great apes. Dutch scientists at the turn into the next century presented detailed descriptions and anatomical drawings of the beast. In 1740, the French naturalist, Georges Louis Leclerc de Buffon, published an illustration of the chimp in one of his many volumes of *Natural History* under the name *chimpezee*. At the same time, one was on exhibit in London and, in 1868, the catalogue of the Jardin des Plantes in Paris featured a splendid engraving of their beautiful female chimpanzee.

Circus-goers and viewers of television variety shows are most intrigued by the closeness of the chimpanzee's mannerisms to those of man, but the beast has much else in common with mankind, for anatomically and psychologically the great apes are nearer to the human animal than to any of their tailed cousins, the monkeys.

Structurally man shares many characteristics with the chimpanzee and gorilla. For instance: the embryo of both of the aforementioned anthropoids and man develops a jointed tail in its fifth week—a tail which shrivels by the eighth week and submerges, leaving a dimple at the bottom of the spine where it sinks below the surface; these dimples can sometimes be observed by students of anthropology in communities in which burlesque has not been outlawed. Apes also can catch many of man's diseases, ones to which other animals are relatively immune—syphilis, typhoid fever, measles and mumps—and they are subject to appendicitis. They react to sedatives, stimulants and poisons the same as man does.

But the greatest anatomical difference between man and the chimp is in the brain. The ape's is roughly one third the size of man's although essentially a miniature of it, no part or organ being missing, the only divergence being a difference of proportion and the degree of development of certain parts. Embryology has not revealed the various stages through which man has advanced in his climb among the anthropoids, but it has clearly shown that in the fetal body the processes of evolution are at work. Somehow the ape, during growth, replaces all the elements of physical delicacy which it possessed in the fetus with ones of strength and brutality, while man in some mysterious way retains them.

Chimpanzees rely much more on visual powers than do other animals, depend less on olfactory. Like all animals, including men and women, they become hostile mainly through frustration and hunger.

The chimpanzee's marvelous imitative factor is what makes it such a proficient circus performer. Some remarkable manlike accomplishments have been credited to this most popular of the apes. George Vierheller, Director of the St. Louis Zoo (a gentleman as well known in that town as Anheuser-Busch), is fond of telling the story of an enlightening night in a Pullman on his way home with Jackie, a chimp he had purchased from a wealthy owner on Long Island, N.Y. Jackie sported tweeds, patent-leather shoes with spats, carried a Malacca stick, flashed a spurious diamond ring, but was believed to be otherwise unusually bright. Jackie had made a nasty scene when he was asked to sleep in the baggage compartment so a chimpanzee compromise had been effected: he was permitted to sleep with Vierheller in his compartment. The zoo director awakened in the clackety-clacking night, found himself alone with the compartment light on. Before he had time to get up to investigate the disappearance of the ape, he heard the donnicker flushing in the adjoining lavatory and Jackie emerged, flipped the light switch, hopped under the covers and was soon blissfully asleep.

At the zoo, Vierheller once had a far more trying experience with chimpanzee imitation. Three of his learned apes, actors in the zoo's famous chimp show, were temporarily housed in wire-fronted crates while their regular quarters were being renovated. One morning they watched fascinated as painters began to redecorate the walls of a room near them. During the workers' lunch hour the apes pushed their way out of their boxes, dashed to the paint buckets, grabbed brushes and started to slosh floor, walls and themselves with color. They were soon discovered and, knowing they were in trouble, took off on the double—an angry shouting attendant at their heels—for the only haven they could think of, the office of the Director.

Their pal and protector was at that moment coming from his headquarters nattily attired in a fresh linen suit on his way to an important luncheon engagement at his club. The two parties met on the staircase with disastrous results to the suit. Vierheller says it is the closest he has ever come to being irked by a great ape.

Chimpanzees reached their imitative peak in America's era of vaudeville. In those times hardly a night went by that a trained chimpanzee was not rattling over the rails to fill an engagement in one of the country's multitude of vaudeville emporiums. From the gleaming Palace to the dreariest window-sill (a vaudevillian's word for a shallow stage) there were chimps imitating men, and imitating each other imitating men imitating each other.

One of the first and possibly most imitated of the ape virtuosos was called Peter the Great, a chimp about six years old. Peter performed a total of fifty-six separate stunts, which included lighting and smoking a cigar, blowing puffs of smoke from either side of the mouth; spitting accurately into a brass cuspidor; spearing banana slices with a fork; pouring tea from a pot, liquid from a bottle—uncorking and corking it; teeth-brushing, hair combing and powdering; undressing and going to bed after lighting a candle and visiting the potty; chasing a young lady while on roller skates; using hammer and screw-driver; bicycling; writing elementary graphic forms and a few of the simpler alphabetical letters (I, L, V, T, F, and W). Peter was followed on the two-a-day circuit by Consul the Great, Consuline, Consul Peter the Great, Alfred the Great and other Greats too numerous to mention.

Observers of that period of apedom were amazed by the total absence of visible direction during Peter's performance, the animal seeming to remember the exact order of the stunts. A psychologist of that time (1909), Dr. Lightner Witmer, a professor at the University of Pennsylvania, undertook to test Peter's mentality. In the Philadelphia *Public Ledger*, Professor Witmer said in part: ". . . I now believe that in a very real sense the animal himself is giving the stage performance. He knows what he is doing, he delights in it, he varies it from time to time, he understands the succession of tricks which are being called for, he is guided by word of mouth without any signal open or concealed, and the function of the trainer is exercised mainly to steady and control."

While it is likely that Peter was using his reasoning power, he probably memorized his role just as any other actor does by what latter-day psychologists call the "chaining" process in learning. Chaining is what happens when one response provides the stimulus for the next. The recitation of a poem from memory is an example of chaining; each spoken line prodding the mind to recall the next. Chaining in animals is usually induced in a positive way by food rewards at each stage of the routine; the gradual withdrawal of the feedings leads the animal to do more and more each time to get the food. Since food rewards mean little or nothing to a chimpanzee, when the system is used on this animal the snacks are replaced by kindness and praise, which animal trainers refer to as "con"-ing. In the case of certain harsh trainers, the negative approach is used, punishment and its withholding being substituted for encouraging words.

Recently an assistant professor of psychology at Barnard College, Dr. Rosemary Pierrel, and a lecturer in psychology at Columbia University, J. Gilmour Sherman, trained a well-adjusted white male rat to perform a series of stunts to demonstrate the chaining process to their students. A written description of the process covers twenty pages in the students' textbook; the performance of the rat, whose name was Barnabel, took one minute and fifty-six seconds.

Barnabel was exhibited in an aluminum and glass case four and one-half feet high. He began his routine by pressing a bar at the lower right-hand side of the enclosure, sounding a buzzer and releasing food pellets for one minute. When buzzer and food stopped, a light flashed at the case's opposite end—stimulus for the next response. At this signal, Barnabel scurried to a circular staircase and clambered to its first landing. From there he hurried across a short bridge and up a sixteen-step ladder to a second platform. There the ingenious Barnabel pulled with teeth and front paws a chain that rolled a little red vehicle to him. The rat climbed in and pedaled merrily away, covering in eight seconds a distance of twelve inches to the foot of a flight of stairs. Bustling to the third and last plateau, the rat slithered through a circular glass tube, seventeen inches long. Upon emerging Barnabel rose on his hunkers and tugged by tooth and claw the halyard of a blue and white Columbia pennant, raising it grandly aloft. He did not salute or pledge allegiance to cheese. When the flag touched the top of its pole, a buzzer sounded telling the actor that cookhouse was open again. Thereupon he popped into a small elevator and was dropped three and a half feet to the ground floor to be again rewarded with food pellets.

Not long ago I watched Miss Beatrice Dante, a French Mam'zelle known around circus backyards as "Madame Fifi," as she put her chimp Charlie (whose real name is Peanuts) through the paces of a routine that no doubt is the result of chaining training. Miss Dante was working at a Florida tourist attraction, and the act was being used as what is known in circus business as a "stall act," one in which a lengthy routine, leisurely presented, pads and stretches a thin program that is light on performers. Charlie didn't perform fifty-six separate stunts; it only *seemed* as if he did. From a hysterically comic Indian opening with the tall, very Gallic blonde showgirl masquerading as Pocahontas in a beaded buckskin chemise, feathered headdress and black pigtails, with war whoops straight from Place Pigalle, the act ran the gamut of chimpology. Charlie not only rode the bicycle and unicycle but did both blindfolded. He jounced on a pogo stick; walked, unaided, on eight-foot stilts; did the rhumba, the mambo, the Charleston, the "Missouri Waltz," and the bunny-hug. He enacted a chimp version of the $64,000 Question, which somehow managed to include the traditional chimp potty-on-head bit—always good for a nervous laugh. He paid further tribute to our modern culture by appearing as a Spaceman and the chauffeur of a "Kiddilac," and by portraying Liberace and Elvis Presley. And there was a stirring military-march finish, climaxed by a shrill shooting of the ape (PAM! poom!) by Miss Dante, followed by the dying-soldier bit by Charlie, proceeding to a dance on crutches. Grim—but that *was* the Finale. (This is entertainment for *children?*)

An act that best demonstrates the chaining process in apeology is that of a young Italian from Bagnara, Amleto Sciplini (known to circus back yards as Scallopini). Sciplini became interested in chimpanzees as a boy, when his father, an attaché to the Italian Consulate in Tangier, North Africa, brought home a chimp baby to be a little *fragalino* for his three-year-old Amletino. Sciplini began circus life as an animal helper on the Swiss Circus Knie at the age of twenty-one, began training chimps in 1947 for the British Barnum, Sir Bertram Mills. Amleto's fabulous act was brought to America in 1956 and has enthralled American audiences with the Ringling Bros and Barnum & Bailey arena circus, one of the few acts considered strong enough to work alone as a center-ring feature.

Sciplini paces his performers by soft-spoken cues, without whip or stick. For a finish the chimp troupe becomes a wild-eyed Latin jazz combo accompanying two couples of shuffling dancers. The chimps also do a fine acrobatic bar act during which one has his pants pulled off—naturally; and there is a baby-buggy bit that never fails to rouse an audience to screams of delight. In this spurt of silliness, mama-chimp pushes diapered baby-chimp through a fast airing in an open carriage climaxed by an unceremonious dumping against the ring curb, after which mama leaps into buggy grabbing the bottle. It gets a big howl, especially from women, for this is exactly what every mother in her deepest subconscious has at some time wanted to do to her own young nuisance.

Another very popular, always amusing, bit comes during a game of leapfrog as the final chimp persists in kicking the bent-over end man instead of leaping. The much-put-upon player finally runs to Sciplini whose back has been turned to the duplicity and pulls the trainer down for a whispered report in his ear of the perfidy. Then the chimp adds a surprisingly human touch. He puts his finger to temple and sadly shakes his head, indicating that his nasty antagonist is apparently "nuts." It's such a natural, human action that it gets a real rise from the audience. The bit is not new to chimp business, though it hasn't been seen in a long, long time. In the early part of this century Reuben Castang, considered by many to have been America's greatest wild-animal trainer, accomplished the same trick with his chimp troupe of ten, including Max and Morris, reputed to have been the highest-paid chimps in history ($1,500 a week—some money in those days). But Castang wasn't the originator of the leap-frog routine either. A fellow named Joe Edwards did it before him, and lord knows who did it before that gentleman and who before him. Show business is so old and chimps have been in it so long that practically every trick in the book has been done by someone somewhere sometime.

For decades zoologists have considered the chimpanzee the most intelligent of wild animals. William T. Hornaday, one-time Director of the New York Zoological Park (the Bronx Zoo) placed second on his list of comparative mammalian intellect one of the other great apes, the orangutan (along with the Indian elephant, the domestic horse and dog), but dropped the gorilla to last place. (Other positions were: third—grizzly bear, beaver, lion; fourth—wolverine; fifth—European brown bear; sixth—grey wolf, mountain goat; seventh—tiger; eighth—big-horn sheep; ninth—coyote, as well as gorilla.)

The ignominious position of the most gigantic primate in Dr. Hornaday's chart is understandable because at the time of his selection—1922—not much was known about the greatest of apes. A psychologist of that day, after conducting a number of experiments at the National Zoological Park, in Washington, D.C., on its then-young gorilla, N'Gi, reached a conclusion that the mammoth ape had the mentality of an average eighteen-month-old baby. Gorillas were greatly misunderstood then and looked upon as monsters of bestiality. None had ever been raised under conditions conducive to permitting the gorilla intellect full play. However, since those unenlightened times, two gorillas have been raised in a household, and the woman who accomplished this revolutionary step in apeology, Mrs. Gertrude Davies Lintz, states flatly that in her experience the gorilla is superior to the chimpanzee in expressiveness, emotional development and intelligence. Her belief is not based on scientific experiments since she claims that to make tests an animal must be docile and imitative, like the chimp.

Mrs. Lintz thinks that the great dignity and reserve of the gorilla, his independent, conservative and aloof manner, keep him from being a particularly good laboratory guinea pig and that he consciously does not co-operate in tests to which he is subjected.

Dr. Robert M. Yerkes, the renowned authority of primate psychology, systematically studied one of the Lintz gorillas and found that she seemed to be motivated by far more complex factors than chimpanzees; to act indifferent to situations when in reality she was deeply stirred, to be stoical to punishment or deprivation. She often baffled the scientist by choosing to do only what she found interesting. While Dr. Yerkes was forced to give the giant ape a laboratory C mark against the A and B of the chimp and orang, he finally decided that the gorilla was psychologically closest to mankind.

In temperament the chimp is less like man than woman, probably because the female is the more primitive of the human species and thus closer to the animal viewpoint. The chimp is quick to anger, just as ready to forgive. It is very solicitous. It becomes gay or depressed without warning or reason. It has strong survival instincts, is stoical in suffering and has a naturally suspicious, possessive nature. Chimps regard rats and mice with the usual housewifely revulsion. They would rather die than actually touch them. The chimp's usual method of killing the creatures is to wait until they have crawled under something such as a floor paper, then pounce and smash with one sharp bonk of the fist. With averted, horrified face the chimp quickly pinches up the paper hiding the loathsome mushy corpse and throws it from the cage.

All the emotions of the human are expressed in a chimp's face: fear, doubt, trust, reliance and affection; disapproval, jealousy, envy, malice and greed; hatred, anger, rage and terror; contentment, satiety and loneliness.

Chimps giggle and laugh, and though they express unhappiness with eyes and voice, they never shed actual tears as gorillas do. (Ringling Bros' great male gorilla used to laugh in the days when he was known as Buddy, but after he became Gargantua, the circus monster, according to his former owner, Mrs. Lintz, he never laughed again and often wept from loneliness, sometimes so much that his massive chest became wet.)

In captivity chimpanzees are habitually clean, being quite fastidious in their personal grooming. They avoid filth and mess, and intensely dislike getting their feet dirty. They have no offensive body odor and are best kept clean by oil rubs, rather than soapy baths which dry the skin too much. Chimps are usually innately modest, some to the point of being ruled by a morbid sense of propriety.

Chimps have been bred in captivity, and the young are born singly as in humans, though there is on record a birth of twins to one Monona, a chimp who lived like a lady in Havana, Cuba, with a couple dozen others of her kind in a veritable chimpanzee paradise kept by an interesting Frenchwoman, Madame Rosalia Abreu. The lady maintained a famous collection of living primates for forty years and at her death a large part of it was acquired by Dr. Yerkes, previously mentioned, for the Yale University Laboratory of Primate Biology of which he was then the director.

Baby chimps, just like human babies, become very much attached to "cozies"—those comforting bits of blankets that persist in babyhood until cuddling and the laundry has shredded them into limbo. By nature, the chimp being carried clings to the carrier's torso front, wrapping back legs about it and hanging from the neck. The infant gorilla can be trundled about in the buttocks-and-shoulders style of the human infant, but the chimp must be broken to this method. Chimps like human babies are most afraid of the dark and of falling, both fears very likely holdovers from their jungle heritage— practical ones for a species that nests with mother by night high in the trees.

Infant chimps love pull-toys, swings and teeter-totters, just as kids do, and both boy and girl apes adore dolls, often making their own from whatever is at hand—lollipop sticks, modeling clay, bits of cloth.

Chimpanzees in captivity get along well with human children except when adults are present. Then they violently hate them, regarding them as rivals for affection. A chimp that never attacks grownups will often gladly take a bite of a child just on jealous principles.

Around the American circus there is a widespread notion that chimps hate clowns also, because of their grotesque make-ups, but the blame of the violent reaction of ape vs. clown lies with the funnyman himself. Our native variety subconsciously considers the chimp a rival clown (or worse yet, a *hulligan* rival clown—a foreigner), a threat to his unsteady domain and treats him accordingly— with nasty, bitter malice. I have been told by European chimp trainers that in England and on the Continent the chimpanzee is regarded by the clown as a fellow artiste; his privacy and dignity are respected, and there is absolutely no trouble of any sort between the two laugh-provokers.

Mentally man is distinguished from the chimp by greater powers of reasoning, concentration and appreciation, the psychological difference between the two primates being relative rather than absolute. A chimp's activity in social life is controlled by stimulus and response as it is in any living thing whether it be plant, earthworm, Picasso, Dr. Einstein or an idiot—the extent of participation depending upon the degree of intelligence. We are much further from being sure of this degree in the animal world than within the framework of mankind, where it is still not completely understood down to the last decimal point.

All of us have shutters on our souls. What we respond to depends upon the fullness of our life. We can only be stimulated by what we see, hear or experience; respond to what we know. This is as true of ape as it is of man. Chimps can absorb social graces when they are exposed to them. Joe Mendi, the vaudeville chimp, was introduced to whiskey by a frequent guest at his owner's home, whose first act on arrival always was to take Joe upstairs to the guest room for a smoke and a little nip. One day, while his masters were absent from the establishment for the afternoon, the chimp contrived to snitch the keys to his cage and that of his lady love. The pair escaped. Joe immediately escorted his friend to the guest room in the main house, and when his owners returned that evening they found Joe and Maggie slumped blissfully in the floor of the liquor closet amid a collection of well-swigged jugs.

A chimp named Yawnie, one of fourteen exhibited at the Chicago Century of Progress fair in 1933 by Mrs. Lintz, was a dark horse, her past a mystery to her new owners. She would fly into an uncontrollable rage when told, "Don't do that," and it was concluded that those words in her previous life meant that she was about to be struck. The new trainer stopped saying them, and the ape immediately lost her fear and bad manners.

Although the chimpanzee's symbolic processes are superior to those of other mammals, they are rudimentary and not so versatile as the human ones. Animal psychologists believe that chimpanzees, in mimicking human activities, are more rigidly bound by sensory conditions (such as food and punishment) and to given routines than is the older human child, which at first is similarly limited; children, they say, go on to higher stages whereas chimps remain on the lower level, never learning the abstract symbols for their actions.

George Vierheller, Director of the St. Louis Zoo, home of the most accomplished and most publicized performing chimpanzees in America, believes that the chimp is superior to a child until they both reach five; then the human forges ahead. Other authorities have placed this parallel level at three years.

If the chimp could have the same advantages of culture for the same thousands of years that the dog and horse have enjoyed in association with mankind, perhaps it would make remarkable social

advances. Chimpanzees, tamed and carefully bred over a long period of time, might be found useful to our society beyond being entertainers; perhaps only as household pets, but I'm afraid that some sharpy would soon be conscripting apes into occupations not requiring too much mental exertion. They might make excellent domestic workers, collectors of highway tolls, time-payment harassers and process servers. Imagine trying to avoid a chimpanzee process server!

There is some precedent for this sort of ape exploitation. An ancient book (*Voyage to the Coast of Africa* by M. Grandpré) tells of a sea-going chimp who helped unfurl and handle sails, spliced rope and attended to the oven in the galley, keeping the live coals from falling out and informing the baker as to the exact moment when the heat was right for the bread dough. Fred Bradna, in his book, *The Big Top*, tells of a chimp trained to act as guard and bartender of an iced-tub of beer in the circus backyard, opening the bottles by a flick of his powerful teeth. The ape boniface of this co-op club was able to limit his customers to paid-up members, driving off by teeth-baring threats of violence and coarse screamings any outsider trying to horn in. Mr. Bradna does not explain how he was able to keep the chimp from helping himself, so perhaps the whole story can be charged up to circus hyperbole, but it is an amusing idea.

Many zoologists feel that the ape's greatest intellectual deficiency is its apparent inability to master words and sentences to form speech that can be understood on the human level. The general psychological superiority of man over ape is emphasized by the human being's capacity for a systematic code of language symbols. According to *his* standards, man can talk and the chimp cannot.

A basic difference between human and chimp babies is that young apes do not babble, whereas man's offspring do, thus learning to use the lips, tongue and breathing apparatus, conditioning them for the speaking of words. But the inability of chimps to speak goes deeper than that. Man has more outer layer of brain grey matter (cortex) in proportion to his weight than has the chimp. Man also has an increased number of nerve cells in a more complex arrangement in the cortical layers. Both of these factors improve man's capacity for more complex functions of acquiring knowledge and sorting it out. In diseases, such as paresis, in which pathological degeneration of the grey matter tissue occurs, it is well known that there is a definite dwindling of ability to cope with symbolic names and meanings.

Mr. and Mrs. Keith Hayes, a man-and-wife team of scientists at Stanford University, found in their chimp, Viki by name, a low-level interest in language. The most important word to their subject was "No," and the young research psychologists estimated that Viki eventually learned to comprehend about fifty word groupings in the form of expressions or commands. They learned that Viki understood recombinations of familiar words within a sentence. She was eventually able to tell what was wanted when words from two separate commands with which she was familiar were used together in a third command. For example, "Kiss me" and "Bring the dog," became "Kiss the dog." But trying to learn too many words confused the chimp, and the pedagogues, in eighteen months of conscientious coaching, were never able to teach their hirsute student to identify her own eyes, ears, nose, hands or toes—and make the lesson stick. Some days she had every member down to a T; at other times she was completely at sea.

Mrs. Lintz found that the chimps which she raised in her home understood about as many words as a three-year-old child; the longer the association with humans, the more the understanding. One of her chimps, Captain Jiggs, knew colors in the abstract, being able to select on request various colors of clothes from his wardrobe. Another of that lady's apes, Maggie, was so fond of the color red that she practically wore out a set of red-plaid car cushions by fondling and patting. Apparently all other colors looked alike to her.

There are limits to an ape's advancement in human environment; a saturation point is reached beyond which it may not be beneficial for the beast to go. Trained show-business chimpanzees usually reach this stage at about age five. Then they react, often violently, against the sum total of what has been foisted upon them and temporarily revert to jungle mores. At the St. Louis Zoo, a favorite chimp performer named Roy, who weighed in at 140 pounds, picked up a trainer, weighing 188, and threw him in the moat. (It wouldn't have been so bad had not the Zoo Board members en masse been visiting the performance that day.) After its violent age has been reached a chimp (though he no longer has the heart or his earlier performing zest) can still be exhibited until he is from nine to twelve years old. After that chimps turn ugly, become too tough to handle and must be retired. No one has tried turning a full-grown chimp back into the jungle to see if he might be happier there. Most old chimps just fade away in a cage—alone, unwanted and growing meaner by the minute.

The greatest permanent collection of performing chimpanzees in this country is at the St. Louis, Missouri, Zoo situated in an eighty-three-acre park on the site of the historic St. Louis World's Fair of 1904. The chimpanzees of this distinguished zoological garden perform in their own specially built arena and are considered by that Mid-Western city's Chamber of Commerce one of its greatest civic assets. The annual gate of the St. Louis Zoo is close to two and one-half million people, over 75 per cent drawn from out of state, a healthy segment from foreign lands. There is no admission charge, yet the Zoo boasts assets of almost three million dollars and earns yearly a net income of almost $100,000 (above expenses of around a half million). Income from taxes (about thirty-eight cents a head per year), sales of animals, interest on U.S. Government obligations, and miscellaneous items annually comes to almost $400,000, not quite covering operating expenses. The deficit is made up, plus a sizable profit, by the net income from the Zoo's refreshment stands; in the year ending March, 1957, this figure was $127,920. That means a lot of thirsty, ravenous souvenir-buyers visit the St. Louis Zoo in season—fifty thousand on a good summery weekend. Mostly they come to see the performing animal shows—elephants, big cats and chimps—whose arenas hold an aggregate of ten thousand at one sitting. The extravaganza of the big apes is the most popular by far, and performances, lasting almost three quarters of an hour, are given thrice daily except Mondays.

The man responsible for building the St. Louis Zoo chimps into such a smashing crowd-puller is George Vierheller, a bouncy, cigar-chomping septuagenarian with a raspy voice like that of an over-worked bally-man on a carny—this delivery a heritage from a throat operation for a stuck fish bone. Vierheller has the puckish face of a gentleman who has aged with happiness about him. He has a distinct gnomish quality: hair white and thick; a magnificent wedge of nose over a spurt of chin, and a smile that comes easily, crinkling his merry eyes into mere slits. The great white-haired father of chimps came to the Zoo when he was a young man of thirty-six and *it* was nothing but a dung-spattered bird cage left over from the World's Fair. His father had been a mailman whose eyes went bad and put him out of the postcard-reading business. Young George, aged twelve, took a job as runner for a grain and stock brokerage firm and by studying at night became a telegrapher at eighteen.

The young telegrapher's wrist gave out in 1914 and he took a political job as clerk of the Board of Elections, passing from there to Secretary of the newly organized Zoological Board of Control in 1918. Three years later he was Superintendent of the Zoo. Then he popped into the Director's seat and has been there ever since—though he doesn't really sit down very much.

In passing through St. Louis, I stopped off to see the world's greatest zoological showman—the Buffalo Bill, John Phillip Sousa, P. T. Barnum of the zoo business. He wasn't in his office on the second floor of the marbled Monkey House, which is charming and antiquated enough to suit the most romantic child's expectation of a monkey mansion. Miss Ettinger, the secretary, told me she *thought* I'd find her boss with Phil, the gorilla, though she couldn't be sure. "He's pretty hard to keep up with," she said. "He scoots all over the grounds; we never know just *where* he might be."

But he was with the mammoth ape all right. Phil is the nearest living thing to King Kong, that horrendous creature of the silent films who took such monstrous liberties with Fay Wray. Phil is coal black, weighs over six hundred pounds, and compared to him Johnny North's highly touted gorilla, the late Gargantua, was a potbellied sissy. Phil's head seemed to me as big as a bushel basket; his fingers were as thick as a child's wrist. He romps in a fifty-foot square cage (with swimming pool) and plays with a tire from a twelve-ton truck.

"He wouldn't hurt you intentionally," said George Vierheller, after he had greeted me. "Watch this," he added. "I always bring him a bottle of Budweiser every morning, but today's Election Day and you can't buy beer, so I have an ice-ball instead." From behind his back he took the sweet-flavored ice-cone and passed it through the bars to Phil who took it, raised it to his lips, then, discovering it wasn't his usual malt tonic, did a delightful double-take at his human friend. Vierheller chuckled at his innocent joke and the gorilla slowly ate the cone, savoring each careful lick. Phil is named for Vierheller, using the Director's middle name. "You couldn't call a gorilla George," he said. "That's a *lion* name."

Phil put his gigantic black face against the bars and looked at me with his deeply set beetle-browed eyes. The look, as human as any I've ever received, had a disquieting penetration. Vierheller put his own face against the hairy one and whispered little nothings to his friend.

"He weighed twenty-six pounds when we got him in 1941," the Director then said to me. "He cost us three thousand dollars, but I wouldn't part with him today for any price—even though he's likely worth more than fifty thousand." Vierheller sniffed the air for the penetration of the acrid, not unpleasant, body odor—more human than animal—of the monster creature. If a gorilla stops stinking, a gorilla owner starts worrying.

Leaving Phil looking disconsolate, we made an informal back-door visit to Roy, the temperamental chimp star who was banned to a cage after throwing his trainer in the moat. At the sight of his friend, the chimp, chattering happily and mooing madly, came rushing across the spacious cage from its front where he had been evil-eying the public.

Vierheller is fond of saying, "Apes are my best friends." Since he established chimpanzee performances at the wonder zoo thirty-three years ago, he claims to have exchanged at least three kisses each day with various members of the ape brotherhood; a grand total of 30,987 simian smootches. (Mathematicians please note: no chimp shows Mondays.) Chimp kisses need not be monotonous. A chimpanzee is able to form with his peculiarly elastic lips a definite point and undulate it completely around the mouth.

Vierheller gave Roy a kiss through the steel barrier that separated them, then put his hand close to the bars and the chimp began to pick at it searchingly. "Not fleas," said Vierheller. "He gets tiny tidbits of salt. They're like candy to a chimp; they all love them." After Roy had his fill of Directorial salt, Vierheller said, "It's just about show time at the chimp arena, so let's go."

He strode off at such a brisk clip I could barely keep up. "An official from the Detroit Zoo is visiting us today, and you and he can watch the show from the roof of the sound-projection booth," continued Vierheller as we raced along the promenade. "You'd never get a seat now; that place'll be jammed—just you wait and see." And so it was.

As Mr. Stoneley, the Detroit zoo man, and I met at the edge of the buzzing mob, Vierheller whispered in his husky carny voice, "Watch your pocketbooks." I was reminded of the sign I once saw alongside the altar of a Mexican cathedral: *"Cuidado con los Rateros"* (Beware of the Pickpockets). The Detroit zoologist and I gingerly climbed the straight ladder leaning against a small building to a tarred roof high in the hot St. Louis sunshine overlooking the chimpanzee amphitheater—a half-saucer of packed humanity facing a broad-roofed hemispherical stage fronted by a wide water-filled, flower-edged moat.

The chimpanzee show has outgrown two arenas since 1925, when the first production opened on a stage in the then-new Primate House, and the ape opera seems well on its way to outgrowing this one. In that first cast were two performers; now there are eleven of the zoo's total of twenty-four chimps, which is more than are in residence at any other U. S. zoo.

The very first entertainer at the St. Louis Zoo was Sam, an orangutan. However, this shaggy redhead was more a busker than a genuine Thespian. His chief stunt was to ride a tricycle, accompanied by his trainer, along the zoo paths, the main object (a Vierheller inspiration) to lead people to the refreshment stand.

The chimpanzee frolics at the St. Louis Zoo these days are elaborately mounted affairs, with expensive riggings and complicated props, specially designed sets and costumes. Both Stoneley and I were fascinated and astounded by the 1957 edition entitled "A Trip to the Moon." Neither of us had ever before seen such an array of cleverly executed chimpanzee tricks.

Following an opening promenade entry of the entire cast of eleven, decked out in sleek satellite suits and outer-space helmets of plastic, there was a fast interlude of unicycling followed by a fantastic turn on an insane high bicycle made from a brass bedstead. Then from teeterboard launching pads, chimps were catapulted through the air like mad rockets, and close on the heels of this acrobatic turn came a bit of beer-barrel rolling on a most complicated high rigging. Then one of the apes performed on the rola-bola, a small board balanced atop a free-rolling cylinder. After this was an exciting romp of trapeze tricks, finalized by several chimpanzees executing giant pinwheel swings the full 360 degrees around the bar as the others played a lively game of leap frog on the stage below. I reasoned that surely this was the act's Finale. "What possibly could follow?" I asked Stoneley. But it was only the beginning. As soon as the ape aerialists climbed from their spinning perches, four of the chimps became a motorcycle stunt team, executing various acrobatic maneuvers on a fast-circling motorbike, their finish trick being an unbelievable four-high pyramid. Then came a barrel roll by a pony with chimp rider; a neat pony-drill with chimp jockeys; and a series of table-catches. In this pleasant bit of chimquestrianism, the ape-rider leaps nimbly from his pony's back as it runs beneath a high pedestal and, as the steed comes from under it, leaps back into the saddle.

This second stanza of the show also included rope-jumping, two chimps whirling the strand for another. I half expected them to chant one of those little-girl rhymes about Rin-Tin-Tin-sat-on-a-pin or Marguerite-go-wash-ya-feet-the-Board-a-Health's-acrost-the-street. Then there was a spate of acrobatics (back flips, front flips, cart-wheels) and some more rope-jumping with a fast finish of "red-hot-pepper." Then came a session on high and low stilts, followed by some rapid roller-skating that climaxed with the skaters zooming from sharply inclined ramps pulled by chimp-driven motorboats on wheels.

Next, a small baby-grand piano was wheeled onstage, candelabra placed on it, and there appeared Liberchimpski, in gold-sequined tail coat, with Brother George. Liberchimpski, after getting a tremendous rise out of the audience with an almost libelous toothy smile, sat at the piano and knuckled out a fair rendition of "Mary Had a Little Lamb." This show-stopper was followed by Elvis Chimp-ley, with guitar and rock-and-rolling tailless torso.

Grand Finale of the chimp jamboree was an invasion of the planet Earth from outer simian space. The interplanetary interlopers whirled through the air in auto-propelled rockets suspended from an aerial track, and bombarded with meteorites (silver-painted basket-balls) the earth-apes circling the stage in battery-powered rocket ships. The exchange was unbelievably noisy and lively, the aim of the flying chimps at times deadly accurate. This was more than a carefully re-hearsed stunt; these guys were *really* out for blood. It was a hysterically wild finish to the most marvelous display of chimp virtuosity I've ever seen—or ever hope to see. A stunned Mr. Stoneley agreed as we climbed down the ladder, one hand on our pocketbooks.

A proud, beaming Veirheller was waiting for us. "First-rate, wasn't it?" he asked. "Now we'll go backstage," he said, "and meet the stars and Mike, their trainer."

The area behind the scenery was almost as large as that in front. "Got to be big," said the Director "to handle all our equipment. Being a permanent operation, we're able to build props and riggings that no traveling show could afford or be able to carry around. Besides we do all our own scene painting back here, too. We change the show every spring. Last year during the Centennial it was 'Chimpanzee Junction' —kind of ole-time vaudeville. We've had a version of 'Showboat' and one year it was a rootin'-tootin' Wild West show with Chimpanzee Indians, Chimpallo Bill and Chimp-annie Oakley, stagecoaches, donkeys and Conestoga wagons."

On racks along the back wall hung several hundred chimp costumes, most of them neatly covered by plastic bags, a couple of dozen changes for each performer. The wardrobe is made by a local concern, which donates it to the zoo as a public service.

"Once in a while," said Vierheller, "when I take one of the boys downtown for a haircut, we drop into one of the big stores, Famous-Barr or Sears, for a new outfit of street clothes. We usually find something nice in the Boys' Department. At first we used to startle the floorwalkers, but they've gotten used to us by now. The chimps love to ride the escalators and look in the triple mirrors. I have to be careful about those trips, though; they're all so jealous of each other."

Then, as a short slight fellow, with a heavy auburn pompadour, sauntered over to us, the Director added, "Here's Mike now—Mike Kostial, our chimp trainer. He's been around the zoo twenty-two years. His father was my first lion trainer; worked a kindergarten act. Mike's almost forty, but he sure doesn't look it. That's what working around animals does for you—keeps you young."

Mike took us along the cages to introduce his accomplished actors. Jocko, Tiny, Jose, Jack, Duke and Danny, Carl, Chico, Jimmy, Smokey and Sambo. "Sambo's the one that we let work at the refreshment stand once in a while," said Mike. "He also knows how to light the boss's cigars."

"Money is no object around here," said Kostial after Vierheller and his out-of-town guest had left to view the Zoo's newest acquisitions. "If I want a certain prop, Vierheller he says 'Get it, I don't care how much it costs.' But maybe it won't work, I say. 'Get it,' he says, 'it'll work.' He has a lot of confidence in his chimpanzees. And we get the very best chimps available. The Zoo buys them on a trial basis, and we don't keep one that doesn't measure up to our standards. We pay a lot more than most places, usually above market price. Chimps now are running around seven hundred dollars."

Mike took one last look around the backstage quarters and then said, "We can get some sandwiches and coffee at the refreshment stand. There's a little private place out in back with a picnic table and benches where we can sit and talk."

On our way we picked up young Dick McGraw, the Zoo's new lion trainer, a perpetually smiling twenty-six-year-old from Kansas City by way of Thousand Oaks, California, where he was a protégé of the famous tiger trainer, Mabel Stark.

"I'm the new kindergarten teacher," said Dick.

"And he's the youngest in the business," added Mike.

The Zoo had just retired its aging big-cat performers, a troupe that was beginning to creak like a moss-back baseball club, and had brought young Dick in to break a new group of fledgings: six one-year-old lions; a sun bear and cheetah aged two; and a pair of lions and a tiger three years old.

Skirting the busy clamor of the refreshment stand's front counter we three went to a small courtyard in back of the low structure. Dick and I sat at a well-weathered wooden table alongside a pile-up of metal wheelbarrows while Mike went for the provender. He came back with a stack of sandwiches and a cluster of bottles of soda pop.

When Mike was sixteen, he told me, he had four chimpanzees under training, but at eighteen he lost interest in chimps, began seriously to notice girl primates and didn't get back again to chimps until about eleven years later, after the war, when he took on ten out-law chimps—ones considered too tough for training.

I asked him what was the first thing he learned about handling chimps.

"Don't show off," he answered. "With any animal, don't show off—and that especially includes girls. When I was just a kid, once I tickled a bear's stomach and she come down on me like a ton of bricks and beat the bee-jeezus outa me. My old man said, 'That'll teach you a goddam lesson; don't show off with animals.' Those old-time trainers were tough. My dad once made me pick up a piece of hot metal just to see if I could take it. I still think the hard way is always the best way."

Mike has two kids (now fourteen and nine) and I was curious as to whether he planned to make them animal trainers.

"No!" he said emphatically, then added quietly, "but that's just what my dad always said about me, too. He tried to make a house-painter out of me; sent me to a vocational trade school. It helped a little; I design and paint all the sets for the chimp shows here."

I knew that an important factor in the ape curriculum of the St. Louis Zoo is a period in which the animal enters the world of human primates. The chimps, of course, go to the home of Mike Kostial in the western suburbs of the city, but other apes have gone to other zoo people's bailiwicks. An orangutan, who lived for several months in a playpen in the home of Zoo official, Moody Lentz, refused to eat and was despondent for days when he was returned to the Zoo. The problem was solved in a characteristic Vierheller way. Every employe was requested to drop by Rusty's cage once each day to give him a word or two of human love, and soon the ape was readjusted to cage life. A young gorilla, Bobo, became so homesick on returning to the Zoo after being reared at the home of ape-house keeper, Frank Florsek, that he developed insomnia. Frank simply brought pillow and blanket from home and slept in the cage with Bobo each night until, after a week, the ape was finally able to sleep soundly. Mrs. Florsek still tucks a little surprise into her husband's lunch box each day for Bobo.

"At my house," said Mike, "the big trouble before the kids grew up was to keep them and the chimps from playing catchers and ripping up the place. Now it's mostly to keep the chimps from turning the lights on at night, wasting electricity, and from raiding the icebox. Duke likes fried chicken, hot dogs, cherry pie and catsup, but you offer him stuff like that at the Zoo and he looks at you like he thinks you're nuts. The chimps at home watch television, too, but I don't think they really enjoy it; they only pretend to so they can be with people."

I asked if the apes wore clothes when at home. "Only the baby ones wear diapers," he said. "We can't take too many chances. Our chimps don't really like to wear clothes, though there are some that does. I knew of a chimp that used to escape a lot from his cage, but he wouldn't leave unless he was dressed in something, even if it didn't exactly fit."

Fitting shoes to chimps is next to impossible. It's like finding shoes to fit the human hand, for the ape really has four hands, as a thick muscular toe jutting from its long, slender foot, is much like our thumb and has the same maneuverability. Any ordinary shoe cramps this great digit and it loses all its utility as a balancing unit. Knitted form-fitting booties can be used on chimps but they soon shred into an irreparable tangle. Rubber boots are suitable, and leather moccasins will last about a month on an active chimp, but tennis shoes or sneakers seem to be the most practical.

"We've broken our chimps to associate clothes with freedom, so they tolerate them," explained the St. Louis Zoo trainer. "They'll put them on by themselves, but we have to take them off, otherwise they'd rip them to pieces. Zippers are a big help in dressing themselves, but they can be embarrassing too—they get too fascinated with how they work and zip their pants up and down in front of the public. That sort of thing can break up an audience and ruin your routine right quick."

Mike Kostial prefers male chimpanzees for a very practical reason. He claims that they are able to perform two years longer than the female. He likes to get his potential performers when they are about three years old and weigh from thirty to thirty-five pounds. "Then they're tops for performance," he said. A first-class chimp will last six or seven years in a good, fast show.

"I look for good disposition mostly," said Mike continuing to outline his personal chimp qualifications. "I don't want no mopers, I like to get one that's feisty—always in trouble. You can tell the real smart ones; they're highly superstitious of everything. And you gotta have one tough guy in every troupe; he's the boss-man. You always want to have a boss around."

The St. Louis Zoo chimp professor said as far as he was concerned unicycle riding is the hardest trick to break, however he has had chimps who were able to do that one-wheel balancing almost without training. One named Nero actually performed the stunt all by himself with no coaching whatsoever. But Nero was special; he also devised for himself a tightrope back-somersault. The bicycle can be mastered by a really intelligent chimp in two days, but average learning time is about three weeks. Stilt-walking is taught low at first, the height increased as the ape becomes more skillful, the method the same as that used on a small boy. In order to play reed instruments, a chimp must first be taught to blow through his mouth alone. To accomplish this, Mike holds his own nose and blows a horn encouraging the ape to imitate him. Kostial has taught his troupe to play basketball (jungle rules), a crude form of tennis, and when I talked to him, he had just about broken in a football eleven. The often-seen trick of chimp head-shaking (to indicate "yes" and "no" or, with fore-finger to temple, the state of being loco) is what Kostial calls a "freak trick," something that the animal does naturally but which must be noticed and then developed into a trick—though not a very dependable one, he feels.

The chimpanzee's hyperactivity and naturally distrustful nature make it a difficult subject for training. In captivity it is an extremely nervous animal and easily absorbs panic from others. (This is why escaped chimps are usually judged to be dangerously mad and shot.)

A chimp trainer must have patience, tireless industry and a natural love for the animal—plus a great deal of firmness, food bribes not being advisable for an ape.

"I try mostly to 'con' them along, but if they get rough with you," said Kostial explaining his training methods to me, "you have to hurt them a little. There is nothing more dangerous per pound than an angry chimpanzee. The little stick we use don't hurt the chimp much; when a chimp is mad, you could swing into him with a two-by-two, like a ball bat, and it wouldn't hurt."

Some trainers of chimpanzees use what is known in the trade as a "hot shot," a stick containing batteries that is able to give out a formidable electric shock, but all of the ape trainers I've encountered believe that kind words plus the occasional authoritative use of a light switch are enough inducement for the animal, and that a kiss gets better results than a banana.

Mike gave me a pretty good description of an exasperated chimpanzee. "He whacks his head, screams and stamps with both feet. His hair stands all bristled up, and he gets a 'come one, come all' look. His eyes are like taking the needle. He goes temporarily insane, into another world. He grabs for your hand and if he gets it, he pulls you in for a bite. I had sixteen holes once in my arm from a chimp attack. They bite your ankles, too, but seldom go for the neck or face. The most painful bite a chimp can inflict is by pinching your fingernails between his teeth—man, that hurts!"

The chimpanzee is an arrogant bluffer, but no trainer calls the bluff unless he is well prepared to back up his stand with all his might. A trainer who weakens might just as well give up trying to work with that particular ape. Chimps are great cheaters, chopping a little from a trick one day, a little more the next, some more the following. Unless this short-cutting is nipped in the bud, soon they are not doing the stunt at all.

"If you have a chimp that's getting old and balky," said Kostial, "it's no good beating him in a last try to get one more year out of him. He'll call you on it; but you can 'con' him into it. A chimp only bites from being forced, from aggravation or being pushed too far. Give him a little sweet talk, and he'll do wonders."

When I asked just how strong is a chimp, Mike said, "I've had one grab my two hands and it was like someone nailed me on a cross. A chimp can handle as many men as he can get ahold of. I've had a thirty-pound animal get me down and bite; they just get ahold and flip you over like a jujitsu wrestler. You see a trainer with a stiff leg, crippled hand or knee caps—chances are he's a chimp man. Al Fleet, Leo Carroll, Ira Watkins—they all got the same thing—a stiff hand from a chimp bite. The orangutan and the gorilla keep chewing on you; the chimp is a hit-and-runner, but he keeps coming back. He knows you can't correct him in front of the audience. You gotta watch them all the time. A big one will secretly squeeze a baby's hand just to start a ruckus; they're just like kids. You gotta watch for fights; if one breaks out it busts up the act."

A chimp that is not angry can be kept on normal good behavior by a simple twist on one of his large ears. A group of chimps can sometimes be kept in line by the use of a visible symbol of something mysterious and all-powerful. Mrs. Gertrude Davies Lintz tells of her own use of a bogeyman, a weird carved head about the size of a man's fist and mounted on a short stick. It had a dark snarling face and a mop of wooly hair. She pretended to be forever frightened of it, shrinking and shivering away from this evil devil with trembling voice, choked with fright. Her lesson, the stock in trade of every English nanny, was so strongly presented that eventually Mrs. Lintz could enter the chimps' playroom in the midst of a free-for-all rumble, lay the hateful object on the floor and cause the biting, shrieking, kicking and hair-pulling apes to retreat in fear to the farthest corners and the hidingest rugs and blankets. Finally Mrs. Lintz's ape family became so conditioned to the bogeyman that she merely had to speak of him to get a desired reaction. But nonetheless she carried the head, detached from its stick, in her pocket for years—just in case some ape decided to retrogress.

Chimps have a very definite quality of solicitude. George Vierheller has witnessed many demonstations of this very human trait in the great ape. One of the fans of the chimp Nero, a St. Louis corporation executive's wife, was once invited to take a spin with the ape around the Zoo promenades in one of the little battery-powered automobiles. Nero started out with such a jerk that the lady oomphed over backwards into the gravel. Nero was appalled. He leaped from his driver's seat, rushed back and helped the fallen lady back into the limousine. She was a true sport and graciously took her seat again, bracing herself a little better. This time Nero very, very gently accelerated, but he kept looking back to see if his friend was still with him.

Mike Kostial frequently takes advantage of this chimpanzee

quality of sympathetic solicitude. In training his chimps once for a rodeo number, he was struck by a pistol carelessly flung by a cattle-rustling ape. Mike went out like a light. The chimp who had been responsible immediately dismounted, ran to his boss and bent over him, patting and churuping until Mike regained consciousness. Now Kostial often fakes falls and faints to get co-operation from performers who are being stubborn.

The St. Louis Zoo has at times turned its educated chimps over to probing psychologists wanting to test them on problems never encountered before. In one of these experiments a scatter of chair, table, a couple of long poles and some barrels in a large room was the means for gaining access to a stock of bananas hung from the ceiling. Each of the apes under observation worked out its own solution, the job of knocking down the fruit averaging fifteen minutes on the first try, dropping to a speedy four minutes on a second run a few days later. In a competition to fit various shaped blocks into their proper holes a four-and-a-half-year-old chimp bested a boy of the same age by seven seconds.

People who have worked closely with chimps have a theory that they burn themselves out by a constant striving to be something other than what they are. A dog is happy just to be a dog; an elephant will be an elephant long after the peanut perishes; tigers never want to change their stripes. But chimps seem to be ever pushing upward, with more than just a will to survive, trying through desperate efforts to learn, to overcome the fatigue and discouragement of their failure to bridge what is likely an unbridgeable gap between themselves and man. A fictional story which appeared in *The New Yorker* magazine some years ago comes to mind. It was by Russell Maloney and concerned the testing by a writer of the preposterous theory that if a group of apes were confined for a long period with typewriters they would eventually turn out all of the world's great literature. I don't remember the details exactly, but it seems to me the chimpanzees were chained to typewriters in a greenhouse, of all unlikely places (but, yes, I'm sure it was a greenhouse; possibly something to do with the tropical-like temperature). Something went wrong with the experiment; the chimps went madly berserk and all had to be eliminated by gunshot. The story ended with the last dying chimp crawling bleeding to his typewriter. He tapped fitfully through his last moments, then slumped to the floor. When the paper was removed it was found to contain the first paragraph of *Uncle Tom's Cabin*.

Psychologists have said that the great apes, while able to profit by their own experiences, are unable to communicate them to others. This is simply intellectual presumption. Because savage primates differ from human ones does not mean that no advanced system of communication exists among them. A great variety of movements and sounds which specifically influence their fellows in certain behavior have been observed in chimps. And certain arts and sciences, embryonic to be sure, are perpetuated as heritage of the species—such as nest building and brachiation. There are even elements of rudimentary esthetic perception among chimpanzees, the beasts in the wild occasionally adorning themselves with clay, bits of fruit and plants and participating in crude dances. We don't really know to what extent apes are able to touch other apes mentally or emotionally, any more than we know that we are able to pass on our own knowledge to species of animals other than two-legged human anthropoids (and there exists some doubt that this exchange is always ideal). Do you really know that an animal understands *exactly* what you are saying to it? I don't believe so. And neither does a little-remembered naturalist of another day, Dr. William J. Long, a Congregational minister, explorer and writer who made headlines fifty years ago by his fiery arguments with President Theodore Roosevelt on nature subjects. Dr. Long, in his posthumously published book (he died in 1952, aged eighty-six) says: "All thought except my own is strange to me; I am never sure of it but can only infer and then estimate it from the actions of the animal under observation." It's a good thing to paste on anybody's whip.

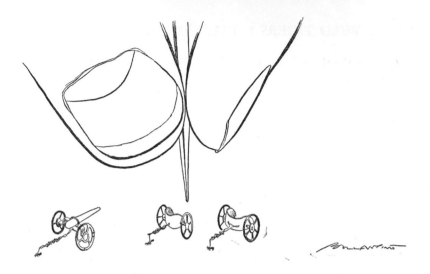

There's No Business Like
Flea Business

Yes, Virginia, there is a Flea Circus where talented trained fleas waltz in hoopskirts, operate a merry-go-round and juggle; where they kick footballs, race madly about in minikin chariots, tote teeny cannons and pledge frenetic allegiance to the flag of the Irish Free State. Such a marvelous academy can be visited after 2 P.M. any day except Tuesday in the lower depths of a penny-arcade emporium in New York off Times Square, on the south side of west Forty-Second Street between Broadway and Eighth Avenue.

This glittery segment of Manhattan's most famous east-west street is a neonized jungle, razzmatazz all the way; a notorious, gaudy midway leading to the topside of Hell's Kitchen, that hard-boiled neighborhood skirting the midtown West Side water front. Day and night the long block is thronged with riffraff, demimonde irregulars and sleazy down-at-heels transients, looking for a few hours escape from the humdrum—a cheap thrill, love, companionship, a bargain or a tempting bellyfull of dubious nutrition.

An unbroken façade of fiercely competitive operations lines each side of the street, and it takes a bit of serious doing to single out the Flea Circus. The flaring fluorescent marquees of ten grind-house movies specializing in canned slapstick, blood'n-thunder violence and sex in all its multifarious manifestations bash the sidewalks with a noonday brightness.

Sizzling pizza parlors vie with hamburger havens reeking of fried onions. There are orange-juice and hot-dog oases to snare the two-bit trade, and there is a busy, bustling Automat for people who like to eat from slots. A peppering of brassy shops offer foreign cameras, rifles with telescopic sights, portable radios, flashy sports clothes, off-beat paperbacks, dog-eared sexology and art-nudes magazines, reprints of Balzac, the Marquis de Sade and Erskine Caldwell. And there are bazaars set up for group games of chance, such as Pokerino and Fascination, the latter a form of electronic Bingo.

Smack-dab in the middle of all this hoop-la is the Amusement Center, an alluring trading post offering on its street level a welter of devices designed to separate nickels and dimes from the gillies. On display are hand-painted neckties sporting full-blown, air-brushed, nude nymphs (some with three-dimensional bosoms); daintily (and hastily) decorated turtles; Statues of Liberty cast in metallic plastic; fluorescent Madonnas; real-silk cushion covers printed in simulated embroidery with the most sentimental echoes of love (with or without fringe). Waiting to be fed within the hustling compound are a variety of ingenious mechanical games, innumerable pinball machines and a handful of antiquated cast-iron movieolas.

Deep inside the large room the paying guests blast away at the battered birds, pipes and creaking targets of an old-fashioned shooting gallery. Other clients take careful bead on electronic rabbits, bears or Space Invaders. By crossing with silver the dusty palm of a waxen grandmother, true believers have the future unveiled (courtesy of Mike Munves Corp. New York). Soldiers and sailors with their girls sit for dripping hypo-stinking photographs in booths skimpily curtained to discourage exploratory military maneuvers.

Against the far back wall of this extraordinary rowdy-dow establishment is the tiny ticket booth of Hubert's Museum, the Annex and Congress of Strange People, which is the sanctuary of Professor Roy Heckler's Marvelous Trained Flea Circus. The turnstile turns for a quarter and the crackle-clatter-clang is left behind. An L-shaped staircase, quite wide, leads down to the museum itself, a pillared expanse of linoleumed basement, once stale-aired, but now pleasantly air-conditioned and painted in muted pinks and blues, its walls hung with tarnished fun-house distorting mirrors, faded posters and salvaged pieces of sideshow paintings of "Famous Freaks of All Time," including the Man with the Revolving Head (180 degrees limit), and the Remarkable Great Waldo, a chap who could swallow (and regurgitate) live mice and whole lemons, and the Most Beautiful Tattooed Lady in the World.

Rimming the room at chest level are several platform stages draped with a nondescript array of dingy cotton print and mouldering velvet hangings, some with gold-braided initials of performers sewn bravely onto them. Separating and flanking these elevations are several small walled-off areas. One of these booths houses the Girl in the Goldfish Bowl and serves as dressing room for the lady contortionist. Another is a tiny stand-up theater in which two United Nations Dancing Girls periodically gyrate modestly to the strains of a horrendous Greek rock-and-roll phonograph record. A third enclosure which appears to be a catch-all storage room is fronted by a line-up of nickel machines for viewing "Paintings on the Head of a Pin." Atop this booth, a clutter of household rubbish, the kind of stubborn bric-a-brac possessions usually found in the attic of a septuagenarian maiden lady, bears a sign proclaiming "Relics of the Collyer Mansion" (home of the Collyer brothers, famous New York recluses of a decade ago). Professor Heckler's bailiwick, the most distinguished of these privy arenas, snuggles between the dais of the Escape Artist and the long double platform on which are exploited the respective crafts of a handless sharpshooter and a pseudo-wild man billed as "The Jungle Creep."

The Flea Circus opens for business on the last metallic ping from the handless sharpshooter's target. The Inside Lecturer, a Negro in grey business suit, swoops out from behind a pillar in back of the knot of spectators. He is distinguished from them by a beaded leopard hat which could be either a Congo bushman's bonnet or a lodge helmet reserved for the most honored potentate.

"Now, folks," he says, "let's all give the gentleman a great big hand."

Then, taking up a position at the lectern before Professor Heckler's still-closed door, the Inside Lecturer becomes an Outside Talker and makes for the Flea Circus what sideshow people call "an opening."

"And now, ladies and gentlemen," he says, "I would like to take

one minute of your valuable time to call your attention to the performance you have all been waiting for, the one *and* only one of its
kind in the entire world. Ladies and gentlemen, I take great pleasure
in offering for your entertainment Professor Heckler and his Trained
Fleas! Here day after day, night after night, week after week, month
after month, year after year people come from all over the world here
especially to see Professor Heckler's Trained Flea Circus, the one *and*
only one of its kind in the entire world. What you see pictured here
to *the* left and to *the* right of the doorway, you will find inside, all
alive and entertaining. When you go in there, you will find sixteen
fleas even though six will entertain you in the circus. The others are
understudies so that in case one of the tiny actors *or* actresses breaks *a*
leg or sprains an ankle or is *in*disposed in any other fashion you will
be sure *of* seeing the entire *and* complete performance at all times."

He knocks sharply on the door to alert the Professor who has
already been alerted by the last crack of the handless sharpshooter's
rifle.

"NUMBAH one!" continues the Talker, raising his voice suddenly, "*will* kick *a* football. Numbah TWO! will juggle a ball that
is three times his size while lying on *his* back. Num-BAH four! will
operate a miniature merry-*go*-round that is no bigger than this silver
dollar I hold here." (He bounces it on the bally-box with a loud
metallic clink.) "NUM-bah five will run the famous chariot *race*, and
the flea which hops the fastest *will* win. NUM-bah SIX! *and* the
feature of this show today is the *dancing* fleas! Little lady fleas dressed
in hoopskirts and costumes of silks and lace, rhinestone jewelry and
each little gown tucked into the waists of these infinitest-timial
creatures. And the fee to *see* all this is only *twenty*-five cents and you
pay me right here. Step right this way, ladies and gentlemen, to see
Professor *Heckler* and his *Trained* FLEA CIRCUS!"

It is a very decent "opening." With his left hand the Talker
slides open the door to the Flea Circus, with the other he collects
what quarters his spiel has cajoled from the listless crowd. Then he
passes in to Professor Heckler what this gentleman refers to as "the
tip"; the paying customers.

When only one patron has been shaken loose of his quarter the
Professor cheerfully refunds the money and reluctantly dismisses the
lone enthusiast. The troupe of trained insect artistes are not shown
unless there is a "quorum present." The Professor's interpretation is
at least two curious souls.

The walls of the Flea Circus room are painted a flamboyant pink and blue and against the ceiling on two sides is a spectacular double-row display of butterflies under glass, some of them of enormous size. Upon close examination these are found to be composites, made of the perfectly matched wings of hundreds of smaller *Lepidoptera*. Below the framed butterflies the walls are plastered with enlargements of newspaper clippings about the Flea Circus. Among them are a great many cartoons, for the establishment has always been an easy spawning ground for pen-and-ink gags. Most of the drawings associate the fleas with dogs, the popular public conception of the insect.

Dog running out of Flea Circus; caption: "Stop thief!"

Dog running into Flea Circus; caption: "Bosco is their talent scout."

Flea Circus professor at dog pound; caption: "I've been promising them a dog for a long time."

The Professor awaiting his "tip" sits against the rear wall facing the entrance. He looks very much like a judge sitting in magistrate's court. A short dapper gentleman, Heckler wears a conservatively cut business suit, usually grey or light blue, with an American Legion button in the lapel, white starched-collar shirt with bow tie, and a watch on his right wrist. The flea master is quite bald, has a poker face and an extremely calm demeanor—ever so sure of himself. Before him is a chest-high table, the top of which is covered with white toweling. A scant ten inches above it hangs a bright light, its cracked hemispheric shade nonchalantly held together with adhesive tape. Directly before the Professor is a felt rectangle bound in a narrow gold picture frame, raised slightly above the table top on low skinny metal legs. This is the flea arena, and casually scattered around it are a half-dozen inlaid-pearl boxes along with a low cylindrical jewel basket upended to form a platform for a tiny gold merry-go-round. Downstage, housed under a small transparent plastic lid, is a group of miniature vehicles: chariots, cannon, wagons, a steam roller and an antique automobile with tiny garnet headlamp. Bordering the table, front and sides, is a broad mahogany rail for the audience to lean upon; back against the walls, dark red bleachers of two steps wait to accommodate any overflow. Just before the performance begins the room is as still as a deep cave, and I always get the eerie feeling that here for a few brief moments sits God about to toy with His pitiful creatures.

The Professor's lecture is given in an extremely deliberate sing-song drawl, each syllable unmistakably pronounced—a delivery that is very much broader than Mr. Heckler's normal speech, which still holds a Tarheel tinge from his native North Carolina (born in Gastonia, 1899).

"*Bee*-fore *start*-ting theee per-form-*mance*," he begins, "I will *show* you *one* of theeee little fell-*ows* at close ob-serv-*va*-shun." He picks up a boxlike magnifying glass attached to a short handle. "I *have* sus-*spend*-ded here a flea at the back of this mag-nif-*fy*-ing glass. Hold it close to the eye to-*wards* the light and pass it a-*mong* you, one to the oth-ther."

It is handed to the nearest member of his by now no-longer-skeptical though still somewhat self-conscious audience. The flea, translucent and rather repulsive, kicking constantly and violently, hangs from an extremely fine wire twisted into a loop which is around its neck, resting in a groove between head and body. The squeamish are relieved that the flea has not been pierced to take the leash.

"That shows you how the-e-e *coll*-lar is placed around the-e-e *neck* of the flea," the Professor continues as the glass makes its impatient rounds. "That's Os-car . . . some-times he *kicks* . . . sometimes he *does*-n't . . . just *like* some *peop*-ple. . . ."

By this time the Professor's voice and calm delivery have his onlookers completely mesmerized. Every movement of his hands is followed by every pair of eyes. As the first pearly box is opened, Professor Heckler casually mentions that all fleas are in harness, that there is no "fear of de-*sert*-shun in the ranks." Even so, the spectators invariably and unconsciously scratch themselves surreptitiously a few times during the subsequent activities, for such is the power of suggestion. As I write this I itch; it is likely that you will itch as you read it.

First on the agenda is the Chariot Race. "There is Marc-*cus* . . . and *Cea*-sar with their *Ro*-man chariots . . . and Nap-*pole*-leon *Boney*-part with his *can*-non," announces the insect mentor as he sets out his racing fleas, removing them carefully from their pearl-covered haven by means of a tweezers pinched to their hairlike wire leashes. Those of Marcus and Ceasar are attached to small golden chariots, that of Napoleon to a cannon with a thin blue glass barrel.

"All-*right*, boys," drones on the Professor, "wake *up* now . . . let's go . . . they're *off* and *run*-ning." With a little persuasion from a straw of fine wire with which the Professor touches their feet, the animated specks get moving and dash rather quickly, but in fits and starts, in a straight line until they bump into the front edge of

the golden frame. It is weird—like a mad scene from a Samuel Beckett play. "*Cea*-sar *first*," announces the Professor, "Nap-*pole*-leon second, and *Marc*-cus *all*-so ran. Not as exciting as a *horse* race, *but* they get there *just* the same." The race never fails to enthrall and warm up the gallery. Though a great empathy remains with the flea, the Professor has the audience in his pocket from now on in.

"Prince *Hen*-ry next. The *flea* that *jug*-gulls a ball." The Director of the Flea Circus takes a flea from another of the cotton-lined boxes, then pauses, examines the insect carefully and returns it tenderly to its berth. "That's *Ben*-ny," he apologizes giving the audience his best poker face. It is a superb bit of showmanship, perfectly timed, and never fails to elicit a small slightly embarrassed titter from the "tip," not sure whether the Professor is kidding or not.

"There . . . *that* looks like *Hen*-ry all-*right*." Heckler places a tiny cotton pith ball about as big as a chick-pea on Henry's upturned feet. "All-*right*, Hen-*ry*, turn it over *nice*-ly and keep it *moo*-ving." Henry drops the little ball. "Pick it *up*, Hen-*ry*. Hold *it*. Now *drop* it Hen-*ry!*" Henry does all this apparently on command.

"It takes a *man* two to three *years* to learn to *jugg*-gull an *ob*-ject with his *feet*," explains the Professor, "what the *flea* accomp-plishes in a few *weeks*. Of course, he has *some*-what the ad-*vant*-tage as he has *six* legs while *man* has only *two*." The pulicology scholars are singularly unimpressed by this scientific revelation.

"And now, Cous-in *Char*-lee, the most A-*mer*-ican-ized flea in the col-*lec*-shun. He once *played* on one of the *lead*-ding college *foot*-ball teams."

Another light laugh. Cousin Charlie takes the same little ball in his feet, then snaps it briskly away from him. He does it again. and again. Professor Heckler seems to enjoy this stunt especially and usually has the flea repeat the kick many times. Every once in a while a humanitarian in the audience will voice a mild objection ("Hey, Perfesser, we oney paid a quarter. Geez, the little guy is kicked enough already. You wear him out, Perfesser"). These excursions into persiflage are infrequent, such is the command of Heckler's austere manner on the paying customers, and the Professor never dignifies such badinage with an answer.

"Next, the Flea Ho-*tel*, show-ing how they are *kept* when not *work*-king, their *feet* en-*tang*-geld in cotton or wool." This hotel is not the magnificent palatial edifice that has been conjured up in the audience's imagination, but simply another pearl-laden box lined with cotton, with a line-up of fleas held in place by a fine wire stretched across their long leashes. No one seems to mind the disillusionment, so completely has the Professor cast his spell.

As Rudolf, "the strongest flea in the collection" slowly pushes the tiny merry-go-round, the listeners are told some of the facts of flea life. Professor Heckler can always get a rise when some timid innocent asks what he feeds his fleas. "BLOOD!" announces the flea pedagogue, good and clear, facing his audience squarely for the first time, "*hew*-man blood drained *right* from the arm of a vol-*lun*-teer." The "tip" shrinks back from the rail a trifle with the same mass revulsion as that shown by a sideshow audience when the snake handler brings out her largest boa constrictor. "We just *place* the flea on a vol-lun-*teer's* arm," continues the Professor, with a significant look at the nearest flea-feeding prospect, "and he is not a *bit* bash-ful about *take*-king his *nour*-rish-ment; *all* he needs is the opp-por-*tune*-nity."

The flea extravaganza concludes with the dancing fleas "dressed in their little *cost*-tumes *dan*-cing to *mew*-sic." The impresario winds an ancient music box. He sometimes has to bop it once or twice before it lofts into a lilting "Santa Lucia," one of its two tunes. The box has been refitted by the Professor with two tiny cylinders instead of the usual single large one ("Don't recollect what's on the other one," he says). An old label pasted inside the lid says the box used to play "On a Sunday Afternoon," "Rip Van Winkle Was a Lucky Man," and "Good Morning, Carrie."

Herr Heckler sets out onto a flat glass disc, the diameter of a highball glass, a tiny colored paper wigwam. "There is Peaches," he says, "and Fifi," adding another, "and Sadie." The three colored hoods (for each covers a flea) scamper about the surface like kids on a slick skating rink "all dressed up in old-fash-shunned hoop skirts. They cannot use hobb-ble skirts because they have too many feet." (The fact that hobble skirts went out of style about the same time as the camisole and the galena detector is of no particular concern.) As the dancing fleas approach a climax in their cavorting, indistinguishable to all except the Professor, he swings into his closing aria, a masterpiece of circus hokum which leaves the audience with a warm contented glow, himself safe from even the slightest imputation of chicanery—rhinestones, palatial hotel, fitted waists or no.

"When one *is* a-ble to *place* a dress on a *ti*-ny thing like *a* flea small enough to per-*mit* them to walk and *waltz*, it is su-*fish*-ent for people of in-*tell*-i-gence that they can-*not* help but *re*-al-ize they have been *well* repaid for their *vis*-it had they seen *noth*-ing else. If you go home and *tell* your friends you have *seen* real *live* fleas per-*form*-ing they will not be-*lieve* you, but just *send* them here and we will a-*tempt* to con-*vince* them. That's *all* for this *time*. If you have en-*joy*-ed our show rec-co-*mend* it to your friends. W*e* thank you."

Professor Leroy Heckler is "in fleas" because his father was "in fleas." The fleas that Professor Heckler the second is exhibiting today are direct descendants of a batch numbering about 150 that was brought to this country from Italy and Spain a few years before the outbreak of the Second World War by a group of German ships' stewards who had been originally contacted for that purpose by Roy's father, the first Professor Heckler, many years ago over in Jersey City, New Jersey, at a German seamen's club, a place similar to the Seamen's Church Institute in New York City. Roy thinks his dad paid about ten cents a flea.

"The price was usually just about what the traffic would bear," he explains, "and the mortality was high—about 50 per cent."

Fleas are usually brought in on the body of a trustworthy seaman or some other co-operative human carrier.

"My most intelligent flea," claims the Professor, "came in on the undershirt of an Italian First Mate from the best suite on one of the finest ships afloat. Naturally, I can't mention the name."

Roy's dad, William Heckler, "had the fleas" on Brighton Beach boardwalk, and the boy became interested when he was about nine years old. The elder Heckler called his exhibition The Flea Theater since it was located in what Roy remembers as a "rather swanky section." To the best of his knowledge there were only two other Flea Theaters at that time, one somewhere else in the East, another in California.

William Heckler was a Swiss who had shipped out as a merchant seaman on German sailing schooners. He made many trips across the Atlantic to America, finally remaining on these shores to become a circus strong man. His grand Spencerian signature graced the payrolls of most of the canvas-covered wonders of those sunburst circus days before the turn of the century, including the famous John Robinson show, and those of Sells Bros and Adam Forepaugh.

Enroute one season he met and married Alice Austin, a native of New Haven whose father Mr. Heckler says was a Yale professor. This marriage of muscle and intellect produced five sons and a daughter, all summertime babies born in the Carolinas where the family wintered. In 1901, when Roy was a kid of two years and his strong-man dad was thirty, there came an opportunity to take over an operating Flea Theater in Orlando, Florida, and the strong-man act was over.

"We was always in a park in them days," says Roy, recounting his early impressions of the family flea business. "The movies was in their infancy, and the thing to do was to go to an amusement park. They were the main recreation for the people then. Most of them was run by the traction companies. There was Hanlon's Point Park out on an island off Toronto more or less run by the Toronto Ferry Company. They had a good flow of people. It was the home of the Toronto International Baseball League park and it was a busy place.

Other parks Roy remembers in connection with the Heckler family's flea gallivantings are Willow Grove in Philadelphia ("a real choice spot for picnics; the excursion trains come from Delaware, Maryland, Pennsylvania and New Jersey . . ."); The Electric Park at Kinderhook Lake in New York State (". . . it was owned by the Hudson Traction Company and you could take a trolley all the way up river to Yonkers then change to one that run clean to Albany . . .") and Riverview Park in Baltimore (". . . out of existence now; it was a big shipyard in the last war where the park originally was . . .").

Winters the Heckler fleas were trouped in Cuba, Central America and the West Indies, where gringo fleas were still a novelty.

Heckler senior's first venture into New York and his entrance to the famous street on which his son still holds forth was at Hammerstein's Roof on Seventh Avenue at Forty-second.

"I can't pin the exact year down," Roy says. "There was an elderly woman in one day, in the neighborhood of fifty years she was. She remembered my dad's premises, but she couldn't pin the year down either. I only remember on the same bill was Princess Rajah, an Oriental dancer, and Singer's Midgets. Baron Leo Singer, he only died eight or nine years ago."

The Heckler educated fleas descended to street level when they became an attraction at Hubert's Museum along about 1925. Flea historians are not numerous but George Jean Nathan, essayist and theatrical critic, has stated that the Flea Circus originated with a Professor Hupf in 1885 at Coblentz, Germany.

"As far as my dad could take it back," comments Professor Heckler, "it was a woman in Germany in the seventeen hundreds invented flea circuses. The Kings of Prussia all had court flea trainers. The flea trainer was looked up to as one of the wise men of the court."

John C. Ruhl, one of the best known of America's pioneer flea entrepreneurs, is often credited with bringing the flea enterprise to this country. "He brought it from Germany," says Professor Roy, "and worked out of California. I knew him well; he died only about fifteen or twelve years ago. When he was an older man, John Ruhl, he worked for my dad."

Ruhl's flea secrets are supposed to have been handed down from his grandfather, Charles Ruhl, who acquired the *modus operandi* from a Siberian exile whom he helped escape to Paris, the prisoner having learned about fleas by studying their behavoir patterns during long, dreary years chained to a salt-mines' wheelbarrow. The legend is very likely untrue, for it bears close resemblance to many other such stories about prisoners and fleas, including one of Professor Heckler's favorites. Several in his small collection of flea anecdotes are borderline cases (including one dandy involving a department-store floorwalker, a blonde cashier and two cold fleas during a coal strike in Shamokin, Pa.), but the following one is printable.

A flea has been painstakingly trained in a prison cell by a long-term convict for years and years (the anecdote blithely ignores the facts of flea life span). The insect was remarkably talented and had been developed by its trainer to a point of being able to do a full two-hour show without repeating a single trick. This flea could perform the most incredible feats. It could hang by its proboscis from a tiny flying trapeze; play the "Poet and Peasant" overture in its entirety on a xylophone made of discarded fingernail parings; balance on one front leg while waving tiny flags of five major nations with the other legs. The prisoner knew he had a gold mine. When he was finally released from pokey he could hardly wait to exhibit his prodigy to an audience. Entering the first saloon nearest the jail gates, he ordered a beer and while the barkeep went to draw it, took the flea's tiny traveling box from his pocket and carefully, tenderly placed on the polished mahogany his cherished creature, the light of his life, his protégé and expected breadwinner. "Say, bartender," he called, "this flea here . . ." He got no further. The barman said, "Oh, yeah, Mac. Sorry about that." He jutted out a fat thumb and squashed the insect. It is the flea business's saddest story. The moral, if any, is always make a good "opening."

In the spring of 1920, shortly after Roy's return from Europe
where he had been a working member of Uncle Sam's Expeditionary
Forces, he put the family fleas through their paces for the first time
on his own, though still under his father's banner. Heckler and son
operated as a partnership, with Roy's brother, William, Jr., assisting,
until 1933 when Papa Heckler took a set of enlightened fleas to an
engagement at the Century of Progress Exposition in Chicago, leaving
Roy home to watch the store at Hubert's—sole trainer, keeper and
curator of that branch of the family fleas. Three years later the elder
Heckler died at the age of sixty-six, and Roy inherited the business,
including all livestock.

In his Flea Circus, Professor Roy Heckler employs only the so-
called human flea, the European house flea whose scientific name is
Pulex irritans. In the United States, itinerant *Pulex irritans* can be
found in most skid row hotels but the natives only in the Mississippi
valley and in California. The California habitat is commemorated in
show business by a tired California flea gag, usually perpetrated by
show girls in the confines of their dressing rooms. Walking the index
and middle finger across a table top in simulation of a pair of legs,
the doll raconteur demonstrates how to distinguish a French, an
English and a Hollywood showgirl. The French and English legs do
the showgirl "garbage walk" perfectly; the Hollywood pair frequently
stop to scratch.

Pulex irritans is of the insect order *Siphonaptera* and is one of
an estimated nine hundred species developed from six families. It is
not accurately known just how many kinds of fleas exist in the world;
new species are discovered yearly. In North America and the West
Indies alone more than two hundred species and nearly seventy sub-
species have been recorded. Only about a dozen species of fleas are
really troublesome to man and beast, but the fleas most fiendishly
annoying to man are the dog flea (which bears the learned name
Ctenocephalides canis) and the cat flea called the same thing *felis*.
David Harum has said, "Fleas are good for a dog because they keep
him from brooding over the fact that he is a dog."

Flea trainers seldom attempt to educate the animal fleas. There
is a feeling that any time spent with an animal flea is poorly invested
since its life span is so much shorter than that of the human flea, the
Pulex irritans. There is also considerable difference in the stamina of
the two species. All fleas are parasitic and to live need a constant supply of warm blood. However, the *Pulex*, conditioned by its human

hosts' habit of long weekends, is able to fast forty-eight hours, while the animal flea can last without food only eighteen hours. Sideshow entomologists believe that this difference in durability is due to the superior nutritive value of human blood. They also nurture a theory that an animal flea does not have a strong-enough constitution to withstand the vicissitudes and environmental changes of the Thespian life, because an animal-born flea lives its entire life in the immediate vicinity of its hairy birthplace, whereas the *Pulex irritans* merely lives *off* its host never *on* him or her. The *Pulex* makes its home in cracks and crevices of floors, walls and furniture and always dines out—breakfast, lunch, tea and dinner.

A *Pulex irritans* flea is shaped something like a bee, is brownish to black in color, and is seldom longer than ⅛ inch, frequently much less. It weighs ¹⁄₂₀ to ⅕ of a grain—stripped (7,000 grains to a pound avoirdupois). A person could carry five thousand fleas on himself and add only one ounce to his weight. However, a flea's weight is considerable in view of its size. In a pamphlet published in 1915 Professor William Heckler attributes this odd relation of weight and size to the insect's compactness and to an extraordinary amount of iron stored within its system.

The *Pulex irritans* flea is covered with overlapping scales of armor similar to fish scales, from which hair projects to prevent irritation. This flea's proboscis is a sawlike beak with a piercing point. Two sharp-edged plates at the beak-front are used to enlarge the incision which the beak makes when it feeds. The *P.i.* flea's six legs are its most remarkable physical feature. They resemble those of a crab or lobster and are extremely strong. Flea legs, of only ¹⁄₂₀ of an inch long, can propel the insect into a high jump of almost eight inches, a broad jump of thirteen inches, more than one hundred times its body length. This same distance is par for a frog, a creature several hundreds of times larger than a flea. If a human's legs were this strong, a man with a pair of three-footers could leap groundwise 700 feet or straight up 450 feet, soaring over the torch of the Statue of Liberty with 145 feet to spare, or just clearing the great Pyramid of Cheops. Its leap is a flea's main protection when being pursued, which is frequently. A flea is also strong enough to effect escape through cloth of the tightest weave. With its hind legs a *Pulex irritans* can kick a ball three times its weight farther than a man can bat a baseball. When dangling from its collar harness, a flea can lift 150 times its own weight. A horse pulls a wagon three to four times what it weighs;

a flea can pull one weighing 300 to 400 times its tip of the scale. The flea (0.2 grain) which operates Professor Heckler's merry-go-round (1 ounce) is pushing an object that is 2,187½ times its own weight.

Fleas may be able to talk to each other, but no man has ever heard one. A flea has adequate eyes and antennae by means of which Professor Roy believes his particular fleas respond to the timber of his voice. An anecdote is told in flea circles about a scientist testing a *Pulex irritans.* He removes one leg; commands the flea to jump. It does, and the science gentleman notes this in his book. He removes another limb; flea still jumps on command. Duly noted. Two more legs come off; flea still responds to the command "Jump." Experimenter takes off fifth leg. Poor flea still leaps when man says "Jump." The final leg is removed; the scientist commands, "Jump!" The flea lies quite still. Scientist writes in his notebook, "With all legs removed the *Pulex irritans* loses his sense of hearing."

Flea training is a matter of reflex conditioning in which the flea's rigid instinctive behavior is exploited. The flea does not perform because of a memory of experience and its sequential education as do mammals and birds of larger brains. The flea's microscopic brain, while one of the most intricately and elaborately organized bits of matter in the universe, has no storage cells for memory. It is doubtful that Professor Heckler has studied the shock-avoidance conditioning methods of Pavlov, the eminent Russian physiologist, but unwittingly he uses his principles in his academic work with fleas.

Heckler professes, as did his father before him, a more mystic approach to the realm of the flea. "Flea training," states Professor Roy, "is more mental than physical. I'm a success because of my patience and sympathetic understanding of fleas. You must know fleas like you know your own children."

In his 1915 pamphlet "Puli-cology," Professor Heckler, the first dean of flea training, states, "It is not as easy for a man to gain the confidence of a flea as that of a spider or cricket, which can be accomplished sometimes within a few minutes by one who understands their nature. . . . The flea is a parasite of man and beast and having been hunted ever since its beginning has undoubtedly developed its faculty of caution. It is for this reason that more time is required to gain its confidence."

Roy Heckler begins the training (or conditioning) of a flea by submitting it to what he calls an intelligence test. He assumes that everyone knows that one flea can be more intelligent than another.

This standard flea-Binet consists of placing the group of initiates into the cotton-filled interior of a glass jar, which is then held close to a lighted electric bulb. When the enclosure becomes uncomfortably warm the shrewdest fleas begin a trip of investigation, circling the jar. Back at their starting point they quickly make up their infinitesimal minds about the coolest side and make a bee line for it. The stupidest fleas run around frantically and eventually die of heat and/or panic.

The qualifying flea is then placed inside on the bottom of a cylindrical glass jar about a foot tall. If he can effect an escape he is well on the road to becoming a flea-circus kinker. Only those fleas with a super supply of strength, persistence and (perhaps) judgment will pass this test. A flea's claws cannot adhere to the slick sides of the glass jar, therefore the insect cannot simply crawl out. Nor can he leap out, for maximum vertical flea-thrust is eight inches. Therefore the flea takes aim, leaps as high as he can onto the glass wall and deftly deposits there a bit of sticky substance before he tumbles back to the floor. Then he keeps trying and trying, leaping until he hits that identical spot again. This time he has enough foothold to take off on the second stage of his journey into outer space.

And now the shade of Pavlov descends. The flea is imprisoned in a horizontally placed glass test tube. Apparently unfamiliar with the confining properties of glass, the insect leaps and bangs his tiny head on the hard ceiling. He leaps again and bangs again. The flea goes on in leaps and bangs, and finally wises up—its soaring days are over. The most important lesson of flea education has been beaten into his head.

When the flea has learned to crawl and walk instead of obeying his instinct to jump and leap, he is placed in the harness that remains with him until he enters Flea paradise. The construction and fitting of the tiny halters, which is done under great magnification, is the most difficult and most important procedure of flea training and requires great skill and patience. Not one of the few persons who have tried to enter Professor Heckler's strange profession has been able to master the tying of the noose around the flea's neck. A group of Columbia University professors once undertook to train a class of fleas and did fine in the elementary stages but even these learned gentlemen were unable to collar a single insect. The trick is to make the tiny twisted loop small enough to restrain the flea but large enough not to choke it at mealtimes, when its neck swells considerably. If the tie is too tight, the captive eventually starves to death.

Through long experience the Professor has become an expert flea-harness maker. The copper wire which he uses was handed down to him by his father, who got it from John Roebling, the man who supplied the cable for the Brooklyn Bridge. It was undoubtedly the finest strand in Mr. Roebling's warehouses, certainly the slimmest I've ever handled. When the white cotton cover is removed (Roy uses a manicure scissors), it is thinner than a horse's tail-hair and every bit as springy-stiff. The roll, six inches long, was about four inches in diameter when it was bequeathed to Roy. A third of it remains, and the Professor figures it is "more'n I'll ever need in my lifetime."

As a final bit of discouragement to indiscreet jumping, the flea's copper leash is fastened to the chain of a miniature brass gibbet. Hanging thus the flea's feet just barely touch the base. If he jumps the heavy chain goes with him and the leap is very suddenly brought up short. Again the flea understands that such foolish action is, as the Professor puts it in his best Chautauqua drawl, "hew-sless."

The flea is now ready for exposure to serious pedagogy. To persons inexperienced with fleas, all fleas look alike, but Professor Heckler can distinguish the members of his company of entertainers. "By the general appearance," he explains wryly, "not by the color of their eyes." He judges strength by the degree of darkness in complexion. A pale flea has little vitality; a black one is agile, full of energy, has great endurance, and is therefore more trainable. The Professor takes about three weeks to train a flea thoroughly. One trick is the limit per flea.

"It took three years to train myself," he avers. "Everything I learned was by my own study and observation. Nothing was ever put in my hand to go at it."

The female flea is more responsive to training and better suited to performing because she not only has a much milder nature than the male but is twice his size. The male is lively enough but is usually overly ambitious and becomes morose and often quite frantic when confined.

By close kindergarten observation the high priest of fleadom determines the sort of trick each flea is capable of. Stodgy ones are broken to the merry-go-round harness; flighty fleas make good dancers; those with especially strong legs will become kickers, jugglers or chariot racers.

There are a great many other things which fleas can be conditioned to do. They can wiggle a staff with a foreleg, an action which transforms them into orchestra leaders, flag wavers, spear carriers or street sweepers. They are good at walking a tightrope and jumping through a hoop the size of an eyeglass lens (for this it is necessary to condition the flea from its no-hop conditioning). And fleas can fence with foils. In the accomplishment of this gentlemen's sport, they are assisted by a spot of glue on their bottoms which holds them to tiny chairs, the weeny blunt swords firmly fastened to front feet. As they try to kick loose these offensive objects the spectator, if he is charitable, will witness a deathless duel.

A flea is taught to juggle by placing a pith ball on its upturned feet. A gentle stroking of the legs and ball with a fine wire soon gives the insect the idea and it begins to pedal the sphere around. When I was a third-grader, every kid except the more repulsive members of the G and E set filled in dull spring afternoons with performances of his own "trained juggling fly," wings spit-glued to desktop, an eraser crumb turning gingerly on frantic upturned legs.

Kicking the ball is a matter of conditioning to a ball soaked in a fluid that has an odor repulsive to the flea. Oil of citronella is good; a strong oral disinfectant such as Listerine, or a dab of five-and-dime perfume, does fine, too. The flea kicks the ball away just to be rid of the awful stink. Eventually the smell can be eliminated; the same ball used for both kicking and juggling.

The dancing fleas need no choreographer; they are merely scampering about trying to find a way out from under their little paper tent-costumes, which are affixed to the flea's copper-wire neckpiece.

Breaking a flea to the chariot or cannon is quite difficult, for it has no inclination to run in a straight line. However, the broadly spaced wheels of the vehicles aid greatly in keeping the contraptions in line.

The Professor figures he has trained close to eighteen thousand fleas in the twenty-four years he has been "in fleas" on his own. The figure is fairly accurate, I judge, and not the usual publicity hyperbole, although the Professor, being well grounded in the art of circus tub thumping, is not adverse to releasing outlandish figures to the press. Once publicly bemoaning the untimely loss of his finest star, Paddy ("the Mansfield of the Flea Arena, a contemporary of Bernhardt"), he stated that this particular favorite had done 50,879 performances. Since the life of a trained flea is of about six months' duration, the great Paddy at that age would have given during his lifetime 8,479½ performances daily, which would have been a lot even at Coney Island in the old days.

Exaggeration or not, from all accounts Paddy must have been a really remarkable flea, for apparently he worked without a harness. One observer in reporting his performance (Paddy was a flag waver) said in part: ". . . only conscience and an apparatus which the professor claimed was only the flag of Ireland kept Paddy from deserting the ranks, for he was the only 'trusty' in all fleadom. . . ."

During the training period, fleas are worked six times a day; as performers they do about twelve shows a day, often more on weekends. A first-class trained flea makes about sixteen hundred professional appearances in its lifetime.

All the props used in the performance of Heckler's Famous Flea Circus were handmade by the proprietor himself. The tiny pieces of rolling stock, the chariots and cannons, have wheels which once were balance gears in watches. In a drawer behind the arena table there is always a boxful of wheels waiting to have their teeth ground off. Mr. Heckler does this with a dandy electric grinding outfit, a proud possession. The chariot bodies are fashioned from cylindrical lipstick cases; the barrel of the tiny cannon was drawn out by a Sideshow glass blower friend named Bill Hart.

"I believe he's dead now," muses the Professor. "That cannon is a real old-timer."

The merry-go-round is also a family heirloom. The gilded horses were originally the heads of stickpins, "slum" stock from a carnival concession. They came to the flea *fantoccini* by way of an Inside Lecturer, who got them from a mugg-joint operator (photographer), who got them from a pratter (a chap who circulates through the "tip" of a carny "joint" [concession stand] "pratting" out [slyly pushing with hips] the undesirable non-spenders). The golden top of the carousel is an old medallion from a dimly remembered relative on the Austin side of the family.

The boxes of inlaid pearl, which are used to house the props and the flea performers, are not the same ones used by Roy's father but several are more than fifty years old. Each one has its own fitted woolsock cover hand-knitted with love by Heckler's daughter, Janet (once a medical laboratory technician, now a mother; the professor also has a son, Roy, a telephone-company worker, and four grandchildren). The covers keep the fleas cozy during their daily trips to and fro between the Museum and the Heckler residence in Bergenfield, New Jersey. The boxes travel with the Professor by bus in an old-fashioned leather brief case. Fellow bus riders never suspect that the dignified fellow across the aisle who could be a tired banker, lingerie salesman or stockbroker is harboring several dozen pedigreed *Pulex irritans.*

The fleas are not taken home each night because the Professor has an overpowering love for the creatures. They are the chief assets of his business and leaving them on Forty-second Street overnight is a risk too great to take. Professor Heckler does not have for his small chums the kind of regard that people ordinarily show toward animal pets.

"I have never become attached to the fleas like you would to a dog or cat," he says. "It's rather the other way around."

The Heckler Flea Circus maintains a stable of understudies for its flea actors. You may have thought that Inside Lecturer was joshing when he mentioned the sprained ankles and broken legs, but actually those are the common incapacitations of the fleas. When one of the little fellows faces the Final Curtain, another just as talented is ready to step into his place in the patched-up limelight. The new flea always assumes the name of the dear departed.

Most of the names in the Heckler company were used by Roy's father, and many go beyond that period in flea history. Some of the names acquired at the baptismal font of the elder Heckler have become outmoded and therefore dropped from the roster. For years, two of William Heckler's stars were named Cook and Peary after the North Pole explorers who were so popularly controversial in the early 1900's. Several generations of lady dancing fleas were called La Castilina, a name bestowed by the dramatic critic, Robert Garland, when, in a fit of pique because he had been refused an Annie Oakley for a performance by La Argentina, the celebrated Spanish danseuse, at the Brooklyn Academy of Music, he reviewed instead the dancing flea at Hubert's.

"La Argentina, the woman," Garland wrote, "may be tonier, but she can be no more gay and graceful than La Castilina, the flea. The Professor picked her up in an Inn at Seo de Urgel in the Pyrenees and now she dances although her heart is breaking."

Like most circuses, the Heckler Trained Flea Circus breeds its own performers. The breeding stock is kept in a cotton-filled jar in which the fleas are able to remain about six months, with regular feedings, of course, before succumbing to the vicissitudes of civilization. In their normal wild state, such fleas are able to live about twice that long. Fleas cannot withstand much cold. They do not hibernate, and unattended fleas usually die at the beginning of cold weather. Only the hardiest can survive a New York winter. Professor Heckler takes every precaution with his valuable charges. His present breeding jar which still bears the label of its original contents ("Vita Imported Snack") is kept cozy and warm by one of Janet's specially knitted socks. The female flea lays three to eight eggs, varying with "the length of time she has been engaged in the industry," as the Professor pithily puts it. The eggs produced by the breeding fleas fall to the bottom of the jar. They are whitish, rather round, translucent, somewhat like snake eggs, but so small that only an experienced flea-egg hunter can discover them. The eggs will hatch in three days to the larval stage unless they are kept away from heat. The Professor keeps his supply in a cool (under 70 degrees) corner of the basement of his Bergenfield home. He claims that eggs will remain unhatched for a period longer than ten years under the right atmospheric conditions.

Professor Heckler doesn't seem to be concerned about running out of fleas to train. "Flea Circuses are becoming extinct," says the Grand Sachem of *Siphonaptera*, "but not because of the dearth of fleas."

The larva gives an indication of the great strength of the adult flea. This worm form, creamy white with a brown tip in its end, doesn't crawl as an ordinary worm, but moves by a kind of seesaw method of extending its body upward and forward, the tail remaining stationary; then lowering this inclined section and re-raising it, elevating the tail as well. When this backwards-pointing incline of worm contracts, the creature has moved a length forward. The flea in a larval stage lives on minute microscopic particles of material and whatever tiny germlike creatures it is able to master. This kind of nutrition keeps it going from five to nine days. Then the worm-flea begins to spin its silken disc-shaped cocoon from a gland much like that which a spider has for spinning webs. The cocoon gives the worm a snug haven for about eighteen days. Like all other insects, the flea, because of its small size, has the advantage of being able to develop from an egg to adult in a minimum time as compared with other creatures of equal brain capacity. Only a minimal volume of tissue is necessary to produce the adult flea; there is great speed of reproduction on a small per capita amount of food. Great populations of fleas can live within a small area. However, let's not get into that, for flea figures have a tendency to get beyond the grasp of the human mind—mine, at least. Suffice to say that eight million fleas can live in the same area as that required for the adequate livelihood of a horse or a cow—about two acres. Fortunately, fleas are not congregationalists, but prefer to live the roving gypsy life as individuals. Most of their Flea Circus antics are really just attempts to escape their enforced servitude. In this respect they are almost human.

The adult flea emerges from its protective cocoon small, but mighty vigorous. It can live five days absolutely without food but then, in the words of that old circus song, it's "root, hog, or die." Sir or madame *Pulex irritans* either finds a human friend from whom to siphon a snack or gangs up with two or three of its hungry fellows to cannibalize a brother flea.

Feeding time at the Flea Circus (not open to the public) is twice a day for the workers—at noon and again at 6 P.M. Often, if the Professor feels that the actors and actresses are feeling poorly, there is an extra feeding. The understudies and proselytes are usually fed just once a day, sometimes twice—depending again on local conditions.

When the bloodthirsty hour rolls around, the Professor latches his door, removes his jacket, rolls up his right shirt sleeve (he is left-handed) and rests his naked forearm on the table, the inside turned up and the back of his half-closed hand resting on a roll of towel. He feeds the loose breeders by placing them in a rather large pickle jar which the Professor then holds cupped high on his forearm. While the fleas feed the Professor reads and smokes a battered cigar stuffed into a stubby amber holder. If he has forgotten to light his smoke before the dinner has begun, he holds the jar balanced tight between his forehead and forearm, so that his left hand is free to operate a lighter. The fleas are usually at the festive board fifteen minutes to a half hour. Fleas eat more in a warm climate (breed more, too) and many shorten their lives by gluttony (and overbreeding).

When the producers are finished, the Thespians get their turn. All are fed in harness with their various cannon, chariots and merry-go-round gear still attached. To keep the vehicles from rolling should he move his arm, the Professor with a tweezers winds a fine gold chain deftly about the equipment to act as a wheel block. The dancers in costume are fed within a double-eight shaped series of connected barricades made of wire heavy enough to prevent the fleas from leaping over it to escape. The Professor determines when his guests' appetites are sated by watching for the tiny red spot left by the full flea as it moves away from the puncture. This mark disappears in about half an hour.

Roy says that the bite of a flea is hardly noticeable. "It is very sub-tle," he says. "That's their protection. They can live off a host

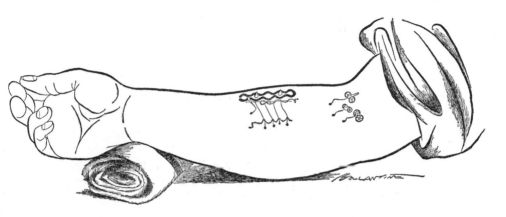

without the person realizing it. A dog flea, now, you know it when he bites you." The longer a flea is kept in captivity the less mark its bite will leave. Roy's father contended that this was because the newcomers are covered with a germlike parasite, carried unwillingly, which is gradually stripped off in feeding and left in the human pore. Any irritation he felt, came from the gathering of the "blood germ" to drive off this unwelcome invader. Another hypothesis regarding flea-bite irritation is that the insect injects a fluid into the host in order to dissolve the blood so that it may pass through the flea's proboscis. Professor Heckler doesn't worry at all about catching a disease from his fleas. A sick flea won't feed, he contends. It just loses its hard glossy surface and turns up its feet. A flea will not stay on an unhealthy person but will always seek out better living conditions. The Heckler fleas, never in contact with any other human or beast, are as antiseptic as a laboratory animal.

A typical bill in the line-up of freaks in the halcyon days of Hubert's Museum might have included besides the Flea Circus, Lady Olga, the bearded lady; Amok, Philippine Headhunter; Lady Grace, Mindreader; The Royal Coach of Kaiser Wilhelm; Henry Burton, Spider Boy; Sylvia-Chester, half-and-half (one shoe 4 triple-A, the other 8½); Miss Lambert, Contortionist; and Frank Lentini, Three-legged Man. Mr. Lentini always referred to his triple extremities as limbs. Everything then was so very elegant. The Inside Lecturer wore a dinner jacket; butchers were vendors and they vended frankfurters not hot dogs. The Needle Swallower wore a tux, and the Dancing Princesses knew at which point artistry stopped and vulgarity took over.

After dark many of Hubert's patrons were socialites and theater-goers in evening dress, for that part of Forty-second Street then, in the early 'thirties, was Manhattan's most luxurious theatrical center. All the finest theaters were there: the Liberty, where Florenz Ziegfeld produced his very first glorified-girl romp; the Lyric, the Sam. H. Harris; the Selwyn; the Candler, which was David Belasco's original theater; the Apollo, home of George White's Scandals; and the New Amsterdam, cradle of the never-to-be-duplicated Ziegfeld Follies.

"I used to give three fast shows just before curtain time," reminisces Professor Heckler, "and after the theater we'd be jammed with everybody waiting until the traffic thinned out to go to the supper clubs. Nobody ever went home in those days. All the theatrical people used to come in, too, when they weren't working. Daniel Frohman made the fleas every two weeks with the most beautiful girls you ever saw in your life. Irving Berlin, too. And Joe Cook, he used to always bring his sons to see the fleas. Fred Allen, he was very fond of Sealo [Charles Barent, so-called Seal-boy, who has flipper like hands, no arms]. He used to get ideas from talking with Sealo. Softest touch in the world Fred was—and this got about. O. O. McIntyre, the columnist, who was read all over the country, he used to give us plenty of write-ups."

Until the late 1930's the sideshow display was located on the street level of the building, and the museum spread across twice the frontage it has now. As recently as 1945 the outfit was so prosperous that the sideshow concession alone paid to the corporation an annual rental of thirty thousand dollars.

In all his years as a flea tutor and freak exhibitor Professor Heckler has never had to go hat in hand to a bank for funds.

"They would probably look at me the same way they do when you're called for jury duty," he reasons. "You tell the court you're an actor or a performer and you're immediately disqualified—out. O-U-T. If I was to tell a banker I'm a flea trainer, there is no telling what might happen."

The lush days have vanished from Hubert's. These days the

audiences run to young toughs in long sideburns, black leather jackets
with brass-studded shoulder straps; sinister, hard-faced irregulars
with soft mouths, pale watery eyes; groups of giggling teenager girls;
tourists, sailors and newly manufactured soldiers.

The banter is more raucous than in the more polite prewar
days, the questions a little more uncouth. "You tell the sex by looking very, very closely," is the Professor's deft side-step to a usual
query. He has become inured to such audience suggestions as,
"Whyn't you dress them dancers in shorty-short shorts, Perfesser?
I like girls in shorty-short shorts."

One Monday evening I observed a typical nine-thirty Flea Circus
house: four girls together; five long-sideburn boys together; a kid in
leather jacket and coonskin hat alone; a Chinese father with four-
year-old daughter; two sets of sailors; a lady in spike heels and white-
fox neckpiece; a woman with half a load on. When they left, the
Professor said of this hobbledehoy conglomeration, "They're all nice
kids, not rough at all. I enjoy having them."

Sometimes the intellectual and social level is higher. One evening when I stopped in at Hubert's the Professor told me he had
entertained that afternoon a pair of Minnesota doctors with wives;
a young couple who had gotten the good word about the Flea Circus
in far-off Israel; and the entire basketball squad of a Midwestern
college ("My, they were tall," said Professor Roy, "and noisy").
He'd had a satisfying "mat-tin-knee."

"The real flea people come out at night," the Professor confided, "and most of them are women. Summertime is our best season
when the tourists flood into New York. Generally in February around
here it gets so slow I close up and take the fleas south to Sarasota.
Next summer things will be real first-class down here. They're in-
stalling air-conditioning, starting, I think, next week and redecorat-
ing complete."

The reputation of Professor Heckler's Flea Circus is world wide.
He has had visitors who have heard about his show from as far off
as Kobe, Buenos Aires, and Copenhagen. One of his favorite newspaper clippings concerns an attempted escape from Belgrade of
a twenty-year-old Yugoslavian theology student and poet named
Dragojvb Ivosevic. The young man had himself, with a loaf of bread,
water and pills to prevent coughing, bolted into a battery box underneath the Orient Express to be released by a confederate in Paris.
When Dragojvb was caught he told the judge his reason for wanting

254 ||||| *WILD TIGERS & TAME FLEAS*

to get to America was to see the Flea Circus. "Fleas?" said the judge before sentencing the kid to eighteen months. "We have them here."

The Flea Circus has always enjoyed a good press, for almost every New York reporter and columnist worth his weight in copy paper has touched on Professor Heckler's spectacle, except perhaps Damon Runyon. When he learned that it had already been covered by the cognoscenti, including George Jean Nathan, Runyon shied away and interviewed a muscle-grinder instead.

One of the best pieces of newspaper copy woven around Professor Heckler's morality play was written by A. J. Liebling when he was a reporter on the N.Y. *World-Telegram,* spring of 1932. It reports the involvement of the Flea Circus in the didoes at a hearing held before License Commissioner James F. Geraghty for the renewal of the licenses of the Republic and Eltinge burlesque theaters. Here is an excerpt:

> "So then," said Inspector Frank J. Donovan, describing the shocking goings-on in the burlesque house, "the Toreador goes up to the girls and he says, 'Pooh, pooh! Pah, pah!' It was very suggestive."
>
> "I don't get it," the Commissioner admitted.
>
> "It doesn't suggest anything," groaned Mr. Minsky (the burlesque impresario). "He's terrible. I should have to come to court to see a bum burlesque show."

Another matter irked the gentleman that Mr. Liebling referred to as "the workingman's Ziegfeld." Commissioner Geraghty, in a rebuttal to an attack on the Flea Circus by Ferdinand Pecora, counsel for the Forty-second Street Association, a group bent on purging the hedonistic block between Broadway and Eighth, stated that in his opinion Professor Heckler (the elder) was a respected pulicologist and his attraction drew a higher class of patrons than the burlesque houses; those interested in science and not the merely aesthetic.

"I would not dare tell my girls," Mr. William Minsky is reported to have said, "that they have been compared with fleas. They would be very much offended."

"Well," commented a lawyer, "at least the fleas wear clothes."

Later Commissioner Geraghty had another opportunity to eulogize Professor Heckler and his galaxy of intelligent insects when the Hubert's Museum license came up for renewal. "One of the most marvelous exhibitions in the city," said the eminent jurist to the crusading property owners of the famous street. The Commissioner then went a step further and completely whitewashed Doraldina, the anomalous double-gaited wonder, and suggested that the patrolman who reviewed the Flea Circus for the License Commission be commended to Commissioner Mulrooney. He added that anyhow the Museum had already been granted a license and lacked only two or three permits for some of its minor organic parts, such operations as "The International Dancers"; "Hidden Secrets"; "The Elmira Miracle Trunk"; and the Siamese twins in a bottle. Plainclothesman Ryan's description of Professor Heckler's extravaganza appeared under headlines which said:

A COP REVIEWS
FLEA CIRCUS
BEFORE HEARING

Plainclothesman Ryan
Describes Show

"Marvelous," says
Commissioner

Geraghty Finds That
Exhibit Is More Scientific
Than Minsky's Burlesque

Plainclothesman Andrew A. Ryan reviewed the Flea Circus at Hubert's Museum 230 west 42nd Street today for License Commissioner James F. Geraghty's hearing at No. 6 Reade Street, Manhattan. His work was more than adequate. "There was a booth at one side of the room," stated Plainclothesman Ryan. "Inside on a table was a square pad that looked like a blotter. On that was cotton and some little boxes around the sides. The Professor passed around a flea under a magnifying glass to show how they are harnessed. He explained he trained them not to jump. Some fleas are harder to train than others. The fleas picked up a little ball and tossed it around. Then some fleas harnessed to a wagon hauled it around. There were some colored things they said were dresses. The fleas put them on and they kind of danced around to the music of a music box. The Professor said these were human fleas trapped in the south of Europe and not animal fleas."

The greatest publicity that the Flea Circus ever got nationally came by way of the movies in the early days of the talkies. One afternoon the Professor received from Hollywood a wire three pages long. It seemed to have been composed with more than one eye on distribution in the public prints. In part it said:

AM BADLY IN NEED OF TRAINED FLEAS FOR MY PARAMOUNT PRODUCTION OF ZAZA. SCENE CALLS FOR FLEA TO GO INTO CLAUDETTE COLBERT'S BLOUSE AND BITE HER. ONLY MUST BE FLEA THAT WILL NOT BITE. MISS COLBERT WOULD NOT LIKE TO BE BITTEN BY A FLEA AND IT MIGHT COST US MONEY LATER IF SHE HAD TO STOP AND SCRATCH AND WE WOULD LOSE TIME. COULD YOU SEND SECOND FLEA AS STAND-IN? THEY SHOULD BE FLOWN HERE AS SOON AS POSSIBLE.

The professor had a feeling that he was sending coals to Newcastle, but he rounded up a pair of his lesser lights, dubbed them Sam and Sadie, put a price of $100 per week entire cost on their heads and shipped them air express to the West Coast after first unsuccessfully trying to insure them for $50,000. The expensive premium didn't frighten Paramount or Dr. Heckler, but the deal fell through because the New York office of the underwriter had no appraiser qualified to tell the age of a flea with certainty, nor could they be sure of the identity of a specific individual flea. The airline, puzzled by the weightlessness of the flea shipment, finally compromised on a freight charge of 85¢ total. The Professor gave feeding instructions to a doubtful stewardess, and the fleas were off for their first cinematic role—a walk-on part, but still a foot in the door.

The fleas were met at the Los Angeles airport by the great star herself, with her director, George Cukor, and her leading man, Herbert Marshall, wearing a flea-tempting mustache. A photographer asked Mr. Marshall to please scratch himself. Mr. Marshall replied, "I thought you were going to ask that, but nothing doing."

Miss Colbert was a trifle nervous. "Look," she pleaded with Cukor, "I'm a good actress, a *very* good actress. I can make believe I've got fleas."

Gloria Swanson had made "Zaza" in the silents without benefit of fleas, but the age of celluloid neo-realism was burgeoning. Mr. Cukor was adamant. Fleas it would be, real fleas; none of that faked-up hokery from the props departments.

The flacks beat their drums, and press stories about Sam and

Sadie made all the papers coast-to-coast. The Memphis *Press-Scimitar* even ran an editorial condemning the use of "Fascist Fleas" and cited the inroads made by the Japanese beetle, the Mexican boll weevil, and the Mediterranean fruit fly. "Why not native California fleas?" asked the outraged Dixie editor.

Well, the fleas never even got to a screen test. A property man trying to transform their measly traveling box into a real Hollywood-style dressing room shellacked it. The gook filled the tiny airholes and Sam and Sadie expired.

"A Little Sad Flea Music, Professor," said the headlines now. "Fleas Scratched Before They Began."

At this point enter one Jim Moran, an enterprising young man who had just returned from Alaska with 250 pounds of glacial ice, some scrimshawed walrus tusks, a polar bearskin cape, a receipt for an ice chest sold to an Eskimo for fifty dollars in cash and a "snowshoe box" full of ivory, *and* (it just so happens) two trained Arctic fleas named Warp and Woof—one from the scruff of the neck of an Alaskan malemute, the other from the underbelly of an Arctic glacier wolf. They were snowblind, explained Mr. Moran, and thus would be able to withstand kleig lights and a glare from talcum powder on the bosom of Miss Colbert. One producer thought they looked more like Los Angeles lower-Main-Street-type fleas. "*Cteno-cephalides canis*," he muttered menacingly, but he was hushed by the press department who hired Warp and Woof anyhow, but without their trainer, for "Zaza" was already finished and in the cans.

In the meantime back at the studio the publicity drums were heating up again. The press boys at Paramount proposed to Professor Heckler that the deceased Sam and Sadie lie in state at Hubert's Museum (second choice Campbell's Funeral Home, where Rudolph Valentino had been so gloriously displayed). The space promoters offered to ship the deceased freight prepaid, and for the sacred services to hire an Italian funeral band ("Did you ever *see* an Italian funeral band?" exclaims the Professor when he recounts this incredible epi-sode in the life of his Flea Circus) plus a horse-drawn, black-plumed hearse ("*Horse*-drawn, mind you!") to transport the flea corpses to the Animal Cemetery where a small plot would be purchased with Paramount funds. As an added inducement, Warp and Woof would be loaned as honorary pallbearers providing the Professor could con-dition them to such work.

The high potentate of fleadom toyed with this startling Hollywood brain storm for about five minutes then rejected it violently. "Heck, no! No dice!" he answered straight wire collect. He sometimes thinks he made a mistake. "We could have done it. The police would have been all right," he muses.

Since the coming of television, the Professor and his fleas have been rediscovered by an entirely new public. He has had the creatures on many network shows including "What's My Line," "We, the People, "Do You Trust Your Wife?" and "You Asked for It." And he and the fleas have been guest stars of Garry Moore and Steve Allen. The appearance of flea actors never fails to puzzle the new viewing-generation even though they are accustomed to finding almost anything on the little grey screen. The letters that pour in after one of the Professor's appearances amuse him greatly. They come from school tykes wanting proof that their mothers weren't lying about seeing a Flea Circus on TV while the kids were in school; from college psychology students wanting to know more for a term paper; and from mistrusting husbands and wives.

Here are excerpts from a pair in this latter class:

Dear Garry Moore:
My husband thinks I've flipped my lid, and it's all your fault. Last Tuesday you had a man on your program who had a flea-circus act. I told my husband how interesting it was. I told him about how the fleas pulled the little carts and danced with skirts on and bounced and kicked little balls. He patted me on the head and told me to take an aspirin and go to bed. I still can't convince him and would appreciate your explaining. I would like to prove to my husband I am just as sane as any mother with four small children.

And this evidence of a domestic crisis avoided:

My husband stayed up after I retired and watched the late show. I believe it was Steve Allen. When I questioned him next morning about who he saw, he told me he watched a flea pushing a merry-go-round. Well, I told him I was sorry I asked if he had to give me a smart answer. Then he told me he also saw fleas with skirts on dancing. Well he has told me some good stories, but I thought he has really outdone himself this time. I dropped the conversation. You can imagine my surprise when I viewed your show yesterday. I called him at work and told him I just saw an Irish flea marching and carrying a flag. You should have heard him laugh.

Every once in a while the Professor has an opportunity to play a date away from the Museum and these he enjoys. "What other theatrical company," he asks, "can travel entirely in a small brief case?"

The Heckler fleas used to be a regular attraction at Southampton's celebrated Greentree Fair on the Whitney estate. Only once did the Professor experience any difficulty with his fleas during an engagement on the road. In 1939 at the Editors & Publishers Convention, held at the Waldorf-Astoria Hotel in New York City, he claims to have been terribly distracted during the performance by bright flashes from the Hope diamond worn by Mrs. Evalyn Walsh McLean.

The Professor's fondest remembrance of his outside engagements was of one at the Henry Talbot estate. "Mr. Talbot he was then President of the New York Stock Exchange—years ago," Mr. Heckler recollects. "I worked for fifteen minutes, then I asked Mr. Talbot where the chauffeur was that drove me out in the hired limousine they had sent for me. He said take it easy, the chauffeur was at the butlers', maids' and chauffeurs' party somewheres else on the grounds and to have another glass of champagne. They had three orchestras playing—Ernie Golden's, a colored one and a Hawaiian one; so I stayed all night and didn't get home until 7 A.M., full of champagne and lobster salad. That party must have set him back fifteen or twenty thousand."

One evening as the Professor was packing his flea troupe for a flying trip to an exterminators' convention in Atlanta, Georgia, pulling the loving white socks over his inlaid-pearl flea hotels, he said to me, "If anyone was to ask what is the nicest thing I have learned from the fleas I'd quote my dad who said, 'Even the small are great in the eyes of those who understand them.'"

Bull-hand

When I was a boy of six, my father gave me one Christmas morning a Made-in-Germany toy elephant. It was all wood except for its leather ears, slight rope tail and the rubber end of its trunk. I have it still, although the elastic snap has long since gone from its aged joints. That was when I first became aware of the animal known as the elephant. As I changed from boy into man, from time to time I saw other elephants, real ones. There were those residents of Pittsburgh's Highland Park Zoo; an occasional carnival transient at the old Exposition Park; and several times each spring and summer, the great herds of various circuses that spread their billowing canvas on the Point Breeze lot: Sells-Floto, Hagenbeck-Wallace, Cole Bros., the mammoth Barnum & Bailey and the then-separate Ringling Bros.

It wasn't until I turned from man into clown that I came face to proboscis with an elephant. This happened in the basement of Madison Square Garden in New York City, which is where the circus (Ringling Bros and Barnum & Bailey) displays its menagerie during the Manhattan run. I had joined the show to be a clown, and on my way to the dressing room, to pack in my trunk three shirts I had just bought, I took a short cut past the elephant line-up. One of the beasts stretched her trunk and deftly removed the envelope from under my arm. As the shirts rose heavenward and stomachward I instinctively leaped after them (they had cost something like six dollars each) and caught the paper package just as it reached the elephant's yawning mouth. Lip clamped to trunk. I was every bit as stubborn. There ensued a tussle, and I had just wrenched the parcel loose when a bull-hand came pounding up, swinging his bull-hook. The envelope had a big, juicy, V-shaped intaglio.

"Ya stupid knuckle-head First 'a-May sunabitch," the elephant boy shouted angrily, "that's Big Mary; she could'a' killed ya. Doncha *ever* do that again. You get ta hell out'a here; let ta bulls alone."

Today if an elephant was eating my life's savings, the deed to my house and my marriage license I wouldn't grapple with it.

As I rattled across the nation that summer, I discovered that not only were the huge animals feared by circus troupers but that the entire elephant department was regarded as an iniquitous den of pestilence. On any circus it is the roughest outfit, and few performers care to set foot across its borders.

After I had left the circus to work as a writer, an editor asked me to do a magazine article about Ringling Bros elephants. The big circus that year (1955) was traveling with fifty-one, the largest number ever taken coast-to-coast in America, eleven more than Hannibal took over the Alps. To handle his grand agglomeration of ponderous pachyderms, John Ringling North had hired a young man named Robert ("Smokey") Jones, who was, according to circus friends, the roughest, toughest, most ornery elephant man in the business. He came from the Dailey show, notorious as a free-swinging, hard-boiled buckaroo of a circus. I had never heard of Smokey, but everybody else had, and what they told me made him sound like the devil incarnate. I quavered but accepted the assignment.

The circus, heading west to California, was just beginning a series of stands in Wisconsin, the nicest circus state in the Union. I knew that at least the show grounds would be pleasant. I caught up with the show in Beloit, and when I arrived on the lot that morning, the Big Top canvas was still on the ground in huge bundles. Kids and men and dogs and tractors were trampling all over the rich green grass, the kind that makes good butter and cheese. The last center pole of the mammoth tent was quivering into place behind its three sisters, pointing skyward like so many lonesome, limbless trees and held erect by long threads of tight cable. There wasn't an elephant in sight.

At this stage of the setting up of a circus, the lot to those who are not "with it," seems a completely disorganized sprawl, but from experience and with a little orientation I knew just where the elephant department would be pitching its particular gypsy camp. I went to that end of the lot, the front just off the Midway; the elephants hadn't arrived from the circus train, but the department was all set up and ready for them.

From a long, red, circus wagon, two wings of canvas had been flung. They were without sidewalls and loosely guyed out from short aluminum poles. One side of this casual shelter was empty except for a bale of hay; the other contained a nondescript slew of battered foot-lockers and low wooden and metal boxes and a couple of beat-up cardboard suitcases—the traditional "crumb-boxes" of the circus working departments (crumb is hobo slang for louse). They were set on the ground in two lines, one against the wagon, the other by the side poles, and in a cluster at the far back end of the awninged space. Down its center was a wide, aluminum-covered board resting on two wooden sawhorses to form a rude table. Near the front of the wagon were two ten-gallon milk cans of drinking water with upside-down tincups atop them. A good-sized mirror with a crudely carpentered frame hung to the side of the wagon above a sheaf of skinny metal tent poles. At the wagon's front corner was a first-aid box painted tan and red. A couple of wood-slatted folding chairs, a red wheelbarrow and several red-painted buckets, badly chipped and crudely lettered ELE, completed the furnishings of this open-air parlor of the pachyderm handlers.

Just outside the stake line was a large oil drum filled with water and a fair distance beyond, a separate small square tent, the elephant departments' donnicker. Drooping on its sagging canvas entrance, in two tones of red, was the warning: KEEp OUT ThiS MEANS YOU.

A sandy-headed bull-hand, stripped to the waist, was leaning into the mirror shaving. Behind him, looking over his shoulder, another hand, in beret and light blue coveralls, was also shaving. Another kid, a tousled blond with hair thick as sheep wool, sat on the grass leaning against one of the boxes. He was singing quietly to himself: "Me and my honey, We cain't agree, I'm gonna leave as sure's you're born, I'm gonna leave soon's it gets warm."

When I asked for the boss, the one in front gave me a long circus look, then said, "You mean Smokey? Smokey Jones? He ain't here yet. He comes up with the bulls. They ain't here yet."

None of the trio seemed especially forbidding, so I asked if I could wait in the shade of the flap for Mr. Smokey.

"He ain't Mr. Smokey, he's Smokey, and I guess you can wait if you wanta."

I stood around and, as all circus people do in the presence of a stranger, the boys clammed up except for the casual singing of the third hand: "My landlord said this morning, To give me the key, Cause this room ain't free, You oughta know this room ain't free."

After a while I asked what kind of a guy was this Smokey. Redhead gave me another long look, then deciding that I'd do said, "Well, he don't drink for one thing, and he hates winos."

"And," said the beret, "he fines ya for bein' drunk, so nobody drinks by daylight no more. And he gives ya a pink slip he catches ya watchin' the show. I ain't even seen the whole elephant act since I been here."

The kid on the ground stopped his warbling to observe, "If you have money, you don't like wine."

"Yeah, you do, too," objected the beret. "I do if I have money."

"He never introduces nobody to anybody," continued Red, ignoring the interruption. "Not even to his wife he never introduces nobody."

"He's a hard man," added the towhead. "And is he neat! He pulls up his pants ten eleven times a day just to check to see his shoe-laces are tied. He can't stand even a one wrinkle in his white shirts or a pitcher on a wall crooked."

Towhead's feet were sockless, his ankles so dirty he could have made his initials with spit on a finger; both shoes were covered with dried mud, and the right one was held on with a piece of string knotted through only two eyelets.

"Here comes our ladies now," said Redhead.

I looked off toward the street, and a long grey line of elephants was heaving into sight, kicking up clouds of dust around their feet. Some of the full-grown ones had infant elephants chained to their necks (by pairs and triplets), and a man or boy either riding the head or straddling the neck. Flanking the lead beast on its left was a horse and rider. The man had a ramrod back, was bull-chested; sun and rain had weathered his face. He looked about squint-eyed, as a sea captain does. He was wearing almost new blue-jeans, a spotlessly clean white shirt and a plaid peaked cap, much like that of a baseball player. The other men were dressed catch-as-catch-can in bedraggled shirts and pants.

When the big lead-guy dismounted near the tent, I asked him if he could point out Smokey to me.

"Hell," he said. "Not *me*—I wouldn't put the finger on *Smokey*. He'd kill me fer sure. You wouldn't like him no-how. He drinks, beats his wife and he's mean to the elephants; I never see a more brutal man. We call him the beatin' boy around here."

After he'd gone in under the canvas pachyderm pavilion, I asked Redhead to tell me which one was Smokey. "Hell, man, you tryin' to give me a hard time?" he answered. "*That* was Smokey. He was just playin' the iggy to sound you out."

I looked over to the rest tent. Smokey was standing there looking at me with a big grin on his face. "Kinda fooled you," he said as I came up. "I jest wanted to see if you really wanted to see me." When I told him why I was there, he showed no reaction but invited me to sit down on one of the crumb-boxes while he selected the slightly higher level of a small folding chair. Close-up Smokey Jones was even more impressive than he had been on the horse. He had a bullet head, its rich brown hair close-cropped. His face was beefy with very strong features, a sort of cross between a Polish steel-mill hand and an Indian brave.

Smokey called his animals elephants, not "bulls," as do most other elephant men, even though traditionally circus elephants have always been females. (The Ringling herd at that time had one male, an African, but this was most unusual.) I first asked Smokey how he had managed to keep his elephants so peaceful this season. During the previous, non-Smokey, season, the Ringling elephants had kicked up a good many ruckuses, and in the non-canvas part of this season there had been a few mild backstage stampedes in Madison Square Garden in New York.

"Well," answered Smokey, "I'll tell you. In Winter Quarters I talked to each elephant and they all promised not to fight this year. I got to know each of these elephants personally before I took them on the road." I asked then how this had been accomplished. Did someone tip him off to all their idiosyncrasies? "Their *what?*" he answered. "Oh. . . . No, you don't have to ask nobody if you're an elephant man. I just take them into the ring barn one by one, and before we come back out I find out what each elephant is like."

Smokey began to whittle down a short ax handle, converting it to a stock for a bull-hook, the chief tool of an elephant handler. It's a sturdy stick a little thicker than a broom handle or a cane and usually not longer than twice the forearm of the handler, though length varies, depending on personal preference. A metal hook with blunt point is imbedded in the club's end.

"You don't have to pick on them," Smokey continued. "My method is: first I ask an elephant nice, then I command. If they still don't do it, I do it for them. You put the hook just against them, let them jab it into their hide if they want to. Next time they'll do what you want without force."

Since a circus elephant is uncaged and goes about fairly free and unfettered, it is necessary to instill in the beast a sense of respect for its handler. The majority of elephant men say this can be accomplished in so large a beast only by fear—a fear of discomfort and punishment. These trainers firmly believe (though there are some who avow otherwise) that mere food reward for positive action and a withholding of it for negative action will not work with the elephant, that actual punishment must follow disobedience. True elephant love, and it definitely exists, is supposed to come to the man who is feared but who also has shown his animal companion that physical punishment will be meted out only if the beast disobeys. When this relationship is established, a decent elephant will work for praise or affection alone, without food rewards. A stubborn elephant can usually be brought to its knees by the gradual tightening of chains attached to the left rear and right front foot until the animal is supporting its entire weight on the two free legs. This soon becomes an exhausting ordeal, and the rebel finally submits with bellowing bawls of protest, eyes bulging and bowels erupting. Once an elephant loses this psychological joust, it usually acknowledges its master, who then sits by the elephant's head saying kind words and making gentling actions. Such action requires real courage, for the beast's man-crippling trunk is still very much available to it. At this point in elephant handling elephant men are separated from the boys.

Sometimes a really malevolent elephant has to be beaten into submission; there is no other way. It is best, elephant men say, to approach an evil elephant, especially a male tusker, from the rear on its left side, the side of chain and command. The beating is given to the fleshy side of the head between eye and ear with an iron tent stake or a bull-hook. Even though the elephant is securely chained, the one-sided scrap takes a lot of man. The joining of the battle is a point of no return. If the man gives up from lack of courage or energy, he will never again be able to handle the balky elephant.

To secure a troublesome elephant in a bull-line, Smokey Jones recommends, instead of the customary iron stakes, a flat steel plate with U-bolt at its center through which rides a chain, its ends fastened to both legs of the elephant. The plate is made round to make it easy for the men to handle by rolling.

"Them grease-ball clowns," continued Smokey, hasping away at his ax handle, "are always worrying about us elephant men beating the elephants. Hell, even Doc Higgins"—Smokey referred to the circus's No. 2 veterinarian—"and there ain't a kinder man livin'— he changed his mind about havin' to wap elephants once in a while." He sighted along the ax handle. "Why, goddammit, a cop carries a club bigger'n that to hit a *human*. Besides, you can't hurt an elephant on the trunk no matter how hard you wap her. It's all gristle."

The true elephant man never permits himself to feel safe at any time around an elephant. "Every one," Smokey told me, "has his own brand of knockout punch. A'course we know which is the bad ones, but you never can tell when one is gonna turn bad. And with the bad ones, they don't give you no warning before they attack. They just let you have it. Whammy!"

In handling his elephants, I learned that Smokey Jones also uses a long bull whip. "The whip crack keeps them in line," he explains. "No hookin' is necessary. Just flicking on the feet is best; it smarts because the feet is tender. A lot is in training," Smokey explained. "You don't have to pick on elephants. These young 'uns had a good trainer, the man who broke me in to the business, Louie Reed; best in the business for my money."

Smokey was interrupted by a dark-faced, mustachioed fellow, who had changed into a blue uniform cap, light blue shirt and uniform pants. "Meet Big John," said Smokey, the man who never introduces nobody to anybody. "Big John Basset from Macon, Georgia. He's my first assistant. I got four of them and I wisht I had eight or nine like Big John." Big John looked embarrassed.

"How much you charge me," he blurted to his boss, "to put another popper on my whip?"

"What kinda popper you want?" countered Smokey.

"Any kind. I don't know one from another."

"You want a good flax popper?" asked Smokey.

"I don't know, Smokey," said Big John, just a bit exasperated. "I practiced last night in the car for two hours. Boy! My hands!"

"You gettin' good?"

"I'm gittin' better."

"You want it now?"

"Nah, between shows is okay."

"There's time now," said Smokey, "there ain't nobody gonna be in there," referring to the matinee audience.

"I plait all my own whips," Smokey said to me, "I can do one in ten minutes flat." He started to put the popper onto Big John's whip. "Elephants," he then said to me, "they know if you're an elephant man or not. You go from one show to another, they can smell you. You got elephant smell all through you, especially on your shoes."

I asked Smokey if he didn't find it difficult to tell one elephant from another. During my performing days, while elephants didn't all look alike to me, I had never been able to identify any one particular elephant for certain.

"Hell," said Smokey, "ain't nothin' to it when you work around them every day. Modoc is unmistakable; she's got such a big jughead all out of proportion to her body. Joske is big all over; she must weigh five ton and she has an awful thick trunk (she don't take much hookin'). Judy is the tall one; Knaudie has a bad eye; and Babe is the stiff-legged one, the roughest on the show for ridin'. Each one has somethin' different. Little Ruth has a large head, but it's beautiful—at least, I think it's pretty. Myrt is so big, you can't miss *her*."

I found out that Smokey knows the names of all his charges and, hardly using his fingers at all, he recited them for me like a beautiful sonnet. "There's Louie," he said, "the male African. And Modoc, Big Ruth, Mary, Knaudie, Big Jewel, Joske, Judy, Big Babe, Lois, Topsy, Little Babe, Icky, Marcella, Myrtle, Ruth (that's Little Ruth), Sabu, Trilby, Emily (the female African), Minyak (the maniac, she's a stomper). And the babies—les' see, I'll do them like they line up: Texas, Padma, Tara, Yamina (Yammy), Rani, Seeta, Rajee, Lizzy, Blondie, Bombee (maybe that's Bambi), Siam, Luna, Lucy, Betty, Calcutta, Indian, Cutie, Henry (or I guess Henrietta), Trixie, Cass, Eva, Little Mary (Big Mary is the mean one; throws off anybody gets on her head), Pinky, Sudan (I call her Suzanne), Mysore, Adele, Fanny, Moe, Jeannie, Rajee (Little Rajee). Let's see, that makes fifty-one in all; and there's three at quarters: Little Jewel, Eva and Ringling Jenny."

In the background I heard one of the elephant boys ask another about the identity of the elephants. "Don't ast me," was the hard answer, "which one is Mary or Root. Ast your assistants; that's what they gets paid for."

"That's one of the new punks," explained Smokey, who had his ear out, too. "We just picked him up in yesterday's town. That's the hardest trouble I have—keepin' help. We're always runnin' short-handed."

On my visit to Smokey's stomping grounds, he was down to nineteen men and four assistants to handle the fifty-one elephants. He had been able to operate with as few as twelve men, but considered this a little dangerous all around, if not downright foolhardy. "I can get lotsa wino's," said the young elephant trainer, "but they ain't no damned good. There's one over there now by the donnicker. He come around this morning down at the train lookin' for a job. I put him on cause I needed another hand—but he won't last. I know him from other shows. He goes real crazy, that one, on that 'Sneaky Pete.' He woke me up once on the Dailey show in the middle of the night and ast me, 'Who am I?' Uh-uh, I don't like that one, but what am I gonna do? Beggars can't be choosers."

Smokey's four assistants hailed from Maine, Georgia, Pennsyl-

vania and Ohio. His polyglot collection of bull-hands came mainly from Southern small towns with a few from Northern industrial cities. Many elephant men are in the trade because they are overpoweringly fascinated by the behemoths and honestly love to be around them. However, I have found out that run-of-the-mill hands usually join out with a strong desire to get even with society because life has warped them with some low roundhouse blow. The surge of power these twisted kids get from pushing around the enormous hulks of elephants is a source of great satisfaction. Many of the youngsters have been streaked by cruelty or battered by neglect and it takes very little to unleash dormant monsters of sadism and masochism.

The pay of an All-American mahout is not attractive. Even on the largest circuses it is incredibly low. The scale for ordinary bull-hands at the Ringling Bros and Barnum & Bailey circus, when the big show was still under canvas, was $16.67 a week, board, berth and transportation thrown in. Assistants' pay during my circus days (as late as 1953) was $40 a week plus board, lodging and travel, and the Elephant Boss took home $85 cash money from the pay-wagon.

Smokey went out to see how the watering of the elephants was coming on, and I tagged along. Elephant watering in the minds of small boys grown to adults is associated with the carrying of countless buckets à la The Sorcerer's Apprentice. But today pachyderms get their water differently. A water wagon (a truck) pumps the water by hose into a half dozen large metal drums, and the elephants are led to this drinking line-up in groups of twelve to eighteen. In other words the mountains come to Mahomet. The Ringling elephants that year were watered twice a day: after their walk from the train, and after the matinee performance. Elephants seldom urinate while performing before the public as they dislike getting their legs wet. They usually relieve themselves while standing still outside the tent awaiting their cue, or upon being returned to the picket line. An elephant takes on about fifty gallons of water per day. One of the screwball notions people have about elephants is that water is drunk through the trunk as though the proboscis were an outsize soda straw. The trunk is merely a five-gallon capacity conveyor of water to the mouth. By contraction, the beast's stomach is able to bring up a small amount of water so that long after its last drink the elephant can reach into its mouth and siphon a trunkful for spraying. Bull-hands firmly believe that an elephant has two stomachs: a large back one for solids, and a smaller one in front for liquids.

The new punk was handling the canvas, nozzleless fire hose, flopping it frantically and sloppily from one emptied drum to another. He was still trying to learn the names.

"What's this 'un's name?" he asked a bull-hook wielder. "Maudie?"

"No, *Knaudie*, you stupid Firsta-May lunkhead."

"Which one leads the whole works?" the new punk persisted. "And which one do *I* ride on?"

"You ride on whichever one Smokey says," was the hard-bitten answer, "and you ride the same one every day. Who you think you are? John Ringling Nort?" Then the bull-hooker reared back and smacked one of his wet charges with the handle of his bull-hook, saying, "Get down, ya lunkhead bastid!"

"Whatja do that fer?" asked the new punk.

"Cat-fer to make kittens' britches. 'Cause she threw my buddy las' night. That's what fer," was the surly answer.

As I stepped a little further down the line, a boy at the next pair of thirsty elephants said, "The worst thing about an elephant is bein' hit by one. By-*jeez*-zus man! They are *powerful*. I got thirty-two stitches in my head from bein' thrown. She used me for a batter ram."

This bull-hand had a fresh tattoo on his forearm, an elephant's head rampant, shiny with oil, and beginning to scab. "I got it at Harvard," he said, "when we played New Haven. See where it's gettin' light around the edges. It's not too very artistic. He didn't know how to draw the trunk so good. I never did like the sound of tattooin'; it sounds like a dentist's drill—but it don't hurt none."

In the grassy field, the Big Top was beginning to puff into an enormous, dusty brown mushroom. Six elephants, in broad leather work harnesses with drag chains, idled with their handlers alongside the stake line, waiting for their job inside to be ready. The working girls' names were painted on their chest-straps: Lois, Ruth, Jewel, Tony, Babe and Myrtle. Lois was romping with her handler, chasing him playfully among the drooping guy-ropes.

I found an opening in the dirty canvas drapery, pushed under and had the feeling of being in an enormous cave, a little boy again under a mother's skirt. The side poles had not yet been placed around the enormous tent's perimeter, so that the canvas swooped right to the ground from its low peaks part way up the center poles. The bale rings wouldn't be pulled to the very tops of those sixty-five-foot wooden spars until all the quarter poles had been positioned. This *main* part of the tremendous job of heisting the acres of canvas would be done by motor winch. Until a few seasons back, it had been managed by combined block-and-tackle and elephants. The loose canvas muffled the tumultuous hustlings of a hundred or more workers swarming the burgeoning amphitheater. The long quarter poles were being stabbed by manpower into their metal eyelets in the vast sag of canvas, the men running the lengthy aluminium tubes like battering rams.

Very soon the poles, hanging between canvas and earth at gawky 30- and 45-degree angles, were ready to be pulled upright by the work elephants. The elephant is used for this work because it can go under the drooping canvas without tearing it, can maneuver in places where a tractor cannot and can more precisely spot the poles. Draught horses are not suitable, as the flapping, flopping canvas frightens them. The job of setting up the poles is fairly simple. A Big Top work-hand hooks the elephant's chain to a metal ring at the base of the quarter pole, the bull-hand walks his lady forward, and the pole skids across the ground and up into place pushing the canvas with it. Three elephants work each side so that the vast tent takes shape evenly.

When the Big Top is finally in the air, bull-hands go into the menagerie area and drive the stakes that restrain the elephant herd. Each elephant is chained by its left back leg and the right front one. The chains are devised so that the animal cannot unhook them with its versatile trunk. The chain hook must be inserted in only one particular link in a just-so position, and to do this a man needs both his hands. The elephant could work it if only she had two trunks.

As I passed along the line of chained monsters, I stopped to talk to a bull-hand who seemed more mature than the fledglings I had thus far encountered. He said his name was Huey but not Big Huey—just Huey Davis. He had been around circuses a long time, said Huey, and was presently in charge of seven infant bulls. He called them his "Seven Wonders." He told me that this town reminded him of his grandmother's home town. "As I was ridin' up on the bulls this morning," Huey said wistfully, "I kept lookin' for her house, and then I realized this wasn't the same town at all. Funny, ain't it, how you get notions like that."

Then Huey, as circus people have a way of doing, abruptly switched subjects, asking me, "You seen that white elephant they got on the Cristiani show? Oney it ain't really white, just sort of yellowish grey with pink splotches. But they say she's a *gen-you-wine* all right and not sandpapered and bleached with peroxide."

In 1884 at a reputed cost of two hundred thousand dollars, and the lives of five crewmen, P. T. Barnum brought from Siam an authentic white elephant, Toung Talong, whereupon the master showman's rival, Adam Forepaugh, transformed an ordinary member of his herd, by bleach and sanding, into an elephant as white as Smokey Jones's shirt.

Huey nudged one of his dirty grey elephants back a little. "You should'a' seen when we had the gold elephant for Mary-lin Monroe to ride in New York. Boy, was that somethin'! They used fifteen pounds of gold powder mixed with postage-stamp glue and water. And you know, like the guy wouldn't wash his duke after he shook hands with the President, well, we didn't wash the elephant all season. She stayed gold until it wore off fine-ly."

Then Huey pointed out to me the difference between Asian and African elephants, the latter being the rarest on exhibition in this country. "The difference is like between a razorback hog and a genuine hog," he explained. "The African is high in the back and more of a ridge. And its trunk is more like put together in sections. But the biggest difference is in the heads. The African is more pointy-like with big ears and the Asian is squarish with big bumps up front, and has just regular small ears."

Huey didn't know it, and I saw no reason to worry him with the knowledge, but the very first elephant on this earth was a small piglike creature with a flattened snout. It was called *Moeritherium* because its fossil remains were found by the dry edge of Lake Moeris in the Libyan desert of North Africa.

Little "Mo," who stood about three feet high on slender legs that bent at their elbows, like those of his kissin' cousins, the hippopotamus and rhinoceros, was among the earliest citizens of the Cenozoic, or mammalian, era of life which began sixty million years ago and, of course, still continues. "Mo" emerged in the Eocene, the first of the five epochs of the Tertiary period, when this fire-ball planet after 940 million years had finally cooled off enough to support mammalian life.

After several million years of stretching out its flexible upper lip in search of nourishment, the *Moeritherium* developed a long Pinocchio-like nose. As the descendants of the creature gypsied about the primeval jungles, they increased in stature and grew long shaggy, yellowish brown hair, became mammoths and pushed out double sets of enormous curving tusks. The mammoths lived almost to the very end of the glacial or Pleistocene period of mankind and from them came the imperial elephants, those early Asian giants, and our own modern-day smaller pachyderms. The mastodon coexisted as an ally of the mammoth in its early days, but it was not concerned in the development of our present-day elephant.

The last time elephant noses were seriously counted in the United States was 1952 and that census disclosed that there were 264 of the mammoth beasts within our borders. Circuses had 124 of them. There were 28 with individual acts; 5 traveling with carnivals; 15 in the hands of animal dealers; and zoos were exhibiting 92. Only 6 of the total were males and 3 of those were in the zoos of Houston, Texas; Tacoma, Washington; and Chicago, Illinois.

Bernhard Grzimek, director of the Frankfurt (Germany) Zoological Gardens, has stated that in 1957 there were two hundred thousand elephants in Africa. There has been no estimate of the number existing in the territories of the Asiatic elephant—India, Ceylon, Burma, Malaya, Sumatra, Siam, Borneo and Indo-China.

The first elephant in London came there in the year 1254 (not counting the one Caesar brought in 54 B.C.), the gift of Louis IX to his brother-in-law, Henry III, who already had a white bear which he quartered in the Tower of London, periodically sending it on leash, by a keeper, to fish for its grub in the Thames.

Yankeedom's first elephant was a female brought by Captain Jacob Crowninshield of the ship *America* to Salem, Massachusetts, on April 13, 1796. She amazed all beholders and was never called anything more than simply "The Elephant." She was promptly bought by a Mr. Owen for ten thousand dollars in gold.

Mr. Owen's handbills stated that his superb attraction had the "Adroitness of the Beaver, the Intelligence of the Ape, the Fidelity of the Dog." They also confided that "he eats 130 weight a day and drinks all kinds of spiritus liquors; some days he has drank 30 bottles of porter, drawing the corks with his trunk." There was also

a warning: "The Elephant, having destroyed many papers of conse-
quence, it is recommended to visitors not to come near him with
such papers." Mr. Owen's colossus is known to have been exhibited
for a Quarter of a Dollar a look (Children 9-pence) until 1818; the
last recorded stop being at York, Pa.

The next elephant immigrant, named Little Bet, arrived in 1811,
and padded around until 1822 when she was shot by five small boys
curious as to whether a bullet would penetrate her hide. One kid was
lucky. He aimed between the eyes.

In 1815, a third elephant was brought to young America by
another sea captain who for one thousand dollars unloaded her on
Hackaliah Bailey, the proprietor of a country inn, The Bull Head
Tavern at Twenty-third Street and Third Avenue, New York City.
Hackaliah was no relation to the famous James A. Bailey. He had,
however, an inherent feeling for showmanship and immediately
packed off his new acquisition by sloop to Ossining and thence
traveled overland afoot to Somers, New York. From there he toured
the countryside with several bears, monkeys and the elephant, which
he called Old Bet. The rag-taggle troupe moved in the dark of night
to prevent free looks, exhibiting in stable yards and barns by day,
for a price. An advance agent with a bell rode ahead on horseback.
From Old Bet, Hackaliah made enough loot to build a fancy resort
hotel in Somers which, naturally, he called The Elephant Hotel. As
the money continued to clink in, Bailey erected in front of his hostel
a granite shaft with Old Bet immortalized in wood atop it. It is still
there. So is The Elephant Hotel, only now it is called the Somers
Town Hall.

Five years after the Grand Gala Opening Fete of The Elephant
Hotel, Old Bet was shot by an irate posse of Maine farmers whose
vegetable gardens, fences and grain fields the giant mammal had
wrecked during a rampage inspired by a stolen jug of Maine-potato
moonshine. Bailey knew exactly what to do with the carcass. He
had it stuffed and sold it to P. T. Barnum, who exhibited it in his
museum until the establishment burned to the ground in 1835.

Every thirty years or so a circus press agent gets the brilliant
idea of conducting an elephant pilgrimage to lay a wreath on Old
Bet's monument. The last such trek took place in 1953 when one
of Hunt Bros Circus bulls did the honors to inaugurate a fund-
raising festival for restoring a church, the Old Tomahawk.

Some years earlier, 1922, Deafy Denman had led an elephant

called Old John up the river (both on foot) to Somers in a similar project to pay homage at the granite shaft. Old John, his feet still tender from the inactivity of Winter Quarters, wore a sort of purple galoshes made of oilcloth and the trip, a distance of about sixty miles, took three days. As man and behemoth passed through upper Park Avenue on a Sunday morning, Deafy felt like the Pied Piper of Hamelin. Kids poured from every tenement and followed the elephant for blocks and blocks, feeding him ice cream, apples and candy. The fabulous sawdust press agent, Dexter Fellows, met the pilgrimage in Somers with a brass band, a cake baked especially by the Ladies' Aid Society and a wreath as big as an elephant tub. John took it and placed it around Mr. Fellows' neck. The return trip was made by truck, and Old John had colic for a week.

Jumbo, the elephant everybody remembers, the pachyderm that added that word indicating great size to the American language (jum'bo, *n.*; *pl.* JUMBOS [-boz]. A big, clumsy thing or person;) didn't get over here until 1883. Jumbo was the greatest elephant the civilized world had ever seen. Official figures, recorded at the London Zoo from whence he came, state he was 10 feet 10 inches at the shoulders, weighed 8 tons and had a trunk 27 inches in circumference. He had been captured in Abyssinia, in 1861, when only 3½ feet high, bought by a Bavarian trader and sold to the Jardin des Plantes in Paris. Shortly after, Jumbo was traded to the London Zoological Society for a rhinoceros. In England he achieved his phenomenal size and became the children's favorite, the recipient of buns and crumpets by the crate.

When Barnum bought Jumbo for ten thousand dollars, the beloved beast's departure raised a public hue and cry which developed into a minor Anglo-American incident with Queen Victoria putting in her royal tuppence worth. She issued an order forbidding the sale, making the British nation officially liable for any damages incurred by a breach of contract. Barnum won hands-down all attempts of the Britons to hang on to Jumbo, and soon had him in the States where he advertised that his ears were as "large as parlour folding doors," and plastered his greatly exaggerated image across the countryside above such blurbs as "JUMBO, The Pride of the British Heart . . . Her Majesty, The Queen, Her Children and Grandchildren & Over One Million & A Quarter of English Children Have Ridden On His Broad Back in Seventeen Years." (The twenty-six children seated in the howdah hardly took up any room at all on the lithographed mammoth.)

Within six weeks after Jumbo's arrival, Barnum had pocketed $336,000 in gate receipts. The bonanza didn't last long, for 3½ years later in 1885 Jumbo was killed at the age of twenty-four by a freight train of the Grand Trunk Railroad at St. Thomas, Ontario, Canada, the impact derailing two cars. Undaunted, Barnum had the hide stuffed. Then he sent to the London Zoo for Alice, an African female. Billed as Jumbo's widow, she was exhibited alongside the stuffed remains. Jumbo's skeleton finally came to rest in the American Museum of Natural History. The preserved hide (1,538 pounds) went to the Barnum Museum of Natural History at Tufts College. Jumbo's head is still the college emblem. Nobody seems to know what happened to Alice.

In the 1830's, what could be accepted as the first group of trained elephants was appearing with the John Raymond Menagerie: four driven in tandem to a band wagon. Barnum was the first circus mogul to take on a large group of elephants, ten Singhalese in 1851. By 1881, the combined Barnum and Cooper-Bailey-Hutchinson shows owned twenty. Opening the 1887 circus season at the old Madison Square Garden, the hated rivals, P. T. Barnum and Adam Forepaugh, joined forces, each exhibiting thirty elephants. In 1886, when the Ringling Bros were Rüngeling Brüders, they owned but two elephants. In 1931, John Ringling, lone survivor of those famed circus kinsmen, had under his thumb and Big Top, what was undoubtedly the greatest assemblage of elephants ever gathered for exhibition in this country; one hundred—one third the total number in the U.S.A. at that time; about twice as many as Smokey Jones was shepherding in the coast-to-coast caravan of Mr. John's enterprising nephew, Johnny.

After I had left the elephant line-up in the menagerie and was back at Smokey's rest tent, I asked this latter-day Hannibal how it felt to be responsible for so many expensive elephants.

"Hell," he said, "I just got them wished on me by Louie Reed. I'm only doin' it for him and my reputation." He spat into the grass and said to Big John, "Tell him what Louie said to you when we left Quarters this spring with the elephants."

Big John grinned crookedly. "Well, old Louie, he said, 'If you don't come into Sarasota we're through.'"

"He meant," Smokey explained, "we gotta finish the season: stick with the elephants all the way and not blow the show. Louie Reed is one man I don't want to be through with me."

"Best in the business," said Big John. "I learned how to handle a shovel an' a broom from Louie. If you didn't do it just right his way, he'd come at you swingin' his bull-hook. He's kinda a little snaggle-tooth anyhow, and he scares the hell outa you—especially the new punks. Mighty good man to break in with."

"The best," amended Smokey. "He is like a father to me. I love him like my own father. Better. Because I never knew my old man." He spat again. "The chief press agent, he come around one day in New York, and he said to me, 'Smokey, you're the greatest elephant man ever, handlin' so many elephants at your age.' (I'm twenty-eight)." He looked toward the "Red Wagon," the circus manager's office on wheels. "Big deal," he said, "they're payin' me a great big fat hundred bucks a week, less'n two dollars an elephant. And you know what one of them things is worth? The babies, about thirty-five hundred dollars each; the whole herd over a hundred grand. But hell, a hundred bucks is more'n any other elephant boss ever got around here and when you figure I started out like them punks, only makin' less money, guess I'm doin' all right. I ain't complainin'.

"We gotta pretty good show," he said. "Fifty-one elephants in the Big Top all at once. And wait until you see them cute little buggers in the baby carriages. Them punks was jungle babies only last summer. Louie Reed, he broke them in down at Quarters last winter." I ventured that elephants in baby carriages sounded like a novel innovation. "Hell," said Smokey, "it ain't nothin' new. Louie told me that they had somethin' like it way back in nineteen-oh-five at the New York Hippodrome. Elephants drivin' fancy phaeton autos, them high old-fashioned ones, across the stage with fourteen girls in them, each one."

From a member of the Circus Historical Society I later learned that Ringling's elephant-baby-buggy idea went back even further, for an elephant born in captivity on the Sells-Floto Circus in 1902 had been trundled around the hippodrome track in a glass-sided snake cage pushed by a full-grown elephant dressed as a Gibson girl. A sideshow banner-line painter, noticing an item concerning the stunt in a circus fan's scrapbook, had passed along the idea to the circus performance director, who slipped it to John Ringling North who loved it and, never a man to do anything on a small scale, immediately ordered a half dozen elephant baby buggies.

There seems to be nothing new in elephant trickdom. All the elaborate, purportedly new, stunts are merely variations of four basic maneuvers: the leg-stand; the lay-down; the sit-up; and the whirl-around. Combined with walking and shuffling, this quartet of old stand-bys forms the basis of even the most complicated of routines.

Years ago, when circuses were sawdust empires, performing pachyderms were exhibited as talented and individual performers. Then elephants walked tightropes, boxed, played ninepins and a crude form of baseball, waltzed, harmonized with sleigh bells, blew harmonicas and trombones, beat drums, rode tricycles, telephoned each other, and shaved themselves, using tubs of creamy lather and outsize straight razors. It is the tendency of the modern circus to present elephants as a spectacle of mass and might, surrounded by dancers, acrobats and clowns, little attention being given to the heavy but strangely graceful, individual performance of the monsters. "We have an art," moan the trainers today, "but it's fast becoming a lost art smothered by spangles and legs. There are days when you can't see the elephants for the girls."

Leaving Smokey, who had begun to shave for the matinee, I sauntered around to the circus back yard, that sacrosanct performers' area beyond the Big Top's back-entrance doors.

A couple of elephant boys were having coffee at the Grease-joint. Talking to them as I came up was a man whom I recognized as Hugo Schmidt, the trainer who presented the elephants in the show's center-ring act. (Smokey did all his work outside the big tent.) I've known Hugo for many happy years and was glad to see him again.

"Yah, yah," he was saying as I arrived at the counter, "you stay away from fooling mit that Louie. He put his tusk right true you one day."

When the unimpressed pair of kids strolled off, Hugo said to me, "*Kleine* ponks, they already know id all. Big *ale*-if-unt trainers. Been First-of-May two months yet."

Hugo is a short, stocky man with an enormous thick chest and a thicker German backwards way of speaking. You have to be around him a while to catch the precise meaning of everything he says. He is one of the circus world's most decent, most honest citizens. He possesses an enormously pleasant moonface, and smiles with crinkly eyes. His head is all but bald, and in the circus he covers its shine with a nicely combed auburn hair-piece. Hugo is that circus oddity, a good father, which under the Big Top is as rare as an okapi. He has two teenage sons, Manfred and Uwe, another boy, Roman, and an infant, Eddie. He is one of the kindest men I've ever known around circuses, which have a plethora of kind people. Hugo Schmidt is also

one of the bravest men I have ever encountered. He faces an elephant charge unflinchingly. I have seen him, by a Götterdämmerung bellow, stop cold, within two feet of his purpling face, a dangerously enraged, onrushing elephant. And finally, Hugo is one of the world's best elephant trainers. He began working with the mammoth creatures, after first dabbling in lions and tigers, thirty-three years ago when he had just turned twenty-one. When I had gotten my paper cup of coffee "all-the-way" (cream and sugar), Hugo and I sat on a nearby wagon pole and talked about elephant training.

He told me that the best elephant trainer the world has ever known was Karl Glutski, a German. And the finest all-round wild-animal trainers he has ever known were Roman Proske and Alfred Court. (Hugo so admires the former, known for his work with big cats, that his seven-year-old was named Roman in Proske's honor.)

In training, Hugo explained to me, the first thing is getting a chain on the elephant's leg, a really challenging job, for they are great kickers. They do not, however, kick like horses but with tremendous force are able to strike out, pistonlike, with a single leg forwards or backwards. They also kick to the side, though not so powerfully nor so accurately. (Because of the elephant's ability to kick, a handler always walks alongside an elephant's front leg—a position in which the man is fairly safe from all but the relatively harmless side swipes and from which he is able to keep an eye on, and control with bull-hook, the only other potential launching site of elephant attack—the trunk.) Once an elephant is hobbled with a chain, the trainer "tames the trunk" by teaching the elephant to hold a stick in it or to "tail-up" trunk to tail with another elephant.

After the trunk has been disciplined comes the tremendous job of making the elephant's enormous hulk respond to the trainer's wishes. The easiest position is taught first, that of lying down. To teach a dog this fundamental trick, its trainer upsets it by holding its legs in pairs. Obviously this cannot be done with an elephant. Neither can the trainer drop the beast by beating or "hooking" down with the bull-hook. The only way that an elephant can be made to compre- hend what is meant by the trainer's command of "down" is to have the beast's leg-support forcibly removed. This is done by a group of strong men applying power to leg chains while the elephant is held in padded slings, supported by block-and-tackle. This use of the block- and-tackle is the only mechanical means ever employed during ele- phant training. "All else," said Hugo, "I do mit my hands."

Once the elephant has been induced to lie down on command, the task of breaking the beast to perform tricks begins—a long tedious business, during which the man achieves as complete a control of the beast as is possible, a working control, for no wild beast is ever brought unconditionally under subjection. Herr Schmidt believes that even temporary subjugation cannot be accomplished by force alone. "I teach respect, not afraid," he explains, "und trust. When you say some-ding you haf to do it. Same like kids. You tell a kid you do some-ding you must do it. No can make disappointment or froos-trate." He is not an advocate of beating for beating's sake. "When ale-if-funt she go crazy," he reasons, "they no care for hook, no afraid from hook. Like a voo-man. When she is no in luf, haf no respect, she do nuddings. Or like *ein* kid. When you haf to beat a kid every time to do some-ding, is no goot. You must teach right from wrong, und respect. If you beat all the time, soon the ale-if-funt she no care, but she begin to hate you inside—same like younker—or voo-man."

Hugo prefers his elephant pupils to be aged five or six, feeling that then the animal is at its intellectual and physical peak. He also favors the ages from fifteen to twenty, for then the animal has had the benefit of jungle training administered by its experienced elders.

Hugo Schmidt finds that elephants will not all accept the same tricks. "Is not exactly the same every elephant," he explains. "You must vatch the char-*act*-ter. In tree, vor veeks you know an elephant. Some take vun year to learn what anudder take only two, tree days. Same like people." Hugo says the most difficult trick to teach is the one-front-leg stand, an ancient trick recently revived by trainer Mac MacDonald of the Polack Bros. Circus. In 1957 Hugo achieved it with his infant bull, Targa. The stunt requires a thorough under-standing by the beast and trainer of balance and weight distribution, as does another formidable trick, the hind-leg stand and walk. Schmidt is the first man on record who was able to train an African male ele-phant to stand on its hind legs. The hind-leg stand requires three months of arduous training before perfection as compared to the mere three days needed to teach an elephant to stand on both its front legs. This stunt is as much a headstand as a legstand since balance is aided greatly by the trunk extending forward along the ground.

The two tricks most dangerous to the performer are the "head-carry," in which the trainer is suspended by the head from the ele-phant's mouth, and the "foot-in-face," in which the trainer lies supine on the ground and permits the elephant to touch the flat of a front foot to his nose-tip. A similar trick is one in which an elephant squats down on all fours, lowering its tremendous weight over the body of the trainer. Those three are the artistes' disaster and death tricks. The head-carry with its seventy-five-pound pressure on the skull can result in a crushed head or a broken neck, if the swings of man and beast get out of adjustment. In the other two stunts there is the strong possibility of bashed-in face or crushed body. I asked Hugo about the dangers of the head-carry. Smiling he answered, "Yah, sure, you can break your neck, but is no so dangerous."

The most spectacular circus-elephant trick is what all circus people call "the long-mount," in which two lines of elephants, their leaders facing each other, simultaneously rear into a front-feet-to-back mount, using one elephant as a keystone. Circuses have traditionally featured the "long-mount" as the elephant-act finale longer than the oldest elephant can remember. It is always the big spine-tingler of any performance.

Hugo Schmidt was an elephant trainer in Europe long before he came to this country in 1948. One of his favorite elephant performers on the other side of the Atlantic was Cora, a most unusual creature, who could whistle as well as do all the tricks. She was very fond of her *liebchen* Hugo and showed her affection by licking his bald head as a dog licks his master's hand. Cora came to Hugo at the ideal age of six and stayed for twelve years, giving him four babies spaced three years apart. From Cora, Hugo learned the intimate details of an elephant's sex life in a way that has been denied most American trainers, since so few elephants have been born in this country.

Perhaps the most famous of our little more than half dozen native-born elephants, none of which lived more than a year, was "Young America" born March 10, 1880, in Philadelphia, the first elephant birth in this country since prehistoric times. The calf's mother, "Hebe," belonged to P. T. Barnum's strongest competitor, a show under the joint management of James E. Cooper, James A. Bailey and James L. Hutchinson, which had the most unwieldy title on record: "Great London Circus, Sanger's Royal British Managerie, and Grand International Shows." The calf's father was so unimportant that his name was not recorded. Hebe gave birth in a stove-heated room and, responding to instinct, immediately after parturition flung the kid away from her, just missing a cherry-red stove. While the keeper ran for help, Hebe broke her chains and, smashing a heavy rail around the heater, picked up the baby and reflung her across the barn. This time it landed in a bed of hay. It took seven men to rechain Hebe. The calf was unhurt, but Hebe would never nurse it, continually kicking it away. So the baby was fed through a rubber hose with a formula of rice and boiled milk. Bailey made a spectacular announcement of the blessed event in the newspapers. Barnum read it and immediately wired an offer to buy the newborn for $100,000. Instead of selling, the shrewd Bailey printed the telegram on a six-sheet poster in letters a foot high with the terse caption: "This is what Barnum thinks of Cooper & Bailey's baby elephant." Barnum, impressed with Bailey's handling of the deal, offered him, in exchange for the baby elephant and Bailey's services as manager, a joint partnership, and thus was born that greatest of all American circus institutions, Barnum & Bailey. The ink was hardly dry on the incorporation papers when "Young America" up and died.

Hugo Schmidt, who has likely seen more births and sexual meetings of elephants than any other man in this country, told me that the mammalian giants engage in a more affectionate courtship than do other animals. A bull elephant cannot be handled for mating purposes in the same way as a stud horse or a tomcat. Elephants require prolonged courtship. For, while a lady elephant can be rushed off her feet by block-and-tackle, an affair of love becomes a more delicate matter. Elephant romance is a gentle endurance contest. The male approaches his lady-fair warily, blows timidly and playfully in her ear, touches her lightly with his long proboscis, and shares any delectable tidbits that he lays onto—little love offerings such as cigarette butts, stale bread and mouldering circus peanuts. He may get the love-wind butted out of him a few times before he scores, but eventually he makes the grade—if the lady wants him to. "Same like people," said Hugo, sighing.

All my life I've heard grandiose tales regarding elephant love-making. Every newspaper engraving plant I've ever been to had its set of faded photographs purporting to be scenes of mad elephantine love-making, with the beasts wallowing in deep pits big as volcano craters.

"*Nein,*" said Hugo, smiling when I asked him for the lowdown, "*nicht* pits, no pits. Is same like all animals. The bull stand up on hind legs behind female. *Und* is no so long, only *drei,* or *fünf minuten.* Vun time is *gut genug,* but they maybe do three, four more time in twenty-four hours."

After elephantine love-making has risen to its natural climax, there ensues a tender honeymoon, prolonged until the young lady suddenly realizes that she is pregnant, a revelation that comes when she is about eleven months along. Pregnancy term of an elephant is 760 days maximum (two years and thirty days). Authorities find it difficult to agree on the exact period of elephant gestation since so few of the giants have ever been pregnant in captivity. Unless caught in the act, it is difficult to determine the date of elephant insemination. Elephants can be extremely pregnant before humans take notice of the condition. Hugo Schmidt says the gestation period is nineteen to twenty-one months; the *Encyclopedia Brittanica* claims eighteen to twenty-one; the St. Louis Zoo believes eighteen to twenty-two; Dr. J. B. Y. Henderson, veterinarian of the Ringling Bros and Barnum & Bailey Circus says twenty-three to twenty-four months.

The average female elephant comes in heat three, four or five times a year. Some never do and others only twice a year. The "must" (or "musth") period of elephant, one of elephantdom's most baffling puzzles, is thought by many students of pachydermatus life, Herr Schmidt included, to be the male's in-heat time (however, females also experience "must"). Others claim there is no real sexual connotation to this gummy discharge which periodically oozes from the temporal glands on the side of the head. A favorite belief among elephant handlers is that the fluid running into the mouth will cause the bull to go insane. Whatever their theory of "must," all bull-hands regard elephants in that state as being especially dangerous. An elephant in "must" is usually chained headed into a corner, its trunk sometimes fettered by a martingale. In the jungle, elephants rub against sharp sticks or branches to pierce the glands and relieve the pressure, native overseers in compounds often doing this job by hand. The period of "must" lasts from two weeks to four months. The better fed the animal, the longer it lasts; if the beast is underfed, "must" period lasts as little as ten days or two weeks. Winter is the commonest season in America; in Asia and India, summer is "must" time. "*Ale-if-funt* is *sehr schwierig*—how you say it, very difficuld," said Hugo.

Then this master of mammoths told me how their babies are born. In the jungle, all the females of the herd gather around to form a protective zone around the mother as she gives birth, and all scream in agonized sympathy with her. The mama opens the birth sack with her trunk. A newborn, about three feet long and exactly two inches taller (according to Hugo), weighs from 160 to 215 pounds. The elephant mother tosses and rolls her calf in the mud ooze of marsh or riverbank to bring out its first squeal, the action taking the place of a human doctor's first spank. Within fifteen minutes the cub can effect a wobbly stand and two hours later nurses (by mouth, not trunk) from two teats which are just back of the front legs on the underside of the mother. They are formed with several ducts, much like a shower head or sprinkler. Elephant babies are weaned at two years. They all scream and protest at the slightest inconvenience; they wouldn't be healthy babies if they didn't. "All younkers alike," says Hugo philosophically, "people babies, animals' babies. *Alles gleich geräuschvoll.*"

The elephant reaches sexual maturity when between fifteen and twenty years old. The twenties and early thirties are its most productive sexual years; the animals calm down in their mid-forties, "same like people." The average female is able to produce four babies during a lifetime.

While Hugo and I were still discussing the facts of elephant life in the circus backyard, Smokey Jones reappeared. You are never very far from anyone on the circus lot. "Hey," he said, "I told you wrong. It takes me twenty minutes to plait a whip. I just took one apart and redid it just to see."

Hugo left to get into his uniform of white leather trimmed with gold, and I walked with Smokey toward the front. I left him and began another tour of the elephant line-up in the menagerie. Doors hadn't opened yet. The Brobdingnagian beasts had all been broom-swept, the chain which protected them from the public was looped in place, and the bull-hand watchers were idling their time, bracing for the onslaught of the towners.

I went over to Huey Davis, who was in his own elephantine world, leaning against the leathery trunk of one of his wards. "You be surprised," he said, "the things people believe about elephants. Like they never forget an' they live to be a hundred 'n' fifty—things like that. That ain't true. They forget lots of things, and I bet there ain't an elephant lived that's ever hit even eighty. And like they never sleep without a one standin' guard. Hell, I've seen them myself on a two-day stand all conked out every one a'snorin' away. Yeah they snore. They lay down on their sides to sleep but only after midnight and only for about two, three hours that way. The rest of their sleep they get in dozes standin' up." He paused to bring one of his ladies back into line. "An' there ain't no mystical hidden burying ground like they all say," Huey continued. "When elephants gets too old, they go to riverbanks and swamps where the eatin' and drinkin' is easier. And when they get too feeble they just sink in the mud and die from starvation and the buzzards finish them off."

The public, passing so trustingly along the elephants' picket line, is blissfully unaware of the treacherous nature of the staked-out Leviathans. The elephant is not an especially vicious animal, but it is a large one. When anything that big becomes angry, the results are apt to have a certain finality. Even a tail swipe from an elephant can break a leg. As one of the hands informed me, "They are bigger'n they look."

Two things to remember when you are around elephants. Beware when the tail stands out straight; and never pat an elephant on its trunk. That's really its nose. Best place is at the shoulders or back of the ears. A good hearty thwack is better than a light touch, which tickles the beast maddeningly.

"Don't forget," said Huey as I left him, "an elephant ain't no play-toy. When you buy an elephant, you're gettin' a scientific thing."

I went out and sat with Smokey under the canvas shade of the elephant wagon. "Many suckers in there?" he asked me, referring to the size of the crowd in the Big Top. I told him the house was light. "It's too hot," he said. "Bet it'll rain 'fore we're off this lot tonight." After one of those long circus silences, Smokey said, "Did you ever know that elephants was used in wars?" Not waiting for me to answer he went on, "They'd paint their trunks and sometimes strap on iron chopper blades. The howdys [howdah] was armored, and they'd feed the elephants wine loaded with pepper before the battles. Wino elephants," he chuckled, "can you imagine? Sometimes they'd go real crazy and turn on their own army. Then the mahout would drive a spike or a sharp chisel through the top of the elephant's skull and man! he'd go down. That was a long time ago in Africa before when Hannibal was there. I been readin' up on it. There was an Assyrian queen, she even tried disguising her *camels* as elephants. Made big suits for them out of black ox skins; it took the royal shoemakers two years to do it. She warred against a king who didn't have no war elephants, but she got crossed up by a couple of blabber-mouth stool pigeons an' she got clobbered."

Then I told Smokey some of the stories I'd heard from a former officer of the British army in India. About the trunk tugs-of-war over a mud-wall between two evenly matched elephants; of elephant fights that are still staged in the back country. And of the patriot elephants immortalized by the British Tommies who fought the battles of India. Of Kuda-Bar-Moll, an ammunition passer who turned the tide in a crucial engagement during the march on Lucknow, in 1858, by touching off a cannonade after field gunners had been annihilated. Of Hathi, who stemmed a retreat of the Poonah regiment at Lahore by holding aloft the regimental colors on the deserted field.

"And I suppose you're gonna tell me," said Smokey, "that she also did a hind-leg stand and sang 'God Save The King'!"

The hands were unchaining the menagerie elephants now and with gruff commands bringing them outside to line up near our shelter. A shrill whistle pierced the muffle of Big Top canvas and the circus band erupted. "Time to get movin'," said Smokey, getting up. "We gotta get ready for 'Spec.'" As soon as all the "Spec" elephants were out of the menagerie, Smokey led them along the stake line of the mammoth Big Top to the back yard, where the bull-hands began to drape the animals with the spangled blankets, headgear, howdahs and other lavish trappings of the pageant, which that season was a melange entitled "Holidays."

"They sure had the floats scattered all over today," one of the assistants was grumbling, "a howdy here, one there; the pay-off float acrost the road . . ."

Some of the boys wore loose purple uniforms, faded by the sun and adorned with rococo twists and swatches of gold braid. Some of them had obviously been originally fitted to other bodies. Several bull-hands wore hats with tall white plumes. Some of the craggy faces, unshaven and puffed a little from loss of sleep, were framed in flippant adaptations of Napoleonic hats and white lace neck ruffles. A few of the fellows, because of the oppressive heat, were bare-torsoed, holding the coats. A good many of the biceps were devoted to tattooed hearts and flowers with a smattering of holy crosses, serpents, and pink and blue nudes. One boy had the letters T R U E L O V E inscribed on the knuckles of his hands. The back of another's hand proclaimed BORN TO WIN.

"Bet you did that yourself," said Smokey to him.

"Yeah," the young man answered sheepishly, "I did it a long time ago with a needle and India ink. I'd give a hunnert dollars, if I had it, to take it off."

"Born to win," scoffed Smokey. "You're a two-time loser right now—on the circus and in the elephant department."

The kid laughed hollowly. One of the hands was holding to a peculiar bulge in his costume blouse.

"Hey, you," said Smokey, "leave them comic books out here when you go in the Big Top. People'll think you're a one-lunger or a rupture."

The "Spec" elephants were all decked out now, lined up and ready for their performance and more were arriving to get dressed for a later number.

"Ain't much to do now but wait," said Smokey to me. "Whyn't you go talk to Doc Henderson over to the vet's wagon? He can tell you how elephants are put together."

So I did. I'd known the spare, tanned Texan for a long while, but somehow we had never gotten around to talking much about elephants, except I knew that the circus veterinarian wanted more than anything else to try breeding them.

"I really believe breeding in captivity can be done," he always said. "Build a compound way off somewheres, for a half dozen or so; buy me a good healthy bull; take good care of the mother—run a blood test, urine analysis, and the rabbit test. They's so much been done nowadays with medicines and vitamins, I bet you could do it."

I know that someday the Doc is going to try to breed an elephant, for he is one serious man around animals and knows, I guess, as much about their innards as anybody in circus business.

As I came up, one of the menagerie hands, aided by a hanging knotted rope, was easing himself down the steep set of wooden steps propped against the open rear end of the long red wagon. He was clutching a paper packet in the grubby hand that was free. "Some pills that were given to me for the baby gorillas," smiled Doc. "I find they work pretty good on the boys, too."

From Doc I learned more than I care to know about the inside and outside of an elephant. The African plains' elephant (*Loxodonta africana*) is the heaviest land animal in the world and the tallest, except for the giraffe. A large skeleton of this species of elephant can weigh up to thirty-five hundred pounds. One of the African elephant's most distinguishing characteristics is its enormous ears, which are approximately one sixth the entire body weight. Its trunk differs from that of the Asian elephant, having deep transverse ridges, which give it that appearance Huey Davis mentioned of being put together in sections. The hide of a good-sized Africaner measures about forty square yards. Skinned and dried this would tip the scale at 130 pounds.

Males often reach a shoulder height of twelve feet. Barnum's stellar attraction, Jumbo, was an African plains' elephant, 10 feet, 10 inches tall, weighing 8 tons. The largest of that species ever brought down on safari was one dropped by a Spanish businessman named José Fenykövi, in Angola, the Portuguese colony in west Africa. It is likely the largest animal ever shot on earth. From ground to withers this bull measured thirteen feet, two inches. Its length from trunk tip to tail tip in a straight line was 27 feet 6¼ inches. Lengthways across, a front foot measured two feet; the back one an inch and one half more.

African-bush or forest elephants are about one third smaller than their plains brothers (averaging in height nine-feet, six inches for the male, the female under eight feet). Their heads are more pointed and tusks grow straight down instead of angling upward and outward. Otherwise they would be troublesome in the jungle thicket.

Asian elephants (*Elephas maximus*) come slightly smaller, go from 8 feet to as high as 11. At nine years, the Asian is about as tall as an average man; at fifteen it is as big as a small truck. Baby elephants grow approximately one foot their first year on earth, about 9 inches the second, then average 3 inches a year to age five when the growth slows down a bit.

The infamous Tusko was an Asian elephant. He measured 10 feet, 2 inches and weighed 7 tons, according to George Lewis, who handled the bull until its death from a blood clot in the heart. Al G. Barnes, who once owned the beast, claimed Tusko was 12 feet, 4 inches with a weight of 10 tons, 240 pounds, but the impresario had undoubtedly breathed a little circus buncombe into these figures.

"A peculiar thing about an elephant," mentioned Henderson, "is her unusually light footfall for such a heavy animal. Some say it's the most delicate of the whole animal kingdom. The lion, tiger, hippo, polar bear, llama, giraffe are all heavier steppers. The elephant really walks on tiptoe. And the padding that encases her foot is constructed of a vast number of cartilaginous plates arranged pretty much like old-fashioned seat springs of a buggy seat." An elephant seldom becomes mired down because its great weight flattens and broadens the foot, which returns to its normal contour as soon as lifted. Elephant men claim that twice the circumference of the foot is an elephant's shoulder height, depending upon how recently the animal has had her toenails trimmed.

An elephant's legs are remarkably formed. They have knuckle-jointed bones, and a cushioning of several thicknesses of tough, resilient gristle between the joints, which helps absorb the animal's tremendous weight, lessens the jarring action and attendant fatigue and is a big aid in walking silently. An elephant has but two speeds, a walk and a shuffle, which is not exactly a run. Maximum stride is about seven feet. An African elephant has been clocked at 24 mph, but about the best an Asian can do is 20 mph. (Best man-speed, based on the mile record, is about 15 mph.) One thing an elephant cannot do with its wonderful legs—jump off the ground.

" 'A' course," added Henderson, "the unique feature of an elephant is her trunk. I posted [post-mortemed] an elephant once, and I'm tellin' you, you just cain't skin a trunk. It's just a web of muscle runnin' every which 'a way; that's why they got such wonderful movement and control in the trunk."

This astounding organ is primarily a nose, but it is also an extension of the mouth and a hand—indeed in African bush language the word means hand. An elephant with one vicious swipe of its trunk can break a man's back, leg or arm, can shatter a lion's rib cage; but it can just as well gently pick up a peanut, lump of sugar or a pin. With its marvelously versatile nose, an elephant can open truck doors and slam them, untie knots, or become a clever pickpocket, noiselessly removing coins, keys or other small objects with the greatest of ease and pleasure. I once saw an elephant in San Francisco's Cow Palace, displeased by her drafty quarters, unscrew electric light bulbs from their sockets, pull a telephone from the wall and rip the directory into shreds. When bothered by flies, elephants use their trunks to spread hay or dirt across their backs, or they waft away the insects with a gunny or toe-sack, flipping it delicately in the best Southern-belle manner. A favorite elephant foible is turning on water faucets. ("I never see one yet," Smokey says disgustedly, "that could turn one off.")

The elephant's elongated nose is the most sensitive part of the Gargantuan body. A sharp blow on the nerve end can paralyze a trunk, and any injury to it results in exquisite agony. One of a circus veterinarian's principal problems with aging elephants is a progressive inflexibility of their trunks. The elephant's nose is its principal means of keeping in touch with the Lilliputian world around it, for an elephant is generally quite nearsighted, with sight equivalent to that of a goat or a deer. In the jungle, the trunk scents water and guides the animal through dense undergrowth. It is from its trunk that the elephant lets loose its wondrous range of sounds, from clarion trumpet blast to piping squeak. The trunk can broadcast an infinite variety of rumbles, bawls, squeals, as well as hurricane gusts of wind. The longish nose thumped rapidly on the ground makes a hollow drumming sound.

Insects and maggots sometimes crawl into the trunk and unless dislodged cause great pain and stir up real fury. In Africa, red ants are a trunk menace, the tickling causing the elephant to beat its proboscis violently against trees or rocks, inflicting injuries that many times result in death. For this reason elephants sleep with trunk ends tightly closed, often curling them into their mouths. They have been known unconsciously to bite themselves during the night, just as humans sometimes bite their tongues.

One of the great misconceptions about elephants relates to the toughness of their skin. The popular notion that hitting an elephant doesn't hurt the beast couldn't be more wrong. The hide is thick but extraordinarily sensitive. "Don't you believe it doesn't hurt," Doc Henderson told me. "Even a fly or mosquito is felt, so they feel the hook all right." The hide thickness averages from ⅛ inch on the head to 2½ or 3 inches at the hind quarters, but the over-all area is from ½ inch to ¾ inches thick.

"Everybody thinks," Doc went on, "that these Asian elephants of ours don't have tusks, but they do. They've just been cut off or worn down. Only three of the whole herd came without tusks. There are two kinds of Asian elephant: the tuskers, called Gundas; and the tuskless Maknas or Hines. We call them mooleys."

The tusk is not an eyetooth or extended canine, as in a wild boar or hippo, but actually a middle incisor of the upper jaw. A tusk grows about two inches per year, and an elephant can have as many as nine in a lifetime. Ivory hunters once wrongly estimated elephant age by the weight of its tusks—each pound signifying one year.

Africans have the greatest tusks, bigger in the east where possibly the longest ever seen were about 13 feet, weighing well over 250 pounds. West African elephant tusks seldom reach more than 6 feet, 6 inches and weigh less than 100 pounds. Asian elephant tusks can grow to about 9 feet, but seldom do. Cross tusks do not indicate a vicious animal, as do crossed horns in a fighting bull (the bizco), but are merely the result of nap-time pressures during babyhood.

Elephants have teeth too, which casual acquaintances of the beast do not often realize; also a tongue that is attached at both ends —front and rear. Each jaw has one large grinding molar in service on each side, another growing one in reserve. As the teeth of the first set become worn down, they are shoved forward by the newcomers and are either chewed up by the animal (remnants have been found in dung) pushed out, or extracted by the trunk. Six sets appear during a lifetime, each successive one larger than its predecessor. The final molar measures approximately three inches by eight. Dentists covet them as paperweights.

Great strength has always been an elephant's most admired quality, yet, for all its size, the beast is not comparatively as strong as man or horse (proven to be respectively 10 per cent and 25 per cent sturdier). The gorilla is stronger than an elephant, and many times more efficient because of its hands and toes.

Elephants are not afraid of anything that they can see in front, even small creatures, such as dogs and mice. But they fear everything approaching from the back, and they greatly fear fire. Their hearing is acute. I have been told by German elephant men that during Hitler's war, the elephants always reacted to the bombs' blasts at least five seconds before their human handlers heard the explosions.

If you are planning to buy an elephant to help around the house, be advised that it makes a difficult pet, requiring pedicures, treatment for corns, calluses and bothersome cuticles. It will need to be swept off and brushed twice a day, scrubbed once a week, and oiled twice a year (neat's-foot rubbed in good) and shaved regularly—with a blowtorch. Foot pads are subject to abrasions, breaks and infections. Toenails develop cracks much like the run in a lady's stocking and they can only be stopped by vigorous filing across the top of the break. If you plan to own two elephants, you will have the problem of tail bites (hot packs and sulfa will straighten them out). Baby elephants come down with colic and pink eye. Imports always arrive in bad shape from their ocean voyages, and new elephants are usually full of intestinal parasites and badly need deworming. Senior elephants develop encapsulated ear abscesses the size of a man's fist.

It is not easy to give pills to an elephant. The tongue is so power-ful that nothing disapproved gets past it. To force pills down the throat, you put your hand in an elephant's mouth only if you feel you can dispense with that useful extremity. Liquids cannot be inserted up the nose as in other animals for the obvious reason of distance. Nor is it a simple matter to take an elephant's temperature. It is so easy to lose the thermometer. An elephant's normal temperature is 99 to 100 degrees. The heart beat is the slowest of all mammals', ranging from 28 to 42 beats per minute. Elephants are very sus-ceptible to chills. Elephant men sometimes treat these with a large dose of brandy, usually requisitioning more than is actually needed, but Doc Henderson recommends an injection of camphorated oil and guaiacol (a colorless liquid distillate of a tropical shrub, guaia-cum). Until a powerful drug called Lentin came along, raw linseed oil was given orally as a laxative. The operation was quite messy as usually four gallons of the oil were spewed out for every one making the downgrade.

Before elephants perform in a circus, they are forced to empty their bowels by being repeatedly reared on their hind legs. The strain of throwing themselves erect usually does the trick. When elephants perform on a stage or in an indoor arena, it is often necessary to be more thorough. Then the elephant man performs a decidedly un-pleasant dung-removing operation known as "raking," in which it is necessary to plunge the bare arm into the elephant up to the man's shoulder.

Before I left Doc Henderson's wagon I asked about the age of elephants and he told me they seldom live more than seventy years. He said, "There is no authenticated record of any elephant reaching more than that age. A certain British Major (I cain't just call his name right now) at the London Zoological Society, he kept records up until 1948. Major Stanley S. Flower—I knew I'd get it. And the Bombay-Burma Trading Corporation kept the records of more'n 1700 of its elephants over a period of 50 years. Not one lived to 70, but 24 passed 65. Only 10 per cent, 167, lived to be more'n 55; the other 90 per cent died under that age. The New York Zoo had an elephant named Jessie lived to be sixty-nine, but she was put out of her misery for 'senile decay' they said."

When I asked the Doc his worst experience with elephants he hesitated. "I was agoin' to tell you about that time one urinated on me during my first elephant abscess operation," he said. "That was the angriest I ever got at an elephant, but I don't guess that's what you mean. My most memorable experience with elephants was that Cleveland menagerie fire. It only lasted three minutes, but four elephants burned to death in it, and a lot of the others got fried ears and seared carcasses. Some of the slices of burned skin hanging from them were that big." He stretched his long arms. "Walter McClain was the bull man then, and the elephants wouldn't budge, burned or not, until he arrived. When he swung in and shouted an order at them, each elephant reached its trunk down, pulled up its front stake (the hands had already pulled the back ones) and they staggered out in perfect formation grabbing one another's burned tails with their singed trunks." He paused, thinking back on the holocaust. "It was awful," he continued, "the hullaballoo, the wild shouting, the heat, the acrid smoke, and the sickening odors. But from beginning to end there was not one peep from any animal. Not one elephant trumpeted. I think they just trusted that us men would get them out of their pickle. It was one of the most touching experiences I've ever had around a circus—or anywhere. That day I acquired a tremendous respect for elephants and all dumb animals."

As we looked across the vast backyard of the circus, the "elephant manège," called "Mama's in the Park," was in full swing. Smokey and his underlings were running Ringling Bros' entire elephant population at a fast and furious pace in and out of the Big Top's canvas back door. Some of the huge creatures wore Keystone-Kop hats and wielded night-billies in their trunks. The "Mamas" wore big floppy flowered bonnets, and pushed baby elephants, chained, sitting in ungainly contraptions that looked as much like baby gocarts as Sherman tanks. Some of the grown females, blanketed in black plastic morning coats, and wearing battered high hats of the same material, masqueraded as men.

"There they are," drawled the long, lean Doc. "One of the four animals most responsive to man's will; not so economically satisfactory as a horse, a cow or a camel, but a great deal more fun."

No other wild animal of adult age can be as quickly trained or as thoroughly domesticated as an elephant. Barnum took advantage of this state of animal affairs when, to promote his American Museum, he hitched an elephant to plow, on his Fairfield County, Connecticut, farm, a six-acre field alongside the N.Y., New Haven & Hartford Railroad tracks. Furrows were turned only when a train went by, for the sagacious showman, never a man to waste elephants, had thoughtfully provided the simulated Hindu plow boy with a timetable. Most of the elephants imported to this country come from their African and Asian compounds with enough rudimentary training to make them conscious of the will of man. The majority of American circus elephants are Asians, largely because the African is so much more expensive. On the Dark Continent, there are only wild elephants. Catching and taming them is a costly business, whereas the Asian elephant is a market staple, just about as available for purchase as horses and cows in the States.

Work is the easiest trick an elephant can do, and for generations work elephants have done the heavy labor of Far East plantations and teak forests. In Africa, the natives have feasted on the elephant's flesh (raw or roasted), constructed stockade fences with the tusks, worked the dried hide into war shields, used the stomach lining for mattresses, woven magic rings and bangles from the long, stiff tail hairs. But while some African elephants have been adopted as household pets, very few had ever been used as domesticated work animals until after the turn of this century, when a project for the educating of African elephants for domestic and industrial purposes was begun by King Leopold II of Belgium in the Belgian Congo at Api, under an indefatigable Captain named Laplume. By 1925 Laplume had produced, for the first time, tame, domesticated elephants in Africa.

To capture a baby elephant in the Congo a score of trappers called Kornaks, armed with rifles and lassos, approach an unwary herd in an extended semicircle. On a pistol signal from the leader all hell breaks loose—shouting, shooting and beating about the bush. The surprised elephants shuffle away, and the men race after them on foot. For about a hundred yards, elephants can maintain a speed of 20 mph, but then they simmer down to between 10 and 12 mph. The well-thewed bushmen soon overtake the elephant calves trailing their elders. The chaser's swift naked legs (he wears only brief lightweight shorts) bring him close behind one of the young escapees. The runner grabs the animal by its flying tail, heels in and stops it long enough to pass a lasso swiftly around a hind leg. When the baby takes off again, which it does almost immediately, the weight of man must be dragged. A second catcher now comes at the beast and pushes against its shoulder. This dangerous position is held just long enough for the first captor to whip his rope rapidly around the trunk of a tree. Now a group of runners move in to goad the animal into repeated attacks designed to distract it from a lasso that is soon tightened around its neck. The captive's neck halter is secured to the girths of one tamed monitor elephant, the leg rope to the other. With the struggling, squirming protesting baby between them, the monitors proceed slowly and quietly to the compound.

Six months after capture, training begins. The colossal kindergarten is tethered in a half circle, each learner surrounded by a knot of black boys. The trainers gently brush the breasts of the beasts with long leafy branches, pet their petulant mouths, stroke their forelegs and hind legs—in other words seduce the young innocents into an almost hypnotic state, singing all the while a murmuring chant. When the beasts are deep in the spell, rocking like so many voodoo worshipers, a number of the crooners break from the group and spring to the backs of the elephants. The drowsy beasts, bellowing with surprise and rage, toss most of the would-be riders. But in time rebellion wears thin, and each elephant accepts his new friend.

The remainder of the breaking in is much like that described earlier by Hugo Schmidt. After five months the elephant seminar becomes a drill squad, learning to march abreast, to go forward, wheel on command, to halt and break into twos and fours, much in the manner of a liberty horse drill. At the seventh month the elephants can be broken to harness and to hauling loads, carrying and trundling.

The Indian elephant, nonetheless, is considered to be the best type for circus purposes, and not solely because they are less expensive. They are believed to be more tractable and more receptive to training, having had a longer association with man. Centuries of breeding for the royal stables has left its mark on the Asian elephant. Royal court elephant standards were very high. To qualify for admission an elephant had to have a chest barrel-deep of great girth; a back straight and flat, shoulder to tail; beautiful head with thick short neck; and a trunk broad at the base, nicely heavy throughout a long triangular-slope to soft pink lip. Large rectangular ears without holes were required. The skin had to be smooth and pliable; mouth and tongue, a ripe red. And above all, the candidate was expected to be a proper lady or gentleman.

When Smokey's elephants went into the Big Top, I followed them, slipping into an empty seat near the ringmaster to watch their performance. After the act, I lingered awhile to watch the flying-trapeze performers. By the time I located Smokey again, it was feeding time for his (and Mr. North's) grey ladies.

Smokey was having a look at the fodder. "You can tell by punchin' your fist into a bag that this feed's too dry," he was telling Big John. "Goddammit, it's all dried out and wormy and old. It should be spongy. I ain't gonna feed that."

While Big John worried over what to do, Smokey told me that the stuff which had been purchased by the twenty-four-hour man, the circus advance arranger, was "Sweet feed." "It has everything in it an elephant needs exceptin' hay," the elephants' overlord explained. "Crimped oats, cracked corn, seed oil, molasses, wheat bran, alfalfa meal, calcium carbonate, and some other minerals like iron and stuff and iodized salt. Ain't never enough salt, so we always adds some." (In their native state elephants search out salt veins in the hard clay banks of the streams they frequent.) Smokey told me that the Ringling daily order for elephant fodder was 600 pounds of sweet-feed and 1 ton of hay, approximately 11 pounds of sweet, 37 pounds of hay per elephant, though, of course, the babies ate considerably less than the grownups. The Ringling younkers also got a ration of sorghum, charcoal powder, resin, soda and extra salt. "Elephant babies need blood," explained Smokey, "and nothin' makes blood like sorghum molasses. Without blood, you're nothin'. I can look in an elephant's mouth and tell if she's got blood. Some mouths is so white, just like a newborn baby."

The St. Louis Zoo feeds each of its full-grown Asiatic elephants 100 pounds of assorted hays daily; lespedeza, timothy, alfalfa, soy bean. Plus: 15 pounds of wheat, bran and oats; 12 pounds of mixed fruits and vegetables; 2 loaves of bread; 1 pound of salt.

Smokey's elephants eke out the corporation-provided diet by foraging among soft-hearted candy butchers, work-hands and the public for doughnuts, coffee (paper cup included), cotton candy, pop, hot dogs, pie, coffee-cake, toasted cheese sandwiches, watermelon rind, ice cream and popsicles, loaves of bread (in one bite with wrapper) and Tums (singly or by the box). For roughage, elephants scrounge coal, dirt and gravel; they love tobacco (contrary to popular opinion) and enjoy sniping butts from the gutters on their walks to and from the circus train.

Smokey claims that an elephant can eat everything except meat (circus red-hots excepted) and fish, though sardines are acceptable if they stay in the closed can. Jennie, a Polack Bros Circus elephant, once made all the wire services by eating $117.45 of the New York Central Railroad's money when an Arlington, Ohio, telegrapher tossed a package containing that amount into the Polack stock car believing it to be the railroad's official baggage car. An unsung elephant named Zip once broke out of its confinement at the winter quarters of Ring Bros circus, a small mud-show, demolished three brand-new cages, threw a camel over a high fence, frightened three kangaroos into kangaroo spasms and ended the rampage by eating a nine-foot length of chain. "She died a' course," said Smokey.

One of the assistants came up to Smokey and told him a couple of elephants in the picket line had been fighting.

"Ain't no fight," said Smokey to him, "if one elephant saps another that's just their way of keepin' order. Knaudie," continued Smokey to me, "she's a good fighter. You need strong back legs for that push and she's got them. When elephants reach sixty, they usually can't stand on their hind legs. In Boston, Judy and Ruth got into a fight, and I give them such a pitchfork fit they'll never do that again." He reached into a cardboard box at his feet (checking his shoelaces at the same time) and hauled out a small gasoline-powered toy racing car and an airplane, with which he began to tinker. "If it wasn't for elephants," he commented, "I'd be doin' somethin' with airplanes. I love them and motorcycles and speed boats and sports cars. When I was a punk I used to steal cars—yeah, I did. Got a kick out of it. But you gotta stop that kind of stuff yourself. It don't do you no good." Circus people have a way of always getting back to an unfinished subject; Smokey was no exception. "Ben Davenport he had a new elephant called Japon. He said to me take her back and let her get acquainted, an' I'll be a sonabitch if she didn't knock over every one of them elephants in the herd—laid them all out, one by one."

Smokey glanced at his wrist watch. "Pretty near time for teardown," he said. "We start early."

From within the menagerie came the clink clink of the picket line stakes being loosened. A bull-hand, wearing an enameled-white straw hat, dumped a wheelbarrow full of stakes in the grass. "Goddammit!" stormed another hand, "now I hafta pick them up." "Don't you go cursin' at me," said the barrow boy, shifting his dangling cigarette, "I'm a'doin' what the boss tole me to do."

"Who tole you?"

"Who's the boss around here?"

"Did Smokey tell you?"

"No, Big John tole me. You kin fight with him."

"You guys cut out that him-hamming around," said Smokey

sternly. "They'll always pay you your money if you wanta' leave. They ain't no doors on a circus."

The hands were fairly quiet now, each puttering at his own tear-down job. Two assistants, with two bull-hands, were driving two parallel lines of stakes in the field before the wagon. At the start of the performance, the working bulls and those not in Spec would be led out from their menagerie picket line and tethered to this outdoor one. The others would be taken directly to the backyard to await their part in the show.

"By God," Smokey commented, looking around at the teardown that was beginning to spread all over the vast lot. "You wouldn't think there'd be so much to one of these things."

When Smokey escorted his long line of elephants to the back-yard that evening, I tagged along, taking care not to get in the way of the snapping whip. As we loped along in the dark alongside the luminescent Big Top, moon sneaking over it, the elephant beside Smokey, Big Jewel, reached out her trunk and nuzzled her boss man. Smokey took hold of the long nose, saying softly, "Hello, Big Jewel," then burst jubilantly into a few bars of a song, ". . . take my hand, I'm a stranger in Paradise . . ." I have marveled many times since at the magic of that moment. "You know," Smokey observed as we rounded into the backyard, "I'd like to have just one kid, one nice kid." We arrived abreast of the Grease-joint just as the band struck its opening blast. "Brother," said Smokey, "we had that timed pretty good."

At the Grease-joint I ran into Doc Henderson having a "Pitts-burgh," black coffee without sugar. "I been lookin' for you," said the lanky veterinarian. "Come over to my wagon; I have something you might want to read." It was a sheaf of dog-eared pages from a scientific journal, an article concerning elephant intelligence. I knew it would be another hour before the appearance of what the official program that year termed the "Peerless Performing Proboscidians," so I took the report to a quiet canvas corner inside the wardrobe tent and sat where I knew I wouldn't be disturbed, on a large trunk containing clown hats used in the Finale. The series of studies set forth had been made by the Zoological Institute of Munster, Westphalia, Germany, to determine an elephant's ability to learn, the limits of its memory, and what association these factors have to the beast's extaordinarily large brain. On a field trip to India it was found that fully trained animals between the ages of twenty and sixty years understood about two dozen commands, the most important being those to move forward, stop, go backward, turn around, and lift foot. Other words dealt with lying down (on belly or side), trunk-lifting and squirting and the techniques of handling objects and dealing with obstacles. The experienced elephants tested during this phase of the research performed their work with a minimum of commands, as do well-bred circus elephants, suggesting to the scientists that the giant beast must be credited with true ideation, that is, the ability to anticipate the results of certain actions.

A separate series of experiments was conducted at the Munster Zoo to learn an elephant's degree of discrimination. The subject was a five-year-old Asian female, whose name the psychologist author did not mention. The apparatus for the test was simple: two small wooden boxes with removable cardboard lids placed on the floor of the elephant den about forty inches apart. In one box was placed a piece of bread, nothing in the other. A symbol on the lid of one box indicated that it contained food, the symbol on the other meant an empty box. The first series of lids were marked with a black cross for the food reward, a black circle for nothing. The symbols remained constant, but their patterns varied, and they were switched frequently from box to box.

The circle was made the negative symbol because the elephant showed an initial tendency to prefer it to the cross. The animal under observation trunked the boxes 330 times over a period of several days to learn, by trial and error, that the cross meant food. Once she realized the correct pattern, the animal opened only the cross-marked lid. After the cross and circle pair of lids had been mastered, the pachyderm professors advanced to a series of others which included: geometric shapes; stripes; curvey lines vs. straight; dots in various arrangements; letters of the alphabet; rudimentary pictures and so forth.

As time went on the elephant was able to distinguish the patterns more rapidly. By the fourth pair she was able to choose right from wrong after only ten trials. As she added to her visual vocabulary, the behemoth was given refresher courses on what had been learned, so that she was able to choose the correct one of each pair when presented in irregular rotation.

In a test covering six hundred trials and lasting only a few hours, the learned Westphalians were surprised to find that their pupil could hold simultaneously in memory the "meaning" of twenty stimulus pairs. The animal showed no symptoms of fatigue but actually improved in performance toward the end. The conclusion was reached that the beast could have gone on to an even greater sight vocabulary. When presented with four patterns at one time, only one positive, the bull recognized the positive one at first sight on about half the occasions; and in the others, after one wrong choice. Given a choice between a positive and a neutral card, she invariably picked the positive. Choice between neutral and negative set up a type of experimental neurosis similar to that produced in man, ant and other animals by conflict situations. The elephant became excited, bit and tore the lids, and often trampled the boxes.

Now experiments were conducted to see if the elephant would recognize symbols when altered. The cross, for instance, was placed in an X position, the lengths of its arms were altered, and so on. But as long as two black bars were crossed, the elephant had no trouble recognizing the food symbol. However, she did not respond to either the cross or the X when it was reversed to white on black. But the elephant was able to grasp the idea of difference in widths of stripes in the striped patterns.

In a test of the perseverance of memory, it was found that the elephant had retained the meaning of twenty-four visual patterns of a possible twenty-six, which she had not seen for a period of one year, a demonstration of that hoary pachyderm chestnut "an elephant never forgets."

A similar series of food-reward tests was run to study the elephant's auditory discrimination and the animal was able to distinguish twelve different tone pitches.

An ass and a zebra, given the same visual tests as the elephant, with slight alterations to suit their differences, didn't flunk the course but only mastered thirteen and ten pairs of cards respectively. A horse got A+, learning the same twenty pairs mastered by the elephant.

As I returned the learned article to the Doc, Smokey was again thundering his charges across the plains of the circus backyard in earth-shaking assaults on the Big Top. As soon as their act inside was finished, the elephants were run at a fast clip from the mammoth tent. Beside their plunging heads thudded the excited bull-hands, shouting and swinging their stocky bull-hooks, digging ears and trunks and thwacking the squealing brutes. As this rampageous horde, kicking up a low choke of dust, swept through the circus town square, all its other activity stopped momentarily to watch the awesome spectacle. Smokey and his cracking bull whip monitored the beasts to a quivering line-up just outside the main area. There the elephants were sorted out, and neck-chained in twos and threes for the long hike to the train. This job seemed to be accomplished by an uncanny knowledge of elephant silhouette on Smokey's part, plus a nice measure of sheer instinct, for by now it was quite dark.

When all fifty-one elephants were in their proper march positions, Smokey mounted old Harold, the elephant horse, and wheeled over to me. "Okay," he said to my surprise, "you git on Knaudie; she's the lead elephant. Pony Red'll help mount you. Red you show him." And he was off, trotting toward the front of his long low ridge of heaving grey mountains. I wasn't prepared for this sudden introduction to the living, breathing actuality of an elephant. "C'mon," said Red. It took two tries to get me up.

At Red's command "Kan-NOW-dee, trunk!", the elephant lowered her head, raising her trunk so that I could, by stepping quite high, plant my left foot on it. Red told me to grap the elephant's forehead harness strap with both hands. Then Knaudie hoisted me high by curling her trunk skyward; I flung my right leg over her neck and scrambled on, quickly shifting my hands. All fifty-one elephants, twenty-three hands and Smokey must have been waiting for me to make contact, for no sooner did I get aboard, than the entire line executed an abrupt right face and we were off through the night in a fast padding shuffle. The suddenness of the takeoff was most startling. I barely had a good seat, and we hadn't gone ten feet, before I was gripped with a real moment of panic such as I had never experienced (nor have I since)—an empty, lost feeling that was terrifying. I knew I was going to fall and knew equally well that I shouldn't, couldn't, wouldn't—dammit. I felt every bull-hand's eye riveted on me. I was somehow being tested by Smokey and by the entire elephant department—including, I'm sure, the elephants themselves. Damn their little pig eyes; I'd show them. In a few moments I got hold of myself; the hysterical surge becalmed. I found that by veering a little to the right I could manage to hang on to my heaving mass-of-muscle perch.

There is no feeling like that of riding an elephant. Every muscle in your body gets a stiff workout; your hips and belly are thrown into a violent, continuous bump-and-grind, worthy of the most talented burleycue queen. There are no potbellied elephant boys.

Two elephant punks were shackled to Knaudie's right, and the chain pushed tight against my foot. At the big elephant's head on my left rode Smokey on Harold the horse. The boss man had a powerful flashlight with a ruby-red head, and I discovered later that the tag elephant wore a large red reflector button on her hind quarters.

Smokey called up, "How're you doin'?"

"F-f-fine uh I un-uh guess." I managed to grunt.

"If you feel like you're slippin' off," he advised, "just yell out 'Come in line' good 'n' loud and everybody will stop and face into the curb. That's our signal."

"Oh-oh-o ho-ho-kay," I replied, heaving and swaying, ramming my tailbone each time on Knaudie's hard spine.

At this point, Harold chose to horse around with Miss Knaudie, stretching his neck to give her sashaying trunk a love nip. His teeth were strong enough, but he didn't have enough mouth. Even so, the elephant gave quite a lurch, and I figured I was a goner again. Then Knaudie thought she'd like to play as well and began to sneak vast sly kicks with one hind leg at the elephant behind her. This didn't sit well with me either. Oh, lord, I thought; you could have said, "No, thank you. I don't want to ride an elephant." Even to Smokey, you could say *that*. For the first five or ten blocks I wasn't conscious of anything except my loins, legs, hands; a taut chain biting into my right ankle; the stiff hairs on Miss Knaudie's knobby head; the broad grey sweep of Harold's rump; Smokey's dazzlingly white shirt back, his bobbing red flashlight; and blurs of asphalt and concrete. That was my world. No sky, no moon, no stars, no trees, no houses, no people.

Then confidence began to creep back into my congealed blood, and I could sneak little looks around. A passer-by in an automobile leaned out and quipped, "Get an elephant." Smokey snarled, "I hate them kind of suckers." He was taking his nightly routine in stride, every so often calling out some impertinence to passing sidewalk love-lies—such drolleries as, "Hell-oh, doll"—pause—"I mean crocka-doll," or "You're old enough, babe; how much money you got?"

All along our route little clumps of people stood at curbside. Piping, screeching kids ran in spurts along with us—some on foot, others cruising on bicycles, which made the elephants skittish.

"Hey, look! They got holes in their ears!"

"Hey, mister! Where is Barnum Ann Bailey? Is she dead?"

"They're dropping bombs!"

"I never touched an elephant."

"They remember."

A couple of times Knaudie sent the shrilling punks scattering with a slimy spray, gagged up from her insides. Harold's shoes made a hollow clatter on the paving.

"It shore feels like rain," observed Smokey. "There ain't a one star out."

From behind came a monstrous soft shuffle, an army of grandfathers in carpet slippers. There was an occasional thumping thwack of club on leathery flesh, a hoarse cry, a trumpeting squeak. I didn't dare look back; I surely would have lost my precarious seat. My thighs ached, my feet were leaden weights, my fingers screamed in a vise of chain and neck. Fighting those tremendous shoulder muscles all the way, I could feel the skin rubbing off my tail-bone millimeter by millimeter. Downhill was the worst; the elephant seemed to tread heavier then, jar me more. Uphill was a delight, especially if I leaned back a trifle. There was a different gait for crossing railroad tracks, a more dainty, cautious one. I soon discovered the secret of elephant riding— a relaxed attitude. After I learned to roll with the punches it was great.

From Smokey, I picked up the basic signals. To go left is "come here," right is "move over" because the American bull-hand, when he walks, is always at the left side of the elephant's head. The orders, oddly enough, work equally well when the man gives them from a perch atop the elephant's head. "Move up" is to go ahead; "back" is steady or stop. Elephants do not reverse very well.

From the dark of a coal yard, a point where the railroad tracks came closest to the street, we were signaled by a waving flashlight. When Smokey rode up to it and found Danny Dooley, the elephant cars' watchman, he became angry, for Dooley's feet are poorly and can't walk very well. "Whoinhell sent *you* away out here?" he demanded. "Why'n't in hell didn' one of them young *punks* come out with the signal?" Dooley muttered something I didn't catch, then with him limping and hopping bravely ahead, flashlight beam bobbing, our long train of heaving shadows weaved its way past coal tipples and water tanks, under low trestles and through some fairly tight squeezes before we came to the elephant cars. They were great, long seventy-two-footers, painted silver. Very narrow cracks separated the wide slats of the wooden sides. The cars had been cleaned out during the day, evidently at some other spot for, while the air was fairly ripe, the flashlights' beams disclosed no enormous dung piles alongside the tracks.

"Come in line!" yelled Smokey, dismounting from Harold.

"Knaudie down!" Miss K. dipped her head and Smokey said to me, "Slide off!" I did, taking three years off my trousers' seat and giving my ankles the jar of their life. After nine years of hanging around circuses, I'd ridden my first elephant.

The haul (which is what the circus calls that distance between lot and train) that night had been about two and one-half miles. I could feel every yard of it in my buttocks. If I had been dragged the entire course, I don't believe my posterior could have been more sensitive. The distance was considered a tough haul. Hugo Schmidt once told me, "For elephant, for everybody is best vun mile or vun-vun-half mile, ah-ber it is ofer vun-vun-half is too much for everybody." The Ringling elephants during a season make some fairly lengthy hauls, the two longest on their route so far that year had been New York City, eight miles, and Akron, Ohio, seven.

Smokey was still riled up about old Danny Dooley and proceeded to tell off the hand who was responsible.

Then Grassy, one of the assistants, got into a jaw with a kid who had been stowing his bull-hooks in Grassy's special locked compartment. Smokey quickly settled the hassle. "You've been puttin' them there six months"; he said, "you can put them there six months more."

The loading operation began immediately. Each car had a heavy wooden ramp leading up to its great yawning door, framing a bull-hand with flashlight hung from pants belt or to a loop around his neck, ready to guide the elephants by bull-hook into their night's lodgings. Each elephant had its regular position inside the sleepers, and there was much shuffling to get them organized for entering. Nineteen of the babies went into the car numbered 224; eight adults and seven infants into 225. Car 226 held ten grownups and four punks. Car 223 was the boys' dormitory, but it also carried three large elephants.

The loading went well though it was almost pitch-black now. The only light besides the electric torches was a small naked-bulb glow inside one of the cars. The darkness was leavened with great heaving noises, animal rumblings, snorts and whimpers, a barking of human orders. "Joss-s-s-kee! Up!" . . . "Marcella, you jughead!" . . . "Jooo-dee!" Some were gentle: "C'mon Baaa-a-a-be"; some rough: "May-ry UP!" Some loving and kind: "Modoc, you come up here baby; steady now, Modoc."

The loading went well until Joske decided that the ramp on her car was impossible to negotiate. It was a great deal steeper than the others because of a sudden dropping away of the ground by the door of that car. Joske dug in stubbornly and growled like a large bulldog. A few drops of rain began to fall. "I knew it," said Smokey, looking at the sky, "Rain! Goddammit! We ain't got troubles enough."

Herr Schmidt came along with three elephants. In the dark I couldn't see him, but that kraut voice was unmistakable. Joske was pulled aside until Hugo's ladies were loaded in another car.

"LOO-nah! *Kom.* Root! *Mar-zella Komen-zee.* Yooah! Go ahait!" Then to the boy inside the car, "Take him, take him!"

Then Hugo and Smokey held a conference—subject Miss Joske, delinquent. "She done this on me once before," said the younger man.

"Yah, yah," said Hugo, "I 'member. Ve hadt to take her to crossing und wait for the train to be moving up. Vaid, I load Rajee then we dry again." Hugo disappeared deeper into the dark and came back with one of the babies. "Rajee," he gently coaxed, "oh, da kleine. Rah-jeeee up. *Rajee.*" Rajah made it to her car with only a few protesting squeals.

"Boy them mosquitoes is bad," said Smokey, lighting a cigarette. Joske still balked on the next three tries. "She's gettin' ready to run," announced Smokey, "dont' pull on her trunk." He took a long, glowing drag from his smoke. "Well, there goes *this* night."

Some of the young hands had tucked in and from the bunks in the next car came snores, sharp outcries, nightmarish snorts, and the kind of heavy, terrorized breathing you hear broadcast from those fake iron-lung walkthroughs on carnivals.

"Git me a chain," Smokey order one of the tense hands. "We'll chain her to that there telegraph pole 'til she calms down." Glancing nervously at the black sky, he added, "I sure to Christ hope that rain holds off."

The noise had attracted a small cluster of towners who stood at what they considered a safe distance, which was not a safe distance. One of them kept laughing nervously.

Then for what must have been an hour nothing happened. Everybody just sat smoking, stretched out flat on the cinders alongside the car or against the ramp. Little cigarette glows pierced the blackness. No one talked and the mosquitoes were fierce. Every so often Joske's chain would clink a little, so I knew she was still at the pole.

"Well, let's try her again, boys," Smokey finally announced. "Git the chains off."

"Chain her up to Jewel and see if she can coax her in," suggested one of the assistants. . . . No soap. "I got a long chain in my possum-belly," said another assistant. "We could put a damn run up the other side the damn car and let Jewel *pull* her in." This didn't seem feasible. Smokey was getting angry.

"You gaddam heifer. Come here!" he snarled at Joske.

"How about that long run on the punks' car?" someone stabbed out of the dark. "Yeah," said Smokey, "Git it and we'll try it. God*dam* those mosquitoes!"

"Now *I* dry," said Hugo when the run was hefted into place by all available hands. "Bas auf!" Hugo shouted with all the power in his thick chest. "Bas AUF! Kom here! Jos-kee! Get aholt her tail und pull her ofer. Jos-kee!" . . . "Look out," cautioned Smokey. "Git back, you guys. I've seen her throw that goddam run!" But now, bit by agonizing bit, Joske inched up the ramp and finally after much low cursing and furious strain all but one long leg was in the car. "Ofer mit the leg, mein lieber," Hugo coaxed again and again softly hitting it with his bull-hook shaft as if he were chopping wood "Bas auf! Joske!" Suddenly with a tremendous heave the leg moved in. There was a flash of lightning and I could see that both Hugo and Smokey were drenched with sweat. The black skies opened, and it began to rain furiously.

"At least God likes elephants," said Smokey. Then, "C'mon," he yelled, jamming me in the ribs with his bull-hook, "there's a diner down at the crossing. If we high-tail it we can make it. C'mon."

It was rough going galloping in the cinders and stones alongside the track. By not leaping soon enough I barked a shin once on a switch, but at least I didn't sprawl.

We slowed down as we splattered up to "the crossing," the place where all circus equipment is loaded onto the train, the crossing of a highway or street with the railroad tracks. Smokey strolled over to the yellow-slickered circus trainmaster, standing in the middle of the tracks directing the "cossing-cats," loading tractors that wheel the wagons up to "the runs"—ramps leading onto the flat cars.

"Did *you* spot this goddam train?" Smokey asked belligerently.

"Yeah, Smokey, don't I always?"

"*You* oughta get promoted."

"What's a' matter, Smokey?" the train boss said. "You're all wet.

Ain't you got sense enough to get in out 'a the rain?" He reached to touch Smokey's shoulder, but the elephant boss jerked away. "Don't touch me, you make me dirty." Then he stalked off to Elsie's Dew Drop Inn which was dry and warm with hamburger smell, French fries and coffee. After three Cokes and a steak Smokey felt better and was ready to forgive his balky elephant but not the trainmaster.

"Some of them elephants can be real mean sometimes," he said. "Trainmasters is always mean."

From "the crossing" came shrill whistle blasts, the chugging of tractors, and rain beat on Elsie's roof.

"Hell," Smokey continued, "tonight that was nothin'. Joske ain't what you call a *bad* elephant. She was just confused by the steep grade. She could 'a' took off on a rampage, but somethin' held her back. Me maybe." Then he told me about some really bad circus elephants who went berserk, including the mighty Tusko. It seems to be the consensus among elephant men that their male beasts become violent more often than the females, and that the terrible-tempered period, while usually occuring during the "must" season, is often caused at other supposedly safe times by jealousy and/or love.

Tusko's problem is thought to have been an overpowering fondness for his owner, that master showman of early circus days, Mr. Al G. Barnes. At least Mr. Barnes fostered that notion. Every time the bossman left Tusko, the great animal would droop and sulk or kick up a colossal rumpus. One of Tusko's most memorable cantankerous outbursts against his frustrated love-life was a roistering barney that took place at Sedro-Wooley, Washington state, about sixty-five miles north of Seattle in the early 'thirties. That swath of destruction included one touring car upended by tusks to the roof of another automobile; demolished chicken coops, pig-pens, innumerable fences, brick walls and hastily locked doors; a telegraph pole snapped off at its base and a two-story frame house pushed several feet off its foundation. Even his platonic lady-friend monitors couldn't restrain Tusko that day. He finally broke into a moonshiner's barn and indulged in an orgy of whiskey-mash slurping. Tusko was found the next morning sleeping it off in the mountains, still wearing his demolished howdah, his Oriental trappings terribly disheveled, and looking like a reveling Shriner the morning after a successful convention banquet.

I asked Smokey for his best stampede advice. The best way to handle one, he said, was to stop it before it started. "If it gets goin'," he added, "just think fast and do whatever you can." He had never been mixed up in one of those terrors. "Unless," he said, "you can count a hoked-up one we did once on the Dailey show for the movies. We had a helluva time gettin' them celluloid cows to goin'. We tried everything—shoutin', yellin', ringin' bells, fire. But they was all so used to Hollywood hullaballoo they wouldn't budge. Ole Lucy, you could've set a sky-rocket off in her mouth and *she* wouldn't move. We finally stirred them up with horses, guns and firecrackers—I don't guess I'll ever have a regular stampede, but if I ever do I'll think of something to do and do it quick." He chuckled. "I tell my boys, when they ask me that, jest git out in front and hold your hands over your eyes. I'm always afraid some lunkhead'll believe me, try it some day and get good and clobbered."

I had always heard that an enraged elephant charges silently with trunk curled under, head tilted back. "Uh-uh," disagreed Smokey, "they can run with the trunk straight out and make a helluva noise with it."

Then we got on to the real baddies, killer elephants, a favorite elephant-man subject.

"Black Diamond, I guess," Smokey said, "is the one us elephant men always talk about. Some say he was love-crazy-queer for his old trainer who left him for a woman. Curley Prickett was his name and he had Black Diamond on a mud-show for about seven years when Al G. Barnes Circus bought him and turned him over to a guy named Grady, or O'Grady—I ferget which. Diamond was supposed to be very jealous of Prickett's wife and Prickett used to sometimes tease the elephant huggin' an' kissin' his old lady in front of it. After Diamond joined out with the Barnes show, Prickett retired into workin' on a ranch for a lady in Texas. When the show come to their town (Corsicana, it was) he took her downtown to see the arrival. The elephants was watering at a trough when they both come up to Diamond and the lady tried to touch the elephant—to pet him, I guess. Well, Black Diamond turned on Curley, caught him with its tusks and threw him over an auto at the curb. Then the elephant knocked the lady down and run one tusk clean through her. And some doctor, a brave man, he made three attempts before he could drag her body away from the crazy elephant. The townspeople raised such a stink about it that finally, after three days, the circus had to shoot Black Diamond. They tried to poison him but he was too smart; he smelled all the poisoned peanuts and oranges they fixed for him. Them Texans was such poor shots they had to pour 170 rounds into Black Diamond before he croaked. Would you like another 7-Up?" I was already floating in the stuff, so I said no thanks.

In the old days, circuses simply hushed up a killing by an elephant (after all, wasn't a roughneck just an expendable nobody?), then changed the murderer's name and palmed the animal off on another show. Thus Queen, who had choked her keeper to death with her trunk, à la boa constrictor, became Empress, a change which didn't deter her from killing five more persons on one bloody rampage. Under a third name, "Mary," she trompled a child during a street parade. Mary, according to some accounts, was given a spectacular send-off. She was hanged from a railroad derrick.

A Barnum elephant, Raja, after he took a dangerous dislike to his trainer, was rechristened Samson and passed along to another circus where he lived up to his new name by literally shaking a man to death.

Occasionally, if a doomed elephant manslayer is a particularly valuable animal, a circus owner will slyly substitute a lesser elephant to face the police firing squad, knowing that few people outside the circus are able to distinguish one elephant from another.

Troublemakers and unmanageable elephants in the past have often turned up in zoos, coming there either as gifts or as bargains too sweet to be resisted. Bad Bolivar at the Philadelphia Zoo was one such, and Ziggy, at the Brookfield Park Zoo in Chicago, another. The latter has the reputation of being the meanest elephant alive in America today. Ziggy had been imported by Florenz Ziegfeld for his famous Follies but was later unloaded onto Singer's Midgets who got him off their cunning little hands by selling the onerous beast to the zoo.

A nefarious killer who took up residence in a zoological garden was Tip (Tipoo-Sahib) who had been brought to America in 1882 by Barnum's bitterest rival, the circus titan Adam Forepaugh. During Tip's first year as a menagerie attraction he killed one workhand, seriously injured two others. Two seasons later Tipoo sent two more circus men to the heavenly Big Lot. Then, in 1888, he knocked off an additional three (two at one time) plus a boy. The following year the fearsome Tip was transferred to New York's Central Park Zoo where he almost immediately severely injured two keepers. After two more vicious attacks on handlers the black-hearted bull was executed by city order in the spring of 1894. His stuffed carcass, a sizable one measuring 10 feet at the shoulder, was first exhibited at the New

York City Museum of Natural History for 33 years, then for 30 more at the Hudson River Museum in Yonkers, N.Y. up the Hudson valley. The elephant mummy is now the property of the Historical Society at Somers, New York, where it keeps silent company with the wooden statue of that early pioneer lady elephant, Old Bet.

Only recently a zoo-elephant attack was reported in the *New York Times*. A forty-five-year-old female Indian elephant named Astra, with an effortless flick of her trunk, catapulted an assistant gardener at the Brooklyn Prospect Park Zoo into the dry-bed of a twenty-foot-deep moat. Results: cerebral concussion, spine and shoulder injuries; and a complaint filed by the State County and Municipal Employees Union against the use of assistant gardeners to tend animal cages. It was Astra's second foray into the assistant gardener department.

"What a night," said Smokey Jones over his fifth Coke. "Bet they had one hell of a sweet time gettin' off that lot. Bet they ain't all off yet. Big John is out there with Lois; Little John (that's Mc-Cauliffe) he has Ruth. They're both good tear-down elephants. You should see Ruth get her head down and roll that wet canvas when nothin' else can move it. Goofus and Mac they have the smoke wagon team—that's the rig what picks up the quarter poles. Ruth and Lois they pull quarter poles down with drag chains. The bull-hand has a long iron rod like a big button-hook that's attached to the drag chains. He puts the hook into a ring on the pole base, the elephant pulls and the Big Top jigs snub the pole down on a rope. It's dangerous work. A good hand with a good elephant can pull two, three poles at a time—if they're guided right."

He studied the neon-reflecting raindrops coursing down the windows of Elsie's Dew Drop Inn. "They'll be drenched when they get to the cars tonight," he said. "C'mon, we gotta blow this joint. I gotta seven A.M. call."

Smokey turned in when we arrived at the coaches but I didn't feel a bit sleepy so I went on the prowl and found a bar near the tracks—noisy, bright with neon and full of showhands. The air was juicy enough to cut with a butterknife, the juke box was blatting full tilt, and everybody seemed to be talking at once. It was one of those Wisconsin-Tyrolean places with German-script mottoes carefully painted on the walls (*Sehen Wir Uns Wieder Mein Tirol . . . Maose Turm Bei Bingen am Rhein*) and dark chromos of things like *Alt Heidelburger Schloss Bei Nacht. Herren* and *Damen* restroom doors were modestly concealed behind a mauve plush curtained partition. Over it was a sign, " 'Till We Meet Again." Above the bar hung a stuffed parrot and a set of moth-eaten moose antlers with small electric light bulbs at their tips. The bartenders were as busy as, to use a favorite clown expression, a horsefly at a rodeo, and the barmaids serving the booths said "Woops" when they bumped anyone, which was frequent in the long jam-packed room.

At the front of the bar were a couple of dripping candy-butchers just in from teardown. "They don't go for *unnfff!* in this town," one was complaining. "I was goin' four ways an' this guy he ast what the nickel change was for when he should'a' had a dime an' you know I always kid with them a little an' I said it's to keep me from workin' this winter an' he throwed it at me and said that's so's you won't have to work this summer neither."

The second butcher snickered. "Man," he said, "I love those elephants. They push that canvas and stomp it and roll it. I had a hell of a ball tonight, a pleasant teardown. I gotta go now and get outa these wet clothes. Thanks for the shot."

I moved on down the bar. A couple of elephant boys in a booth spotted me and called me over. I pulled up a curvaceous bent-wood chair and sat at the outside of the enclosure. They were having a merry time. As I sat down one was saying, ". . . an' the Deacon he could take an 18-pound sledge and, holdin' it at the very end—none of this 12 inches in—touch the tip of his nose with it, left hand *or* right."

Pony Red was jammed into one corner of the booth. ". . . I went into them barber-shop baths under the Oriental Restaurant," he was saying, "and you shoulda seen the inscriptions on the donnicker walls. Lissen; I wrote some of them down." He read from the back of a wrinkled pay voucher. " 'Please Do Not Throw Cigarettes in the Toilet. It Makes Them Soggy and Hard To Light.' " All hands doubled up with laughter. " 'We aim to please. You aim too, please,' Get it?" explained Red. "Too, t-o-o."

"Jee-*zuz*," I heard a familiar voice say, "is this all you got to do?" It was Big John soaked to the skin but grinning. "Can I buy a beer? Your money ain't no good here." He squeezed onto one of the bench ends and sat half-facing the room.

"Man, it was rough out there," he said referring to the teardown. "I just come from another joint down the street, but none of the boys was there."

Across the room at the bar a wino was talking very loudly. "I'm the Ringling's head elephant man—two hunnert a week." Our table stopped talking to listen. "How ya like that?" The wino slapped a lady next him on the thigh, spilling beer into her lap. "The other day my elephant grabbed a girl's leg and wouldn't let her go. All I have to do is give her an orange. I'm also Adolph the clown. I had cocktails with Hitler and Eva, too. I says to Eva, 'Have another drink.' O.K., I will." He paused to upend a bottle enclosed in a paper bag. "I used to have ponies an' zebras too that ride bareback on elephants . . ."

As the wino trailed off Big John said, "We showed here once with the Barnes show. Didn't have a corporal's guard at any show. We starved to death." Red was now telling a joke in his corner.

I begged off the next round (the empties were accumulating alarmingly) and left.

I slept well that night until a rude shove awakened me as I was becoming hopelessly involved fitting galoshes and long strands of pearls to a line-up of one hundred elephants with pink trunks. It was Big John. One hard shove, no more.

"Smokey says you wanted to ride in with us in the elephant sleeper," he said as I blinked awake. "Well, c'*mon* then. Get movin'. We won't be stopped here for long."

I pulled into pants and shirt, didn't stop to lace shoes, and followed John out of the car. We ran forward along the cindery track, hopping the unevenly spaced tie-ends, until we came to Car 223. We had hardly leaped aboard through the wide door opening which had two heavy wooden planks horizontally across it, when the train jerked into motion.

"Jest made it," said Big John, less breathless than I was. He settled to the hay-strewn floor, hanging his legs over the doorsill. I did too, but cautiously kept my legs inside the car. There was no other place to sit but on the floor. Most of the bull-boys were up and dressed, looking sleepy-eyed and bleary. My beering companions of the night before nodded what greetings they were able to muster and I returned the compliments. Some of the rag-tag outfits could have been slept in. Also aboard was an elephant who looked very blasé and very tall inside the car. The name "ICKY" was painted on the wall beside her. I assumed this was Icky.

A section of three-high bunks behind a wooden partition took up about one third of the car. The quadrangle of this boys' dormitory was extremely ascetic, decorated only with a small display of picture postcards and beer coasters thumb-tacked to the partition's barred screen-door. There were 3 elephant cards, one of them a comic (elephant pushing trunk through flap of camp tent; caption: "Why, Henry!"); 1 bucking bronco card; 1 Miami bathing beauty sitting on a gigantic orange. Pasted at the top of a small mirror nailed to the car's wall was a poem hand-written in painful scrawl:

> Once there was an elephant
> Who tried to use the telephant
> No! No! I mean an elephone
> Who tried to use the telepone
> Howe'er it was, he got his trunk
> Entangled in the telephunk;
> The more he tried to get it free
> The louder buzzed the telephee
> I fear I better drop the song
> of elephop and telephong
> by selaphane
> who has a belephone

"Where we at?" asked one of the boys of no one in particular, "Sixty-fi' miles out yet. We'll never git in. Supper'll be when the band plays."

"Where's that wino that joined out yesterday?" asked Big John.

"He got into a clem with a razorback last night," someone answered. "Man! he got turned every way but loose. He slept in the car until two A.M. then he blew."

"He better not come back," another voice said, "if the boys in the horses ever catches him. He glommed onto a suit an' a watch an' some other things outa their car between shows."

"He oney stole a watch," corrected a sooty-faced sprig lying full-length on the floor, his head resting on the elephant's left front foot.

A long skinny kid with bare non-tattooed torso stood at a little barred ventilating window looking melancholically at the passing strings of box-cars. His faded blue-jeans hung so low on his boney hips that four inches of underwear shorts were exposed.

Two kids squatting in a corner, their bent legs taking up the train's motion, played checkers, using beer bottle-caps for markers.

We passed a manufacturing plant, two large buildings joined

by a low arcade. "Hey, lookit the braz-zeer factory," shouted someone, "the middle part is where they make the straps." Nobody
laughed.

"That's a corn flakes factory, ya dopey bastard," said someone
scornfully, "ya can read it on every box—Battle Creek, Wisconsin."

"I wisht I had some potato salad," said the other.

The train wrenched to a sudden stop with a crashing jar. Big
John sprang to the ground. "C'mon," he said to me. "We go wake
Smokey up. He'll be mad I let him sleep this long." We ran back
along the stock cars and flats until we came to the sleepers. Outside
Smokey's stateroom window, Big John clattered a large iron bolt up
and down on the metal louvers and banged it on the car's steel side,
shouting at the same time, "Let's go now! Let's go now!" He seemed
to relish waking up his boss. Soon the slats flashed a couple of times
and we knew that Smokey was stirring. "You can wait for him on
the platform," said Big John, "I gotta run back before this thing
starts off again."

When Smokey came out buckling his belt the train was rolling
again. We sat on the hard iron steps of the open platform and
watched the scenery amble by.

"You know what I like best to do?" asked this superman bull-
leader. "Wash elephants. I *love* to wash elephants. I'd like to wash
them every day, but you know what they'd tell you around here about
wastin' water. Ain't one elephant around here's been washed in
twenty years. If there was a river or a lake near the lot I'd take them
in myself." Some more scenery rocked by. "More'n anything else,"
Smokey said suddenly after a long silence, "I'd like an elephant ring
with a small diamond for the eye." We rattled alongside a long
lake, grey blue in the morning light.

"Sometimes it's hard to get elephants outa water," said Smokey
continuing his miles-back conversation. "In Peru, Indiana, the big
flood in 1913, Hagenbeck and Wallace turned loose twelve elephants so's they could swim to high land, but you know they swum
around and around until they drown-ded. Ordinarily elephants is
good swimmers, they're so bouyant. Once on the Floto show, Louie
told me, some elephants stampeded at Rock Springs, Wyoming, fell
into the Green River rapids and went over the falls. But they all
come out okay, just a little bit scared. Not a one drown-ded."

The train didn't stop until we were almost into town—about fi'
miles out according to Smokey. This time he ran, with me a poor

second, to another car where Smokey knew the porter always had an early pot of coffee brewing. At 10:22 by Smokey's wrist watch, we were "spotted"; that is, the sleepers were parked for the day.

"They had the poles to engine last night 'stead the other way around," Stitchy the coffee-making porter explained to us (his nickname came from being a wintertime canvas-tailor). "They had to turn all the flats around last night 'afore we left town." (An unloading technicality: to be pulled off the flats, wagons must always have their poles, or tongues, facing the unloading point; self-powered units must be headed towards it.)

Later, we went to the siding where the bull-hands were unloading the elephants. When all 51 were out and standing in a long swaying line, their rumps backed into the train, the bull-boss turned to me and said, "Okay, you're gonna ride the last elephant this morning and this here's your bull-hook. Don't you let her straggle behind." Butterflies hatched in my innards. Me and Big Jewel exchanged a long searching look. "Trunk please, Miss Jewel." She heisted me with it and I settled into her neck.

"Goin' away!" yelled Smokey from the head of the line, which means take them to the lot. Harold the horse swung around and clattered off; 51 grey hulks sashayed around and padded away at a middling fast clip. "Jewel move up!" I commanded in as gruff a voice as I could muster. "JEWEL move *up!*" I prayed that she would. She did. We sluffered off. I held the bull-hook gingerly across my lap, trusting that Big Jewel would regard me as a paid-up member of the bull-hand's local. If I behaved myself maybe someday she would discover me sitting in the cheap seats at the circus, reach out with her trunk and move me into an expensive box. "JOOL! Move-up! Jo-o-o-o-ul *movup!*"

Yes, love, that's easily said:
But as long as you grow older everyday
You don't ask for love
You got to make use of the short time that's yours.
A human being is not an animal!

Ja, Liebe, das ist leicht gesagt:
Doch, solang man täglich älter wird
Da wird nicht nach Liebe gefragt
Da muss man seine kurze Zeit benützen.
Ein Mensch ist kein Tier!

BERT BRECHT
From the Weill-Brecht opera, *Mahagonny,*
as sung by LOTTE LENYA
in the character of *Jenny Smith.*

GLOSSARY 🐘

aerial ballet: A performance of rhythmic gymnastics aloft by the "ballet broads" (circus chorus girls) usually on webs (vertical canvas-sleeved cotton ropes), sometimes including iron-jaw, trapeze and cloud-swing performers and a center-ring star.

baggage horse; (pl.) *baggage stock:* A horse or horses used to pull heavy spectacle floats; in pre-caterpillar-tractor days, a horse or horses used to pull the heavy parade wagons and all wagons to and from the "runs" where they were loaded on railroad flatcars.

bally: An abbreviation of *ballyhooly truth,* an English music-hall tag *circa* the early 1880's, perhaps derived from *whole bloody truth* or holy bloody truth; a term for eloquence aimed at the pocketbook; advance publicity of a vulgar, misleading kind; circus-wise, either the appearance of a performer (an "attraction") alongside a midway "talker" to illustrate his flamboyant eloquence about the wonders of the sideshow, or the talk itself, or the box from which it is delivered.

banner line: Paintings of sideshow attractions, usually in a display lined up on either side of a sideshow entrance, sometimes on individually framed metal plates, more often on seperate sections of canvas (banners).

big cage: The barred or steel-meshed arena in which wild-animal acts are performed.

Big Top: The main performance tent, also called *the big rag* and *Big Bertha.*

bounce (v.): To make noise, hullabaloo; i.e., a "bouncy" cat act is one in which there is much roaring, snarling and fierce-looking—albeit often harmless—action; (n.) the roar or rush of a lion, tiger or other wild cat.

breaking: Elementary training of an animal.

Buckeye boy: Male native of Ohio, the Buckeye state.

bull-hand: Man who helps to care for, and sometimes to display and work, elephants; a handler.

bull-hook: An elephant goad with handle (usually wooden) and metal hook, resembling a short boat hook (in India, the *ankus*).

bulls: All the elephants in a circus herd, whether male or female.

busking: Performing for handouts in a bar, restaurant or other public house, or on the sidewalk or street before it; English vagrants' slang *circa* 1850's probably derived from standard English of the eighteenth century; *busk*, to go about probing for salvageable items, using a corset steel as a ragpicker would (a busk, from French *busc*, and Italian *busco*), or from the nautical term, *busk*, to cruise as a pirate.

cage boy, cage-hand: A wild-animal attendant, *not* a handler; one who commonly feeds and waters wild animals and cleans their cages, but sometimes a trainer's assistant working outside the big cage.

carny: A corruption of *carnival*; also applied to a person who is "with" a carnival (an integral part of its operation).

clem (v.): Hobo cant *to starve*; (n.) circus jargon for a fight.

clown alley: Originally, in the circus men's dressing tent, an aisle occupied exclusively by clowns. When a man becomes a clown he "goes into clown alley," although in most circuses today there is actually no such place.

cookhouse: The low-squatting tent under which the circus feeds itself three times a day.

crumb-box: The box, foot locker or suitcase in which a circus work-hand keeps his personal belongings. Lack of traveling space prohibits his carrying a full-sized trunk as do performers. In hobo cant a crumb is a louse, due to close resemblance.

crumb-up (v.): Circus work-hand jargon for bathing, washing up or any personal hygiene.

dog-and-pony: A traveling circus of modest size, featuring small domesticated-animal acts.

donnicker (or donniker, or doniker): The circus outhouse; from *dunnaken* (or dunneken, or dunnyken, or dunagan), late nineteenth-century colloquialism for a privy, from seventeenth-century cant *dannaken*, a combination of *danna*, underworld cant for human excrement, and *ken*, sixteenth- to late nineteenth-century word for room, possibly from the Hindustani *khan(n)a* (a house or room) which appears in various Gypsy dialects.

equestrian director: The gentleman who controls a circus performance from the arena floor, generally referred to as the *ringmaster*, although in the purest sense the ringmaster is a monitor who controls horses in a circus ring during an equestrian act.

First-of-May: A circus rookie experiencing a first season.

fighting act: A big cat act with fast timing and lots of "bounce," giving the impression that the trainer is fighting off a bunch of jungle-wild animals.

four-ways: A *way* is a code word for five cents, used in the jargon of candy butchers (vendors in a circus Big Top) to keep each other informed, and the public in ignorance, of the price of their wares, constantly fluctuating above the official rate, according to what the traffic will bear.

The Garden: Madison Square Garden in New York City (Eighth Avenue between Forty-ninth and Fiftieth streets), traditionally the first—and longest—stand of the season for the Big One—Ringling Bros and Barnum & Bailey Circus. To the performer sun-baked during Florida rehearsals *The Garden* means the dank, dark North, expensive meals and hotel bills, backstage drafts and springtime grippe; there's also, however, an exciting connotation of spring and hopeful renascence.

gazooney: A youngster, a kid; also called *punk* and *gunsel.*

gilly: A person uninitiated or alien to the circus; in England, a member of the audience. From British sailor jargon, *gilguy,* a wrong rope on a boat, hence a wrong guy.

gilly-galloo: Compounds the insult of the above by the addition of *galloo,* a corruption of *gelubt,* Dutch for eunuch.

generally useful: The phrase in a circus performer's contract which makes him available for whatever work the management wishes to put him to.

gimmick: Originally *gimix,* a small tool or machine; circus-wise, a mechanical aid, not apparent to the audience, for making a difficult trick easier to perform.
Also, *gaff:* from a finger ring with small hook worn by a sharping card-dealer, from fishing spear of the same name.

guyed-out: To be drunk, *i.e.,* tight as a tent.

greaseball: Term of opprobrium for clown, derived from one who doesn't flat-down with powder his shiny grease paint; also called a *shine.*

Grease-joint: A circus backyard quick-lunch wagon, serving circus people and their guests exclusively.

haul (n.): The distance from the "runs" (inclined runways used by rolling stock between railroad flatcars and roadway) to the "lot," *i.e.,* the field or other area in which a circus sets up its tents. The haul is always marked, night and day, with ball-torches indicating right turns. A wise circus hand always knows whether "tomorrow's town" has a long or short haul, how many miles the horses and elephants will have to walk, sometimes even the street names.

him-hammin': Hemming and hawing, stumbling around a subject instead of speaking the truth.

hippodrome track: A redundant term for the oval track running around the inside of a circus Big Top between the tiers of seats and the exhibition rings and stages.

hooking: Raking and jabbing of an elephant with the bull-hook.

hulligan: Slanderous designation of a foreigner, especially a member of a European act, by intolerant American circus performers; a corruption of *hooligan,* the name given in the old days to the dressing tent of the Wild West show's cowboys and Indians, always a rowdy bunch. Hooligan derives from *Hooley Gang,* a group of young toughs of late nineteenth-century London.

iggy (from ignorant): To "give 'em the iggy" is to play dumb, an attitude often assumed by circus people when confronted by quidnunc towners or the local "fuzz" (police).

inside lecturer: In the circus sideshow, a talker who directs the attention of the audience to each attraction and points out its wonders.

iron-jaw: An aerial acrobatic performance in which the participant suspends himself by clamping jaws to a mouthpiece.

juke (or jook): To duck or dodge away from a blow; a regionalism of western Pennsylvania and Ohio.

kinker: Originally, a ground tumbler, from the stretching of acrobats to get kinks out of their muscles; now accepted as any seasoned circus performer.

lash whip: A whip used in animal training and performing, fashioned of a long rawhide lash connected to a heavy stock and having a cord cracker at its tip. Not a crop or quirt.

liberty horses: Horses that perform, riderless, in displays of muscular control and obedience, usually in changing group formations resembling a drill.

lunge line or rope: A lunging rein attached to a horse's bridle, or a restraining rope or chain attached to a wild beast's collar or harness.

make a bally: *See* bally.

Midway: A wide avenue fronting the circus Big Top and leading to its main entrance, and containing sideshow, various "joints" (concession stands), ticket and administration wagons.

outside talker: An eloquent gentleman who proclaims the attractions of a circus Sideshow from a bally box or stage outside the tent. Never called "barker" by circus people.

opening: An introductory speech made by an outside talker.

pick-out (pony, horse, dog or other animal): One trained to select objects at the trainer's cue or command.

picture act (or act-beautiful): A performance mainly consisting of a series of tableaux, especially gracefully arranged combinations of animals.

pinhead: A microcephalic human; one with an extremely tiny or pointed head, a classic circus-Sideshow attraction. Examples: Zip, the What-Is-It?; Cuckoo, the Bird Girl.

pink slip: A discharge notice given a circus work-hand, indicating that he cannot be rehired by another department on the show, but must leave the circus. If fired with a *white* slip he may be rehired by another boss for another type of work. To get a pink slip is to be "run away from the show," "run down the track" or "run off the lot."

pop: a single time, item or package.

popper: A cracker or snapper on the tip of a whiplash made of plaited hemp or flax.

possum-belly: a closed box suspended beneath a railroad car or circus wagon, and used for storage.

props: A corruption of properties, the accessories of a theatrical performance. In a circus, props include elephant tubs, jugglers' paraphernalia, wire-walkers' apparatus, etc.

pumpkin fairs: Small-time country fairs full of pumpkins and bumpkins.

punks: Children, kids, gazooneys, gunsels.

razorback: A circus trainhand who loads and unloads the show's rolling stock; so called from the command, "Raise your backs," given in earlier circus days when a group of these workers lifted, by the power of their backs, and turned short cage wagons so that they loaded crossways on a flat car instead of lengthwise, thus saving space.

riggings: Tackle, gear; the ropes, wires, cables and pulleys used to adjust and secure the gymnastic apparatus used in aerial circus acts: trapezes, webs, high-wires, tight and slack wires, etc.

ring barn: A round or octagonal barnlike building, usually at a circus winter quarters, equipped with a standard-sized 42-foot circus ring for practice of horses.

ring carpet: A ground cloth used within a circus ring.

ring No. 1 (or 2 or 3): In a circus the No. 1 ring is that nearest the main entrance. No. 2 is center ring and No. 3 is nearest the back entrance.

ringstock: Performing horses as opposed to baggage or work horses. Ringstock includes liberty, dressage and race horses; the rosin-backs of the riding acts; standard-breds, carriage horses, hackneys and saddle horses; ponies and Wild West horses. Also refers to the horse department.

Risley act: The foot-juggling of humans, one of the circus's most ancient acts, although its name comes from the name of a famous nineteenth-century expert in the art.

rola-bola: A rolling cylinder upon which is balanced a short board on which gymnasts perform, most often in teams of two. The word usually designates the act, although it is sometimes applied to the performer.

rope caller: The straw boss of a Big Top guying-out crew, who chants rhythmic directions to his men as they work their way systematically around the big tent, pulling and shaking, taking up the slack in the canvas. The call varies from show to show, but usually it goes something like this: "Take it, shake it, make it, break it, walk along." Occasionally, when the big boss commands, "Speak your Latin," you will hear a rope caller singing a much older song: "Ah, heebie, hebby, hobby, hole, golong."

run: The distance between circus towns.

runs (pl.): *See baggage horse or haul.*

sap (v.): The striking of a blow by an elephant's trunk; from the slang term for blackjack, a small leather-wrapped club with weighted head and elastic shaft.

seat block: A solid, heavy cube of wood used in preliminary training of big jungle cats to furnish them a secure, non-tipping, non-rattling home-base. Later, lighter-weight tubs or pedestals of metal and wood are substituted.

shandy: An electrician or member of circus-lights department (from chandelier).

sidewall: Vertically hung canvas curtains forming the outside walls of a tent. To sidewall (v.) is to sneak into a circus tent during a performance.

smoke wagon: A long wagon, usually pulled by elephants, that circles the Big Top of a circus during its teardown, collecting the quarter poles.

Sneaky Pete: Cheap wine.

Spec (or Spectacle) (from spectacular): Traditional parade pageant of the circus within the Big Top; includes most of the personnel and animals, and embroiders some imaginative or historical theme.

spindle: A metal tripod topped with a horizontally revolving disc on which a paw or hoof may be placed.

stall act: An act lengthened by superfluous bits of business, used to hold an audience for some special reason (often mercenary) or to pad an inadequate program.

still act: A picture act.

strip (n.): In clown parlance, a gag ending with the sudden metamorphosis of an actor by the unexpected removal of clothing—usually trousers.

stock whip: A lashless whip with stock and braided leather end.

styling: Inviting applause at the end of a trick or an act by a grandiose gesture frozen into a stylish pose.

tanbark: A most satisfactory footing for animal performers; it is composed of tiny pieces of tree bark whose tannin has been spent in leather tanning.

teardown: The nighttime business of taking the circus apart and packing it off to its train.

thread-the-needle: A drill maneuver of horses.

tip: A crowd of prospective customers at a circus or carnival.

tournament: An archaic term for the circus spec.

trouper: A player in a traveling theatrical troupe. On a circus the word carries a connotation of great affection and approval.

Under canvas: A circus showing in tents, as opposed to giving performances in a building, ball park or stadium without a Big Top.

Write-up: Any mention in print of a circus performer or his act is a "write-up"—never called a story, mention, review, or report. An insertion concerning a circus trouper in the *Congressional Record, Who's Who in America,* or the *Almanach de Gotha* would still, by his standards, be a "write-up."

ACKNOWLEDGEMENTS 🐿

I thank the circus for taking me into its canvas fold. I am forever indebted to hundreds of circus troupers, too numerous to mention individually, for much of the knowledge of the circus and its animals which you will find in this book.

I want to honor here my long, continuing friendship with the great clown, Felix Adler, who became my very first friend of the circus back yard in knee-pants days long ago.

I especially thank the animal trainers about whom I have written for their tremendous help in explaining their techniques and methods, and I am extremely grateful for the time these busy people so generously gave me for interviews.

I pay humble homage to that grand queen of the tigers, Miss Mabel Stark, and I salute the great Professor Roy Heckler, Master of Fleas. My heartfelt thanks goes to Clyde Beatty, Trevor Bale and Pat Anthony. Damoo Dhotre, Paul Fritz, Oscar Konyot, Dick McGraw and Roman Proske also helped me to report the big cats. I learned the most about elephants from Louis Reed, Hugo Schmidt and Robert "Smokey" Jones. Eugene "Arky" Scott and Floyd Smith were also helpful in the pachyderm division. I thank Jack Joyce for an understanding of camels, and Hank Craig, Mike Kostial and Amleto Sciplini for an insight into chimpanzee life. A deep curtsy to the old masters of beardom, Emil and Cato Pallenberg, and a quiet thanks to Albert Rix, the first bear trainer I ever knew. I am grateful to Miss Josephine Rosal for lifting the veil from the mysteries of snake charming, to Louis Pasteur for information on cobras, and to towner friend, Ben Key, for other snake lore. I wish to thank Bobby Nelson for his contribution on the art of pig training. I greatly appreciate the information regarding sea lions so freely given by the Roland Tiebors, Sr. and Jr. And to Anne and John White, many thanks for taking me back with them to earlier circus times.

I wish to thank especially Adolf Frohn, the world's premier porpoise trainer, because my story about him, which appeared in *Holiday* magazine, was the spark which started this work.

I am grateful to Arthur M. Concello, executive Director of Ringling Bros and Barnum & Bailey Circus, for the enormous courtesies extended me by that organization over the years. I am grateful to J. Y. Henderson, D.V.M., chief veterinarian of that show, and to Pat Valdo, Esquire, its General Performance Director. I want to thank Frank McClosky, General Manager of the Clyde Beatty Circus, for kindnesses shown me en route with that outfit. The Cristiani Bros. Circus was especially cooperative.

George P. Vierheller, Director of the St. Louis Zoo, was graciously obliging. Certain historical material was found at the Museum of the American Circus and the Circus Hall of Fame, both in Sarasota, Florida. I owe special thanks to Melvin C. Miller of that city. I am very much obliged to Parley Baer of North Hollywood, California. I thank Marian Murray, Roland Butler and John and Alice Durant for providing pertinent information. Fred Woltman, Harry Dann and Paul Horompo were helpful. I am grateful for the aid given by Tom Parkinson of the Chicago office of *Billboard* and by Irwin Kirby of the New York office of that publication. Mrs. Vivienne Mars, Librarian of the Harry Hertzberg Circus Collection of the San Antonio, Texas, Public Library, provided much assistance. I thank Duane Thorpe and Vincent Fago for special help.

I thank Lois Long for permission to reprint a quotation from her father's book, *The Spirit of the Wild* by Dr. William J. Long.

I thank the Sarasota *Herald-Tribune* for the use of a bit from the column, "Sawdust & Spangles," which appeared in that newspaper during the winter of 1954.

I am very grateful to Lotte Lenya for granting permission to use a quotation from the Kurt Weill-Bertolt Brecht opera, *Mahagonny*, and to Harper & Brothers for permission to quote from Mark Twain's *Huckleberry Finn*. Some of the material in the chapter on Clyde Beatty originally appeared in different form in *Cavalier* magazine.

I have relied somewhat on leading writers of circus life and animals, and I give thanks especially to Gertrude Davies Lintz, John Latouche, Gertrude Orr, Bernhard Grzimek, Edward Anthony, Alfred Court, Roman Proske, Al G. Barnes and Hartzell Spence.

I send a big center-ring "style" to that very special troupe of wild tigers and tame fleas without whom this book would not have been written: Al and Sesyle Hine, Jerry Bangs, Tom Barron, Milton Caniff, Bill Charmatz, Stephen Colhoun, Dr. Henry Harold Conley, Catherine Crane, Harry Devlin, Adele Earnest, Byron Goto, Robert Greenhalgh, Eugene Guibert, Leonard Kessler, Walter Klussmann, Charlotte Light, Herman Linden, Aili Mangel, Charles E. Martin, Fred Pfening, Dan Quirk, Conway Sawyer, Sidney Simon, John Slater, Jane Tibbett, Paul Williams and associates, and Eric C. Wilson.

And great spangled kudos to R.L.B. for immeasurable practical assistance, advice and encouragement.

Bill Ballantine

INDEX 🐾

elephants *(continued)*
Ringling Bros', 169; list, 268
sex life, cycle, 284–87
size, 276, 293
skin, 295
smell, sense of, 295, 313
speed, 294, 299
strength, 296
swimming, 319
teeth, 296
training, 265–7, 298
  age of pupils, 283; beating in, 266,
  283; block and tackle, 282; chaining,
  282; commands, 303–4, 307–9, 320;
  hooking, 283; respect and fear, 265,
  283; whips, 267
tricks, 278, 283–4
trunk, 293, 294–5, 307–8
Tusko, 293; rampage, 312
tusks, 295–6
unloading, circus, 320
value of, 278
war, 288
watering, 270
white, 273
work, 271, 298–9, 303, 315–16
zoological information, 273–4, 292–6
Elephas maximus, 293
Elizabeth I, Queen of England, 51
Ella, the Wonder Bear, 65, 66, 68
Emmitt, Alligator-Skin Boy, 187–8, 197,
  198–9
Eocene Epoch, 156, 273
equestrian directors
  Bradna, 47, 59, 76, 214; Hauser, 136;
  ringmasters, 38–40
equestrians. *See* Bradna, Ella; Desval,
  Olympia; Duttons, Riding; Hannefords; Loyal, Giustino; Loyal-Repenski; Strepetow, Lilly; Wirth, May.
  See also Billy Button; Huckleberry
  Finn; January act; Pete Jenkins
Escalante, Josefina, 181. *See also* Rosal,
  Josephine
Excelsior, talking horse, 4, 5, 12

fairs, 68, 72, 74, 201, 212, 241. *See also*
  amusement parks
Farmer Burns' pig act, 13
Fellows, Dexter, 276
Fenykövi, José, 293
Fields, Al G., 13
fighting, of animals, 128–29, 130–31, 146,
  226, 302
"fighting-acts," 116, 124, 132
Fireproof Man, 191. *See also* Singhalee,
  Mossa Kutty
Fissipedia, 53
Flea Circus, The, 229–259
  club-dates, 259

Flea Circus, The *(continued)*
fame of Heckler's, 253
hall surrounding, 230–31
lecture during, 233–38
neighborhood, 229–30
"opening," 231–32
properties, 247
publicity, 254–58; Hollywood, 256–
  58
room, inner, 233
television, on, 258
flea jokes, 233, 240, 241, 243
flea trainers. *See* Heckler, Professor Leroy;
  Heckler, William, Jr.; Heckler, William, Sr.; Hupf, Professor; Ruhl,
  Charles; Ruhl, John C.
fleas, 229–259
breeding actors, 248–9
bite of, 251
Castilina, la, 248
cat, 241
cold, 247, 248–9
dog, 241, 257
durability of, 246–7
feeding, 237
  of actors, 250; of breeding stock, 250
habitat, 241
harness, 244–5
hearing (anecdote), 243
human, 241–9
  strength, 242; weight, 242
individuality of, 245
injuries to actors, 248
intelligence test, 243–44
liberty performer, 247
lifespan of trained, 246
names of actors, 247–248
ontological development, 249
price of, 238
sex of performers, 245
taxonomy, 241
television, 258
training, 243
training myths, 240
tricks of, 229, 234–37, 245–46
understudies, 248
zoological information, 241
Fleet, Al, 226
Florine, Martha, 95
Florsek, Frank, 223
Flower, Major Stanley S., 297
Fogardus, Madame, Clever Canines &
  Feathered Sweethearts, 13
Fo-Hi, Chinese Emperor, 10
Fonda, Mrs. C. D., 36
force-feeding, 180. *See also* snakes
Forepaugh, Adam, 277, 314
Forty-second Street, New York City, 229–
  30, 252, 254
Forty-second Street Association, 254

tigers (*continued*)
 mauling, 92, 94, 110–11. *See also* trainers, scars of
 misconceptions about, 122–4
 Rajah, 91
 rollover, 91, 128
 size of, 121
 size of acts, 96, 102, **117**
 Sleika, spinner, 116
 training of, 88–90, 120–26
  age for, 88; early, 89, 90; observation
   in, 89; type for, 88
 tricks, 90, 91, 111–12, 126, 128
 versus bears, 54
 versus lions, 82. *See also* lion-tiger
  hate
 wild imported, 120
 wrestling with, **91**, **95**. *See also* lions,
  wrestling
tragulids, 156
trainers
 "arena shock" in, 137
 "anxiety palpitation" in, **113**
 as fathers, 27, 61, 105, 107, 108, **138**,
  279, 283, 289
 bear. *See* bear trainers
 camel. *See* camel trainers
 chimpanzee. *See* chimpanzee **trainers**
 dog. *See* dog trainers
 elephant. *See* elephant trainers
 female, 1, 40–47, 57, 59, 66, 85, 95, 120,
  129, 168, 172, 181, 207, 209, 210,
  215
 flea. *See* flea trainers
 future for, 138
 horse. *See* horse trainers
 Japanese, 96
 lion. *See* lion trainers
 mule. *See* mule trainers
 pig. *See* pig trainers
 prayer of (tiger), 111
 resemblance of trainer to trained, 59,
  69, 87, 118
 scars of, 75, 76, 87, 92. *See also* mauling
 sea lion. *See* sea lion trainer
 snake. *See* snake handlers
 tiger. *See* lion and tiger trainers
training
 achieving control, 61, 283
 adventitious, 91–2, 126, 151, 167
 beating in, 58, 61, 90; description, 266
 "bogey man" in, 226
 bull-hook in, 265, 283, 295
 "chaining," mental process in, 206–7
 chaining in, 282
 chair, 129
 collar, 89, 124
 commands, 61, 88, 152–3, 303–4, 307,
  308, 309, 320
  by fingernail click, 8, 36; by gesture,

command (*continued*)
  36, 120; "seats!", 20, 21, **78**, 89,
  102, 107, 150; by voice. *See* training, voice in; by whistle, 120
 communication, 228. *See also* training,
  rapport in
 "conning" in, 225
 cruelty in, 123
 fear in, 78, 265, 283
 flicking, 129
 food rewards, 20, 23, 59, 90, 207, **225**,
  265
 force, 22, 61, 90, 120, 283
 future of, 138
 "hot shot" in, 120
 humiliation in, 120
 mutual understanding in, 122, 228. *See*
  also training, rapport in
 observation in, 58
 poking, 123, 129
 rapport in, 88, 90, 126, 148
 reflex-conditioning in, 243
 respect, 61, 122; and fear, 265, **283**
 "squeeze-cage," 124
 tricks. *See* specific animal, *i.e.*, tigers,
  tricks
 use of sympathy to elicit co-operation,
  226–7
 varied methods, 124
 voice in, 61, 88, 90, 96, 97–8, 102, 107,
  111, 120, 152–3, 282, 308, 309, 320
 whips in, 20, 22, 58, 61, 77, 89, 90, 92,
  123, 267, 287
Trees, Eddie, 97
trouper, circus, qualities **of, 11**
Tufts College, 277
Tylopoda, 156

Uncle Sam, 5
Ursidae, 53

Valdo, Pat, 101, 151
Van Amburgh, Isaac, 113
vaudeville, 13, 24, 41–6, 205
 animals in, 43–6; chimps in, 205; **first**
  white-Negro act to tour South, 42; **mule**
  in, 41
venationes, 49–50
Venice, California, 86–7
veterinarian, circus. *See* Henderson, **Dr.**
 J. Y.
Victoria, Queen of England, 276
vicuña, 156
Vierheller, George, 204–5, 212, 216–18,
 221, 226; career, 217
Vitanza, Anthony Patrick, 71. *See also*
 Anthony, Pat
voice, in training, 61, 88, 90, 96, 97–8,